UNCTAD/ITE/IIT/7

UNITED NATIONS CONFERENCE ON TRADE AND DEVELOPMENT
Geneva

Bilateral Investment Treaties in the Mid-1990s

United Nations
New York and Geneva, 1998

Note

UNCTAD serves as the focal point within the United Nations Secretariat for all matters related to foreign direct investment and transnational corporations. In the past, the Programme on Transnational Corporations was carried out by the United Nations Centre on Transnational Corporations (1975 – 1992) and the Transnational Corporations and Management Division of the United Nations Department of Economic and Social Development (1992 – 1993). In 1993, the Programme was transferred to the UNCTAD. UNCTAD seeks to further the understanding of the nature of transnational corporations and their contribution to development and to create an enabling environment for international investment and enterprise development. UNCTAD's work is carried out through intergovernmental deliberations, technical assistance activities, seminars, workshops and conferences.

The term "country" as used in this study also refers, as appropriate, to territories or areas; the designations employed and the presentation of the material do not imply the expression of any opinion whatsoever on the part of the Secretariat of the United Nations concerning the legal status of any country, territory, city or area or of its authorities, or concerning the delimitation of its frontiers or boundaries. In addition, the designations of country groups are intended solely for statistical or analytical convenience and do not necessarily express a judgement about the stage of development reached by a particular country or area in the development process.

The following symbols have been used in the tables:

Two dots (..) indicate that data are not available or are not separately reported. Rows in tables have been omitted in those cases where no data are available for any of the elements in the row;

A dash (-) indicates that the item is equal to zero or its value is negligible;

A blank in a table indicates that the item is not applicable;

A slash (/) between dates representing years, e.g., 1994/95, indicates a financial year;

Use of a dash (–) between dates representing years, e.g., 1994 – 1995, signifies the full period involved, including the beginning and end years.

Reference to "dollars" ($) means United States dollars, unless otherwise indicated.

Annual rates of growth or change, unless otherwise stated, refer to annual compound rates.

Details and percentages in tables do not necessarily add to totals because of rounding.

The material contained in this study may be freely quoted with appropriate acknowledgement.

UN2
TD/UNCTAD/ITE/IIT/7

UNCTAD/ITE/IIT/7

UNITED NATIONS PUBLICATION
Sales No. E.98.II.D.8
ISBN 92-1-112430-1

Preface

It is now widely recognized that foreign direct investment can play an important role in economic growth and development. Consequently, governments strive to create a favourable climate to attract such investment. They do so by providing an enabling regulatory framework which includes reducing investment restrictions, granting certain standards of treatment, legal protection and guarantees, and strengthening measures aimed at securing the orderly functioning of markets.

Bilateral treaties for the promotion and protection of foreign investment are an element of that framework. Exclusively dedicated to investment, the legal issues they address are among the most important for foreign investors. Bilateral investment treaties were introduced for the first time four decades ago and have since remained largely unchanged in terms of their format and the issues they cover. However, some new issues were introduced over the years, and there are also important differences in the formulation of their provisions that deserve scrutiny.

The United Nations has analysed bilateral investment treaties for many years as part of its work on foreign direct investment, which is presently carried out by the Division on Investment, Technology and Enterprise Development of the United Nations Conference on Trade and Development (UNCTAD). In 1988, it published its first comprehensive study of bilateral investment treaties (UNCTC, 1988). That study was followed in 1992 by the publication of a comprehensive list of treaties signed since 1959, which was prepared jointly with the International Chamber of Commerce (ICC) (UNCTC-ICC, 1992). Since then, the list of bilateral investment treaties has been updated and published in the *World Investment Reports*. At the same time, analyses of new trends and issues regarding these treaties have been reflected in a number of studies, the latest being chapter V of *the World Investment Report 1996: Investment, Trade and International Policy Arrangements*.

A number of significant developments have taken place in recent years that suggest that the time is ripe for a new analysis of bilateral investment treaties. The number of treaties concluded has risen dramatically since the publication of the 1988 study, while investment flows to developing countries during the same period have increased rapidly. In fact, more than two-thirds of the total 1,513 treaties signed by the end of 1997 came into existence in the 1990s. Apart from this rapid growth in the number of treaties, a considerable number of new countries have become active participants in this treaty practice in the late 1980s, with the total number of countries and territories reaching 169 by the end of 1997. Furthermore, the number of treaties being concluded between developing countries and between these countries and countries with economies in transition has also risen substantially in recent years.

These new developments, in turn, have policy implications for the role bilateral investment treaties play as instruments of international policy on foreign investment, and these implications need to be analysed. A key question in this regard is whether bilateral investment treaties have had an impact on attracting investment flows. It is also of interest to examine to what extent bilateral investment treaties have found acceptance in the international community and, in particular, among developing countries. To the extent that these treaties have been concluded in large numbers, cover most countries in all regions and have similar provisions, a question that may be raised is whether they have an influence in shaping and clarifying the principles and concepts of international law applying to foreign investment. A related question is whether bilateral investment treaties have influenced the elaboration of regional and multilateral investment agreements and, if so, how; and what the interrelations are between investment agreements at all levels. The contents of the new treaties also need to be analysed, and their differences and similarities with those negotiated in previous decades need to be identified in order to appreciate the evolution and present policy approaches to foreign investment. Finally, an issue that deserves special attention is whether and how bilateral investment treaties address development concerns and, in particular, what can be done to increase their potential as instruments to advance the development of the developing countries.

In parallel with these developments, the increasing recognition of the importance of foreign direct investment in the global economy has led to a number of initiatives at the regional and multilateral levels which, in turn, have placed foreign direct investment issues high on the international economic policy agenda, raising the possibility of increasing international cooperation in this area. First, the conclusion of the Uruguay Round of Multilateral Trade Negotiations resulted in multilateral agreements that, for the first time, addressed directly issues relating to foreign direct investment in the context of the General Agreement on Tariffs and Trade/the World Trade Organization. Second, the number of regional agreements that have incorporated investment rules has increased considerably in various parts of the world. Third, negotiations began in 1995 in the Organisation for Economic Co-operation and Development on a multilateral agreement on investment. Fourth, more recently, the countries members of the World Trade Organization, at its first ministerial conference held in Singapore in December 1996, agreed to establish a working group to examine the relationship between trade and investment. This group was requested to draw upon the work of UNCTAD, among others, in this area. Pursuant to paragraph 89 (b) of "A Partnership for Growth and Development", adopted by UNCTAD IX in Midrand, South Africa, in 1996, UNCTAD's work in this area includes "identifying and analysing implications for development of issues relevant to a possible multilateral framework on investment" (UNCTAD, 1996a, para. 89 (b)).

Given the significance of bilateral investment treaties as instruments relevant to the treatment of foreign investors, this study is intended to assist policy makers, business executives, academics and other interested groups in dealing with these treaties and, in particular, to contribute to a better understanding of the issues involved in their negotiation, conclusion and application. More generally, it is hoped that the study will contribute to international discussions on international policy arrangements in the area of investment, paying special attention to the development dimension.

A working draft of this study was made available to the Expert Meeting on Existing Agreements on Investment and Their Development Dimensions, held in Geneva on 28–30 May 1997, as a background document for the discussions. These discussions and the outcome of the meeting, in turn, are reflected in the final version of this study. The study, which is dedicated to one type of investment agreement only, does not, however, pretend to exhaust the analysis of issues involved in international investment law, or the development dimensions of such issues. Specific issues will be discussed in more detail in the forthcoming series of papers on issues relevant to international investment agreements and their development dimensions.

The study is divided into four chapters. Chapter I, by way of introduction, reviews the purposes of bilateral investment treaties and their origins, evolution and geographical distribution, looking in particular at recent trends and how these trends have affected some of the earlier assumptions about these treaties. Chapter II discusses briefly the negotiating process of such treaties; given that more and more countries are negotiating more and more such treaties, it is meant to provide a practical guide for negotiators, particularly those from developing countries. Chapter III analyses individual clauses in bilateral investment treaties, focusing in particular on the definition of the terms and principles involved, how these are used, the differences and similarities between present and former treaty practice, and the implications of individual treaty provisions for development. Chapter IV examines the impact bilateral investment treaties have on investment flows. Finally, the study provides general conclusions. Annex I contains the list of bilateral investment treaties signed as at 1 January 1997, while annex II reproduces a selection of model treaties prepared by individual countries or groups of countries.

Geneva, October 1998   **Rubens Ricupero**
                                                    Secretary-General of UNCTAD

Acknowledgements

This study was prepared by a team comprising Kenneth J. Vandevelde, Victoria Aranda and Zbigniew Zimny, on the basis of a text prepared by Kenneth J. Vandevelde, under the overall direction of Karl P. Sauvant. Inputs were received from Farok J. Contractor, Joseph Mathews, Sankaran P. Raghunathan and Jeswald Salacuse. Research assistance was provided by Siri Dalawelle, Changsu Kim and Lizanne Martinez. The production of the study was carried out by Vanda de Brie, Florence Hudry and Jenifer Tacardon, and it was prepared for publication by Teresita Sabico. It was copy-edited by Paul Stephenson.

The study benefited from comments from a number of experts. Substantial comments were provided by Argyrios A. Fatouros, Mark Koulen, Maryse Robert, Patrick Robinson, Pedro Roffe, Margrete Stevens, M. Sornarajah and Wang Hejun. Comments were also provided by Samuel K.B. Asante, Ruvan de Alwis, Sew Sam Chan Tung, Persephone Economou, Rudolf Dolzer, Masataka Fujita, Stephen E. Guisinger, Bertrand Marchais, Rajneesh Narula and Dominick Savatore.

The study also benefited from the discussions of the Expert Meeting on Existing Agreements on Investment and Their Development Dimensions, held in Geneva in May 1997, which focused on bilateral investment treaties, as well as from the expert papers submitted to that meeting which reflected country experiences in dealing with bilateral investment treaties; the papers are included in the list of references.

Contents

Chapter I

INTRODUCTION

A. Purposes

For nearly 40 years, countries have been concluding bilateral treaties with a view towards promoting and protecting foreign investment.[1] These treaties, known generically as bilateral investment treaties (BITs), impose certain obligations on the contracting parties with respect to the treatment of foreign investment, and they create dispute-resolution mechanisms to enforce those obligations.[2]

Traditionally, home countries (mainly developed countries) have relied on BITs as a mechanism to ensure protection for their investment in developing countries, while developing countries have entered into BITs as part of their strategies to attract foreign direct investment (FDI).[3] However, as some developing countries achieve the status of home countries, they pursue the twin objectives of investment promotion and investment protection in negotiating BITs.[4] BITs are not usually concluded between developed countries.[5]

---

[1] Unless otherwise stated, throughout the study BITs are referred to by the names of the two countries that are signatories to them. For further identification of the relevant treaties, the list contained in annex I of this study includes information on the date of their adoption and, where available, the date of entry into force. The texts of most BITs mentioned in this study can be found in the United Nations Treaty Series and in the collection of bilateral investment treaties maintained by the International Centre for Settlement of Investment Disputes (ICSID) (ICSID, 1972 –).

[2] For the recent literature on BITs see, among others, Voss (1981), Mann (1981), Bergmann (1983), Klebes (1983), Kunzer (1983), Hashem (1984), Gann (1985), Laviec (1985), OECD (1985), Sornarajah (1986, 1994), Akinsanya (1987), Denza and Brooks (1987), Kohona (1987a, b), Ocran (1987), UNCTC (1988), Vandevelde (1988), Matsui (1989), Salacuse (1990), Paterson (1991), Khalil (1992), Reading (1992), Vandevelde (1992, 1993a, 1993b), World Bank (1992), Dolzer and Stevens (1995) and Karl (1996).

[3] In some cases, the conclusion of BITs by a capital importing country is a condition for the issuance of political risk insurance by a capital-exporting country. Capital exporting countries that have linked conclusion of a BIT with their political risk insurance programmes include Germany and France, which are among the countries with the most extensive BIT programmes. Developing countries thus sometimes conclude BITs in order to become eligible to participate in such insurance programmes. In addition, the Multilateral Investment Guarantee Agency (MIGA) – which offers political risk insurance for investors – has also encouraged the adoption of BITs as a test to ensure that investments are sufficiently protected, thus minimizing political risk (Convention Establishing the Multilateral Investment Agency, chapter III and Operational Regulations (UNCTAD, 1996b, vol. 1, p. 213)). (Political risk insurance programmes are discussed in further detail in section I.B. below.)

[4] On this point see, for example, China (1997).

[5] Developed countries are members of the Organisation for Economic Co-operation and Development (OECD) and are bound by commitments adopted by the members of the Organisation in the area of foreign investment.

There are numerous preconditions for the successful mobilization of FDI, including attractive markets, adequate infrastructure and sufficiently trained manpower, to name just a few. It also requires satisfactory policy and legal frameworks. Developing countries typically seek a framework that encourages the flows of capital and technology to their territories while, at the same time, maintaining control over the effects of FDI on their economies, to ensure in particular that it contributes to growth and development. From the investor's perspective, however, national frameworks on foreign investment, particularly if they seek to restrict and control managerial flexibility, may raise a number of concerns about the conditions for entry and operation of an investment, the stability of benefits granted and the commitments made by a host Government, the security of the investment, and the resolution of investment disputes. Also, foreign investors are often hesitant to rely on host country laws alone for the protection of their investments because of the fear that host Governments may change their laws and may not fully respect investors' interests when administering the laws. For this reason, countries seeking to protect their firms abroad have often turned to international law to deal with FDI issues and relations.

1. Protection of foreign investment under international law

Bilateral investment treaties are one of the policy instruments available to provide legal protection to foreign investments under international law and thus to reduce as much as possible the non-commercial risks facing foreign investors in host countries. In this respect it is useful to recall that there are two principal sources of international law: customary law and international treaties.[6] Under customary international law, the ability of a foreigner to make an investment in a host country is subject exclusively to the territorial sovereignty of that host country. It is well established in international law that a State has the right to control the movement of capital into its territory and to control the entry and activities of aliens.[7]

On issues concerning the treatment of investments once they have been made, customary international law has been a contentious matter among countries and scholars. In 1970, the International Court of Justice, in the Barcelona Traction, Light and Power Company Limited case (Belgium v. Spain) involving the exercise of diplomatic protection, summarized the state of the debate as follows :

> Considering the important developments of the last half-century, the growth of foreign investments and the expansion of the international activities of corporations, in particular of holding companies, which are often multinational, and considering the way in which the economic interests of states have proliferated, it may at first sight appear surprising that the evolution of law has not gone further and that no generally accepted rules in the matter have crystallized on the international plane (International Court of Justice, 1970, pp. 46–47).[8]

---

[6] The sources of international law are spelled out in Article 38 (1) of the Statute of the International Court of Justice. In addition to treaties and custom, which are considered the principal sources, the article mentions a number of subsidiary sources, namely (a) general principles of law, (b) judicial decisions and (c) writings of publicists. For a detailed discussion on this topic see, for example, Oppenheim (1992).

[7] On the customary international law affecting foreign investment, see, among others, Shawcross (1961), Fatouros (1962), Brierly (1963), Schwartzenberger (1969), Diez de Velasco (1978), Brownlie (1991) and Sornarajah (1994).

[8] It should be noted, however, that the issue under contention in the quotation from the Barcelona Traction, Light and Power Company Limited case referred to the inadequacies of customary international law in the narrowly circumscribed field of protecting a corporate citizen as distinguished from the shareholders of that company. The case did not address the wider subject of the principles of customary international law governing the treatment of foreign investment.

The doctrine of State responsibility for injuries to aliens and their property[9] has long held that a State is entitled to exercise diplomatic protection for its nationals who are injured by acts contrary to international law committed by another State, from which they have been unable to obtain satisfaction through local remedies.[10] A number of countries, mainly developed ones, have asserted that a breach of international law could arise because a State does not respect the "minimum standard of protection" required by customary international law with regard to the treatment of aliens, in particular, foreign investors.

That view was not unanimously accepted, however, by countries as an accurate statement of customary international law (Sornarajah, 1994). At the end of the nineteenth century, the Latin American countries took the position that, under international law, States are required to accord aliens the same treatment they accord their own nationals under national law, but no more than that. Where an alien or a foreign company has been injured by actions of the State that do not discriminate between aliens and nationals, there is no breach of international law. It follows from the same principle that foreign companies are not entitled to preferential treatment; claims by aliens against the host State must be decided solely by the domestic courts of that State and not by arbitral or other international tribunals; and diplomatic protection by the State of the alien's nationality can be exercised only in cases of direct breach of international law. This position was reflected in many Latin American constitutions and in contracts with foreign investors.[11]

Moreover, in the post-Second World War period, the developing countries undertook a number of initiatives in multilateral fora aimed at asserting their economic sovereignty and independence. The results were reflected in a series of United Nations General Assembly resolutions that affirmed States' permanent and inalienable sovereignty over natural wealth and resources.[12] The position of most developing countries with respect to customary international law on foreign investment at that time appears to be summarized in article 2 of the United Nations Charter of Economic Rights and Duties of States, which provides:

1.   Every State has and shall freely exercise full permanent sovereignty, including possession, use and disposal, over all its wealth, natural resources and economic activities.

2.   Each State has the right:

(a)   To regulate and exercise authority over foreign investment within its national jurisdiction in accordance with its laws and regulations and in conformity with its national objectives and priorities. No State shall be compelled to grant preferential treatment to foreign investment;

(b)   To regulate and supervise the activities of transnational corporations within its national jurisdiction and take measures to ensure that such activities comply with its laws, rules and regulations and conform with its economic and social policies. Transnational corporations shall not intervene in the internal affairs of a host

---

[9] For a discussion of the origins and early developments of the principles of customary international law relating to the protection of aliens and their property abroad see, for example, Borchard (1915), Freeman (1938), Amerasinghe (1964), Lillich (1983), Garcia Amador (1984).

[10] The right of diplomatic protection was discussed by the Permanent Court of International Justice in the Mavrommantis case (Greece v. the United Kingdom) (Permanent Court of International Justice, 1924). The Court made clear that, under international law, diplomatic protection is a right of the State, not of the individual or company.

[11] The traditional Latin American view of international law with respect to foreign investment is best known as the "Calvo doctrine". It was named after the Argentine jurist Carlos Calvo, who elaborated this doctrine in a treatise published in 1868 (Calvo, 1868). Since the mid-1980s and early 1990s, however, Latin American countries have adopted investment regimes that seem to depart from the Calvo Doctrine.

[12] See, for example, United Nations General Assembly resolutions 1803 (XVII) (UNCTAD, 1996b, vol. 1, p. 21), 3201 (S-VI) (vol. 1, p. 47), 3202 (S-VI) (vol. 1, p. 52) and 3281 (XXIX) (vol. 1, p. 57).

State. Every State should, with full regard for its sovereign rights, co-operate with other States in the exercise of the right set forth in this subparagraph;

(c)   To nationalize, expropriate or transfer ownership of foreign property, in which case appropriate compensation should be paid by the State adopting such measures, taking into account its relevant laws and regulations and all circumstances that the State   considers pertinent. In any case where the question of compensation gives rise to a controversy, it shall be settled under the domestic law of the nationalizing State and by its tribunals, unless it is freely and mutually agreed by all States concerned that other peaceful means be sought on the basis of the sovereign equality of States and in accordance with the principle of free choice of means. (UNCTAD, 1996b, vol. 1, p. 61).

However, the Charter of Economic Rights and Duties of States, and article 2 in particular, were not accepted by a number of major developed countries.

Given the controversy surrounding customary international law relating to foreign investment, international agreements could provide a source of clear and certain rules.[13] At the regional level, countries have succeded in adopting agreements dealing partially or solely with foreign investment, and the number of such agreements is growing. In particular, many developing countries have been party at one time or another to regional and subregional integration schemes. While economic cooperation and collective self-reliance on the basis of regional agreements have been pursued for wider purposes, one of their underlying considerations has been that they may also serve as a means to strengthen the bargaining power of developing countries with respect to foreign investors by means of common trade programmes, coordinated development, and cooperation in policies regarding foreign investment (UNCTC, 1988). At the multilateral level, the adoption of agreements on investment has proved to be far more difficult.[14] Although a number of global agreements address partial aspects of the issue,[15] a comprehensive multilateral agreement on foreign investment does not exist.[16]

Thus, over the years, for many countries BITs have provided the second best solution in the absence of a universal investment agreement. Indeed, many developing countries found that acceptance of certain rules as *lex specialis* between the two contracting parties was not inconsistent with critical positions on the same principles as a source of general customary international law. As a result, BITs constitute at present a principal source of substantive and, especially, procedural rules for the international protection of FDI. But it is debatable whether they reflect general principles of customary international law.[17]

As noted in the previous United Nations study on bilateral investment treaties (UNCTC, 1988), the policy of negotiating BITs received support from the investment clauses inserted in interregional agreements concluded by the European Community, such as the Fourth Convention

---

[13]   See footnote 6 on the main sources of international law.

[14]   Efforts to create conventional multilateral rules for foreign investment started in the early 1940s in the framework of the Havana Charter. Positions on FDI issues at that time were too far apart to allow consensus. Even within the OECD, a draft convention on the protection of foreign property abroad could not enter into force. For a more detailed discussion on the historical background and evolution of the international framework on investment, see Sauvant and Aranda (1993) and UNCTAD (1996b, c).

[15]   For a detailed discussion of the various attempts to elaborate multilateral instruments on FDI, see, for example, Sauvant and Aranda (1993) and UNCTAD (1996c, chapter V).

[16]   It should be noted, however, that, in a number of United Nations General Assembly resolutions it was possible to find compromise language and, as a result, some of them were adopted by consensus. A prominent example is General Assembly resolution 1803 (XVII) of 1962.

[17]   See below for a discussion of the various views on this topic.

of Lomé and several association agreements with individual countries.[18] At the multilateral level, article 23 of the Convention Establishing the Multilateral Investment Guarantee Agency mandates the Agency to undertake activities aimed at facilitating "the conclusion of agreements, among its members, on the promotion and protection of investments" (UNCTAD, 1996b, vol. 1, p. 223).

At present, apart from BITs,[19] other bilateral treaties dealing with important aspects of investment relations include bilateral treaties for the avoidance of double taxation. In these treaties, of which there are many, the parties agree to observe certain commitments for the allocation of tax revenue between the jurisdictions involved, in order to avoid and resolve the conflicts that occur when income and capital of firms operating abroad are considered as taxable in more than one jurisdiction. In the area of competition law and policy, some countries have also concluded in recent years bilateral agreements for cooperation in various aspects relating to the enforcement of competition rules (UNCTAD, 1997a). In addition, bilateral free trade agreements containing investment chapters similar to chapter 11 of the North American Free Trade Agreement (NAFTA) have been signed between a number of countries.[20]

2. Promotion of foreign investment

Bilateral investment treaties, through improved protection of FDI – a purpose that matters especially for home countries – are aimed at promoting FDI between the two country partners and, more specifically, at attracting FDI to host countries – a purpose that matters especially for these countries. Bilateral investment treaties may encourage foreign investment in a number of ways. The basic assumption is that the existence of a BIT with clear, simple and enforceable rules to protect foreign investors increases investor confidence, improving the investment climate. In particular, it reduces the political risks that an investor would otherwise face, and a reduction in risk, all other things being equal, encourages investment. It is important to emphasize that a BIT does not ordinarily impose an obligation upon the parties to take concrete measures to encourage their nationals to invest in the other country. Under BITs, the objectives of attracting foreign investment, technology and expertise are operationalized through the following strategies:

- Facilitating and encouraging entry of FDI in the host country's territory by nationals and companies of the other contracting party;
- Guaranteeing foreign investors high standards of treatment including, in particular, fair and equitable treatment, non-discriminatory treatment, most-favoured-nation and national treatment;
- Providing, as discussed in the preceding section, legal protection under international law and guarantees for investments, notably with respect to the transfer of funds and expropriation, including the standards for the compensation to be paid, and thus reducing the likelihood of arbitrary nationalization (small as it is in today's FDI climate);
- Guaranteeing access to international means of dispute resolution in the event that a dispute concerning an investment arises;

---

[18] On this point see, among others, Lebanon (1997).

[19] See below, under "Origins and evolution", for a discussion of earlier bilateral treaties dealing with investment issues.

[20] These include the free trade agreements between Bolivia and Mexico (chapter 15) (10 September 1994); between Costa Rica and Mexico (chapter 13) (signed on 5 April 1994); and Canada and Chile (chapter G) (signed on 5 December 1996). In addition, Chile, for example, has signed "bilateral complementary agreements" with the following countries: Mexico (signed on 22 September 1991); Venezuela (signed on 2 April 1993); Colombia (signed on 6 December 1993); and Ecuador (signed on 20 December 1994). It also signed such an agreement with the Southern Common Market (MERCOSUR) (on 25 June 1996).

- In some cases, addressing issues that foreign investors consider important but that are not addressed in a country's national law; providing more reliable and transparent conditions for investors than national laws and enhancing the stability and predictability of the regulatory environment;[21]
- Satisfying a precondition for the provision of political-risk insurance often found
- In national, regional and multilateral insurance agencies and thus facilitating insurance and resulting possibly in reducing insurance premiums;
- Allowing economies in transition to provide guarantees for foreign investors while they undertake national legislative reforms (and thus contributing to the success of such reforms by attracting the necessary foreign capital, technology and management know-how);[22]
- Protecting intellectual property as a form of FDI, a protection that is valuable in particular to investors in high-technology and some service industries where companies rely on intangible assets such as patents, copyright and brands.

BITs are only one among several confidence-building measures that can be used to improve a host country's investment climate. Thus, signing a BIT may be a way of inducing firms at least to consider undertaking investments in a given country.[23] Moreover, while a BIT may not directly result in an influx of foreign capital (see chapter IV), it may be one of several diplomatic and other steps to improve relations with a foreign country from which various additional economic advantages, such as increased trade and economic cooperation, are sought. Just as friendship, commerce and navigation treaties (see below under "Origins and evolution") were intended by the United States as a means of starting political and economic relations with other countries, similar considerations may be a motivating factor for some BITs.

Consequently, countries actively seeking FDI consider BITs as an important component of their enabling regulatory framework, further spurred by the increasing competition among countries for FDI.[24] At the same time, countries need to bear in mind that BITs, in and by themselves, will not secure FDI. Other determinants of investment flows also come into play.

3. The development dimension

The presumed effect of BITs on development rests on the premise that the protection of foreign investment encourages investment flows to developing countries, and this, in turn, contributes to their economic development. In this respect, it is worth noting that FDI can, indeed, be an important vehicle for the transfer of resources such as capital, technology and managerial skills, which are vital to a country's economy and for the integration of a country into international production and distribution networks. These and other components of the FDI package can also significantly contribute to improving the international competitiveness of firms and the economic performance of countries (UNCTC, 1992; UNCTAD, 1995). BITs may help to attract certain types of investments that are particulary conducive to development. The long-term nature of some of the most important FDI projects for development (e.g. in infrastructure) increases investors' exposure to political risks. Investors in these projects therefore pay more attention to the protection clauses in a BIT (e.g. on expropriation, preservation of rights or settlement of disputes).

---

[21] On this point, see, for example, the Philippines (1997).

[22] On this point see, among others, Romania (1997).

[23] Some countries have emphasized the relevance of BITs when facing questions regarding the risk rating of a country by evaluating agencies; on this point, see, among others, Lebanon (1997).

[24] See, among others, Germany (1997) and the Philippines (1997).

Given the many determinants that influence locational decisions, however, policy measures aimed at protecting foreign investment alone are not sufficient to attract the level and quality of investment flows that developing countries seek. Consequently, BITs sometimes complement their protection provisions with investment promotion commitments. Thus far, however, home country commitments in this respect are usually quite vague and weak. And there are no specific commitments in BITs regarding investors' behaviour, although all foreign investments are bound by the laws of their host countries.[25]

At the same time, however, and despite the potential benefits of BITs for development, countries need to carefully consider the advantages and disadvantages of these treaties before concluding them. It is true that, under most BITs, a host country maintains wide discretion to control the establishment of foreign investment from the other party in its territory. However, by entering into a BIT, a country assumes obligations that may prove costly at some time in the future. More specifically, BIT obligations may create obstacles to the ability of a host country to change certain of its economic policies or to develop new policies in the future. In other words, in concluding a BIT – or any other international agreement, for that matter – a country reduces its future flexibility to pursue particular economic strategies or take specific measures.

The goal for a developing country in concluding a BIT, then, is to maximize its benefits in the form of increased flows of FDI, while minimizing its costs in the form of obligations and commitments that may prove burdensome or expensive in the future or may impinge on its development efforts. The achievement of this goal requires a clear understanding of the consequences of assuming particular BIT obligations so that the costs and benefits of each specific obligation can be weighted. The task of achieving this balance can be particularly difficult for developing countries that are not capital-exporting countries.

Still, developing countries that wish to commit to the standards of treatment and protection of investors typically stated in BITs while retaining a margin of freedom to deal with their specific development concerns can use of a number of techniques, including the introduction of exceptions and derogations to, and temporal exemptions from, such standards. These and other bargaining techniques can lead to mutually satisfactory results, as nearly 40 years of BIT negotiating processes (discussed in chapter II) have demonstrated.

* * *

In sum, BITs are symmetrical in form, in the sense that they establish identical rights and obligations for both countries. However, their provisions typically focus on the treatment to be accorded to foreign investors by the host country only. They do not prescribe corresponding home country obligations (other than some general obligations as treaty signatories), or investor obligations. This raises the question of whether BITs are balanced instruments, in the sense that they provide mutual (if not symmetric) benefits to both parties. The answer to this question requires a parallel examination of two related aspects: first, whether the issues addressed in BITs and the manner in which these are addressed cover adequately the concerns of developing countries (the issues typically addressed in BITs are examined in chapter III); and, second, whether BITs help developing countries in attracting FDI for development (this aspect is addressed in chapter IV).

---

[25] In fact, some treaties, like the Indonesian and Australian treaties, protect only foreign investment that conforms with host country laws (see below under chapter III for a more detailed discussion on this point).

B. Origins and evolution

BITs are not the first bilateral treaties to provide protection for foreign investment. Beginning in the late eighteenth century, the United States and, to a lesser extent, Japan and a few other Western European countries, concluded a series of treaties, known as Friendship, Commerce and Navigation (FCN) treaties, Treaties of Establishment or Treaties of Amity and Commerce, that included various property protection provisions, such as restrictions on a host country's right of expropriation. After the Second World War, when bilateral trade agreements lost significance due to the establishment of the multilateral trading system under the auspices of the General Agreement on Tariffs and Trade (GATT), investment protection became a major purpose of these treaties. The FCN treaties differed from BITs in two main respects: first, the former addressed numerous subjects other than investment, including trade, maritime and consular relations; and, second, while BITs have been concluded predominantly between developed and developing countries, FCN treaties have been concluded also between developed countries (e.g. between the United States and European countries). A significant number of these FCN treaties remain in force.[26]

Also, after the Second World War, the United States initiated a political risk insurance programme as part of the Marshall Plan of foreign assistance to Europe. Over the next several decades, other countries developed similar programmes to insure investment in developing countries. Under these programmes, the home country insures the foreign investments of its nationals against certain non-commercial risks, such as expropriation or currency transfer restrictions. Some of these countries, notably the United States, also initiated a series of investment guarantee agreements to facilitate the operation of their political risk insurance programmes. Under these agreements, the home country and the host country agree that, in the event that an investor is paid compensation by the home country insurance agency, the insurer shall be subrogated to the claims of the investor and shall be entitled to seek resolution of the claims through binding arbitration. Investment guarantee agreements, however, do not confer protection on foreign investment. Rather, they establish a remedy for the home country where it has been required to pay compensation to an investor under its insurance programme.

In 1959, the Federal Republic of Germany negotiated the first two BITs, with Pakistan and the Dominican Republic, soon to be followed, in chronological order, by France, Switzerland, the Netherlands, Italy, the Belgium–Luxembourg Economic Union, Sweden, Denmark, and Norway in the 1960s (annex I). The BITs concluded by European countries in the early years included many of the same kinds of provisions that had appeared in the FCNs and the investment guarantee agreements. Unlike the FCNs, however, they were devoted entirely to the protection of investment, and, unlike the investment guarantee agreements, they included substantive terms for the protection of investment.

Most of the early BITs were concluded between Western European countries and African countries. As many as 26 African countries concluded BITs in the 1960s, whereas only 10 Asian countries did so in the same decade. Latin American countries, adhering to the Calvo doctrine, were more reserved, with only two countries concluding BITs in the 1960s.[27]

---

[26] The United States concluded such treaties with some 30 developing countries, although some of these treaties never came into effect. For a more elaborate discussion of the FCN treaties, see Wilson (1949, 1951, 1953, 1956, 1960), Hawkins (1951) and Walker (1956, 1958). For a discussion of the effects of FCN treaties and BITs on international investment see Fatouros (1962).

[27] On the State practice of the Calvo doctrine in Latin America, see Roffe (1984).

The negotiation of BITs gained new impetus in the 1970s. As noted, during that period, the developing countries were actively promoting multilateral investment instruments associated with a "New International Economic Order" in various international fora, emphasizing control of transnational corporations (TNCs) by host countries. That did not prevent them from concluding BITs, many of which contained clauses stating principles that they opposed in multilateral forums.[28] In other words, developing countries were against certain principles and standards when these were put forward as general international law norms, but were prepared to accept, for the pragmatic reason of attracting FDI, the same norms as *lex specialis* in the context of special bilateral relationships created by BITs. Among the developed countries, Austria, Israel, Japan[29] and the United Kingdom[30] began their BITs programmes during the 1970s.[31] Among the developing countries that concluded their first BIT in this decade were Haiti, Jordan, Kenya, Mali, Singapore and Yemen. Also some Central and Eastern European countries, such as Romania and Yugoslavia, signed their first BITs during the same decade.

Until the early 1980s, developing countries had relied heavily on external loan financing for their development needs. But with the onset of the debt crisis and the subsequent sharp reduction in commercial bank exposure in these countries, attracting and retaining foreign investment emerged as an important option for development financing. At the same time, the experiences of various countries led an increasing number of developing countries to recognize the positive effects of FDI for development. As a result, many developing countries that had not concluded BITs before (e.g., Bangladesh, China, Ghana, Guyana) introduced this practice as part of their efforts to attract FDI. China concluded its first BIT in 1982 and pursued a vigorous BIT practice, concluding 25 treaties by the end of 1980s. The total number of treaties signed by the end of 1980s jumped to 386 from a total of 167 at the end of the 1970s (see figure I.1).

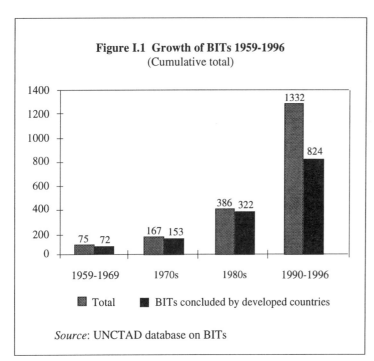

Figure I.1 Growth of BITs 1959-1996
(Cumulative total)

Source: UNCTAD database on BITs

Most Latin American countries had not been traditionally involved in the conclusion of BITs. As noted earlier, this was mainly due to the doctrine and State practice followed by these countries with respect to the treatment of FDI. On the other hand, the United States – the main source of FDI to that region – signed guarantee agreements with most Latin American countries, as a complement to the political risk insurance granted by the Overseas Private Investment Corporation. Over time, countries in the region relented in their opposition to BITs. In fact, since the late 1980s, Latin American countries have been

---

[28] See, for example, with respect to the standard of compensation on expropriation, article 2 (2) (c) of the Charter of Economic Rights and Duties cited above.

[29] For a detailed analysis of the Japanese BITs, see Matsui (1989).

[30] For a detailed analysis of the United Kingdom BITs, see Denza and Brooks (1987).

[31] The United States began its BIT programme formally in 1977, although no treaty was actually concluded for several years.

actively pursuing BIT negotiations, again as a mechanism for attracting FDI (Organization of American States, 1997).

As mentioned above, initially BITs were concluded predominantly between developed and developing countries. Typically, the developed country prepared a model treaty that it proposed for negotiation with various developing countries. A country preparing a model treaty often based the text on models already in use by other countries. These models also drew upon the 1967 Draft Convention on the Protection of Foreign Property (UNCTAD, 1996b, vol. II, p. 113)), which was prepared and adopted by the OECD but never opened for signature. As a result, the model treaties prepared by developed countries were often quite similar or even identical in many respects. However, there were also fundamental differences between, for example, the United States model and those of European countries in respect of issues such as admission of investment, performance requirements and admission of key personnel. Developing countries eventually also developed their own models, notable examples being the models developed by Chile and China and the three models proposed by the African-Asian Legal Consultative Committee (AALCC models A, B and C, reproduced in annex II).[32] In addition, some multilateral agreements such as the Fourth Lomé Convention have established broad principles for the negotiation of BITs.

C. The present universe of bilateral investment treaties

During the 1990s the number of BITs has increased dramatically. By the end of 1996 a total of 1,332 such treaties existed, of which 824 were concluded by developed countries with other countries (figure I.1). This was a marked increase from the 322 BITs signed by developed countries by the end of the 1980s. The number of BITs concluded between developing countries and economies in transition has also increased dramatically during the 1990s, from 64 by the end of the 1980s to 508 at the end of 1996. Since the late 1980s, countries with economies in transition, including those that emerged as independent States after the dissolution of the former Soviet Union, have also rapidly expanded their network of BITs with both developed and developing countries. Currently 162 countries and territories from all regions have concluded at least one BIT (table I.1 and figure I.2).

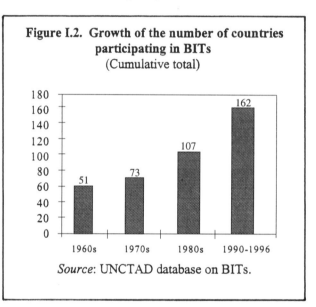

Figure I.2. Growth of the number of countries participating in BITs
(Cumulative total)

Source: UNCTAD database on BITs.

Table I.1. Countries/territories that have concluded bilateral investment treaties, end 1996

Countries and territories[a]	Developed countries				Developing countries		Economies in transition of Central and Eastern Europe and Central Asia[b]
	Western Europe	United States	Japan	Other developed countries	Within their region	Outside their region	
Albania	10	1	-	1	-	5	7
Algeria	5	-	-	-	1	4	1
Antigua and Barbuda	1	-	-	-	-	-	-
Argentina	13	1	-	3	9	9	9
Armenia	4	1	-	-	-	7	4
Australia	-	-	-	-	1	9	5
Austria	-	-	-	1	-	12	13
Azerbaijan	2	-	-	-	-	2	3
Bahrain	1	-	-	-	-	-	-
Bangladesh	6	1	-	-	5	-	1
Barbados	4	-	-	1	2	-	-
Belarus	8	1	-	-	-	4	6
Belgium and Luxembourg	-	-	-	-	1	28	11
Belize	1	-	-	-	-	-	-
Benin	3	-	-	-	-	-	-
Bolivia	10	-	-	-	5	2	1
Bosnia and Herzegovina	-	-	-	-	-	2	1
Brazil	8	-	-	-	2	1	-
Bulgaria	14	1	-	1	-	8	13
Burkina Faso	2	-	-	-	1	-	-
Burundi	3	-	-	-	-	-	-
Cambodia	1	-	-	-	2	-	-
Cameroon	5	1	-	-	-	-	1
Canada	-	-	-	1	7	2	7
Cape Verde	5	-	-	-	-	-	-
Central African Republic	3	-	-	-	-	-	-
Chad	4	-	-	-	-	-	-
Chile	13	-	-	1	13	4	5
China	16	-	1	3	20	16	24
Colombia	2	-	-	-	2	-	-
Congo	5	1	-	-	-	-	-
Costa Rica	4	-	-	-	1	-	-
Côte d'Ivoire	7	-	-	-	-	-	-
Croatia	3	1	-	-	-	5	8
Cuba	6	-	-	1	6	3	3
Cyprus	2	-	-	-	-	-	5
Czechoslovakia							
Czech Republic	2	-	-	1	-	12	15
Democratic Republic Republic of Congo	5	1	-	-	-	1	-
Denmark	-	-	-	1	-	23	14
Dominica	2	-	-	-	-	-	-
Dominican	2	-	-	-	-	-	-

Countries and territories[a]	Developed countries				Developing countries		Economies in transition of Central and Eastern Europe and Central Asia[b]
	Western Europe	United States	Japan	Other developed countries	Within their region	Outside their region	
Republic							
Ecuador	5	1	-	1	6	2	2
Egypt	12	1	1	1	5	12	11
El Salvador	3	-	-	-	3	-	-
Equatorial Guinea	1	-	-	-	-	-	-
Eritrea	1	-	-	-	-	-	-
Estonia	11	1	-	1	-	1	5
Ethiopia	2	-	-	-	-	1	-
Finland	-	-	-	-	-	15	15
France	-	-	-	2	1	52	19
Gabon	5	-	-	-	1	-	1
Gambia	1	-	-	-	-	-	-
Georgia	4	1	-	1	-	3	7
Germany	2	-	-	2	1	86	22
Ghana	5	-	-	-	-	2	2
Greece	1	-	-	-	-	9	12
Grenada	1	1	-	-	-	-	-
Guatemala	-	-	-	-	1	-	-
Guinea	3	-	-	-	1	1	1
Guinea-Bissau	1	-	-	-	-	-	-
Guyana	2	-	-	-	-	-	-
Haiti	3	1	-	-	-	-	-
Honduras	4	1	-	-	1	-	-
Hong Kong, China	9	-	-	2	-	-	-
Hungary	15	-	-	3	-	15	10
Iceland	-	-	-	-	-	1	-
India	5	-	-	1	2	-	6
Indonesia	13	-	-	1	9	4	8
Iran (Islamic Republic of)	1	-	-	-	4	-	10
Iraq	-	-	-	-	1	1	-
Israel	2	-	-	-	3	1	11
Italy	-	-	-	-	1	39	13
Jamaica	6	1	-	-	1	1	-
Japan	-	-	-	-	3	1	-
Jordan	5	-	-	-	4	3	1
Kazakhstan	7	1	-	1	-	8	7
Kenya	3	-	-	-	-	-	-
Republic of Korea	14	-	-	1	13	10	11
Kuwait	5	-	-	-	5	5	7
Kyrgyzstan	2	1	-	-	-	6	3
Lao People's Democratic Republic	5	-	-	1	7	-	1
Latvia	14	1	-	2	-	3	5
Lebanon	1	-	-	-	1	1	3
Lesotho	2	-	-	-	-	-	-
Liberia	4	-	-	-	-	-	-
Libyan Arab Jamahiriya	-	-	-	-	3	1	-
Lithuania	13	1	-	1	-	6	7

Countries and territories[a]	Developed countries				Developing countries		Economies in transition of Central and Eastern Europe and Central Asia[b]
	Western Europe	United States	Japan	Other developed countries	Within their region	Outside their region	
Madagascar	5	-	-	-	-	-	-
Malawi	1	-	-	-	-	1	-
Malaysia	13	-	-	-	11	6	10
Mali	2	-	-	-	2	-	-
Malta	7	-	-	-	-	2	1
Mauritania	3	-	-	-	1	-	1
Mauritius	3	-	-	-	-	1	-
Mexico	2	-	-	-	1	-	-
Republic of Moldova	5	1	-	-	-	4	6
Mongolia	7	1	-	-	5	-	6
Morocco	13	1	-	-	4	5	5
Namibia	2	-	-	-	-	-	-
Nepal	3	-	-	-	-	-	-
Netherlands	-	-	-	1	1	40	16
New Zealand	-	-	-	-	-	2	-
Nicaragua	4	1	-	-	1	1	-
Niger	2	-	-	-	1	-	-
Nigeria	3	-	-	-	-	-	-
Norway	-	-	-	-	-	7	8
Oman	6	-	-	-	1	2	-
Pakistan	7	-	-	-	7	1	5
Panama	4	1	-	1	2	-	-
Papua New Guinea	2	-	-	1	-	1	-
Paraguay	9	-	-	-	4	2	2
Peru	12	-	-	1	6	4	2
Philippines	6	-	-	2	5	1	2
Poland	16	1	-	3	-	19	19
Portugal	1	-	-	-	-	12	9
Qatar	2	-	-	-	-	2	1
Romania	20	1	-	3	-	40	18
Russian Federation	5	1	-	-	-	7	8
Rwanda	3	-	-	-	-	-	-
Saint Lucia	2	-	-	-	-	-	-
Saint Vincent and the Grenadines	1	-	-	-	-	-	-
Saudi Arabia	3	-	-	-	1	1	-
Senegal	6	1	-	-	1	2	1
Sierra Leone	2	-	-	-	-	-	-
Singapore	6	-	-	-	7	-	2
Slovakia	1	-	-	-	-	1	13
Slovenia	5	-	-	-	-	1	5
Somalia	1	-	-	-	-	-	-
South Africa	7	-	-	1	-	2	-
Spain	-	-	-	-	-	28	9
Sri Lanka	11	1	1	-	6	1	1
Sudan	4	-	-	-	1	-	1
Suriname	-	-	-	-	-	1	-
Swaziland	2	-	-	-	-	-	-
Sweden	-	-	-	-	-	22	13
Switzerland	-	-	-	1	1	61	18

Countries and territories[a]	Developed countries				Developing countries		Economies in transition of Central and Eastern Europe and Central Asia[b]
	Western Europe	United States	Japan	Other developed countries	Within their region	Outside their region	
Syrian Arab Republic	3	-	-	-	1	-	-
Taiwan Province of China	-	-	-	-	2	2	1
Tajikistan	-	1	-	-	-	8	2
Thailand	5	-	-	-	9	1	5
The former Yugoslav Republic of Macedonia	2	-	-	-	1	1	4
Togo	2	-	-	-	1	-	-
Trinidad and Tobago	2	1	-	1	-	-	-
Tunisia	13	1	-	-	10	10	4
Turkey	10	1	1	1	7	2	20
Turkmenistan	2	-	-	1	-	7	4
Uganda	3	-	-	-	1	-	-
Ukraine	12	1	-	1	-	13	12
United Arab Emirates	4	-	-	-	3	3	4
United Kingdom	-	-	-	1	1	63	22
United Republic of Tanzania	4	-	-	-	-	-	-
United States	-	-	-	-	9	11	19
Uruguay	8	-	-	1	-	1	3
USSR (former)[d]	11	-	-	1	-	3	-
Uzbekistan	7	1	-	-	-	6	9
Venezuela	9	-	-	1	8	-	2
Viet Nam	10	-	-	1	8	2	11
Yemen	5	-	-	-	2	1	-
Yugoslavia	5	-	-	-	-	4	7
Zambia	2	-	-	-	-	1	-
Zimbabwe	5	-	-	-	-	1	1
Total	732	40	4	61	287	873	669

Source: UNCTAD.

[a] The broad categories of regions used in this study are as follows:

Western Europe: European Union countries, Iceland, Norway and Switzerland
Other developed countries: Canada, Australia, Israel, New Zealand and South Africa
Developing country regions: Africa, Latin America and the Caribbean, Asia (West Asia, South, East and South-East Asia) and the Pacific
Transitional economies of Central and Eastern Europe and Central Asia (including the countries of the former Yugoslavia)

[b] Including the countries of the former Yugoslavia

[c] The Czech Republic and the Slovak Republic have upheld all bilateral treaties for the promotion and protection of FDI concluded by Czechoslovakia

[d] All international obligations undertaken by the USSR have been assumed by the successor States

Another interesting development in BIT practice in the 1990s is the increasing number of BITs concluded between developing countries, usually from within the same region, pointing to the change in the status of some of these countries from exclusively home countries to home and host countries. Whereas there were only three such BITs in the 1960s, the total number now stands at 159 (figure I.3). The number of BITs concluded within developing regions has also increased considerably, led by Asia and the Pacific (75), and followed by Latin America and the Caribbean (37) and Africa (17) (figures I.4 and I.5).[33]

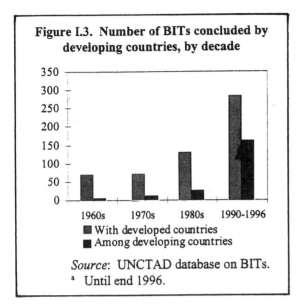

Figure I.3. Number of BITs concluded by developing countries, by decade

Source: UNCTAD database on BITs.
[a] Until end 1996.

The broad use of BITs among countries in all regions in recent years is attributable to a number of factors. The move towards market economies in the formerly socialist countries of Central and Eastern Europe led to a widespread recognition of private sector development as a promising path towards economic growth and development. Shrinkages in foreign aid placed renewed emphasis on the need to create favourable conditions to attract private investment in developing countries, which also began to recognize the potential of FDI as a source of economic growth, new technologies, access to markets, etc., and took steps to attract FDI. Today, virtually all countries acknowledge the importance of FDI and are frequently in competition with each other to attract investment projects. All these factors led to the conclusion that developed and developing countries (as well as transition economies) had a common interest in guaranteeing legal protection for FDI. In other words, ideological differences gave way to more pragmatic attitudes (Sornarajah, 1994). In that context, previous arguments concerning

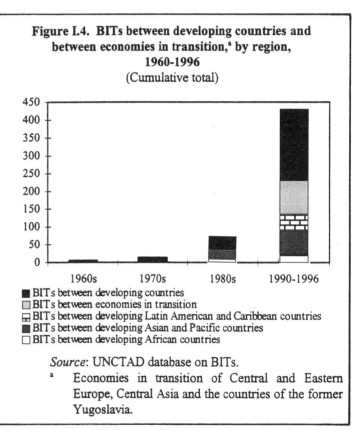

Figure I.4. BITs between developing countries and between economies in transition,[a] by region, 1960-1996
(Cumulative total)

- ■ BITs between developing countries
- ▦ BITs between economies in transition
- ▥ BITs between developing Latin American and Caribbean countries
- ■ BITs between developing Asian and Pacific countries
- □ BITs between developing African countries

Source: UNCTAD database on BITs.
[a] Economies in transition of Central and Eastern Europe, Central Asia and the countries of the former Yugoslavia.

---

[33] In fact, the Islamic Republic of Iran has concluded 15 BITs, and all but one (signed with the Federal Republic of Germany in 1965) were concluded with developing countries and economies in transition. The fact that all these BITs have been concluded with countries that belong by and large to the same region highlights how regionalism may contribute to the conclusion of BITs and set the horizon for further development of a broader framework and arrangments for investment. On this point, see, for example, Iran (1997).

whether BITs are one-sided agreements in favour of the capital-exporting country became less relevant than in past decades, as developing countries made special efforts to create conditions favourable for attracting FDI.

A closer look at individual regions and countries (figures I.6 and I.7), reveals the following patterns:

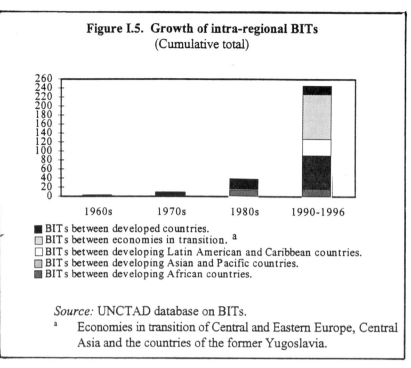

Figure I.5. Growth of intra-regional BITs
(Cumulative total)

■ BITs between developed countries.
□ BITs between economies in transition. a
□ BITs between developing Latin American and Caribbean countries.
▨ BITs between developing Asian and Pacific countries.
▨ BITs between developing African countries.

Source: UNCTAD database on BITs.
a Economies in transition of Central and Eastern Europe, Central Asia and the countries of the former Yugoslavia.

• Not surprisingly, the largest number of BITs have been concluded by countries in Western Europe as a group, reflecting their status as traditional capital-exporting countries. Indeed, they are parties to 732 BITs, representing about 55 per cent of all the BITs concluded to date.

• Early BITs were almost exclusively between developed countries and developing countries. For example, in the 1960s, 71 out of 72 BITs were concluded with a developed country as one of the parties. Africa was more actively involved in concluding BITs during that decade than any other developing region.

• Among capital-exporting countries, Germany ranks as the country that has concluded the largest number (113) of BITs (figure I.8 and annex I). The United Kingdom ranks second, with 87 BITs, and Switzerland ranks third, with 81 BITs.

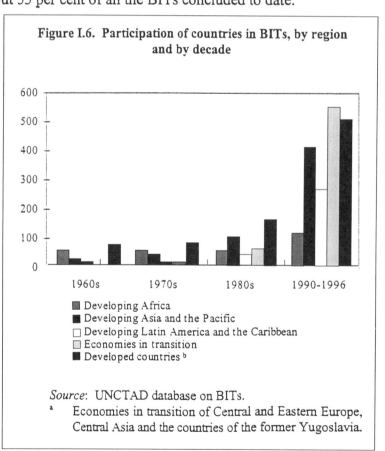

Figure I.6. Participation of countries in BITs, by region and by decade

▨ Developing Africa
■ Developing Asia and the Pacific
□ Developing Latin America and the Caribbean
▨ Economies in transition
■ Developed countries b

Source: UNCTAD database on BITs.
a Economies in transition of Central and Eastern Europe, Central Asia and the countries of the former Yugoslavia.

- Japan, in spite of its extensive outward investment in Asian developing countries and developed countries, has concluded only four treaties to date.

- With 39 BITs, the United States, the largest outward investor, ranks below the Belgium-Luxembourg Economic Union in terms of the number of BITs.

- Among capital-importing countries, Romania ranks first in terms of the number of treaties concluded, with 82 BITs. China is a close second, with 80 BITs. Poland, with 58 BITs concluded, is the third.

- African countries continue to conclude BITs, although at a slower pace than in the previous decades. To date, some 45 African developing countries have at least one treaty. Altogether they have concluded 284 BITs, of which 17 are among countries in the region.[34]

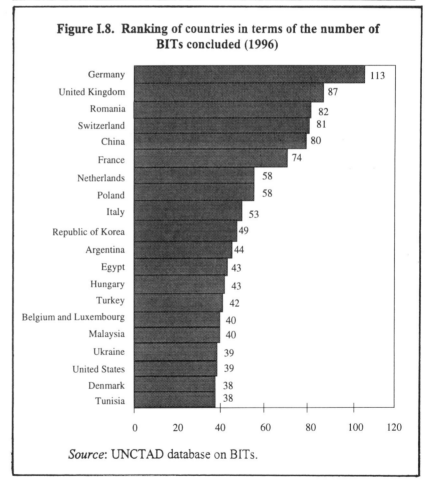

Figure I.7. Average number of BITs per country, by region (1996)

Source: UNCTAD database on BITs.
[a] Economies in transition of Central and Eastern Europe, Central Asia and the countries of the former Yugoslavia.

Figure I.8. Ranking of countries in terms of the number of BITs concluded (1996)

Country	Number of BITs
Germany	113
United Kingdom	87
Romania	82
Switzerland	81
China	80
France	74
Netherlands	58
Poland	58
Italy	53
Republic of Korea	49
Argentina	44
Egypt	43
Hungary	43
Turkey	42
Belgium and Luxembourg	40
Malaysia	40
Ukraine	39
United States	39
Denmark	38
Tunisia	38

Source: UNCTAD database on BITs.

---

[34] Despite the number of BITs concluded, most African countries continue to have serious difficulties in attracting FDI. On this point see, for example, Gabon (1997).

- A number of developing countries in South and South-East Asia and the Pacific have become more active in concluding BITs recently. Countries like Cambodia and India began to sign BITs in the 1990s. Currently, about 33 countries in the region have concluded a total of 567 BITs. Intraregional BITs are also on the increase, with 74 such BITs concluded so far.

- Developing countries from West Asia were active in concluding BITs as early as the 1960s and have continued to do so to date, although not in large numbers. The fact that Arab countries are signatories to a number of regional agreements for the protection and promotion of investment among themselves[35] may have obviated the need for signing BITs between countries in the region, some of which are important capital-exporting countries. In spite of this, a number of countries in the region have signed BITs with other developing countries in the region and in Northern Africa, as capital exporting countries. Currently, 14 West Asian countries are parties to one or more BITs.

- Latin American countries have embarked on signing BITs in increasing numbers during the 1990s. At present, 21 countries in the region have concluded one or more BITs; the regional total is 264 treaties (Organization of American States, 1997).

- The Caribbean countries for the most part did not become actively involved in BIT negotiations until the 1980s, despite the fact that the first BIT to enter into force was signed by the Dominican Republic with Germany in 1959. However, since then they have signed 34 treaties (Organization of American States, 1997).

- The Latin American and Caribbean region as a whole has concluded 298 treaties, of which 37 are between countries within the same region.[36]

- Since the late 1980s and early 1990s, countries in Central and Eastern Europe have started concluding BITs with developed countries in large numbers. After the dissolution of the Soviet Union, the successor States also started their own practice of entering into BITs. They were also concluded extensively with other countries in the region and with developing countries as well. To date, of the 669 BITs concluded by the economies in transition as a whole (figure I.9),[37] 104 BITs are among themselves and 205 BITs are with developing countries.

* * *

In spite of the rapid increase in the number of BITs concluded, the network of BITs among countries of various regions is far from complete. (Indeed, if every country or economy in the world concluded a BIT with every other country or economy, the number of BITs would be about 20,000.) As a result – and leaving aside FDI within the OECD area – a substantial portion of FDI flows is not covered by BITs. For example, although the United States is a major investor in China, to date there is no bilateral investment treaty between these two countries.

---

[35] For example, the Agreement on Investment and Free Movement of Arab Capital among Arab Countries, signed in 1970 (UNCTAD, 1996b, vol. II, p. 121); the Convention Establishing the Inter-Arab Investment Guarantee Corporation, signed in 1971 (vol. II, p. 127); and the Unified Agreement for the Investment of Arab Capital in the Arab States, signed in 1980 (vol II, p. 211).

[36] Only a number of small island countries in the region have not concluded BITs.

[37] For the purpose of this study, transitional economies include countries in Central and Eastern Europe, Central Asia and the countries of the former Yugoslavia.

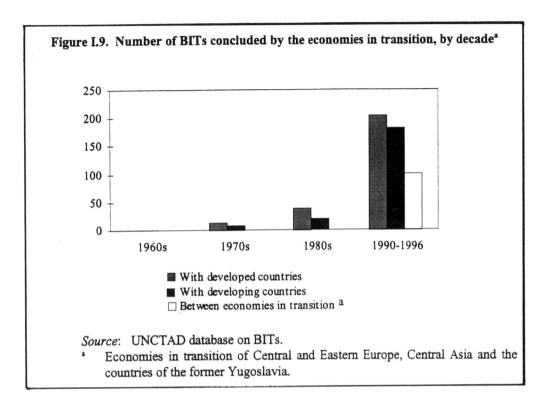

Figure I.9. Number of BITs concluded by the economies in transition, by decade[a]

Source: UNCTAD database on BITs.

[a] Economies in transition of Central and Eastern Europe, Central Asia and the countries of the former Yugoslavia.

Chapter II

NEGOTIATING A BILATERAL INVESTMENT TREATY

Bilateral investment treaties (BITs) are the result of negotiations. Through the negotiating process, the benefits of BITs for either party can be either enhanced or diminished. Therefore, to achieve the best results, it is important that countries consider carefully not only the substance of the treaty provisions but also the negotiating process. Indeed, despite the great similarity among BITs and despite the relatively few issues that they treat, any two BIT negotiations are seldom identical. The special needs and conditions of the countries concerned, as well as the skills of the individuals involved in the negotiations, can undoubtedly influence the outcomes. This chapter examines key aspects of a typical BIT negotiation.

A. The present context

As noted in the preceeding chapter, in the early years, BITs generally involved a developed, capital exporting country and a developing, capital importing country. The negotiation was almost invariably initiated and driven by the developed country, and it was common to regard a BIT as constituting a series of concessions made by the developing country to the developed country. The assumption was that the developed country sought as much protection as possible for its investment abroad, while the developing country sought to promise no more than what was necessary to attract new investment.

Changing circumstances have altered this assumption. First, the international economic climate has changed dramatically, with the result that many developing countries are now actively seeking to attract FDI, indeed competing for it.[1] Consequently developing countries often see a BIT as a means of signalling their favourable attitude towards inward investment and are more willing than in the past to offer concessions to foreign investors. Second, as already noted, it is increasingly the case that BITs are not necessarily concluded between a developed country and a developing one; developing countries and transitional economies are concluding BITs among themselves,[2] either as capital exporters or as protected platforms from which other countries may export capital. For example, the BIT between China and Singapore was intended to protect both Singaporean investors

---

[1] On changing attitudes towards FDI see, for example, Wiesner (1993).

[2] See, for example, Reading (1992).

and foreign companies established in Singapore coming from home countries which have no BIT with China. (A substantial share of Singapore's outward FDI is by foreign affiliates in Singapore.)

The result is that the traditional setting of BIT negotiations is no longer a true reflection of current practice. Rather than passively responding to proposals to negotiate from individual developed countries, developing countries may now decide as a matter of policy to negotiate and conclude a large number of BITs within a relatively short time. Moreover, while negotiators must still determine the appropriateness of particular treaty language for the circumstances of a given country, they less often see negotiations as a process in which a gain by either party necessarily represents a loss to the other. In this respect, the general trend in national policy frameworks for FDI has facilitated the conclusion of BITs. This does not mean, of course, that developing countries do not have important interests that need to be safeguarded in BIT negotiations. Indeed, one of the main purposes of looking at the BIT negotiating process is to ensure that developing countries make the best use of this process to advance their interests.

Despite the changes in the setting for BIT negotiations, the steps in the negotiating process remain relatively unchanged.

B. General considerations

The goal of negotiations is to achieve agreement on the formulation of a BIT that advances common interests while accommodating conflicting ones.[3] Consequently, an important task for the negotiators at the outset of BIT negotiations is to identify the areas where the interests of their country are the same as those of the other side and those where they are in conflict with those of the other side.

There is no single approach to negotiating. Some negotiators begin by stating extreme positions in which they ask for far more than they ever hope to obtain. Others prefer to find ways of advancing their own interests while leaving room for the other side also to do reasonably well; the key to this latter approach is for negotiators not to argue about positions (i.e. what each side says it must have), but rather to discuss the underlying interests on which those positions are based.

Negotiating style can be instrumental in successful negotiations. A good understanding of the other side's negotiating style may enable a negotiator to reach a better agreement. For example, some negotiators prefer to reach agreement on general principles before discussing detailed provisions, while negotiators from other countries prefer to "build" a treaty from agreement on specific provisions. In general, one must remember that international negotiations not only cross political frontiers, but also cultures. As a powerful factor in shaping communication and behaviour, culture conditions the negotiating process in fundamental ways. Cultural factors might explain, for example, why certain countries that are important home countries have concluded only a relatively small number of BITs (e.g. Japan). On the other hand, one should avoid any overly deterministic view of the impact of culture on negotiations.

It is often assumed that the side with the most resources has the greatest bargaining power and therefore the ability to force agreement on its terms. Thus, in the case of negotiations between an industrialized country and a developing country, it is often assumed that the developing country is in a weak bargaining position and that genuine negotiations between weak and strong cannot take place. However, the history of international negotiations does not always bear out that assumption.

---

[3] On BIT negotiations in general, see Vandevelde (1988) and Robinson (1993).

Very often what "power" means in international negotiations is the ability to influence the decisions of the other party. The challenge for the weaker country in a BIT negotiation is to devise strategies and to mobilize its resources so as to enhance its ability to influence the other side's decision-making (Habeeb, 1988).

C. Negotiating phases

The negotiation of a BIT can be divided into a series of distinct phases.

1. Determining the need

Negotiations essentially begin when a country determines that one or more of its investment policy goals – generally either the goal of protecting its investment abroad or the goal of attracting investment to its territory – could be advanced by negotiating a treaty. If the potential benefits seem great enough to justify the costs incurred in negotiations, the country is likely to begin the process of identifying prospective treaty partners.

2. Selecting treaty partners

Various factors are considered by a country in selecting the countries to approach:

- The status of diplomatic relations: favourable diplomatic relations are typically an important condition for BIT negotiations;
- The extent to which nationals of the prospective BIT partner have already invested in the other country or the likelihood that they may invest in the future, if the investment climate is favourable;
- The extent to which its own nationals have invested or could be expected to invest in the other country in the future (the status of trade relationships may give clues as to the potential for FDI);
- The general attitude of prospective BIT partners towards FDI;
- The broader economic and political interests that may be served by a BIT negotiation.

While capital-exporting countries have concluded BITs with countries that are the hosts or potential hosts to significant quantities of investment by their nationals and companies, historically that has not been a necessary condition for successful negotiations. Similarly, while many countries are eager to conclude treaties with countries that are likely to be the source of FDI, conclusion of a treaty with a country that does not appear to be a likely source of investment in the foreseeable future may still have benefits that justify the effort to negotiate. Such benefits may include demonstrating to investors from other countries a commitment to providing a safe investment climate or demonstrating to the local population a commitment to attract FDI. This said, however, developing countries with meagre resources might find it necessary to prioritize the list of potential treaty partners.

3. Preparing a model negotiating text

Countries that are active in BIT negotiations often begin their involvement with the preparation of a model negotiating text, sometimes referred to as a prototype. (For some examples, see annex II and UNCTAD, 1996b) This text, in effect, represents the ideal treaty, or at least an acceptable treaty from the particular country's perspective.

The development of a model negotiating text serves several purposes. It provides an opportunity for the Government to study the entire question of investment protection, to consult with various interested governmental and private-sector organizations, and to formulate a national policy on the question. It also helps to identify potential problems associated with the conclusion of a BIT, provides an opportunity to resolve any such problems before negotiations begin, and helps to ensure that the model negotiating text that emerges from the consultations will enjoy broad political support inside the country.

The preparation of a model negotiating text also serves to communicate to other countries the type of treaty desired by the country that has prepared it. Potential treaty partners can study the text before deciding to negotiate and perhaps determine whether the parties are sufficiently in agreement about the desirable content of the treaty to warrant spending time and other resources in the negotiations. At the same time, the opportunity to study the language carefully and formulate questions before negotiations begin can expedite the negotiations considerably and prevent the last-minute problems that can arise when negotiators find themselves working with new language that neither party has had much time to analyse.

The preparation of a model negotiating text also promotes uniformity in the language of the BITs concluded by a single country, thus facilitating their implementation and interpretation.

Finally, the use of a model text provides a negotiating advantage for the country that has drafted it, since such a text sets the agenda and indicates the ideal outcome for the drafting country on every issue addressed by the treaty. While the non-drafting or receiving country is free to contest any provision with which it disagrees, if it does not question a given provision, the drafting country obtains by default its preferred language on the issues addressed by that provision.

4. Determining the other party's interest

The precise means by which a country makes contact with its prospective treaty partner varies from case to case. Many countries inquire directly through formal diplomatic channels. Others adopt a more indirect approach, preferring not to be the party formally to request negotiations. Regardless of how the initial contact is made, the second country has to make a basic decision as to whether it has any interest in entering into negotiations with the country that has proposed the treaty, taking into account all circumstances, including the considerations described above.

5. Responding to the proposal to negotiate

The process by which the country approached responds to an invitation to negotiate and, where relevant, to the model negotiating text, is analogous to the process by which the drafting country prepares the treaty text. The receiving country must assemble a group of experts to determine whether negotiations would be desirable and to review the proposed text. Such a review must ascertain both whether conclusion of the treaty would be consistent with that country's foreign and economic policy and whether it would be feasible as a practical matter. The feasibility study should consider the legal framework within which the BIT would operate. It must focus in particular on whether the treaty is consistent with domestic law and whether there is sufficient political support for the treaty in the receiving country to ensure that the treaty will receive approval from the constitutionally appropriate body and that the obligations imposed by the treaty can be met. This precaution will prevent embarrassment later on if the country is unable to ratify a signed BIT because of a lack of parliamentary support.

Another initital task is to review and evaluate the other country's proposal so as to determine, among other things, the effect of the treaty on other international agreements to which the country is a party, and on foreign policy positions it has taken in other arenas.

Finally, a potential signatory to a BIT should make a realistic assessment of the costs of the treaty for the country. Inevitably, there will be divergent views on these issues, but any such matters must be resolved before negotiations begin. In particular, developing countries might need to assess whether the loss of flexibility with regard to specific investment measures that might arise as a result of signing the BIT would be compensated for by significan increases in FDI flows.

Assuming that the review ends in a decision to proceed with negotiations, it is nevertheless likely to result in a list of political or practical issues that must be addressed in negotiations. Once a country has determined that it is interested in negotiating a BIT with the proposing party, it communicates its decision to that country. At that point, the two countries must agree upon the time and place for the first session of formal negotiations.

6. Preparing for formal negotiations

The key to a successful negotiation is thorough planning and preparation before discussions with the other side begin. The first step in preparation is to organize a team of experts from the relevant government departments to study the matter and prepare a negotiating strategy based on the country's interests. Very often developing countries will face difficulties arising from a lack of qualified personnel; however, every effort should be made to ensure that the team includes a lawyer and an economist from the relevant ministry. In some developing countries there might be a need for technical assistance and training of negotiators before a team with the necessary knowledge of the issues involved can be assembled. The difference that a well-trained team can make in the BIT negotiating process can far outweigh the financial cost of such training and technical preparation. A number of government departments should have a voice in the negotiating process, not merely for the substantive reason that their expertise will be useful in negotiating a treaty that will advance the country's interests, but also for the purely pragmatic reason that a government agency unjustifiably excluded may oppose approval or ratification of the treaty. In addition, the team may need to consult with private organizations such as local chambers of commerce and specific sectors that may be significantly affected by FDI. Widespread consultations help to ensure broad support for the country's negotiating policies and to avoid sudden disagreements that may be exploited by the other party. The team must be given a clear mandate defining the extent of its authority to commit its country to the treaty.

In general, the team should be chosen both for the institutions its members represent and for their professional expertise. In particular, the team should include an expert from a foreign investment agency or department. If a country is contemplating the negotiation of several BITs over a longer period, it may be wise to establish a permanent task force or negotiating team for this purpose so as to build up its expertise and experience.

The receiving party faces two alternatives in responding to the model negotiating text: accept the proposed model negotiating text as the basis for negotiations or propose its own model text as a counterdraft. In the early days of the BIT programmes, many developing countries lacked the resources to prepare their own model texts. A model text, however, need not be a country's own original product. There are a number of models prepared by developing countries that can be used (see annex II and Vol. III, annex B, in UNCTAD, 1996b). Alternatively, a country may simply select any one of the hundreds of existing treaties and propose it as a basis for negotiations.

As noted above, there are numerous benefits associated with the preparation of a model negotiating text. The chief advantage of proposing a counterdraft is likely to be that it eliminates the negotiating advantage of the other country. It removes the receiving country from the posture of implicitly accepting by default any language in the drafting country's model text that it does not explicitly question or oppose.

While the counterdraft tactic may seem obvious, it is not frequently used in BIT negotiations for a number of reasons. Too much delay can reduce the momentum that pushes forward a negotiation. It may not be productive to spend time debating which text shall constitute the basis for negotiations. If the parties cannot agree on which text to use, they may attempt to prepare a consolidated text, in which provisions addressing similar issues are laid side by side to permit easy comparison. If the treaties are organized differently, however, this can be a difficult task.

The importance of a counterdraft, in any event, should not be overstated. In most cases it is sufficient that the negotiating team is ready to make counter-proposals to specific provisions in the proposed draft.

As part of their preparation for negotiations, each country is likely to obtain copies of other BITs concluded by the country with which it is negotiating.[4] These BITs contain language that has been acceptable to the other country in the past, and it will be difficult for that other country to refuse to agree to the same or similar language in present negotiations. It would also be advisable to collect and study existing agreements that may have provisions with implications for foreign direct investment and its treatment, such as double taxation treaties and commerce and navigation treaties in force between the two negotiating parties. Similarly, prior to negotiation it would be advisable to verify whether the negotiating parties are signatories to international conventions that are usually referred to in BITs, such as the Convention on the Settlement of Investment Disputes between States and Nationals of other States, and the United Nations Convention on the Recognition and Enforcement of Foreign Arbitral Awards.

If the receiving party decides not to offer a counterdraft, it may blunt the controlling effect of the model treaty by suggesting that the model be put aside temporarily while the two teams discuss the basic principles and concepts that should govern the investment relationships between the two countries. The negotiators may then record their general understanding in the form of simple principles that would become the framework for the treaty instead of the model originally proposed.

Alternatively, if the model treaty is accepted as the basis for negotiation, the receiving party may be well advised not to proceed to discuss the draft treaty provision by provision, in the order stated in the draft. Rather, the receiving party may identify the principal issues to be discussed and present them for consideration in the order it judges appropriate. At the very least, this approach enables that party to shape the order of the agenda. Moreover, the receiving party may choose not to negotiate on the basis of exceptions to the rules and principles proposed in the model treaty but, instead, it may frame its concessions in the form of positive formulations. For example, if the draft treaty presented prohibits ten types of performance requirements and there are five the receiving party may wish to retain, it may decide not to seek exceptions to those five but rather to list the five that can be eliminated as a specific concession on its part.

---

[4] As noted above, the texts of many BITs can be found in several collections, including the United Nations Treaty Series and ICSID (ICSID, various years). In addition, the American Society of International Law also publishes BITs from time to time and the Organization of American States has started to publish texts of BITs between countries in the Americas on the Internet.

Finally, the choice of language in which the negotiations are to be conducted is something to be kept in mind, since the experts on the team may not speak the other party's language. In these situations, a third language, acceptable to both negotiating parties, may be agreed upon.

7.   The formal negotiating rounds

The two countries must agree initially on the location of the negotiations. Most countries prefer to host the negotiations to avoid the expense of travel and to facilitate consultations between the negotiating team and other members of the Government if unanticipated problems arise. It is not unusual to alternate negotiations between the two countries. Questions of cost are important factors for developing countries in deciding on the venue of the negotiations and may lead the parties to choose the process of written diplomatic exchange rather than face-to-face negotiations. The process of diplomatic exchange to conclude a BIT should, if possible, be avoided. Because of the issues it raises, a BIT generally is not best negotiated by the process of diplomatic exchange, which could be drawn out over a long period of time without resolving outstanding issues. Face-to-face negotiations may be more productive; they allow for interpersonal exchange and facilitate accommodation and compromises. If a developing country finds that it cannot afford to send a delegation abroad, it would be better advised to host the negotiations at home where it can field its strongest delegation, leaving the process of diplomatic exchange for the final resolution of less difficult issues or the main issues previously discussed during face-to-face negotiations.

A typical negotiation proceeds as follows: a first round of negotiations will eliminate minor issues and identify any major problems; a second round is directed at attempting to resolve the major problems; between negotiating rounds, countries can often resolve a variety of issues through normal diplomatic channels, using embassy personnel to communicate questions, objections and suggested solutions to the members of the negotiating team from the other country.

The first round of negotiations typically begins with an explanation of the model negotiating text by the drafting party. If the receiving party wishes to propose a counterdraft, it may do so through diplomatic channels prior to the first round or it may present the counterdraft at the first round. Presenting the counterdraft before the first round permits the other party to analyse it and potentially expedites the negotiations, but may also send a signal that the negotiations are going to be difficult, thereby slowing the momentum before negotiations even begin. In either event, if there is a counterdraft, the proponent of the counterdraft may use the first round as an opportunity to explain its reasons for rejecting the original model negotiating text as a basis for negotiations and to draw attention to what it regards as the important differences between the drafts, thus laying the groundwork for the preparation of a consolidated draft, if that is the route chosen.

After the initial presentation of proposals and counter-proposals, the issues are identified and discussed. The resolution of these issues can take place in various ways:

- **Acceptance**. The party receiving the proposal may agree to accept a provision after hearing an explanation of its nature and purpose.
- **Clarification**. In some cases, the receiving party does not fully understand the meaning or intended effect of a provision and seeks clarification of the language. Often the issue can be resolved by an oral explanation of the provision by the proposing party.
- **Redefinition**. The receiving party may feel that the meaning of the provision is unclear and the parties may therefore agree to redefine or define more specifically the terms of the provision.

- **Reformulation**. The receiving party may agree with the fundamental underlying principle, but object to the precise language used for political or other reasons, thus requiring modification of the language though not the principle.
- **Substantive modification**. The parties may agree on a provision only after the original proposal has been substantively modified due to concessions made by one or both of the parties.
- **Use of protocols and exchange of letters.** Any modification, explanation or reservation can appear in the treaty itself or in a separate document known as a protocol, or in an exchange of letters or notes. Such documents have the same binding force as the treaty itself, and are an integral part of it. The parties may use this technique rather than modify the treaty itself for any of several reasons; for example, they may wish to minimize any appearance of having made a substantive change.
- **Omission**. The receiving party may oppose the provision, and the proposing party may ultimately agree to omit the disputed provision from the treaty.

This description of negotiating patterns, however, does not imply that there are any set patterns or predetermined approaches to a negotiation. Indeed, the key point to be stressed is that each negotiation is a unique and peculiar process requiring flexibility and accommodation. Also, it should be noted here that many issues are resolved on the basis of political accommodation, using a package approach with linkages internal to the BIT, and, sometimes, even external to it.

8. Conclusion and ratification

When all issues have been resolved, the negotiators generally signal their agreement by initialling or signing the treaty text. If one or both parties wish to draw attention to the conclusion of the treaty, the negotiators may initial the text at the end of face-to-face negotiations and then schedule a formal signing ceremony later.

In many countries, a signed BIT requires ratification by a legislative body before it becomes binding.[5] Thus, BITs often provide that the treaty will enter into force some period of time after the parties have notified each other that all domestic requirements for approval of the treaty have been completed. Typically, this notification occurs through the exchange of instruments of ratification. In such cases, the treaty may provide that it will enter into force, for example, 30 days after the parties exchange the instruments of ratification. It is important for each country to determine whether the treaty will require the enactment of any implementing legislation.[6]

Once they are ratified, BITs are promulgated. It is also advisable that the agencies responsible for the implementation of the treaty make sure that the existence of a BIT is made public in ways that reach the potential investors to whom it would apply.

---

[5] The legislative body may refuse to ratify on any of several grounds, including that it violates some constitutional principle. For example, the Constitutional Court of Colombia declared the BIT between Colombia and the United Kindom to be unconstitutional.

[6] Some countries have stressed the importance of having good knowledge of the details of the ratification procedure as well as information about the legal character of a BIT in the legal systems of the countries involved. This means knowing, for example, whether a BIT will require approval by the Government, by the parliament or by presidential decree; and whether it consequently becomes an international treaty which prevails over national laws. On this point see, among others, Czech Republic (1997).

Chapter III

MAIN PROVISIONS OF BILATERAL INVESTMENT TREATIES

Bilateral investment treaties cover similar issues, which are few in number and which relate exclusively to investment. Their principal provisions address a host country's obligations towards investors from the other treaty partner, but the treaties also cover, directly or indirectly, other aspects of the relations between the host and the home countries involved.[1] The usual provisions of such treaties are discussed in the following sections.

A. Title and preamble

Although the title and the preamble do not directly create rights and obligations, they may be relevant to the interpretation of the treaty to the extent that they constitute part of its context and reflect its object and purpose. Article 31 (1) of the 1969 Vienna Convention on the Law of Treaties provides that "[a] treaty shall be interpreted in good faith in accordance with the ordinary meaning to be given to the terms of the treaty in their context and in the light of its object and purpose"; it further provides that "[t]he context for the purpose of the interpretation of a treaty shall comprise, in addition to the text, ... its preamble ... " (United Nations, 1987). Although not specifically mentioned, the title of the treaty should also be considered part of its context and, therefore, a reflection of the treaty's object and purpose.

Some early BITs refer to themselves in their titles as treaties for the protection of foreign investment; for example, the BIT between Sweden and Egypt is entitled "Agreement between the Government of Sweden and the Government of the Arab Republic of Egypt on the Mutual Protection of Investments". The almost universal practice now, however, is to refer to both protection and promotion. A typical example of this practice is the "Agreement between Japan and the Democratic Socialist Republic of Sri Lanka concerning the Promotion and Protection of Investment".

---

[1] The issues examined in this chapter are analysed in the context of BITs only. However, the analysis does not exhaust all aspects of the issues when examined from the broader perspective of customary international law and other international investment agreements. To analyse these and other issues of international investment law and their development dimensions, UNCTAD is preparing a series of papers on issues relevant to international investment agreements.

In view of the developing countries' desire to attract FDI, arguably a formulation that expresses both protection and encouragement would be more advantageous to them, since this formulation could be interpreted as expressing an intent by each country – and especially by the capital exporting country – to encourage its nationals to invest in the other country. In fact, it could be argued from the title that there may be a general duty on the part of the home country to promote investment in the host country. On the other hand, the word "encouragement" in the title could also be interpreted to mean that each country is to encourage the other country's nationals to invest in its territory. In the latter case, there might therefore be a basis for arguing that the treaty's title indicates an intent by the host country to take actions to encourage investments from the other country, an argument that foreign investors might raise, for example, to avoid or lighten investment-screening procedures used by the host country.

The titles of BITs often include the word "reciprocal" or "mutual" (e.g. treaty for the "reciprocal encouragement and protection of investments"). By expressly mentioning reciprocity or mutuality in their titles, BITs acknowledge their formal reciprocal nature, that is, the fact that they grant identical rights and obligations to both treaty parties. But this term can also suggest that both parties to a BIT expect to derive benefits from it, although the benefits derived from BITs need not be identical for both countries (it is not necessary to achieve equal levels of FDI, for instance). In other words, in the final analysis, if the objectives of a BIT are fulfilled, each country should be satisfied that it is benefiting from the operation of the treaty. In the case of developing countries, the benefits to be derived from a BIT could be measured by the extent to which it contributes, directly or indirectly, to its growth and development.[2]

The preamble of a BIT is typically brief, comprising only three or four paragraphs. These paragraphs usually recite the same small number of objectives underlying the treaties, including the enhancement of economic cooperation, the promotion of private investment (which is sometimes linked explicitly to economic prosperity) and the protection of investment. A typical example is the preamble of the BIT between Malaysia and the United Arab Emirates (table III.1).

Variations in the language of the preamble, however, are sometimes significant. For example, the Swiss model treaty of 1979 makes a reference at the outset to "economic cooperation based on international law", while reaffirming the right of the host country to define the conditions under which an investment is admitted. There is also a reference to cooperation between private and public companies of the two countries. The models A, B and C prepared by the African–Asian Legal Consultative Committee (AALCC) (see annex II and Vol. III, annex B, in UNCTAD, 1996b) mention the promotion of "wider co-operation between the countries of the Asian–African region to accelerate their economic growth and to encourage investments by developing countries in other developing countries".

In another fairly common variation of the preamble, the parties recognize that "agreement on the treatment to be accorded to investment will stimulate the flow of capital and technology and their economic development"; they also include a reference to fair and equitable treatment (table III.1). Identifying economic development as one of the objectives of the treaty is, of course, a matter of interest to developing countries. Such recognition would help to ensure that individual clauses in BITs are interpreted in ways that support their growth and development, or at least in ways that do not obstruct it.

---

[2] Similarly, the word "reciprocal" does not imply that the parties are obliged to maintain the same level of openness in terms of admission of investments or to accord identical protection to that accorded in the other country's territory.

Table III.1. Examples of preambles in BITs

BIT between Malaysia and the United Arab Emirates (1991)	BIT between Argentina and the Netherlands (1992)
Preamble The Governments of ...;	Preamble The Government of ...; and The Government of ...;
Desiring to create favourable conditions for greater economic co-operation between them and in particular for investments by investors of one Contracting State in the territory of the other Contracting State; Recognizing the need to protect investments by the Contracting States and by natural and juridical persons of the Contracting States and to stimulate the flow of investments and individual business initiative with a view to the economic prosperity of the Contracting States; ...	Desiring to strengthen the traditional ties of friendship between their countries, to extend and intensify the economic relations between them, particularly with respect to investments by the investors of one Contracting Party in the territory of the other Contracting Party. Recognizing that agreement upon the treatment to be accorded to such investments will stimulate the flow of capital and technology and the economic development of the Contracting Parties and that fair and equitable treatment of investments is desirable, ...

While the wording of preambles often reflects the texts proposed in the developed country models, some treaties have gone a bit further and have used the preamble to define specific areas in which cooperation is sought. Thus, for example, the agreement between Egypt and Greece mentions "production, industry, commerce, exploitation of natural resources, energy, tourism, transports, agriculture, science and technology". The BITs concluded by Switzerland with Egypt and Sudan stress cooperation in the areas of "production, commerce, tourism and technology", and the treaty with Singapore refers specifically to "science, technology, industry and commerce".[3]

* * *

Given the role of the preamble as a reflection of the treaty's object and purpose, it is important that the language of the preamble should not express intentions that are not shared by the countries concerned or that impinge upon an obligation contained in the body of the treaty. For example, if the preamble states that "each country is desirous of establishing a free flow of investment with the other", a statement in the body of the treaty to the effect that "each contracting party shall consider favourably applications for investments of capital in its territory ..." could be taken to mean that such consideration is to be of a "pro forma" nature and that permission to invest will be given automatically, when in fact the intention of the host country may be to ensure that investments are made in accordance with the laws and procedures applicable to all FDI. On the other hand, a country could also view the preamble as an opportunity for including language (such as "desirous of seeking ways to encourage the flow of capital for developmental purposes") that, when coupled with appropriate provisions in the treaty, might be used as a basis to argue that the home country should take positive action to encourage its nationals to invest in the developing

---

[3] More recent examples of this practice include the treaties signed by Switzerland with Uruguay and Turkey.

country, particularly in industries or activities that the latter country wishes to attract as part of its development strategy.

B. Scope of application

The purpose of definitions in legal instruments is to determine the object to which the instrument's rules shall apply and the scope of these rules' applicability. Definitions, therefore, are not neutral. They form part of the normative content of the instrument.

The typical BIT protects investment made by investors of one contracting party in the territory of the other contracting party. The scope of a treaty's applicability thus depends on the definition of certain terms, particularly "investment", "investor" and "territory". Definitions of these terms are a key element of any BIT. They determine which investments and investors are to benefit from its provisions and which are excluded from the coverage of the treaty. The definitions section may also specify the precise relationship that must exist between the investor and the investment for the investment to be protected.

Generally, home countries seek to give these definitions the broadest possible scope. Host countries, on the other hand, sometimes prefer to limit their coverage so as to protect certain national interests.[4]

1. Definition of terms

(a) Investment

The concept of "investment" does not have a generally accepted definition and is constantly evolving as new forms of investment are created and developed by entrepreneurs, financiers and TNCs. In the absence of a generally recognized definition of investment, the definition of this term in BITs is of critical importance. While investment is usually understood as involving a commitment of resources over period of time, with a view to future benefit, important variations exist in the formal definitions found in international instruments. They generally fall into two broad categories. Instruments dealing with the cross-border movement of capital and resources tend to define investment in narrow terms, and stress foreign control over a company as a necessary element of such a definition.[5] Instruments aimed at the protection of investment, on the other hand, tend to use broad and comprehensive definitions that are asset-based, to cover not only the capital that crosses the borders, but also other kinds of assets of an enterprise.[6] BITs follow the second approach.

Recent BITs contain a relatively standard definition of investment. It emerged in the 1960s and has undergone relatively few changes since then (table III.2). The most commonly used definition is "every kind of asset".[7] It is also common to add an illustrative list of assets that are

---

[4] For a detailed discussion of the scope of BITs and other international investment instruments, see Parra (1995).

[5] See, for example the definition of investment in annex A of the OECD Code of Liberalisation of Capital Movements (UNCTAD, 1996b, Vol. II, p. 17).

[6] For a more detailed discussion of the types of definitions used in international instruments, see UNCTAD (1996b, Vol. I, Introduction).

[7] In the case of the United States treaties, the term used is "every kind of investment" (see, for example, the BITs between Albania and the United States, article I (1), and between Bulgaria and the United States, article I (1)).

included within the definition. The following are categories of assets that typically appear in recent BITs:

- Traditional forms of property, sometimes described as **movable and immovable property**. This category generally includes property rights such as mortgages, liens and pledges. Tangible assets are forms of property clearly protected under traditional customary international law, as an extension of the protection of aliens.

- **Companies and interests in companies** (e.g. shares or bonds). Companies are treated in BITs both as assets (hence they are part of the definition of "investment") and as actors (hence they are part of the definition of "investor"). As assets, interests in companies may include equity as well as debt. Thus, a host country that seizes a company could be considered to have expropriated the property of both the owners and the creditors of that company.

  As this suggests, most BITs do not distinguish between direct investment and portfolio investment; the language of the treaties generally is broad enough to cover both forms of investment. Thus, a single share of stock in a company, though it is portfolio investment, would be protected by the treaty to the same extent as a number of shares sufficient to permit the owner to exercise control. In some treaties, portfolio investment is expressly addressed.[8] In some other BITs, however, it is clearly stated that only direct investment is protected: for example, the BIT between Denmark and Lithuania (article 1 (1)) defines investment as "every kind of asset connected with economic activities acquired for the purpose of establishing lasting economic relations between an investor and an enterprise...". Similarly, the treaty between Germany and Israel (article I (1) (a) (i)) defines investment as "investment in an enterprise involving active participation therein ...".

  Whether portfolio investment was an asset protected under traditional rules of customary international law has been an open question. The outcome of the Barcelona Traction case suggests that it was not protected. In fact, in reaching that conclusion, the International Court of Justice suggested that bilateral and multilateral agreements on investment protection would be the obvious way of ensuring its protection.[9] One reason why portfolio investment was not protected under traditional customary international law might have been that the risk involved in some portfolio investments for the investor may not be as high as that involved in a direct investment, since the former investment could normally be pulled out more easily than the latter (Sornarajah, 1994). It has been observed that the inclusion of portfolio investment under the protection of a BIT does not raise particularly important concerns for the host country because such investment does not involve foreign control. On the other hand, portfolio investment could raise a number of important problems if it was included under agreements aimed at the liberalization of foreign investment entry.

- **Intellectual property**, including copyrights, industrial property rights and know-how. Business goodwill is often included in this category as well. Traditionally, such intangible assets as intellectual property were not thought to be assets that came within the ambit of

---

[8] See, for example, the BIT between France and Sri Lanka (article 1).

[9] The International Court of Justice in the Barcelona Traction, Light and Power Company Limited case (cited above) denied Belgium *locus standi* to maintain an action against Spain to protect the interests of the Belgian shareholders of a Canadian company whose investments in Spain had been affected by actions of the Government of Spain.

Table III.2. Examples of definitions of investment in BITs

BIT between Italy and Romania (1977) Article 2 (1)	BIT between Bangladesh and Italy (1990) Article 1	BIT between Ecuador and the United Kingdom (1994) Article 1 (a)
Definition of investment For the purpose of the present agreement: "Investment of capital" shall mean a contribution to the achievement of an economic objective, including any category of goods and services in which capital is invested. In particular, but not restrictedly, "investment of capital" shall mean: (a) ownership or movable and immovable assets and any other real right acquired or constituted in conformity with the legislation of the country in which the invetsment was made; (b) rights of participation in companies, enterprises or other economic initiatives, including any capital allocation to which the investor is entitled and any other form of share participation; (c) monetary claims or other rights relative to services having an economic or financial value; (d) industrial or intellectual property rights, technical procedures, trademarks, trade names and goodwill, know-how; (e) concessions granted by law or by contract, including those for research and exploitation.	For the purposes of this Agreement: The term "investment" shall be construed to mean any kind of property invested before or after the entry into force of this Agreement by a natural or legal person being a national of one Contracting Party in the territory of the other, in conformity with the laws and regulations of the latter. Without limiting the generality of the foregoing, the term "investment" comprises: (a) movable and immovable property, and any other rights in rem including, insofar as they may be used for investment pruposes, real guarantees on others' property; (b) shares, debentures, equity holdings and any other negotiable instrument or document of credit, as well as Government and public securities in general; (c) credits for sums of money or any right for pledges or services having an economic value connected with investments, as well as reinvested income as defined in paragraph 5 thereafter; (d) copyright, commercial trademarks, patents, industrial designs and other intellectual and industrial property rights, know-how, trade secrets, trade names and goodwill; (e) any right of a financial nature accruing by law or by contract and any licence, concession or franchise issued in accordance with current provisions governing the exercise of business activities, including prospecting for cultivating, extracting and exploiting natural resources.	Definition of investment For the purposes of this Agreement: (a) "investment" means every kind of asset and in particular, though not exclusively, includes: (i) movable and immovable property and any other property rights such as mortgages, liens or pledges; (ii) shares, stock and debentures of companies or interests in the property of such companies; (iii) claims to money or to any performance under contract having a financial value; (iv) intellectual property rights and goodwill; (v) business concessions conferred by law or under contract, including concessions to search for, cultivate, extract or exploit natural resources.

customary international legal protection (Sornarajah, 1994). However, in recent times their economic value has come to be of critical importance and central to investment protection (United Nations, Transnational Corporations and Management Division, 1993). The inclusion of intellectual property rights and other intangible rights within the definition of investment in BITs has indeed contributed to dispelling any doubts that existed in classical customary international law about their recognition as assets to be protected under international law (Sornarajah, 1994).

- **Contractual rights.** This category may include rights such as those created by concession agreements conferring on an investor the right, for example, to search for, extract or exploit natural resources. Concessions are included in most model agreements, including the AALCC models A, B and C and in the majority of BITs signed in recent years. For example, the treaty between Denmark and Peru refers to "business concessions conferred by law or by contract" (article 1 (1) (e)). It may also include other long term contractual rights, such as licensing, management, franchises or turnkey contracts. Protected contract rights may include in addition certain relatively short-term rights, such as claims to money or performance. At the same time, however, contracts calling for immediate – as opposed to long-term – payments (e.g. a contract for a one-time sale of merchandise) would not generally be considered an investment.

Some treaties also explicitly include licenses and permits within the list of assets. For example, the treaties signed by the United States with Moldova and Sri Lanka (article I (1) (a) (v) in both treaties) define investment as including "any right conferred by law or contract, and any licences and permits pursuant to law". While issuance of a license or permit initially may be a matter of the host country's discretionary powers, once granted, the license or privilege becomes an asset protected by the BIT.

It has been suggested (Sornarajah, 1994) that the inclusion of licenses and permits in the definition of investment is a recognition of the fact that many of the rights that the investor obtains in host countries are administrative rights based on permission to conduct certain activities in the host country upon which the whole course of the investment project may depend.[10] Most BITs, however, do not include an explicit reference to licenses and permits; nevertheless, depending upon the circumstances, a particular license or permit, may meet the definition of investment.

As noted, the lists of protected assets in BITs are not exhaustive, and this is due to a number of reasons. First, most BIT drafters recognize the difficulty of drafting an exhaustive list. Second, there has been a conscious desire to leave the definition of investment somewhat open-ended so that it can absorb new forms of investment as they emerge.

A question to be considered by a host country is whether it wishes to accept such an open-ended definition of investment, since it might result in protecting future business forms that the parties did not specifically agree to protect as investments at the time the treaty was concluded.[11] Similarly, host countries might not find it appropriate to grant permit rights the same kind of protection that they give to other assets of foreign origin. At the same time, a narrow definition of investment may exclude certain new forms of investment that the host country may wish to attract

---

[10]   For example, in the case of Amco Asia Corporation (et al.) v. Indonesia (1985), some of the issues under contention concerned administrative controls (ICSID, 1985).

[11]   This question was under consideration in the OECD negotiations on a multilateral agreement on investment (MAI) with respect to financial assets. It has been suggested that there may be good reasons to include these assets in an international investment agreement on condition that they are acquired for the purpose of establishing lasting economic relations with an enterprise (Germany, 1997).

as part of its development strategy. A broad definition obviates the need to renegotiate the treaty in these situations. It is therefore for each country to consider the implications of various definitions of investment and determine whether they accord with national policy.

BITs often define "investment" as investment that is made in accordance with the laws of the host country; a typical example is the treaty between Bangladesh and Italy (table III.2).[12] The BIT between Australia and Indonesia contains an interesting variation in that the investment must be made "in conformity with the laws, regulations and investment policies applicable from time to time" (article 1). In the BIT between Malaysia and the United Arab Emirates (article 1), the formula in the case of Malaysia is "approved investments", whereas in the case of the United Arab Emirates it is "investments approved and classified as investments by the competent authorities of the United Arab Emirates in accordance with its legislation and administrative practices."

Local laws, of course, may require approval of the investment, and the approval may be subject to certain conditions. Where such a definition appears, investments that do not conform to local law, obtain any required approvals, or meet the conditions included in any required approvals, would not be protected by the treaty because they would not be considered "investment" within the meaning of the treaty.[13] Some BITs make this point explicitly, by providing that the treaty shall apply only to investment made in accordance with the laws and regulations of the host country.[14]

These types of qualifications permit a country to refuse treaty protection to investments that it considers unworthy of such protection. Thus, by confining protection to investments that are in conformity with its legal requirements, a country is able to ensure that only investments considered desirable from the point of view of its development goals are given protection. Developing countries therefore can take advantage of these qualifications by identifying a clear set of development priorities and criteria to be taken into account in determining whether an investment should receive treaty protection. It should be pointed out, however, that while as a sovereign State a host country may change its laws, regulations and policies, these changes may affect adversely the stability of its investment climate; the credibility of a Government may also be affected should laws and policies be frequently changed.

A different approach for ensuring that treaty protection is granted only to investments made in accordance with the national laws of the host country consists of subordinating the admission of investment in the host country to that country's domestic law. (See below under "Admission of investment".)

Bilateral investment treaties often include a provision to ensure that the alteration of the form in which assets are invested (e.g. where a lender converts debt into equity) will not affect their classification as investment for the purpose of treaty protection. For example, the BIT between Canada and Hungary (article 1 (b)) provides that "[a]ny change in the form of an investment does not affect its character as an investment." Some of these BITs, however, also include the condition that the alteration of the form of the investment must not be contrary to the initial approval of the investment granted by the host country. Thus, the BIT between Belgium–Luxembourg and Cyprus

---

[12] Other recent examples of this approach include the BITs signed by China with other developing countries. The clause also appears in the BITs signed by Australia and Indonesia and in the BITs signed between India and the United Kingdom; Canada and Trinidad and Tobago, and Chile and Norway, to mention some.

[13] The question of whether an investment qualifies as "approved investment" for the purpose of receiving treaty protection was raised in a recent case involving the BIT between the Belgium–Luxembourg Economic Union and Malaysia (arbitration case of Philippe Gruslin v. the Government of Malaysia (unpublished) (ICSID, 1998)).

[14] See, for example, the BIT between Argentina and Sweden.

(article 1) states that "[a]ny alteration of the form in which assets are invested shall not affect their classification as investment, provided that such alteration is not contrary to the approval, if any, granted in respect of the assets originally invested." The principal purpose of this condition is to ensure that reinvestment is not used to circumvent restrictions placed by the host country on the original investment.

A variation of this practice is to provide that reinvestments must not be contrary to the laws of the host country. For example, the BIT between Albania and Croatia (article 2 (2)) stipulates that "[a] possible change in the form in which the investments have been made does not affect their substance as investments, provided that such a change does not contradict the laws and regulations of the relevant Contracting Party."

(b) *Returns on investment*

Most BITs protect returns on investment. For example, they may guarantee the free transfer of returns on investment out of the host country. Treaties that protect returns separately from investment often include a definition of that term. The most common definition, used consistently since the 1960s, is "amounts yielded by an investment".[15] Most BITs that define the term also include a non-exhaustive list of monetary flows that are considered returns. This list typically includes profits, interests, capital gains, dividends, royalties and fees.[16]

(c) *Investor*

The aim of a BIT is to encourage and protect investments by investors of the two countries that are party to the treaty. Consequently, the treaty must define those investors that have a sufficient link with their respective countries to merit protection. In particular, the capital importing country may be reluctant to grant the benefits of a BIT to persons and companies having only a tenuous relationship with its treaty partner. To allow the treaty to benefit persons or companies that are primarily associated with third countries with which it has no treaty relationship would be, in effect, to abandon its prerogative to negotiate corresponding privileges and obligations from those countries.

The definition of the term "investor" usually includes natural persons and juridical entities, often referred to generically as "companies". Some BITs do not use the term "investor" and refer directly to natural persons and companies.

i. *Natural person*

With respect to natural persons, most BITs give protection to persons who are "nationals" of each of the contracting countries concerned. The typical definition of a national of a party is a natural person recognized by that party's internal law as a national or citizen. For example, the treaty between Jamaica and the United Kingdom employs the following language:

(c) "nationals" mean:

(i) in respect of the United Kingdom: physical persons deriving their status as United Kingdom nationals from the law in force in the United Kingdom;

---

[15] This definition has been used, for example, in the treaties signed by Denmark, Finland, Germany, Norway and the United Kingdom.

[16] See, for example, the AALCC model B, article 1 (e).

(ii) in respect of Jamaica: physical persons deriving their status as Jamaican nationals from the laws of Jamaica.

Under customary international law, a State's granting of nationality to an individual need not be recognized by other States if there is no genuine link between the individuals and the State whose nationality they are claiming.[17] Most BITs, however, do not seem to require such a genuine link. Thus, an individual is a national of a contracting party for the purposes of the BIT as long as that contracting party's internal law recognizes the individual to be a national.

In some cases, BITs require more of a link than nationality. A few BITs require that the person should also reside or be domiciled in the country of nationality.[18] In other BITs the requirement is that investors should be permanent residents.[19] The reason for this additional requirement of residence or domicile is to ensure that nationals covered by the treaty have a real link to the other country, a consideration that may be important if such other country has significant numbers of citizens residing in third countries and without a significant connection to the home country whose nationality they legally possess. One issue not explicitly addressed by BITs is whether a natural person who possesses the nationality of both parties under their respective laws may claim treaty protection.[20]

ii. Company

The term "company" is generally given a wide definition and includes corporations and other juridical entities. The BIT between Tunisia and Turkey (article I (1) (h)), for example, defines "company" as "any kind of juridical entity, including any corporation, company, business association or other organization that is duly incorporated, constituted or otherwise duly organized under the applicable laws and regulations of a Party".

Some treaties specify that the definition includes public and private entities, regardless of whether they are organized for profit or have limited liability. Thus, the treaty between Peru and Thailand (article 1 (2)) defines "company" as "any juridical person incorporated or constituted under the law in force in the territory of either Contracting Party whether or not with limited liability and whether or not for precuniary profit". The AALCC models A and B include a separate definition for State entities.[21] Other BITs are silent on these matters, but the definition in such BITs is generally broad enough to include any of these entities, as is evident in the language of the BIT between Tunisia and Turkey.

As noted, the key definitional question with respect to companies as investors relates to the conditions under which a legal person is considered to have a sufficient link to a treaty country to

---

[17] See the Nottebohm Case (Liechtenstein v. Guatemala) (International Court of Justice, 1955).

[18] See, for example, the BITs between Germany and Israel (article I (3) (b)) and between Denmark and Indonesia (article I (a)).

[19] See, for example, the BITs between Argentina and Canada and Canada and Trinidad and Tobago.

[20] In the case of most BITs signed between Argentina and other countries in the American continent, and the BITs signed by Ecuador with Chile (article 1 (3)) and El Salvador (article 1 (2)), the treaty does not apply to investments made by natural persons from the home country if they have been domiciled in the host country for more than two years, unless it is proved that the investment was admitted from abroad (Organization of American States, 1997).

[21] In its introductory report, the AALCC explained that such a definition addressed a situation often found in developing countries in which investments, whether in the shape of capital or technology, are likely to be made at times by State entities that cannot be appropriately brought within the definition of companies.

be deemed a company of that country for the purpose of treaty protection. Three situations raise particular problems for determining whether an investment by a company is covered: investments made by a company organized in a treaty country by nationals of a third country; investments made by a company organized in a third country by nationals of a treaty country; and investments made by a company originating in a treaty country in which nationals of a third country have a substantial interest.

Typically, BITs extend protection to companies that are deemed to have the nationality of one of the contracting countries, but they vary in how they attribute nationality to companies. Three different criteria have been used by treaties in different combinations. These are the place of incorporation; the location of the seat (sometimes referred to as the "siège social", "real seat", or the "principal place of business"); and the nationality of ownership or control.

Each of these different criteria brings with it certain advantages and disadvantages. The place of incorporation is the easiest to determine. Treaties that use the place of incorporation or organization as a basis for ascribing nationality to juridical entities include those concluded by Denmark, the Netherlands, Switzerland, the United Kingdom and the United States. It is also used in treaties between developing countries, such as, for example, the BIT beween Singapore and Sri Lanka. Thus, the treaty between Nigeria and the United Kingdom (article 1 (d)) defines companies to include "corporations, firms, associations and other legal persons incorporated or constituted under the law in force in any part" of a contracting party. The problem with this criterion is that the country where the company is organized may have no other connection to the company. A country may find itself defending the interests of a company in which none of its nationals has any rights. Indeed, foreign nationals may form a company under the laws of a contracting party simply to gain treaty protection. For this reason, some BITs reserve for each contracting party the right to deny treaty protection to a company that is incorporated under the laws of a contracting party, but is controlled by nationals of a third country and/or has no substantial business activities in the territory of the contracting party. For example, the treaty between Romania and the United States contains a provision to prevent nationals of third countries from obtaining BIT protection by incorporating in one of the signatory countries (table III.3).

Ownership or control, by contrast, establishes a much more important link between the investment and the country of nationality, but it is sometimes difficult to ascertain. A company may be owned by thousands of investors from many different countries, with the nationality of the dominant investors changing from time to time as shares in the company are traded. Treaties using ownership or control as a basis for establishing the nationality of juridical entities include those concluded by the Netherlands, Sweden and Switzerland. A typical example is the BIT between Lithuania and the Netherlands (table III.3).

The inclusion of "ownership and control" as one of the criteria for attributing corporate nationality for the purpose of BIT protection represents a significant departure from traditional customary international law, as spelled out in the Barcelona Traction case discussed above, in that a corporation has the nationality of the State in which it was incorporated and, therefore, only that State has the right to exercise diplomatic protection. In fact, the Barcelona Traction case raised doubts as to whether shareholders could be protected under existing customary international law, and that might have been a significant precipitating factor in the development of BITs. Indeed, securing the protection of shareholders was becoming increasingly important in the context of the creation of locally incorporated joint ventures, in order to grant protection to the foreign minority partner (Sornarajah, 1994). Another technique for securing shareholder protection under BITs has been the inclusion of shares as assets coming within the definition of investment discussed above.

Table III.3. Examples of definitions of companies in BITs

BIT between China and Japan (1988) Article 1 (4)	BIT between Germany and Swaziland (1990) Article 1 (4)	BIT between Romania and the United States (1992) Article I (1) (b) and (2)	BIT between Lithuania and the Netherlands (1994) Article 1.b
(4) The term "companies" means: (a) in relation to Japan, corporations, p a r t n e r s h i p s, companies and associations whether or not with limited liability, whether or not with legal personality and whether or not for pecuniary profit; and (b) in relation to the People's Republic of China, enterprises, other economic organizations and associations. Companies constituted under the applicable laws and regulations of one Contracting Party and having their seat within its territory shall be deemed conpanies of that Contracting Party.	The term "companies" means (a) in respect of the Federal Republic of Germany: any juridical person as well as any commercial or other company with or without legal personality having its seat in the German area of application of this Treaty, irrespective of whether or not its activities are directed at profit, (b) in respect of the Kingdom of Swaziland: corporations, firms or associations incorporated or constituted under the laws in force in the Kingdom of Swaziland.	(b) "company" of a Party means any kind of corporation. company, association, partnership, or other organization, legally constituted under the laws and regulations of a Party or a political subdivision thereof whether or not organized for pecuniary gain, or privately or governmentally owned or controlled; ... 2. Each Party reserves the right to deny to any company the advantages of this Treaty if nationals of any third country control such company and, in the case of a company of the other Party, that company has no substantial business activities in the territory of the other Party or is controlled by nationals of a third country with which the denying Party does not maintain normal economic relations.	[T]he term investor shall comprise with regard to either Contracting Party: i. natural persons having the nationality of that Contracting Party; ii. legal persons constituted under the law of that Contracing Party; iii. legal persons not constituted under the law of that Contracting Party but controlled, directly or indirectly, by natural persons as defined in i. or by legal persons as defined in ii. above; who invest in the territory of either Contracting Party.

Some BITs add a definition of some of these terms in a protocol or exchange of letters. For example, the protocol annexed to the BIT between Egypt and the United States defines "control" as "[having] a substantial share of ownership rights and the ability to exercise decisive influence". The same protocol stipulates that, in cases in which there is a difference of views as to the existence of control, the parties shall resolve the disputes in accordance with the dispute-settlement provisions specified in the treaty.

Basing nationality on the location of a company's seat may represent something of a middle ground. It establishes a more genuine link than mere incorporation and is often easier to ascertain and more stable than the country of ownership or control. The use of the seat as a basis for ascribing nationality is common in BITs concluded by, for example, Belgium, Germany and Sweden. Thus, the BIT between Germany and Swaziland defines German companies as those having their seat in the German area of application (table III.3)

Often these three elements are combined so that a company must satisfy two or more criteria in order to be covered by a treaty. Thus, many recent treaties require the company both to be incorporated in a treaty country and to have its seat or controlling interests in that country as well. A typical example is found in the BIT between China and Japan (table III.3).

The AALCC models A and B contain two alternative definitions. The first alternative consists of a joint definition of companies using the incorporation criterion, with the possible addition of the control criterion. The second alternative suggests a separate definition left to each party to determine.

Unilaterally denying the benefits of the treaty to a company with a supposed link to the other country can be a potential source of conflict. As a result, mechanisms for consultation on this issue may be built into a treaty. For example the BIT between the United States and Zaire, after allowing one party to deny the benefits of the treaty to a company for the reasons indicated above (see quote from the BIT between Romania and the United States in table III.3), also states:

> ... provided that whenever one Party concludes that the benefits of this treaty should not be extended to a company of the other Party for this reason, it shall promptly consult with the other Party to seek a mutually satisfactory resolution to this matter. (article 1 (b) (ii)).

Once it has been determined that a person or entity is a protected investor, the question arises as to what relationship an investor must have to an investment for the investment to be protected by the BIT. Most BITs do not address this issue in any detail. They generally provide that the asset must be an investment "of" or "by" nationals or companies of a contracting party. This seems to imply that nationals or companies of the contracting party must own or control the investment. Such ownership may be fractional, as where nationals of a contracting party own only a small interest in an investment, or indirect, as where nationals of a contracting party own interests in an entity that owns the investment. Some BITs signed by the United States [22] state specifically that investment shall be considered as investment of a contracting party if it is owned or controlled "directly or indirectly" by nationals or companies of that contracting party. The implication of this wording is that ownership of the investment by nationals or companies of a contracting party through multiple corporate layers is sufficient for the investment to be considered investment of nationals or companies of that contracting party.

There are, however, other issues in relation to the determination of the nationality of a company that BITs do not seem to address. Other issues not addressed are how to deal with companies having the nationality of both parties to a BIT, and how changes in nationality of an investment during the term of a BIT affect the operation of its provisions (Dolzer and Stevens, 1995).

(d)   *Territory*

The earliest BITs typically did not define the term "territory". A definition began to appear regularly in the 1970s. In the context of BITs, territory is defined for the particular purpose of investment protection. Often, the territorial protection of an investment in many BITs does not coincide with the delimitation of the territory under the law of the contracting parties. In fact, in many BITs, the definition of territory does not specify what land areas shall be considered the territory of a country; rather, this definition serves to indicate what maritime areas shall be considered part of a contracting party's territory. The typical definition includes within "territory" those maritime areas over which the contracting party exercises sovereign rights or jurisdiction in accordance with international law. For example, the BIT between Lithuania and Sweden (article

---

[22]   See, for example the BIT between Jamaica and the United States (article I (1) (a)).

1 (4)) defines territory to mean "in respect of each Contracting Party the territory under its sovereignty and the sea and submarine areas over which the Contracting Party exercises, in conformity with international law, sovereignty, sovereign rights or jurisdiction". This generally includes the continental shelf and the exclusive economic zone. The result is that investment in offshore mineral exploitation facilities will be considered investment within the territory of the maritime country.

While the territorial scope of an investment treaty normally coincides with the delimitation of the territory of the contracting parties, a treaty may contain territorial extension clauses. For example, the BITs concluded by the United Kingdom provide that territory, in the case of the United Kingdom, includes those territories to which the applicability of the BIT is extended by diplomatic note.[23] Conclusion of a BIT with the United Kingdom is often followed by one or more exchanges of notes applying the BIT to areas outside the metropolitan territory of the United Kingdom.

An important related question is whether the provisions of BITs apply to sub-national authorities, particularly in countries in which such authorities enjoy wide discretion and autonomy regarding the regulation of foreign investment. Most BITs do not address this issue explicitly, but some do; for example, the BIT between Poland and the United States (article XIII) states that "the Treaty shall apply to the political subdivisions of the Parties". The Vienna Convention on the Law of Treaties (article 27) provides that the existence of a contradictory internal law is not a justification for the failure to perform an international treaty. Article 29 provides that, unless a different intention is evident in the treaty or is otherwise established, a treaty is binding upon each party in respect of its entire territory.

2. Application in time

An important question regarding the coverage of BITs is whether treaty protection extends to investments made before, as well as after, the conclusion of a BIT.

Host countries may sometimes be reluctant to provide treaty protection to investments that were established prior to the entry into force of a treaty. They may see the provision of such protection as a windfall to the investor, who was willing to make the investment without the promise of treaty protection. Moreover, such prior investment might not have been approved had the authorities then realized that the investor's rights later would be expanded by treaty. For example, a host country might have approved an investment project on the assumption that its restrictive exchange-control laws would apply to limit the project's right to repatriate income and capital. If, by treaty, the currency transfer rights of existing projects were to be expanded, this might place an increased and unexpected burden on the host country's foreign exchange reserves.

Home countries, by contrast, generally want their BITs to apply to existing investment. This avoids giving later investors a competitive advantage over earlier investors, which could distort the operation of the market and arouse the opposition of existing investors to the conclusion of the treaty.

Despite these opposing interests, the contracting parties usually do agree to extend the protection of the treaty to existing investments. Indeed, even where host countries conclude BITs for the sole reason of attracting new FDI, excluding from BIT protection all existing investors –

---

[23] See, for example, the BIT between the United Kingdom and Sri Lanka (article 1 (e) (i)). As a result of the diplomatic note in this BIT regarding the extension of territorial scope to the United Kingdom's overseas territories, the treaty was applied to a Hong Kong company in the recent arbitration case of Asian Agricultural Products Ltd. v. Republic of Sri Lanka (ICSID, 1990).

many of which are a potential source of new investment – this might reduce investors' confidence in the host country's investment climate. Consequently, by denying protection to pre-existing investments, host countries might be blocking an important source of potential new foreign investment. In fact, this is an issue which has become less problematic in recent years as a result of the widespread trend towards liberalization: many BITs state explicitly that the treaty applies to investments established prior to the entry into force of the treaty, as well as those established subsequent to entry into force. They sometimes do so by including a separate article stating that the treaty applies to existing investment. Thus, for example, the BIT between Estonia and Switzerland (article 6) provides that:

> The present Agreement shall apply to investments in the territory of a Contracting Party made in accordance with its laws and regulations by investors of the other Contracting Party prior to the entry into force of this Agreement.

Or they may define the term "investment" to include investment established before the treaty entered into force.[24]

Not all BITs, however, apply to existing investments. Some BITs provide that the treaty shall apply to investments established after entry into force of the country's foreign investment law.[25] Other BITs, notably some of those concluded by Germany,[26] require that existing investments should be approved before receiving treaty protection. For example, the BIT between Egypt and Germany (article 9) requires investments made before the entry into force of the treaty to go through the prescribed admission procedures in order to enjoy treaty protection. It should be noted, however, that Germany' current practice is to cover existing investments in BITs. Another approach is simply to provide that the treaty shall not apply to investments made prior to signature or entry into force of the treaty.[27]

Some treaties, such as a few to which the United Kingdom is a party, do not specifically state whether the BIT will apply to existing as well as future investments. To avoid problems of interpretation over the treaty's scope of application, it may be wise for the parties to reach a clear understanding on this issue before concluding a treaty.[28]

3. Entry into force, duration, termination and amendment

(a) *Entry into force*

In many countries a signed treaty may enter into force only if ratified in accordance with internal law.[29] Treaties drafted by these countries provide that they enter into force after each party

---

[24] See, for example, the BIT between Bangladesh and Italy (article 1) quoted in table III.2.

[25] See, for example, the BIT between Indonesia and the United Kingdom (article 2 (3)).

[26] See, for example, the BITs signed by Germany with Indonesia (article 8 (2)), Malta (article 9 (2)) and the Islamic Republic of Iran (protocol, para. 11).

[27] Such an approach is found in, for example, the BITs between France and Morocco (article 12) and between Germany and Sri Lanka (article 9).

[28] The position of the Vienna Convention on the Law of Treaties on this issue is that unless a different intention appears from the treaty or is otherwise established, its provisions do not bind a party in relation to any act or fact which took place or any situation which ceased to exist before the date of the entry into force of the treaty with respect to that party.

[29] The internal act of ratification, which may be required for the treaty to enter into force, should be distinguished from the question of whether the treaty needs to be enacted into domestic law (where its provisions affect existing internal law).

has notified the other that its internal requirements (e.g. ratification) have been satisfied.[30] If these notifications occur on different days, then a treaty will enter into force on the latter of these days.[31] In many cases, a treaty enters into force a certain number of days after the notifications have been given. The most common period is 30 days after the notifications have been exchanged.[32]

(b) *Duration and termination*

One of the major purposes of a BIT is to ensure a stable legal environment for investors. For this reason, the standard practice since the 1960s has been to specify that a BIT shall remain in force for a fixed term during which there is no provision for termination. The most common minimum term is 10 years. This period is found in BITs concluded by France, Germany, the United Kingdom and the United States. However, some BITs provide for a term of 15, 20 or even 30 years[33], while in others the initial term is for as little as five years[34] or even one year.[35]

After the fixed term has ended, the treaty may be terminated by either party, usually with one year's notice.[36] Some BITs provide for a different period of notice, such as six months.[37]

If a BIT is not terminated at the end of the fixed term, then it continues in force. In general, countries have adopted two different approaches to specifying the duration of a treaty after the fixed term expires. Under one approach, a treaty continues in force indefinitely, subject always to the power of either party to terminate the treaty with written notice.[38] Under the other approach, a treaty continues in force for additional fixed terms.

The latter approach is followed by most BITs. This ensures investors a stable legal environment beyond the fixed initial term of the BIT. The period specified most commonly in the clause is 10 years, but it is 15 years in some BITs and 20 in others. These additional terms are not necessarily of the same duration as the original term. In some Swiss BITs, for example, the initial term is 10 years, but the additional terms are two years each.[39]

In any event, the initial term in combination with this additional period can provide protection of substantial duration. In the BIT between Malaysia and the United Arab Emirates, for example, the initial term of 30 years is combined with continued protection for 20 years after termination, with the result that investment is protected by the treaty for 50 years, even if the treaty is terminated at the first opportunity. Treaty protection may last for the life of the investment. Some BITs concluded by France,[40] for example, provide that, in the event of termination, they shall remain applicable, apparently indefinitely, to investments established prior to termination.

---

[30] See, for example, the BIT between Cuba and the United Kingdom (article 13).

[31] See, for example, the BIT between Canada and Trinidad and Tobago (article XVIII).

[32] See, for example, the BIT between Nicaragua and the United States (article XVI).

[33] For an example of an initial term of 30 years, see the BIT between Malaysia and the United Arab Emirates (article 15).

[34] See, for example, the BITs between Germany and the Philippines (article 13 (2)) and between Germany and Zambia (article 14 (2)).

[35] See, for example, the BIT between Switzerland and Burkina Faso (article 11).

[36] See, for example, the BIT between Norway and Peru (article 14).

[37] See, for example, the BIT between Germany and Papua New Guinea (article 13).

[38] This approach is followed, for example, in the BIT between Denmark and Peru (article 16).

[39] See, for example, the BIT between Switzerland and the United Republic of Tanzania (article 6 (2)).

[40] See, for example, the BITs signed by France with Egypt (article 13), Haiti (article 6), Indonesia (article 10), the Republic of Korea (article 9 (4)), Morocco (article 13) and Yugoslavia (article 9).

One issue raised by this clause is whether an investment must be established prior to notice of termination to be protected. Treaties adopt one of two approaches. Some stipulate that investment must be established prior to the notice of termination; for example, the BIT between Lithuania and Norway (article XIV) provides that "[w]ith respect to investments made prior to the receipt of notification of expiry, the provisions ... shall remain in force for a further period of ten years from the date of notification". Others provide that an investment must be established prior to the effective date of the termination; thus, the treaty between Australia and the Republic of Korea (article 11 (3)) states that "[i]n respect of investments made prior to the date of termination of the present Agreement the provisions ... shall continue to be effective for a further period of ten years from the date of termination of the present Agreement".

(c)   *Amendment*

A few BITs include a provision stating that the treaty may be amended by agreement of the contracting parties.[41] Such a provision may not be necessary because, under the Vienna Convention on the Law of Treaties, a treaty can always be amended by agreement of the parties. Where such a provision is included, it usually indicates that the amendment shall enter into force when the contracting parties have notified each other that their internal requirements for approval of international agreements have been satisfied.

* * *

The definitions of "investment" and "investor" in BITs determine what and who is entitled to receive treaty protection. They therefore raise important policy questions for host countries. Countries considering BITs may need to ask themselves whether by using a narrow definition of investment they are limiting their opportunities to attract new forms of investment that could be desirable for their economic development or whether by choosing an open-ended definition they are extending treaty protection to certain forms of investment (including future forms of investment) that they might later prefer not to have that level of protection (the question of the inclusion of portfolio investment is particularly important here). Developing countries that are concerned about the quality of the foreign investment they may attract and that are trying to devise effective screening systems may still use a broad and open-ended definition of investment, but may limit the benefits of the treaty to investment approved by the parties or may build in other safeguards. In this manner, countries are able to maintain a certain flexibility.

With respect to the definition of "companies", an important task for negotiators is to ensure that the companies covered under the treaty have a real link with the home country, and to avoid giving treaty protection to companies that have no substantial business activities in that country. In the present era of globalization, no single test for attributing corporate nationality can guarantee appropriate coverage of foreign investors. In these circumstances, using several tests together may provide a more reliable method of defining foreign companies for the purposes of treaty protection.

Another question facing policy makers, particularly in developing countries, is whether they wish to grant treaty protection to investments made before a BIT becomes operative, and whether investments made during the life of the treaty should continue to receive BIT protection after the treaty ceases to exist. As noted before, each approach has its advantages and disadvantages, and there are no easy answers to these questions, but it is important that BIT negotiators, in particular those from developing countries, realize the full implications of the approaches they take and ensure that such approaches are consistent with their long-term policy objectives.

---

[41] See, for example, the BIT between Nigeria and the United Kingdom (article 12).

C. Admission of investment

As noted in the Introduction, the rule of customary international law deriving from the principle of the territorial sovereignty of States is that a State has the right to regulate or prohibit the admission of aliens and their property into its territory. This principle has been reflected in many international instruments.

Most countries are unwilling to grant foreign nationals or companies an unqualified right to make investments within their territories. The reasons for this are varied. Countries are often reluctant to allow foreign control over the most important means of production. Some countries may be concerned about foreign ownership of industries that are vital to national security, while other countries may be concerned about foreign ownership of industries of special importance to the development effort or of special cultural value or significance. In other cases, domestic businesses may demand protection against foreign competition. The result is that many countries impose certain restrictions or conditions on the entry of FDI in specific industries.

For reasons such as these, BITs do not usually confer on investors of one contracting party the right to establish investments in the territory of the other contracting party.[42] In other words, under the typical BIT, the host country has sole discretion to decide whether investment shall be permitted in its territory. Once the host country decides to permit an investment, however, the investment becomes entitled to all the protections afforded by the applicable BIT (although the question does arise, as to whether an investment is entitled to receive treaty protection only if it continues to satisfy the conditions imposed on its entry by the host country).

Most BITs do nevertheless address the question of entry and establishment. Typically, they provide that each contracting party shall admit investment of nationals and companies of the other contracting party, but only in accordance with the laws of the host country. A typical example is the BIT between Estonia and Switzerland (table III.4), which reflects what has consistently been the practice since the earliest treaties of this kind. Such a provision rules out any interpretation that claims that the investments covered under a BIT are not subject to the general admission requirements and procedures established by the host country (e.g. the requirement that FDI projects should be approved by a specific ministry or authority).

Some early treaties, such as the BIT between Belgium and Singapore (table III.4), have more specific requirements. Other BITs state that an investment is only protected as from the date of approval. For example the treaty between Germany and Uganda limits its application in Uganda to investments which have been approved under Uganda's regulations for the protection of foreign investments, or which have received special approval for the application of the treaty. Others make more detailed references to the applicable procedures. Thus, the BIT concluded by Germany with Malaysia provides that an investment in a project must be classified by the appropriate ministry in Malaysia in accordance with its legislation and administrative practice as an "approved project".[43] Sometimes, the agency involved in the issuance of admission documents is also mentioned.

Furthermore, under some early agreements (e.g. the BIT between Pakistan and Sweden), the host country will give approval only "in the exercise of its full discretion", while a number of early BITs concluded by Germany contain details on criteria and procedures for admission. Thus,

---

[42] On this general question, see Shihata (1996).

[43] Similar clauses also appear in the BITs between Germany and the United Republic of Tanzania and between Egypt and Switzerland.

Table III.4.   Examples of provisions on admission in BITs

BIT between Belgium–Luxembourg Economic Union and Singapore (1978) Article 3	BIT between Estonia and Switzerland (1992) Article 2 (1)	BIT between Argentina and the United Kingdom (1990) Article 2 (1)	BIT between Canada and Trinidad and Tobago (1995) Article II (3)
The Agreement shall, to the extent that a written approval is required, only extend to investments, whether made before or after the coming into force of this Agreement, which are specifically approved in writing by the Contracting Party in whose territory the investments have been or will be made. An investment so approved shall be subject to the laws in force in the territory of the Contracting party concerned and to the conditions, if any, upon which approval shall have been granted.	Each Contracting Party shall in its territory promote as far as possible the investments by investors of the other Contracting Party and admit such investments in accordance with its laws and regulations.	(1) Each Contracting Party shall encourage and create favourable conditions for investors of the other Contracting Party to invest capital in its territory, and, subject to its right to exercise powers conferred by its laws, shall admit such capital.	Each Contracting Party shall permit establishment of a new business enterprise or acquisition of an existing business enterprise or a share of such enterprise by investors or prospective investors of the other Contracting Party on a basis no less favourable than that which, in like circumstances, it permits such acquisition or establishment by: (a) its own investors or prospective investors; or (b) investors or prospective investors of any third state.

Trinidad and Tobago (table III.4).[44] This approach implies that the host country must treat clauses have sometimes been included stating that an investment must fit into national development plans.[45] Some early BITs might even use the admission clause to impose special conditions or derogate from other treaty standards. Thus, the BIT between Germany and Rwanda contemplates the possibility of imposing "special conditions" with regards to the following: the administration of a capital investment; the economic activity of the company; the reinvestment of profits; and professional training and the employment of local personnel.

While it is clear that BITs do not generally create a right of entry, there can be no doubt that many of these treaties put the emphasis on facilitating the entry of investment from the other party in the host country. This emphasis is in harmony with liberalization trends at the national level as most countries have considerably relaxed their requirements for the approval of investment.[46] A typical example of such a clause can be found in the BIT between Argentina and the United Kingdom (table III.4).

Some home countries have gone further in granting certain rights of entry to investments from treaty partners. The BITs concluded by the United States, and also some recent BITs signed by Canada, have adopted this approach. Specifically, these BITs provide that the host country must grant most-favoured-nation (MFN) treatment and national treatment with respect to the entry and establishment of investment. A typical example can be found in the BIT between Canada and applications for admission by investors of its treaty partner in the same manner that it treats

---

[44] See also, for example, the BITs signed by the United States with Jamaica (article II) and Nicaragua (article II).

[45] See, for example, the BITs signed by Germany with Mali, Rwanda and Thailand.

[46] See, for example, the difference between one of Jamaica's earlier BITs, with Switzerland (article 4 (2) (1)),which requires approval of an investment as a precondition for free transfer, and Jamaica's later BITs with Argentina, China and the United States.

applications by its own national investors or those from other countries. In other words, nationals and companies of one contracting party are granted the same right to invest in the territory of the other contracting party as nationals and companies of that other contracting party and nationals and companies of any third country. This right, if not qualified (by, for example, the phrase "in like situations"), would be particularly broad, given that the definition of companies in these BITs includes State-owned enterprises. Thus, investors of one contracting party would have the right to establish investment in the territory of the other contracting party in industries in which either public or private entities of that other contracting party have established investments. Another implication of this approach is that, unless otherwise stated in the treaty, "pre-establishment" decisions made by host countries that violate the national treatment or MFN treatment requirement may be challenged under the BIT dispute-settlement provisions.

The United States model treaty, as well as the United States treaties concluded so far do not preclude, however, the host country from applying measures necessary for maintaining public order and national security,[47] or from prescribing special formalities for the establishment of investments. However, such formalities are limited only to those that do not affect the substance of the rights granted by the treaty. Thus, the treaty between Egypt and the United States (article II (1)) states that each party "shall, in applying its laws, regulations and administrative practices and procedures, permit investments to be established on terms and conditions that accord [national treatment]." It further provides that the parties retain discretion to approve investments according to national plans and priorities on a non-discriminatory basis consistent with the above provisions (article II (3) (b)).

These types of provisions might create difficulties for a number of host countries. For instance, their internal laws may deliberately prohibit foreign investment in certain industries or activities because, for example, the Government wishes to promote the emergence of a domestic enterprise sector as part of its overall development efforts. Sometimes this is further accentuated by a belief that domestic firms may not be able to compete with transnational corporations with greater financial or other resources. In such circumstances, they may prefer to grant MFN treatment rather than national treatment at the pre-establishment stage.

Like other countries, however, the proponents of this approach are sensitive about foreign investment in certain industries or activities. The BITs concluded by the United States, for example, permit each contracting party to designate in an annex the industries with respect to which it reserves the right to deny MFN or national treatment. Thus, the treaty beween Grenada and the United States grants MFN and national treatment with respect to the entry of investment from each country but "... subject to the right of each Party to make or maintain exceptions falling within one of the sectors or matters listed in the Annex to this Treaty" (article II (1)). More specifically, the list with respect to Grenada consists of the following areas: air transportation; government grants; government insurance and loan programmes; ownership of real estate; and use of land and natural resources. The list with respect to the United States includes: air transportation; ocean and coastal shipping; banking; insurance; government grants; government insurance and loan programmes; energy and power production; custom house brokers; ownership of real estate; ownership and operation of broadcast or common carrier radio and television stations; ownership of shares of the

---

[47] In should be noted that the first group of BITs signed by the United States only received Senate approval or ratification in 1988 when the following proviso was included in the resolution approving the treaties: "either Party may take all measures necessary to deal with any unusual and extraordinary threat to its national security."

Communications Satellite Corporation; the provision of common carrier telephone and telegraph services; the provision of submarine cable services; and use of land and natural resources.[48]

The annexes of some treaties between the United States and Central and Eastern European countries include a statement indicating the intention to remove some of the industries and matters from the list of exceptions as the process of privatization and demonopolization progresses.[49] Early BITs concluded by the United States allow countries to deny only national treatment with respect to the establishment of foreign investment in industries listed in the annex.[50]

The BITs concluded by the United States furthermore prohibit retroactive limitations on establishment. Thus, neither contracting party may prohibit investment after it has been established. Moreover, these BITs do not provide for the inclusion of additional industries in the annex once a treaty has been concluded.

The application of the concepts of national treatment and MFN treatment to FDI projects, no two of which are exactly alike, is far more difficult than their application to international trade in tangible goods. At the same time, the qualifying words "in like situations" that are sometimes included may also allow for some differing treatment on entry, if the projects themselves or the surrounding circumstances are sufficiently dissimilar.[51]

Because the BITs that provide for MFN and national treatment at the pre-establishment stage are more protective of foreign investment in this regard than most BITs, the question arises as to whether investors covered by other BITs, as a result of the MFN clauses in those other BITs, would be entitled to the right of establishment afforded by a BIT with, say, Canada or the United States. In many cases this will not be the case because the MFN clauses in these other BITs do not apply to investment at the pre-establishment phase and therefore MFN treatment would only be extended to post-investment conditions.

A rather different approach to the admission of investment, found in some BITs concluded by the Belgium–Luxembourg Economic Union,[52] is to state that a BIT applies only to investment in certain industries. Thus, not only would the host country have the right to exclude investment from other industries, but, where it did permit such investment, that investment would not be protected by the treaty.

* * *

The admission clauses in BITs are amongst the most important from a development perspective. Entry restrictions and conditions for entry are some of the ways through which developing countries give expression to their development strategies with respect to foreign investment – or, more precisely, their desire to develop a vibrant domestic enterprise sector. Developing countries may therefore be concerned about clauses that may tie their hands in a manner that is inconsistent with their policy objectives and priorities. It is true that the prevailing approach

---

[48] The lists for national treatment and MFN treatment may differ considerably. For example, in the annex to BIT between the Jamaica and the United States treaty, the United States identifies 17 exceptions to MFN treatment, and Jamaica identifies four. With respect to national treatment, the United States identifies 13 exceptions and Jamaica only one.

[49] See, for example, the BIT between Poland and the United States (article XII (4) and annex, para. 4).

[50] See, for example the BIT between Egypt and the United States (article II).

[51] See below for a fuller discussion on the meaning of national and MFN treatment.

[52] See, for example, the BITs between the Belgium–Luxembourg Economic Union and Egypt (article III (1)), Indonesia (article 3 (1)) and the Republic of Korea (article 3 (1)).

in BITs is to commmit the signatory countries to create favourable conditions for investment. Yet, to date, most BITs leave the question of entry and establishment subject to national laws, and national investment regimes even in the most liberal countries typically keep a number of industries and activities closed to foreign investors in order to protect national interests.

The foregoing review of provisions on admission offers a broad range of choices for policy makers, from best-efforts provisions, to more firm commitments to facilitate and encourage entry, to granting admission on the basis of MFN and national treatment. At the same time, it is characteristic of all BITs that the parties retain some degree of flexibility to control the admission of FDI from the other party. Some BITs do so by referring to the laws of the host country on matters of admission, approval and so on, while others allow for the inclusion of a list of industries or activities that may be exempted from the operation of the general admission clause.

It is, of course, up to each individual host country to pursue the approach that best suits its interests, keeping in mind that, while the prevailing philosophy in most countries is to encourage FDI, for many developing countries the ability to reap the benefits of FDI for development may depend on whether they have a degree of control over the way in which the foreign investor operates within the national economy.

D. Investment promotion

For many countries, particularly host developing countries, the principal purpose of a BIT is not merely to protect existing investment, but to encourage the establishment of new foreign affiliates or the expansion of old ones. As already noted, the premise underlying BITs is that the act of concluding BITs with other countries, and observing them, will, in itself, promote inward FDI.

Since the 1960s, however, many BITs have gone a step further and included a specific commitment by each contracting party to encourage investment from the other contracting party in its territory. A typical formulation is that found in the BIT between Turkey and the United Kingdom (article 2) which states that "[e]ach Contracting Party shall encourage and create favourable conditions for investments of nationals or companies of the other Contracting Party in its territory ...". The exact meaning of this provision is difficult to determine because it is formulated at a high level of generality with few, if any, specific obligations. Further, the concept of "favourable conditions for investments" is subject to numerous interpretations. For example, it could refer to laws and regulations, or to the physical conditions necessary for investment, such as roads, communications, power supplies and infrastructure.

To avoid any implication that the host country is required to admit any specific investment as a result of an "encouragement" clause, the obligation to promote investment is sometimes a qualified one. One common approach is to provide that the obligation of each contracting party to promote investment in its territory is subject to the laws or, even more broadly, policies of the host country. An example of this approach is the treaty between Japan and Sri Lanka[53] (table III.5).

A second approach is to require each contracting party to promote investment in its territory "as far as possible".[54] A typical example of this approach is article 2 of the BIT between Germany and Saint Lucia (table III.5).

---

[53] Other BITs using this approach are those concluded by the Belgium–Luxembourg Economic Union, France, the Netherlands and Sweden.

[54] The treaties concluded by Denmark, Germany and Switzerland, for example, use this approach.

One may ask whether, in the spirit of reciprocity underlying these treaties, BITs should impose an obligation on the home country to encourage its nationals and companies to invest in the territory of its treaty partners. Most BITs do not. In fact, home countries are reluctant to make too much of a commitment in this regard. First, the capital-exporting country may regard the principal purpose of the treaty as protecting existing investment rather than promoting new investment. Second, the capital-exporting country may regard a BIT as an instrument to reduce rather than increase government interference in international investment flows. Third, the capital exporting country may be concerned that a promise to promote outward investment flows will create domestic political opposition to the treaty. Fourth, a capital exporting country that has BITs with a large number of countries may find that it can make no more than a nominal effort to promote investment in the territory of each of these other contracting parties.

Some BITs and model clauses, on the other hand, describe specific actions that one or the other contracting party must take to promote investment. Thus, the AALCC models commit home countries to offering appropriate incentives to investments in the territory of the other contracting party "which may include such modalities as tax concessions and investment guarantees" (model A, article 2 (i)). This practice is reflected in some BITs concluded between developing countries, which have also included active measures that both countries must take to promote investment flows between them. An example of this approach is article 2 of the BIT between Malaysia and the United Arab Emirates (table III.5). The BIT concluded by Poland with the United States requires the former country to establish a contact point to facilitate the identification in its territory of investment opportunities and to act as an intermediary in dealings with State agencies.[55]

A different approach is that found in article 2 (3) of the treaty between the Belgium–Luxembourg Economic Union and Cameroon (table III.5). This provision acknowledges the asymmetrical nature of the relationship between a capital-exporting developed country and a developing country, for it does not impose a similar obligation on Cameroon to promote investment in the Belgium–Luxembourg Economic Union.

* * *

For many developing countries, in particular the least developed countries, granting the high standards of treatment, protection and guarantees to foreign investments that are common in BITs might, in and by themselves, not be sufficient to attract FDI in the quantity and quality needed to achieve their development objectives. Moreover, their Governments may lack the necessary infrastructure and resources to introduce effective investment promotion programmes. In these circumstances, efforts by the home country BIT partner to encourage its own investors to invest in the host developing country could make a difference.[56]

Thus, beyond the general commitments typically found in BITs in this respect, BITs partners might wish to explore more specific measures to encourage their nationals and companies to invest in their respective territories. For example, embodied in a special "technical cooperation

---

[55] Another example of specific promotion provisions is to be found in the recent Jamaican BITs, such as article 2 (1) of the BIT with China: "Each Contracting Party shall encourage and promote investment by investors of the other Contracting Party in its territory. To this end, the Contracting Parties shall consult with each other as to the most effective ways to achieve that purpose." See also the BIT between Argentina and Jamaica.

[56] Germany, for example, has the following mechanisms to promote FDI flows: investment guarantees against non-commercial risks; certain credit facilities for small and medium-sized enterprises provided by the Kreditanstalt für Wiederaufbau in Frankfurt; and involvement of the government-owned Deutsche Entwichlungs-Gesellschaft, Cologne, in joint ventures through equity participation or the provision of loans with equity features (Germany, 1997).

clause" in a BIT, such measures could include the dissemination of information to their investment communities on business opportunities, the sponsorship of investment missions by representatives of their companies, and the provision of advisory assistance on ways to encourage the transfer of capital and technology. These and similar commitments from home countries could enhance the development dimension of BITs.

Table III.5. Examples of provisions on promotion in BITs

BIT between the Belgium–Luxembourg Economic Union and Cameroon (1980) Article 2 (3)	BIT between Japan and Sri Lanka (1982) Article 2 (1)	BIT between Malaysia and the United Arab Emirates (1991) Article 2	BIT between China and Jamaica (1994) Article 2 (1)
Aware of the importance of investments in the promotion of its policy of cooperation for development, the Belgium-Luxembourg Economic Union shall strive to adopt measures capable of spurring its commercial operations to join in the development effort of the United Republic of Cameroon in accordance with its priorities.	Each Contracting Party shall, subject to its rights to exercise powers in accordance with the applicable laws and regulations, encourage and create favourable conditions for nationals and companies of the other Contracting Party to make investment in its territory, and, subject to the same rights, shall admit such investment	(4) (a) Each Contracting State shall endeavour to take the necessary measures and legislation for granting appropriate facilities, incentives and other forms of encouragement for investments made by investors of the other Contracing State. ... (6) The Contracting Parties shall periodically consult between themselves concerning investment opportunities within the the territory of each other in various sectors of the economy to determine where investments from one Contracting State into the other may be most beneficial in the interest of both Contracting States. (7) To attain the objectives of the Agreement, the Contracting States shall encourage and facilitate the formation and establishment of the appropriate joint legal entities between the investors of the Contracting States to establish, develop and execute investment projects in different economic sectors in accordance with the laws and regulations of the host State.	Each Contracting Party shall encourage and promote investment by investors in the other Contracting Party in its territory. To this end, the Contracting parties shall consult with each other as to the most effective ways to achieve this purpose.

52

E. General standards of treatment

In addition to stating standards under which foreign investments will be admitted to a country, a BIT invariably stipulates the treatment that the host country must grant the investment once it has been established. A preliminary distinction can be made between general treatment standards, that is, standards relating to all aspects of the existence of a foreign investment in a host country, and specific treatment standards addressing particular issues. The general standards of treatment typically found in BITs include one or more absolute standards (i.e. standards that state the treatment to be accorded, although perhaps in terms whose exact meaning has to be determined by reference to the specific circumstances of application) and one or more relative standards (i.e. standards that define the required treatment by reference to the treatment accorded to other investment). It should be noted, however, that the terms "absolute" and "relative" are not universally accepted. This classification therefore is meant solely for the purpose of presentation, and no legal implications should be drawn from it.

1. Absolute standards

(a) *Fair and equitable treatment*

Very often BITs include one or several general principles that, together or individually, are intended to provide overall criteria by which it is possible to judge whether the treatment given to an investment is satisfactory, and to help interpret and clarify how more specific provisions should be applied in particular situations.[57]

Many BITs provide that the host country is to accord "fair and equitable treatment" to investments from the other country. A typical example is article II of the BIT between the Netherlands and the Philippines (table III.6).

Fair and equitable treatment is a classic standard in customary international law closely related to the traditional standard of due diligence, although its meaning has not been precisely defined. The official commentary on article 1 of the OECD Draft Convention on the Protection of Foreign Property states that the phrase "fair and equitable treatment" indicates "the minimum international standard which forms part of customary international law" (OECD, 1968, p. 117).[58] According to this view, which has been supported by some scholars (Huu-Tru, 1988, p. 577 and pp. 604–614), this standard covers an array of international legal principles, including non-discrimination, the duty of protection of foreign property and the international minimum standard. On the other hand, as noted in the Introduction of this study, the status and content of certain standards of international law and their applicability to foreign investments has been questioned by some developing countries.

According to another view, the strength and usefulness of the fair and equitable treatment standard lie in its relative lack of abstract content which appears to be aimed at ensuring the prudent and just application of legal rules (Juillard, 1979; Mann, 1981; Laviec, 1985; Salem, 1986). According to this view, the inclusion of this standard in BITs serves several purposes; not only does it provide a basic standard, it also provides a basic auxiliary element for the interpretation of the

---

[57] On the purpose of general principles in BITs, see Gudgeon (1986).

[58] According to this interpretation, one of the implications of the fair and equitable treatment for host countries is that treatment which meets the national standard might nonetheless be challenged as a breach of the "fair and equitable" standard.

Table III.6. Examples of provisions on absolute standards of protection in BITs

BIT between the Netherlands and the Philippines (1985) Article 3	BIT between Malaysia and the United Arab Emirates (1991) Articles 2 and 13	BIT between Denmark and Lithuania (1992) Article 3	BIT between Brazil and Chile (1994) Article III
2. Investments of nationals of either Contracting Party shall, in their entry, operation, management, maintenance, use, enjoyment or disposal, be accorded fair and equitable treatment and shall enjoy full protection and security in the territory of the other Contracting Party. 3. Each Contracting Party shall observe any obligation arising from a particular commitment it may have entered into with regard to a specific investment of nationals of the other Contracting Party.	2.(2) Once established, investments shall at all times enjoy full protection and security, in a manner consistent with international law. 2.(3) Each Contracting State shall at all times ensure fair and equitable treatment to the investments of investors of the other Contracting State. Each Contracting State shall ensure that the management, maintenance, use, enjoyment, acquisition or disposal of investments or rights related to investment and its associated activities in its territory of investors of the other Contracting State shall not in any way be subject to or impaired by arbitrary, unreasonable or discriminatory measures. * * * 13. (3) Each Contracting State shall observe any obligation it may have entered into in the documents of approval of investments or the approved investment contracts by investors of the other Contracting State.	Protection of investments 1. Investments of investors of either Contracting Party shall at all times be accorded fair and equitable treatment and shall enjoy full protection and security in the territory of the other Contracting Party. Neither Contracting Party shall in any way impair by unreasonable or discriminatory measures the management, maintenance, use, enjoyment or disposal of investments in its territory of investors of the other Contracting Party. Each Contracting Party shall observe any obligation it may have entered into with regard to investments of investors of the other Contracting Party.	Protection and treatment 1. Each Contracting Party shall protect the investments made in its territory by investors of the other Contracting Party in accordance with its legislation, and shall not create obstacles, through unjustified or discriminatory measures, to the management, maintenance, use, enjoyment, expansion, sale or, if applicable, liquidation of such investments. 2. Each Contracting Party shall provide non-discriminatory, just and equitable treatment, in accordance with the principles of international law, to the investments made in its territory by investors of the other Contracting Party, and shall guarantee that no obstacles will be created to the exercise of these rights.

other provisions in the agreement and for filling gaps in the treaty. However, there is little authority on its application.[59]

The use of the standard of fair and equitable treatment in BITs dates from the OECD 1967 Draft Convention on the Protection of Foreign Property. While the concept of "fair and equitable treatment", either alone or in combination with other general standards, appears in the majority of BITs, including the most recent ones, it is generally not mentioned in agreements concluded by certain Asian and African countries (e.g., most treaties signed by Pakistan, Rwanda, Saudi Arabia and Singapore). Nor is the clause mentioned in the model agreements recommended by the AALCC. On the other hand, despite the possible minimum-international-standard connotation of this clause, the BITs signed by Latin American countries do contain it. The clause also appears in BITs concluded by China.

[59] For a general discussion of the meaning of the standard of fair and equitable treatment, see United Nations Centre on Transnational Corporations (UNCTC) (1990).

(b)   *Full protection and security*

Many BITs, after providing for fair and equitable treatment, add explicitly that investment from the other contracting party should be provided with "full protection and security" or "most constant protection and security".[60] Other variations in the wording are not unusual. This standard was already used alone in the earliest BITs signed before the OECD Draft Convention on the Protection of Foreign Property, before the concept of fair and equitable treatment had been introduced. In fact, full protection and security is an old standard commonly used in FCN treaties.

The provision does not impose strict liability on the host country to protect foreign investment. In effect, the standard does not represent a deviation from the due diligence rule.[61] Thus, the term "full protection and security" connotes the assurance of full protection and security for foreign investors as contemplated or required by customary international law. At the same time, the clause on full protection and security is unusual in that it contemplates protecting investment against private as well as public action, that is, the clause requires that the host country should exercise reasonable care to protect investment against injury by private parties.

(c)   *Prohibition of arbitrary or discriminatory measures*

Non-discrimination, in its general sense, means that the host country must abstain from discriminatory action towards foreign investors in general or towards specific groups of foreign investors. While the principle as such is generally accepted, a number of important exceptions are also recognized (see below, under national treatment and MFN treatment).

Although, arguably, the standard of fair and equitable treatment implicitly excludes arbitrary or discriminatory treatment, some BITs explicitly prohibit such treatment.[62] A similar provision appears in many FCN treaties negotiated by the United States, for which some judicial authorities exist. For example, in the case concerning Elettronica Sicula S.p.A. (ELSI) (International Court of Justice, 1989), involving an investment made under such a treaty between Italy and the United States, the International Court of Justice rejected the argument by the United States that various actions taken by the Mayor of Palermo with respect to a United States investment were arbitrary or discriminatory within the meaning of this provision. One reason for the Court's conclusion was that the measures were subject to review under Italian law (Hamrak, 1992).

In many BITs, the word "unreasonable" appears in lieu of "arbitrary". An example of this approach is the BIT between Denmark and Lithuania (table III.6).[63] When the provision uses the conjunction "and" instead of "or", as in "unreasonable and discriminatory measures", it may be that the host country would have greater latitude for action; it would be free to discriminate as long as the discrimination was not unreasonable (or arbitrary). For example, a host developing country that grants special incentives to national investors, but denies them to foreign investors, could argue that such differentiation is reasonable in view of its status as a developing country. To support its

---

[60] For an example of the former formulation, in addition to the examples shown in table III.6, see the BIT between Canada and Hungary (article III (1)). For an example of the latter formulation, see the BIT between Peru and Thailand (article 3 (2)).

[61] On the meaning of this clause, see the case of Asian Agricultural Products Ltd. (AAPL) v. Republic of Sri Lanka (ICSID, 1990). See also analyses of this case by Sharma (1992); and Vascianne (1992).

[62] For example, all BITs signed by Latin American countries, except those signed with Canada, have non-discrimination clauses.

[63] See also the BITs between Ghana and Switzerland (article 3) and between Lithuania and the Netherlands (article (3) (i)). Another example of such a clause can be found in the BIT between the Kyrgyz Republic and the United States (article II (2) (b)).

argument, it could point to similar differentiation in treatment prevailing in many countries around the world. At the same time, the host country might also argue that such "reasonable" differentiation was not discrimination.

(d)   *Duty to observe commitments concerning investment*

Another clause in use requires each contracting party to observe any obligations that it may have incurred with regard to investment, although this type of clause is less frequently used than the previously discussed absolute standards. A typical example of this clause is to be found in the BIT between Denmark and Lithuania (article 3 (1)), which provides that "[e]ach Contracting Party shall observe any obligation it may have entered into with regard to investments of investors of the other Contracting Party" (table III.6).[64]

This clause is directed in particular at investment agreements that host countries frequently conclude with individual foreign investors.[65] It would appear, however, that, unless otherwise stated, this provision could also apply to undertakings by the two contracting parties concerning investment. Indeed, the language of the provision is so broad that it could be interpreted to cover all kinds of obligations, explicit or implied, contractual or non-contractual, undertaken with respect to investment generally. It may be for this reason that the BIT between the Netherlands and the Philippines departed from the Netherlands prototype and adopted more specific language on this point (table III.6). Another example of a more specific formulation of this matter is the BIT between Malaysia and the United Arab Emirates (table III.6).[66]

Investment agreements between host countries and foreign investors are often subject to the local laws of the host country, depending upon their precise formulation (see below under "settlement of disputes"). A provision of the kind discussed here might possibly alter the legal regime and make the agreement subject to the rules of international law. In any event, as a result of this provision, violations of commitments regarding investment by the host country would be redressible through the dispute-settlement procedures of a BIT.

(e)   *Treatment consistent with international law*

Some BITs have a provision that requires the host country to provide the investments covered by the treaty with treatment no less favourable than that required by international law. These include, for example, BITs concluded by the Belgium–Luxembourg Economic Union, France and the United States. Thus, the treaty between Belgium–Luxembourg and Malaysia (article 3) specifies that fair and equitable treatment "may in no case be less favourable than that recognized under international law". The provision also appears in some BITs signed between Latin American countries, such as the BIT between Brazil and Chile (table III.6).[67]

This provision ensures that the BIT is interpreted so as to provide at least the minimum standard of protection required by international law. It is analogous to the one discussed in the preceding section in that it has the effect of incorporating another separate set of norms into the BIT

---

[64] The clause often appears, for example, in BITs concluded by Germany, the Netherlands, the United Kingdom and the United States.

[65] On the use of such clauses generally, see Waelde and Ndi (1996).

[66] Through this type of provision it is sought to bring together, as a single category, both formal contractual arrangements between State and investor (e.g., concessions, State contracts) and obligations the State has undertaken by virtue of the instrument of approval of the investment (as to which it is usually said that they have a contractual element, although they are normally administrative acts).

[67] Other examples of BITs involving Latin American countries that contain such a provision are the BITs between Barbados and Venezuela (article 2 (2)) and between Ecuador and Venezuela (article III (1)).

– in this case, the principles of international law. Thus, treatment of investment by a host country that falls below the international law standard would violate the BIT. Moreover, this provision in a BIT would allow the principles of international law applicable to investment to be invoked in the event of dispute.

A number of developing countries, in particular, consider that the concept of an international minimum standard for the treatment of aliens abroad[68] has often been used in the past to secure privileged treatment for foreigners in economic matters, to exploit these countries' natural resources, and even to justify military intervention by home countries (UNCTC, 1988). For this reason, as noted in chapter I, the content and applicability of certain international standards to foreign investment has been questioned by some countries in multilateral forums.[69] Bilateral investment treaties, of course, take no position on the issue of the content of customary international law applicable to foreign investment.

Finally, this provision may serve as a choice-of-law clause for the dispute-resolution mechanisms of the treaty, where those mechanisms are not governed by a more specific choice-of-law clause. Because investment must be treated no less favourably than is required by international law, the resolution of any dispute concerning the treatment of investment under the treaty would necessarily be governed by the provisions of international law.

* * *

The standard of fair and equitable treatment plays a significant role in BITs. In addition to filling gaps and providing a context for the interpretation of specific provisions, one of its main advantages is that it provides a relatively easy means for raising questions about the treatment of investors. In its absence, the party concerned would have to resort to allegations about infringements of a specific BIT rule or provision. Instead, the obligation to accord fair and equitable treatment provides a legitimate channel of communication between the parties involved for examination of specific concerns. In the context of the settlement of an investment dispute under a BIT, fair and equitable treatment would give conciliators and arbitrators an opportunity to resolve problems not only by reference to strict legal rules but by considering the entire situation and context of the issue (UNCTC, 1991).

2. Relative standards: most-favoured-nation treatment and national treatment

Bilateral investment treaties use two different standards that are directed at preventing discriminatory treatment of different classes of investment: the MFN treatment standard and the national treatment standard.

(a) *Definitions and purpose*

i. *Most-favoured-nation treatment standard*

This standard guarantees that investment by nationals and companies of one contracting party in the territory of the other contracting party will be treated no less favourably than investment by nationals or companies of any third country. Thus, an MFN clause prevents a country from imposing conditions on the investments from the other contracting party that are less favourable than

---

[68] See, among others, Brownlie (1991) and Sornarajah (1994).

[69] The different positions on this issue have been described in several studies undertaken in connection with the negotiations of the Draft United Nations Code of Conduct on Transnational Corporations. See, for example, Robinson (1986) and Vagts (1986); for a more recent analysis of this question, see Sornarajah (1994).

those granted to investments of a third country. It also means that if one of the parties gives any special advantage or privilege to investment from a third country, it must grant that same advantage or privilege to investment from its treaty partners. A typical MFN clause is that found in the treaty between Chile and Malaysia (table III.7); a different formulation, with potential for a different interpretation, is found in the treaty between Denmark and Indonesia (table III.9).

Table III.7. Examples of provisions on MFN treatment in BITs

BIT between Chile and Malaysia (1992) Article 3	BIT between China and Sweden (1982) Article 2
Most favoured nation	(2) Investments by investors of either Contracting State in the territory of the other Contracting State shall not be subject to a treatment less favourable than that accorded to investments by investors of third States.
1. Investments by nationals or companies of either Contracting State on the territory of the other Contracting State shall ... not be subjected to a treatment less favourable than that accorded to investments by nationals or companies of third States.	
...	(3) Notwithstanding the provisions of paragraph (2) of this Article, a Contracting State, which has concluded with one or more other States an agreement regarding the formation of a customs union or free trade area, shall be free to grant a more favourable treatment to investments by investors of the State or States, which are also parties to the said agreement, or by investors of some of these States. A Contracting State shall also be free to grant a more favourable treatment to investments by investors of other States, if this is stipulated under bilateral agreements concluded with such States before the date of the signature of this Agreement.
3. The provision in this Treaty relating to treatment no less favourable than that accorded to investments of third States shall not be interpreted to oblige a Contracting Party to extend to investors of the other Contracting Party the benefits of any treatment, preference or privilege by virtue of:	
(a) any customs union, free trade area, common market or monetary union, or any similar international convention or other forms of regional cooperation, present or future, of which any of the Contracting Parties might become a party; or the adoption of an agreement designed to achieve the formation or expansion of such union or area within a reasonable time; or	
(b) any international convention or agreement related totally or principally to taxation, or any national legislation related totally or partially to taxation.	

The MFN treatment is a treaty-made standard that has its origins in trade agreements, where it was originally formulated and applied on the basis of reciprocity (Kline and Ludema, 1997). More recently, however, the unconditional application of the standard has prevailed (UNCTC, 1990).

ii. National treatment standard

This standard guarantees that investment by nationals and companies of one contracting party in the territory of the other contracting party will receive from the host country treatment no less favourable than the treatment given to investment by nationals or companies of that host country. An early example of a formulation of the national treatment standard can be found in the BIT between Germany and Kenya; a more recent example is the BIT between Jamaica and the United Kingdom (table III.8).

Table III.8. Examples of provisions on national treatment in BITs

BIT between Germany and Kenya (1964) Article 2	BIT between Jamaica and the United Kingdom (1987) Article 3
(1) Investments owned by, or under the control of, nationals or companies of either Contracting Party in the territory of the other Contracting Party shall not be accorded by that Party treatment less favourable than that it accords to any other similar investment in its territory. (2) Neither Contracting Party shall subject activities of nationals or companies of the other Contracting Party in connection with their investments, as well as the management, use or enjoyment of such investments, to conditions less favourable than it imposes on activities in connection with any other similar investment in its territory.	(1) Neither Contracting Party shall in its territory subject investment or returns of nationals or companies of the other Contracting Party to treatment less favourable than that which it accords to investments or returns of its own nationals .... (2) Neither Contracting Party shall in its territory subject nationals or companies of the other Contracting Party, as regards their management, use, enjoyment, or disposal of their investments, to treatment less favourable than that which it accords to its own nationals .... (3) Special incentives granted by one Contracting Party only to its nationals and companies in order to stimulate the creation of local industries are considered compatible with this Article provided they do not significantly affect the investment and activities of nationals and companies of the other Contracting Party in connection with an investment.

The principle of national treatment has been used in two different but not unrelated contexts: under international agreements, the national treatment principle established by express provisions seeks to assure that no less favourable treatment will be accorded to aliens than to nationals, as well as to their property. On the other hand, the principle of national treatment is also one of the doctrines of international law supported and applied by some developing countries for the treatment of aliens and their property, also known as the Calvo doctrine. In this context, the national treatment standard aims at providing only equality of treatment. It sees national treatment as establishing that no more favourable treatment will be accorded to aliens. The concept of national treatment referred to in this study relates to its first meaning, that is, as it is used in BIT practice. It should be noted, however, that concerns that "treatment no less favourable" may allow preferential treatment of foreign investors vis à vis national firms have led some countries to refer to "the same" or "similar" treatment (UNCTC, 1990).

(b) Operation of the provisions

The general assumption in the past has been that a country was most likely to favour its own nationals, and therefore a provision on national treatment would usually be more advantageous to foreign investors than one on MFN treatment. In some instances, however, countries may treat foreign investment more favourably than local investment. Since one form of treatment may be superior to the other in particular cases, many BITs require that host countries provide both forms of treatment to foreign investment. A typical example of this approach is the BIT between Hungary and Israel (table III.9). Where both are required, the implication is that the host country must apply the form of treatment that is more favourable under the circumstances, and a number of BITs, such as those concluded by Germany, the Netherlands and the United States, explicitly say so (table III.9).[70]

Table III.9. Examples of provisions dealing with MFN and national treatment in a single clause in BITs

BIT between Denmark and Indonesia (1968) Article 3	BIT between Hungary and Israel (1991) Article 3	BIT between Armenia and the United States (1992) Article II (1)
Neither Contracting Party shall in its territory impose on the activities of enterprises in which such approved investments are made by nationals or corporations of the other Contracting Party conditions which are less favourable than those imposed in its territory on activities in connection with any similar enterprise owned by nationals or corporations of the other Contracting Party or national or corporations of third countries.	1. Neither Contracting Party shall, in its territory, subject investments or returns of investors of the other Contracting Party to treatment less favourable than that which it accords to investments or returns of its own investors or to investments or returns of investors of any third State. 2. Neither Contracting Party shall, in its territory, subject investors of the other Contracting Party, as regards their management, maintenance, use, enjoyment or disposal of their investments, to treatment less favourable than that which it accords to its own investors or to investors of any third State.	Each Party shall permit and treat investment, and activities associated therewith, on a basis no less favorable than that accorded in like situations to investment or associated activities of its own nationals and companies, or of nationals or companies or any third country, whichever is the most favorable, subject to the right of each Party to make or maintain exceptions falling within one of the sectors or matters listed in the Annex to this Treaty. Each Party agrees to notify the other Party before or on the date of entry into force of this Treaty of all such laws and regulations of which it is aware concerning the sectors or matters listed in the Annex. Moreover, each Party agrees to notify the other of any future exception with respect to the sectors or matters listed in the Annex, and to limit such exceptions to a minimum. Any future exception by either Party shall not apply to investment existing in that sector or matter at the time the exception becomes effective. The treatment accorded pursuant to any exceptions shall, unless specified otherwise in the Annex, be no less favorable than that accorded in like situations to investments and associated activities of nationals or companies of any third country.

Countries are often less willing to grant national treatment than MFN treatment; that is, they may wish to reserve the right to discriminate in favour of domestic investors without reserving the right to discriminate in favour of only certain foreign investors. Thus, while a number of BITs do not guarantee national treatment to investment (e.g. early BITs concluded by Norway and Sweden and the majority of BITs concluded by China[71]), virtually every BIT requires that investment covered by the treaty should receive MFN treatment. On the other hand, national treatment is considered of such importance by certain countries (e.g. Germany) that they would

---

[70] In Latin America, the following BITs state that a contracting party shall grant MFN treatment to investors of the other contracting party if this treatment is more favourable than the one it accords to its own investors: Argentina–El Salvador; Bolivia–Peru; Chile–Guatemala; Chile–Paraguay; Chile–Uruguay; Chile–Venezuela; El Savador–Peru; and Paraguay–Peru.

[71] In fact, until the 1990s, China did not agree to incorporate the national treatment standard in BITs as a matter of principle, although it was granted in the BIT between China and Germany (article 3 (IV)). Since the early 1990s, as China pursued its economic reforms and continued to open up to the outside world, it began to provide for national treatment in BITs with certain qualifications. The most important qualification is that national treatment shall be limited by existing laws and regulations; such a qualification appears in, for example, the BIT between China and Morocco (article 3 (1)). In some BITs recently concluded by China, (e.g. the BIT between China and the Republic of Korea (article 3 (2)) the national treatment clause appears without qualifications. Pursuant to the 1996 Report of the State Council in which it declared its policy to accord foreign investors full national treatment on a step-by-step basis, China has expressed its intention to adopt a more and more open policy on this matter.

prefer not to sign a BIT rather than omit a national treatment clause (UNCTC, 1988). It should be noted, nevertheless, that both standards have appeared in BITs since the early 1960s.

A party to a BIT that has an MFN provision must provide investors of the other contracting party with every form of favourable treatment that it extends to investors of any third country. Thus, because virtually all BITs include an MFN provision, any form of favourable treatment given to foreign investors by a host country should be extended, in principle, to investors of every other country with which the host country has concluded a BIT containing an MFN clause.

Occasionally a country has included a guarantee of favourable treatment in an earlier BIT that it later does not wish to extend to any other country. One solution would be to renegotiate the earlier BIT so that the guarantee is removed, which would eliminate the entitlement of other countries to the same treatment. However, if the other party to the earlier BIT refuses to renegotiate the treaty, another solution would be to include in all subsequent BITs a provision that the early BIT cannot be invoked for the purposes of determining the country's obligations under the MFN clause of those BITs. However, this solution would only work if every subsequent BIT party agreed to the provision. If one party did not agree to it, then that party would have a right to the favourable treatment agreed in the earlier BIT, and all other BIT parties would therefore be entitled to the same treatment, notwithstanding their agreement to exclude the MFN provision included in the earlier BIT.

The generalizing effect of an MFN provision also applies, in principle, to the national treatment provision of a BIT: if a country promises national treatment to any BIT contracting party, then all other BIT contracting parties would be entitled to national treatment as a result of the MFN provisions in their BITs. Thus, while some BITs do not explicitly include a promise of national treatment, the contracting parties may still be obligated to provide national treatment by the MFN treatment provision.

In essence, the effect of an MFN provision is to raise the level of protection guaranteed by each BIT concluded by a country to the level guaranteed by that country's most protective BIT. Thus, to a considerable extent, the differences between the BITs concluded by a country may become irrelevant. For example, if a country has concluded a BIT in which it promises to pay prompt, adequate and effective compensation in the case of expropriation, and a second BIT in which it makes no such promise, the MFN provision in the second BIT would require the country to pay prompt, adequate and effective compensation for expropriated investment covered by the second BIT.

The wording of an MFN or national treatment provision, therefore, is of special importance. In particular, it is important to ascertain which entities or activities are entitled to MFN or national treatment. In many BITs, it is the investment that is entitled to MFN or national treatment. Other BITs guarantee MFN or national treatment to investment and returns, while still others confer the right of MFN or national treatment on investment and investment-related activities or on investment and associated activities. As noted before, terms such as "returns" or "associated activities" that appear in the MFN or national treatment provision are often defined elsewhere in a BIT. A typical definition of "associated activities" used in United States BITs can be found in the BIT between the United States and Zaire (now the Democratic Republic of the Congo) (article II (2)), which includes:

> ...the establishment, control and maintenance of branches, offices and other facilities for the conduct of business; the organization, acquisition, management and liquidation of companies; the making, performance and enforcement of contracts; the acquisition of property; the leasing of real property for the conduct of business; the acquisition, maintenance and protection of copyrights, patents, trademarks, trade names, trade secrets, licenses and other industrial property rights and the borrowing of funds.

A further question arises as to whether it is the investment, the investor, or both that are to receive MFN treatment. Thus, a provision that refers to "enterprises and the activities of enterprises" would seem to exclude investors in the enterprise from MFN treatment in such matters as, for example, taxes. To guard against this result, some treaties, such as the BIT between Jamaica and the United Kingdom, include separate provisions granting the investor and the investment MFN treatment (table III.8). Arguably, however, in some contexts the term "investment" could be interpreted to cover "investors" because of the inextricable linkage between the investment and the investor.

Interpretation of the MFN and national treatment provisions also requires determining which entities or activities serve as the reference point for ascertaining the type of treatment to be provided. For example, in the case of national treatment, the question may arise as to whether an investment is entitled to treatment as favourable as that provided to an investment by State enterprises of a treaty partner. This question is often answered by the definition of the term "company". If the term is defined to include public as well as private entities, then a provision requiring each contracting party to provide national treatment would require that investment covered should receive treatment as favourable as that accorded to an investment by State enterprises of the host country. On the other hand, a BIT may expressly provide that national treatment shall not include treatment afforded to the host country's State enterprises, as is done, for example, in the protocol to the BIT between Germany and Mali (para. 3 (c)).

Very often the MFN or national treatment provisions are limited to investments that are "in the same circumstances"[72] or "in like situations"[73] or that are made by a "similar enterprise",[74] thus mitigating some of the most sweeping effects of the application of the MFN and national treatment clauses. Such provisions, however, do not identify the criteria by which similarity or likeness is to be established. The determination might depend, for example, on whether the two investments are in competition with each other. In OECD practice, for example, the specific criteria to be taken into account include whether the two enterprises are in the same industry, the impact of policy objectives of the host country in particular fields and the motivation behind the measure involved. In any case, unless the standards of MFN and national treatment are being applied to two identical companies in the same industry at the same time, comparisons for this purpose are highly problematic (UNCTC, 1990).

Another question that arises is whether the MFN or national treatment obligation applies to special treatment granted to certain individual investors or to all investors of a particular nationality. Some BITs may be interpreted as requiring the most favourable treatment if it is accorded to any investor, even if it is not accorded to all investors of a particular nationality.[75] Other BITs, however, may apply the treatment of investors of a particular nationality as MFN treatment only if all investors of that nationality receive the treatment.[76] Of course, where there is only a single investor of a particular nationality in a given situation, then it will be difficult to decide whether the special treatment accorded to that investor shall be considered treatment accorded to an individual investor or treatment accorded to all investors of that nationality in the same situation.

---

[72] See, for example, the BIT between Belize and the United Kingdom (article 3 (1)).

[73] See, for example, the BITs concluded by the United States.

[74] See, for example, the BIT between Indonesia and Norway (article III) of 1969. It should be noted, however, that the text of the new treaty between Indonesia and Norway, signed in 1991, does not contain such a phrase.

[75] For example, Vandevelde (1992), suggests that the general intent of BITs concluded by the United States is that MFN or national treatment requires treatment afforded to the most favoured enterprise.

[76] See, for example, the BIT between Germany and Pakistan. See also the OECD Draft Convention on the Protection of Foreign Property (article 1 (7)) (UNCTAD, 1996b, Vol. III, p. 113).

(c)   *Exceptions to most-favoured-nation treatment and national treatment*

In addition to the various qualifications often found in the definitions of the standards of MFN and national treatment that may limit considerably the scope of their application, many BITs seek to further limit the obligation to provide MFN or national treatment by including additional qualifications, exceptions or derogations.

One exception to the granting of MFN and national treatment relates to restrictions based on public order or national security. The protocol to Germany's model treaty, for example, contains the typical reservation concerning measures "taken for reasons of public security and order, public health and morality".

A second exception relating to MFN treatment concerns special privileges accorded by virtue of a country's membership of a customs union or free trade area. Customs unions and free trade areas generally provide for favourable treatment of foreign investment as well as foreign trade. The effect of this exception is to permit a country to extend favourable treatment to investment by nationals and companies of other countries in the customs union or free trade area to which it belongs, without having to extend that treatment to other countries with which it has a BIT, but which are not members of such a union or area. Treaties vary in the way they refer to the types of arrangements that fall within exceptions. They may refer, for example, to an "economic union" or a "regional economic organization" as well as customs union or free trade area.[77] A typical exception clause is that found in the BIT between Chile and Malaysia (table III.7). The granting of MFN treatment in a BIT is therefore of concern not only to countries that are already members of such groupings, but also to host countries that plan to enter into such special arrangements in the foreseeable future.

A third exception related to MFN treatment (and sometimes national treatment too) applies to treatment accorded under international treaties or domestic legislation relating to taxation. In other words, the exception permits a country to provide favourable tax treatment to investment by nationals or companies of another country without according the same treatment to investment by nationals and companies of other countries with which it has BITs. For example, the treaty between the Republic of Korea and Mongolia (article 7 (b)) states that the MFN and national treatment provisions "shall not be construed so as to oblige one Contracting Party to extend to the investors of the other Contracting Party the benefit of any treatment, preference or privilege which may be extended by the former Contracting Party by virtue of ... any international agreement or domestic legislation relating wholly or mainly to taxation". The reason for the tax exception is that many countries prefer to address international tax relations through separate treaties dealing specifically with tax matters. The exception allows a country to conclude a tax treaty granting special tax treatment to the investment of another country in return for other concessions without having to be concerned that other countries will have a right to the same treatment by virtue of the MFN provision in their BITs. Another reason for addressing tax relations through a separate treaty is that the complexity of tax matters may render such matters unsuitable for inclusion in the kind of standardized provisions that are typical of BITs.

Some BITs apply the MFN provision only to treatment granted under treaties concluded subsequent to the entry into force of the BIT in which the MFN provision appears. For example, a number of BITs concluded by Sweden allow the contracting parties to grant treatment to

---

[77] Although the Association of South-East Asian Nations (ASEAN) is not an economic union or free trade area, all ASEAN member countries have provisions in their BITs excluding advantages given in the context of the regional association. On the question of regional economic integration organizations, see Karl (1996).

investment under agreements concluded before the signature of the BIT, without having to extend that same treatment to investment covered by the subsequently concluded BIT.[78]

A fourth exception to MFN and national treatment consists of the exclusion from the application of the standards any benefits and advantages given to other investments. An example of this approach is the BIT between Denmark and Indonesia (table III.9), which does not refer to "treatment" but rather to the "imposition of conditions", and it applies to both national treatment and the MFN obligations. This language could be interpreted as meaning that a host country is not obliged to give MFN and national treatment with respect to benefits and advantages granted to investments. Thus, it would prevent a host-country Government from imposing performance requirements on investments from a treaty partner if it does not impose similar requirements on investments from the host country or from third countries; however, it might not oblige the host country to grant the same subsidies and exemptions to investments covered by the treaty that it has granted to its nationals or to investments from third countries.

A different approach is found in Protocol No. 2 of the BIT between Indonesia and Switzerland, which allows derogation from national treatment of Swiss investors "in view of the present stage of development of the Indonesian national economy". However, Indonesia, pursuant to the terms of the treaty, would grant "identical or compensating facilities to investments and nationals of the Swiss Confederation in similar economic activities".[79]

Another type of exception, typical of the BITs signed by the United States and applying to both MFN and national treatment, excludes certain industries from MFN or national treatment. An example of this approach is the BIT between Armenia and the United States (table III.9). These BITs authorize the contracting parties, at the time a BIT is concluded, to designate in an annex to the treaty certain industries to which the obligation to provide national or MFN treatment (entry and establishment and as well as after the establishment of an investment) shall not apply.

As noted in the discussion on the admission of investment, a number of treaties provide for the possibility of derogating from national treatment and MFN treatment in provisions governing the admission procedure. Thus, the protocol to the BIT between Germany and Uganda states:

> (d) In the interest of the national economy either Contracing Party may, in approving an investment by nationals or companies of the other Contracting Party, make specific stipulations deviating from the treatment provided for in Article 2. If specific stipulations of that nature have been made, the provisions of Article 2 shall, to that extent, not be applicable. Such specific stipulations to be effective shall be made in detail in the document of approval (para. 2).

Finally, it may be noted that, where the parties wish to subject both MFN and national treatment to differing limitations and qualifications, it may be easier to do so by addressing each standard in a separate article of the treaty.

* * *

The standard of national treatment is an important principle for home countries, but is a cause for concern in most host countries, since such treatment may enable foreign enterprises to

---

[78] See, for example, Sweden's BITs with China (article 2 (3)), Egypt (article 2 (3)), Malaysia (article 2 (3)), Pakistan (article 3 (3)), and Yugoslavia (article 2 (3)); see also paragraph 2 (b) of the protocol to Germany's BIT with the Republic of Korea.

[79] Development considerations seem to play a role in the case of Germany's approach to national treatment, insofar as it has accepted certain exceptions to the national treatment principle, provided that these are undertaken for development purposes only (e.g. to develop small-scale industries) and that the measures do not substantially impair investments from a German investor (Germany, 1997).

compete in the local economy to the detriment of domestic enterprises. This concern is particularly acute in developing countries, since their national enterprises may be particularly vulnerable to competition, especially from large transnational corporations. Moreover, host Governments sometimes have special policies and programmes that grant advantages and privileges to domestic enterprises in order to stimulate their growth. If a national treatment clause in a BIT obligates a host country to grant the same privileges and benefits to foreign investors, the host Government would in effect be strengthening the ability of foreign investors to compete with local business. To address this problem, developing countries have often sought to qualify or limit the application of national treatment in their negotiations, and have thus avoided the potentially most detrimental effects of national treatment on the host country.

The MFN standard, on the other hand, is less problematic for developing countries in terms of its potential effects on domestic firms. However, it can also have far-reaching and often unforeseen consequences in terms of elevating the standards of treatment of third countries' investors, including indirectly granting national treatment to third countries' firms. Consequently, policy makers would be well advised to consider appropriate formulations of MFN provisions to avoid difficulties of interpretation.

F. Expropriation

As discussed in chapter I, one of the primary reasons that many developed countries initiated BITs in the 1960s was to protect their investments abroad against the risk of expropriation[80]. BITs prescribe the conditions under which expropriation may take place. The broad definition of investment that appears in most BITs is of particular relevance here. Since "investment" may include "interests" in companies, equity shareholders in, or creditors of, a company may have a claim arising from the expropriation of their interests in the company if the company is taken over by a host country.

1. Defining expropriation

There have been efforts to draw a distinction between expropriation and nationalization as these terms are used in customary international law. In one view, for example, "nationalization" refers to the seizure of an entire industry of an economy as part of a change in economic policy, while "expropriation" refers to seizure of a particular property by a country.

While the terms "expropriation" and "nationalization" are generally left undefined in BITs, these treaties do not appear to have been drafted with such a distinction in mind. Rather, BIT provisions on expropriation typically apply to actions by a country that substantially impair the value of an investment, regardless of whether they amount to an isolated event or whether they are part of a major structural change in the economy. Many BITs make this clear by expressly stating that expropriation includes measures "tantamount" or "equivalent" to expropriation. Thus, the BIT between Egypt and Japan (article V) includes " expropriation, nationalization, restriction or any other measures, the effects of which would be tantamount to expropriation, nationalization or restriction", and the BIT between the Republic of Korea and Sri Lanka (article 7) mentions "measures having effect equivalent to nationalization and expropriation". The same formulation appears in the AALCC model A.

---

[80] On the topic of expropriation, see, for example, Borchard (1915), Dunn (1932), Foighel (1957, 1964), Friedman (1953), Garcia Amador (1958), Wortley (1959), White (1961), Katzarov (1964), Lillich (1972, 1973-1975), Weston (1975), Dolzer (1981), Huu-Tru (1990), Murphy (1991), Amerasinghe (1992), Mouri (1994).

As a result of this broad language, most BITs also apply the expropriation provisions to "indirect expropriations". In fact, some treaties make explicit reference to indirect expropriation. Thus, the BIT between France and Pakistan (article 5) refers to "measures of expropriation or nationalization or any other measures the effect of which would be direct or indirect dispossession". Indirect expropriation occurs when the country takes an action that substantially impairs the value of an investment without necessarily assuming ownership of the investment. Accordingly, indirect expropriation may occur even though the host country disavows any intent to expropriate the investment and characterizes its actions as something other than expropriation. Where the action is equivalent to expropriation, however, the conditions imposed by the expropriation provision apply.[81] In the Starret case before the Iran–United States Claims Tribunal, the Tribunal, in a similar situation noted that:

> It is undisputed in this case that the Government of Iran did not issue any law or decree according to which the Zomorod Project or Shah Goli expressly was nationalized or expropriated. However, it is recognized in international law that a measure taken by a State can interfere with property rights to such an extent that these rights are rendered so useless that they must be deemed to have been expropriated, even though the State does not purport to have expropriated them and the legal title to the property formally remains with the original owner.[82]

Certain countries are more explicit about the meaning of indirect expropriation. Thus, while the model treaty prepared by Germany mentions "any other measure the effects of which would be tantamount to expropriation or nationalization" (article 4 (2)), the protocols of many treaties concluded by Germany add the following definition of expropriation:

> Expropriation shall mean any taking away or restricting tantamount to the taking away of any property right which in itself or in conjunction with other rights constitutes an investment.[83]

In addition, the protocols specify that any government measure severely impairing the economic situation of an investment gives rise to an obligation to pay compensation.

Some BITs concluded by the United States specify that such measures include, in particular, but are not limited to, "the levying of taxation, the compulsory sale of all or part of the investment, or impairments of the management, control or economic value of a company" (United States and Zaire (now the Democratic Republic of the Congo) (article III)).

Most BITs are also understood to apply the expropriation provision to "creeping expropriations". This term refers to an expropriation carried out by a series of acts over a period of time. Any of these acts taken in isolation may appear to be a legitimate regulatory action, but ultimately their cumulative effect is to destroy substantially the value of an investment. In that situation, BITs generally regard an investment as having been expropriated.

2. Conditions of expropriation

As noted above, BITs impose certain conditions on expropriation if it is to be considered lawful. Practically all BITs adopt some variation of the traditional rule of international law that a State may not expropriate the property of an alien except for a public purpose, in a non-discriminatory manner, upon payment of compensation, and in accordance with due process of law.

---

[81] For an in-depth study of the legal aspects of indirect expropriation taking into account judgements of international tribunals, see Weston (1975) and Dolzer (1986).

[82] Case No. 24 of the Iran–United States Claims Tribunal, quoted by Dolzer (1986). For a general discussion of the cases on this issue before the Iran–United States Claims Tribunal, see Khan (1990).

[83] See, for example, the BIT between China and Germany (protocol (4)).

The various elements of the traditional rule have taken different formulations in different treaties, some more and some less protective of the investor's interests. The treaty between Costa Rica and the United Kingdom is an example of a provision that emphasizes investor interests. A formulation that is less protective of the investor's interests is contained in the treaty between China and Japan (article 5) (table III.10). Indeed, although the article of the treaty between Costa Rica and the United Kingdom uses the same elements as the article from the treaty between China and Japan, there are many important differences between them, which will be discussed in the following sections.

(a)   *Public purpose*

Nearly all BITs require that the expropriation should be for a public purpose or, in some treaties, in the public interest. In practice, this condition imposes few restrictions on the expropriating country. In the contemporary world, countries are very reluctant to challenge another country's determination of what is a public purpose since there is no agreed definition under international law, and international tribunals are likely to defer to the host country's determination (UNCTC, 1988). Nevertheless, some commentators have attempted to hypothesize situations that would violate this condition. Expropriation as an act of political reprisal, for example, may not be for a public purpose.[84]

A few countries have included some limitations on public purpose in the BIT text. Thus, for example, the BIT between Costa Rica and the United Kingdom (table III.10.) requires that the expropriation be for a public purpose "related to the internal needs" of the host country, a provision that would prevent a host country from taking property for reasons of foreign policy. A similar provision is also found in other BITs signed by Denmark and the United Kingdom.[85]

Some BITs, such as, the treaty between France and Malaysia (article 3), omit any reference to public purpose. The BIT between Singapore and Sri Lanka (article 4) permits expropriation "for any purpose authorised by law". The AALCC model B (alternative 1) states that "a country may exercise its sovereign rights in the matter of nationalization or expropriation"; alternative 2 includes the requirement of "public purpose" in brackets.

(b)   *Non-discrimination*

Many BITs require the expropriation of any investment to be non-discriminatory. Some commentators seem to assume that this provision is directed particularly at expropriations based on nationality, race or national origin, but in fact the provision prohibits any expropriation that treats investors differently without legitimate justification. At the same time, some forms of discriminatory expropriation would be prohibited by the general provisions requiring MFN and national treatment. Also, the impairment of investment by arbitrary or discriminatory action is prohibited separately by many BITs.

(c)   *Compensation*

All BITs require the payment of compensation for expropriation, and this condition is undoubtedly at the heart of the expropriation provision in most BITs. While the requirement itself is generally not questioned, the standards for determining the amount of compensation have been

---

[84] See, for example, in the arbitration case of the British Petroleum Exploration Company (Libya) Limited v. Government of the Libyan Arab Republic (1974) (International Law Reports, 1979).

[85] The phrase "related to the internal needs" was objected to by Jamaica and is not included in its BIT with the United Kingdom.

Table III.10. Examples of provisions on expropriation in BITs

BIT between the Netherlands and the Sudan (1970)	BIT between Costa Rica and the United Kingdom (1982)	BIT between China and Japan (1988)
Article XI The investments of nationals of either Contracting Party in the territory of the other Contracting Party shall not be expropriated except for the public benefit and against compensation. Such compensation shall represent the equivalent to the depreciated value of the investment affected, it shall be actually realizable, freely transferable, and shall paid without undue delay.	Article 5 Expropriation (1) Investments of nationals or companies of either Contracting Party shall not be nationalized, expropriated, or subject to measures having the effect equivalent to nationalization or expropriation (hereinafter referred to as expropriation) in the territory of the other Contracting Party except for a public purpose related to the internal needs of that Party and against prompt, adequate and effective compensation. Such compensation shall amount to the market value of the investment expropriated immediately before the expropriation or before the expropriation became public knowledge, shall include interest at the normal commercial rate until the date of payment, shall be made without delay, be effectively realizable and be freely transferable. The national or company affected shall have a right, under the law of the Contracting Party making the expropriation, to prompt review, by a judicial or other independent authority of that Party, of his or its case and of the valuation of his or its investment in accordance with the principles set out in this paragraph. (2) Where a Contracting Party expropriates the assets of a company which is incorporated or constituted under the law in force in any part of its own territory, and in which national or companies of the other Contracting Party own shares, it shall ensure that the provisions of paragraph (1) of this Article are applied to the extent necessary to guarantee prompt, adequate and effective compensation in respect of their investment to such nationals or companies of the other Contracting Party who are owners of those shares.	Article 5 .... 2. Investments and returns of nationals and companies of either Contracting Party shall not be subjected to expropriation, nationalization or any other measures the effects of which would be similar to expropriation or nationalization, within the territory of the other Contracting Party unless such measures are taken for a public purpose and in accordance with laws and regulations, are not discriminatory, and, are taken against compensation. 3. The compensation referred to in the provision of paragraph 2 of the present Article shall be such as to place the nationals and companies in the same financial position as that in which the nationals and companies would have been if expropriation or nationalization, referred to in the provisions of paragraph 2 of the present Article, had not been taken. Such compensation shall be effectively realizable and freely transferable at the exchange rate in effect on the date used for the determination of amount of compensation. 4. Nationals and companies of either Contracting Party whose investments and returns are subjected to expropriation, nationalization or any other measures the effects of which would be similar to expropriation or nationalization, shall have the right of access to the competent courts of justice and administrative tribunals and agencies of the other Contracting Party taking the measures concerning such measures and the amount of compensation in accordance with the applicable laws and regulations of such other Contracting Party. 5. The treatment accorded by either Contracting Party within its territory to the nationals and companies of the other Contracting Party with respect to the matters set forth in the provisions of paragraphs 1 to 4 of the present Article shall not be less favourable than that accorded to nationals and companies of any third country.

the subject of much debate.[86] The international standards of compensation set by the community of States in the nineteenth century; and reflected in the so-called Hull formula of "prompt, adequate and effective" compensation, were first called into question by the Soviet and Mexican revolutions and later, by the decolonization process after the Second World War. As noted in the introduction, developing countries argued during that process in various multilateral forums that such standards were contrary to their interests. Instead, they proposed standards such as "appropriate" compensation, which gave the host country more flexibility in determining the compensation to be paid, while taking into account the specific circumstances of each case. This view was reflected, for example, in article 2 (2) (c) of the Charter of Economic Rights and Duties of States (UNCTAD, 1996b, Vol. I, p.57).

When it came to the conclusion of BITs, however, many developing countries were prepared to accept formulations of the standard of compensation close to the Hull formula, as a matter of *lex specialis* and with the purpose of attracting FDI from selected economic partners. The formulas for compensation found in recent treaties, however, are quite diverse.

The large majority of BITs use the traditional rule that such compensation must be "prompt, adequate and effective". It appears in the model agreements proposed by the United Kingdom and the United States, among others, and it has also been used in a number of treaties between developing countries. If the Hull standard is not further elaborated upon in a BIT, the standard might be subject to different interpretations as to what is "adequate", "prompt" and "effective" (UNCTC, 1988). For this reason, many BITs define the meaning of these words; the BIT between Costa Rica and the United Kingdon is a typical example of this approach (table III.10).

Other BITs use different terminology that nevertheless may lead to similar results. A BIT may require, for example, payment of "full value" or "just compensation."[87] Such terms are often understood to mean fair market value immediately prior to the date when the expropriation occurred or became public knowledge.[88] Thus, most BITs concluded by Germany follow the German model treaty and explain that "compensation shall be equivalent to the value of the investment expropriated immediately before the date the expropriation or nationalization was publicly announced" (article 4 (2)). Then, in the protocol, it is further explained that "value" means market value. If the latter cannot be determined, other "criteria of value" are to be applied.

The AALCC model A provides that compensation is to be worked out "in accordance with recognized principles of valuation such as fair market value".[89] But where the market value cannot be readily ascertained, the compensation shall be determined "on equitable principles, taking into account inter alia, the capital invested, depreciation, capital already expatriated and other relevant factors" (article 7 (ii)). The same formulation is found in the second alternative of model B (article 7 (ii)); the first alternative refers to "recognized principles of valuation" (UNCTC, 1988).

---

[86] For a discussion on the assessment of compensation upon expropriation, see, for example, World Bank (1992).

[87] It is worth noting that the term "just compensation" began to be used in the United States FCN treaties in the period between the two World Wars. It was taken from the Fifth Amendment to the United States Constitution, where it is understood to indicate fair market value.

[88] A significant variation to the standard of "becoming public knowledge" is to be found in all of Jamaica's BITs. To ensure that the date of determining market value is the date of an authorized announcement by the Government, the Jamaican BITs use the term "was made known by the authorities" or "was publicly announced" instead of "became public knowledge". Moreover, to guard against leakages unduly affecting market value, the Jamaican BITs contain the following provision: "In determining market value, the Contracting Parties agree that due weight shall be given to any factors which might have affected the value before the compulsory acquisition was made known by the authorities". (See, for example, the BIT between Jamaica and the United Kingdom (article 6).)

[89] See, for example, the BITs signed by Sri Lanka with the Republic of Korea (article 7), Singapore (article 6) and Romania (article 6).

Market value (or similar concepts such as fair market value, actual value, real value or commercial value) is one of the methods most commonly used for the valuation of expropriated assets. Fair market value may be determined through several methods, depending upon the circumstances. In the case of a commercial enterprise, for example, fair market value may be considered the value of the enterprise as a "going concern", which would include goodwill and other economically valuable assets associated with the enterprise. The value of an enterprise as a going concern is determined in some cases by the discounted cash-flow method, in which the total amount of an enterprise's future net income is discounted by the time value of money, the projected inflation rate, and the probability that such income will actually be received, to derive the present value of the enterprise's future income. Where an investment has not been in operation long enough to be valued as a going concern, its fair market value may be determined by ascertaining the replacement value of the assets, or even their book value. Most BITs do not go that far in specifying the method of valuation to be utilized and they use, instead, more general language as a guide to the application of this standard.[90]

Compensation based on a fair market value is also often understood to include interest from the date of expropriation to the date of payment. Many BITs include this requirement explicitly (e.g. the BIT between Japan and Sri Lanka). Some BITs, such as those concluded by Germany, the United Kingdom and the United States, also specify the rate of interest. The BITs concluded by the United States, for example, often require a "commercially reasonable rate".[91] In the BIT between Costa Rica and the United Kindom (table III.10), compensation includes interest at a normal commercial rate until the date of payment.

The language in the BIT between China and Japan (table III. 10) does not expressly include the payment of interest, and could also be interpreted as providing for compensation at less than the fair market value. However, the meaning of this clause is clarified in an explanatory note annexed to the treaty stating:

> It is confirmed that with reference to the provisions of Article 5 of the Agreement, the compensation referred to in the provisions of paragraph 3 of the aforesaid Article shall represent the eqivalent of the value of the investments and returns affected at the time when the expropriation, nationalization or any other measure ... are publicly announced or when such measures are taken, whichever is earlier, and shall carry an appropriate interest taking into account the length of time until payment.

Still, this provision does not specify the type of valuation method to be used. For example, the difference between the "market value" and the "book value" of an investment may be substantial. Similarly, the difference between "interest at a normal commercial rate" and an "appropriate interest" may also be substantial.

As noted, a number of countries prefer to use more flexible formulations of the compensation standard than those suggested by the phrase "prompt, adequate and effective"; they may prefer, for example, "fair and equitable compensation". The treaties between India and the United Kingdom and between China and the Philippines, among others, follow this approach. At the same time, it has been suggested that terms such as "fair" compensation can, in practice, also lead to more specific interpretations that are close to those typically associated with the Hull formula (Dolzer and Stevens, 1995).

---

[90] Other recent BITs explicitly requiring compensation based on a fair market value include those between Canada and Hungary (article IV), Bangladesh and Italy (article 5 (2)), Albania and Croatia (article (2)), Chile and Finland (article 5), and Nigeria and the United Kingdom (article 5 (1).)

[91] See, for example, the BIT between Kazakhstan and the United States (article III).

In fact, China's BITs have followed several different approaches with respect to the standard of compensation upon expropriation.[92] Thus, the BIT signed by China with Sweden (article 3), prescribes compensation "the purpose of which shall be to place the investor in the same financial position as that in which the investor would have been if the expropriation or nationalization had not taken place." The BITs signed by China with Austria and with Germany, respectively, refer to the value of the investment immediately before the expropriation became public knowledge. However, the treaties signed by China (e.g. with Viet Nam and Slovenia) simply refer to "compensation" without qualifying the term.

Among the BITs that do not use the Hull formula, some make explicit reference to the book-value method of valuation. It may consist of either the net book value (depreciated assets value) or the updated book value (also called the adjusted book value, taking inflation into account), or just the tax value of the assets. The treaty between the Netherlands and the Sudan states that the compensation should represent the equivalent of the "depreciated value of the investment affected" (table III.10).

Since nationalizations have often take place in the context of fundamental changes in the control over strategic industries of the domestic economy, some countries have argued that the requirement to pay "full market value" would impede their sovereign right to reorganize their economic system. These countries have therefore suggested that additional factors should be considered, such as excessive profits in the past, the extent of amortization of the initial investment, undue enrichment as a result of historical exploitation, unpaid taxes and any outstanding labour benefits (UNCTC, 1988).

With respect to the modalities of payment, many BITs state explicitly that payment must be "without delay" or without "undue" delay. Such a provision also leaves room for interpretation. Consequently, some BITs explicitly require the expropriating country, prior to the expropriatory act, to make provision for the determination of the time of payment of compensation.[93]

BITs often require furthermore that compensation should be freely transferable and effectively realizable. These latter terms overlap to some extent. Compensation is "effectively realizable" if an investor can obtain the benefit of the compensation immediately. An example of compensation that is not "freely transferable" would be government bonds that cannot be sold. Compensation is freely transferable if it can be repatriated. Payment in a freely convertible currency would generally satisfy both conditions.

Most BITs do not specify the exchange rate in the expropriation article, although some do. Thus, the BIT between China and Japan quoted above provides that "... such compensation shall be paid without delay. It shall be effectively realizable and freely transferable at the exchange rate in effect on the date used for the determination of amount of compensation.". Nearly all BITs, however, have a separate provision on currency exchange, and that provision, which generally applies to expropriation compensation as well as other payments related to an investment, usually specifies an exchange rate.[94]

---

[92] For a detailed discussion of the BIT practice of China, including the special features of the BITs signed with developing countries and other socialist countries, see Shishi (1988).

[93] See, for example, the BITs between Egypt and Romania (article 3 (1)), Germany and Israel (article 4 (2)), Germany and Romania (article 3 (1)), Indonesia and Norway (article IV (3)) and France and Indonesia (article 6 (3)). It is also interesting to note that early treaties, such as the one between Jamaica and the United Kingdom (article 6), provide for payment over a three-year period in cases where compensation involves a large sum. Significantly, no doubt influenced by the liberalization era, Jamaica's later BITs do not have this provision (e.g. the BIT between Jamaica and the United States).

[94] See also the section on "Transfer of funds", below.

(d)   *Due process and judicial review*

Many BITs require that any expropriation should be consistent with due process of law. Although the term "due process" has been exhaustively analysed as a matter of domestic law, particularly in the United States, there is little authority concerning the meaning of this term in the present context. Nonetheless, the requirement of due process is a standard element in the BIT practice of a number of countries.[95] In addition, most BITs prohibit separately the impairment of the investment by arbitrary means.

Many BITs also include a separate requirement that the legality of an expropriation should be subject to judicial review. For example, the model treaty of Germany provides that the "legality of any such expropriation, nationalization, or comparable measures and the amount of compensation shall be subject to review by due process of law" (article 4 (2)). This wording now appears in most treaties concluded by Germany, as well as in recent treaties signed by other countries (e.g. the BIT between Chile and Sweden, in article 4 (2)). The United Kingdom model agreement entitles the investor to "prompt review, by a judicial or other independent authority ... of his or its case and of the valuation of his or its investment in accordance with the principles set out in this paragraph". Some agreements concluded by the United Kingdom replace the words "his or its case" by "of whether the expropriation is in conformity with domestic law". The AALCC model A stipulates that, in the absence of an agreement between the investor and the host State, the determination of compensation shall be referred to "an independent judicial or administrative tribunal or authority competent under the law of the expropriating State or to arbitration under an agreement beween the investor and the host State" (article 7 (ii)).

The requirement of judicial review to some extent reinforces the protection provided by the clause requiring that any expropriation should be in accordance with due process.

The BIT between China and Japan cited above does not require a review of the expropriation; rather, it gives the injured investor "access" to local courts, tribunals and agencies. The meaning of "access" is not clear, but it can be argued that the term does not imply an obligation to review the expropriation in a judicial sense.

The Netherlands model agreement requires simply that the measures be taken "under due process of law", without reference to judicial review. The same applies to the Swiss model and to the majority of treaties signed by France.

(e)   *Consistency with contractual obligations*

Some BITs, such as those concluded by France and the United States, include a fifth condition, namely, that an expropriation should not be contrary to any commitment the host country has entered into with respect to the investment. In some BITs, the inclusion of this condition would be redundant because they already include a general requirement that the host country should observe any obligations entered into with respect to investment.

Whether the condition appears as a general treaty rule or as a rule specifically applicable to expropriation, its effect could be to prohibit a contracting party from expropriating an investment if it has previously agreed not to expropriate the investment. The violation of such an agreement

---

[95] Developing countries have sometimes insisted on using the wording "in accordance with domestic legal procedure" instead of "under due process of law" for fear that due process of law might be interpreted as having to meet the so-called "international minimum standard".

would presumably violate the BIT and might be subject to proceedings under the investor-to-State or State-to-State dispute provisions of the BIT.

* * *

Given the theoretical controversies surrounding the standards of compensation upon expropriation, BIT provisions on this issue have been of crucial importance to foreign investors. While expropriation can still be an extreme measure of last resort available to countries, the incidence of major nationalizations, which reached its peak in the 1970s, has declined sharply since the 1980s. In fact, it is the trend towards privatization rather than nationalization that defines the economic policies of the 1980s and 1990s. Nevertheless, expropriation remains a critical issue in foreign investment relations, both in theory and in practice, as new forms of "indirect" or "creeping" expropriation may be, and are, practised. Thus, the issue of whether "regulatory" takings (for example, in the context of anti-trust law) amount to a compensable taking may become increasingly challenging for policy makers in the years to come.

G. War and civil disturbance

Customary international law distinguishes between expropriation and the destruction of property due to military necessity. The general consensus is that no compensation is due for losses caused by military necessity.[96] Most BITs, however, offer investors a limited degree of protection against such losses. The most common provision guarantees that investors covered under the treaty shall receive MFN treatment with respect to any compensation for loss of property caused by war, insurrection, riot, rebellion or other civil disturbance. A typical example is the BIT between Hungary and Norway (table III.11).

In other words, the host country need not pay compensation. However, if it compensates investors of any third country, it must compensate investors covered by the treaty, and to the same extent.[97] Some BITs also guarantee to apply national treatment to investors covered by the treaty with respect to compensation for such losses.[98] Of course, any country that agrees to national treatment in one BIT must provide national treatment to all other investors who are covered by a BIT guaranteeing MFN treatment with respect to compensation.

It is important to specify not only the standard to be followed with respect to such losses, but also the particular type of damage protected under this clause. For example, article V of the treaty between the United Kingdom and Ukraine is quite specific (table III.11).

By contrast, the provision in the treaty between China and Japan refers to "the outbreak of hostilities or a state of national emergency" (article 6). While a state of emergency may be relatively easy to determine since it often involves a government declaration, the meaning of "hostilities" is vague and subject to varying interpretations.

---

[96] For a discussion of customary doctrine and a BIT provision applicable to the destruction of property during combat, see Asian Agricultural Products Ltd. (AAPL) v. Republic of Sri Lanka (ICSID, 1990). The primary focus of the case was on the applicability of particular provisions of the BIT between Sri Lanka and the United Kingdom to circumstances of military and paramilitary activity. Against this background, the Tribunal gave broad consideration to the standard of diligence owed by government forces to foreign investors under general international law (Vasciannie, 1992).

[97] The MFN formula has also been adopted in BITs concluded by China.

[98] Examples of this include the BITs between the Republic of Korea and Mongolia (article 4) and between Malaysia and the United Arab Emirates (article 5 (i)).

Table III.11. Examples of provisions on war and civil disturbance in BITs

BIT between Hungary and Norway (1991)	BIT between the United Kingdom and Ukraine (1993)
Article V	Article 5
Investors of one Contracting Party whose investment suffers losses in the territory of the other Contracting Party owing to war, revolution, or other armed conflict, state of national emergency or other similar events shall be accorded treatment no less favourable than that accorded to investors of any third State as regards r e s t i t u t i o n , i n d e m n i f i c a t i o n , compensation or other valuable consideration. Such payments shall be freely transferable.	(1) Investors of one Contracting Party whose investments in the territory of the other Contracting Party suffer losses owing to war or other armed conflict, revolution, a state of national emergency, revolt, insurrection or riot in the territory of the latter Contracting Party shall be accorded by the latter Contracting Party treatment as regards restitution, indemnification, compensation or other settlement, no less favouable than that which the latter Contracting Party accords to its own investors or to investors of any third State. Resulting payments shall be freely transferable. (2) Without prejudice to paragraph (1) of this Article, investors of one Contracting Party who in any of the situations referred to in that paragraph suffer losses in the territory of the other Contracting Party resulting from: (a) requisitioning of their property by its forces or authorities, or (b) destruction of their property by its forces or authorities, which was not caused in combat action or was not required by the necessity of the situation, shall be accorded restitution or adequate compensation. Resulting payments shall be freely transferable.

Another clause that appears in many BITs provides that any compensation paid for such losses must be freely transferable, or otherwise addresses the transferability of such compensation. This clause may not be strictly necessary in many BITs because the general provision on currency transfers, which guarantees free transferability of payments related to an investment in many cases would be broad enough to apply to compensation for losses suffered as a result of war and civil disturbance .

A few BITs make a distinction between damages caused by war and civil disturbance without direct action by the host States and damages caused by action by the State itself in situations of war and civil disturbance. In the latter case, they provide for an obligation to compensate investors, even if investors of the host country or third countries are not compensated for similar losses. Some BITs concluded by the United Kingdom, including the BIT with Ukraine (table III.11), provide that investors who suffer losses in the territory of the other contracting party during war or civil disturbance shall receive restitution or adequate compensation when such losses are caused either by government requisitioning of their property or by government destruction not attributable to combat or military necessity. Similarly, some BITs concluded by the United States require that in either of these situations compensation consistent with the expropriation provision should be paid.

The AALCC model A (article 8) contains the provision on "compensation of losses" in square brackets, with a choice of national treatment or MFN treatment, while a second paragraph follows the wording of the example of the United Kingdom. The explanatory notes observe that some experts have reservations about the "fairly new" concept of compensation for losses. The AALCC model B provides for restitution or adequate compensation without further qualifications (UNCTC, 1988).

* * *

The inclusion of a provision on compensation for losses caused by war and civil disturbances in BITs is justified because situations of war or civil war are often exceptions to insurance contracts (or may need special coverage) and are often treated differently from government action in time of peace. Requisition by the army in time of war may not be covered by provisions on expropriation in normal circumstances. Consequently, it may be "abundance of caution" to include this provision, since it is by no means clear that the matter is covered by other provisions.

H. Transfer of payments

1. Purpose of the provision

The provisions on the transfer of payments are considered by both investors and countries as among the most important in a BIT. They concern an aspect as on which the interests of the host country and the foreign investor may differ widely. For host countries, including most developing countries, the sudden repatriation of large profits or the proceeds from sale or liquidation can have an adverse effect on their balance of payments, thereby hindering economic development and defeating the objective of the BIT. Thus, balance-of-payments difficulties can reduce considerably a host country's ability to grant investors unrestricted rights to make monetary transfers in connection with their investments. However, foreign investors regard the timely transfer of income, capital and other payments as an indispensable requirement to operate and benefit from their investment projects, and to meet their obligations vis-à-vis shareholders, contractors, creditors or licensors.

A broadly applicable limitation on the right of countries to impose controls on currency exchanges is found in the Articles of Agreement of the International Monetary Fund (IMF) (article VIII (2)) (IMF, 1945). This limitation, however, applies only to controls on currency exchanges for current, as opposed to capital, transactions. Furthermore, the majority of IMF member countries have reserved the right under article XIV to "maintain and adapt" exchange-control mechanisms in existence at the time they joined the IMF, a right that in practice has afforded considerable flexibility to these member countries. For these reasons, the IMF articles provide relatively little protection for foreign investors. Capital-exporting countries thus continue to insist on the inclusion of the right of free transfer in BITs.

Virtually every BIT has a provision on the transfer of payments, but there are important differences among them in the wording of this provision. Home countries generally seek specific and broad guarantees. They look for a provision that guarantees to investors the right to transfer payments related to an investment into a freely convertible currency without delay at a specified exchange rate. In other words, the provision addresses investors' concerns that they may not be able to withdraw the investment or the returns generated by the investment from the host country at some point in the future, or that the investment and returns will be denominated in a currency that is not freely convertible. The BIT between the Russian Federation and the United States is an example of this approach (table III.12).

2. Transfers covered

The first issue normally addressed in such a provision is the type of payments to which it applies. These involve three categories of funds, namely, the repatriation of the capital invested, transfer of returns generated by an investment and dividends to the investor's shareholders, and current payments made in relation to an investment (i.e. amounts that may be needed to pay current expenses, the interest and principal on loans, or other obligations incurred by the investor).

Most BITs adopt one of two different approaches. The first approach is to guarantee the free transfer of all payments related to, or in connection with, an investment. Many of the BITs concluded by Germany and the United States and virtually all BITs concluded in Latin America and the Caribbean follow this approach. This approach is preferred by investors because of its breadth, but it may be resisted for the same reason by developing countries that have low foreign-exchange reserves. Because of the uncertainty that may arise over which payments are covered by this provision, many BITs that follow this approach include a non-exhaustive list of payments that are to be covered. Typically, this list includes: returns on investment such as income, profits, dividends and interests; funds for repayment of loans; royalties and other fees; and proceeds from sale or liquidation.[99] The list frequently contains earnings of employees, but some BITs limit the amount of earnings for which there is a right of free transfer, or restrict the right to transfer earnings to nationals of the home country.[100] The list may also include compensation paid as a result of an investment dispute, as in the case of the BIT between Sri Lanka and the United States (article IV (1) (c)). Compensation for expropriation is often included, though many BITs cover that separately in the expropriation provision.[101] A typical example of the language used can be found in the BIT between Chile and Norway (table III.12).[102]

A variation on this approach can be found in many of the BITs concluded by the United Kingdom. They also guarantee free transfer of a broad category of payments, specifically "investments and returns" or "capital and returns". Because these terms may themselves be defined in the treaties, these BITs do not include an illustrative list of transfers that are covered by the provision.

The second approach is simply to list the types of payments covered by the provision. Typically, this list is quite similar to the illustrative list in BITs that adopt the first approach, with the difference that the list is exhaustive rather than illustrative.[103]

Notwithstanding the right of free transfer, some BITs authorize the contracting parties to require reports of currency transfers, to administer withholding taxes, and to protect the rights of creditors or ensure the satisfaction of judgements rendered in adjudicatory proceedings.[104]

Finally, it should be noted that the currency-transfer provision could amount in effect to a guarantee that foreign currency will be made available to the investor. Thus, the provision may go beyond a mere prohibition on legal restrictions regarding currency transfers.

---

[99] See, for example, the BIT between Germany and Swaziland (article 5).

[100] See, for example, the BITs between Indonesia and Norway (article VII (c)), Indonesia and the Netherlands (article 6 (1)), Kenya and the Netherlands (article VIII (1)), the Netherlands and Thailand (article VII (c)), and France's BITs with Jordan (article 6), Paraguay (article 6), Singapore (article 5 (1) (e)) and the Sudan (article 6).

[101] See, for example, the BIT between Germany and Swaziland (article 4 (2)).

[102] The latest Jamaican BITs, for example, do not guarantee "free transfer" but "the right to the free transfer" (in the treaty between Argentina and Jamaica, article 4) or "shall permit... to transfer" (in the treaty between China and Jamaica, article 4). This change reflects the liberalized market regime for foreign exchange, in which foreign exchange comes not from a Central Bank but from the commercial banking system.

[103] The second approach is typical of BITs concluded by Denmark, France and Sweden.

[104] This is the case of the BITs signed by the United States, (see, for example, the BIT between the Kyrgyz Republic and the United States (article IV (3)).

Table III.12. Examples of provisions on the transfer of payments in BITs

BIT between the Netherlands and the Philippines (1985)	BIT between the Russian Federation and the United States (1992)	BIT between Chile and Norway (1993)
Article 7	Article IV	Article 5
1. Each Contracting Party shall in respect of investments permit nationals of the other Contracting Party the unrestricted transfer in freely convertible currency of their investments and of the earnings from it to the country designated by those nationals, subject to the right of the former Contracting Party to impose equitably and in good faith such measures as may be necessary to safeguard the integrity and independence of its currency, its external financial position and balance of payments, consistent with its rights and obligations as a member of the International Monetary Fund. 2. The exchange rate applicable to such transfer shall be the rate of exchange prevailing at the time of remittance. 3. In cases where large amounts of compensation have been paid in pursuance of Article 5 the Contracting Party concerned may require the transfer thereof to be effected in reasonable installments.	1. Each party shall permit all transfers related to an investment to be made freely and without delay into and out of its territory. Such transfers include: (a) returns; (b) compensation pursuant to Article III; (c) payments arising out of an investment dispute (as defined in in Article VI); (d) payments made under a contract, including amortization of principal and accrued interest payments made pursuant to a loan agreement; (e) proceeds from the sale or liquidation of all or any part of an investment; and (f) additional contributions to capital for the maintenance or development of an investment. Companies or naturals of each Party shall be permitted to convert such transfers into the feely convertible currency of their choice. 2. Transfers shall be made in freely convertible and, except as provided in Article III, paragraph 1, at the market rate of exchange on the date of the transfer with respect to spot transactions in the currency to be transferred. 3. Notwithstanding the provisions of paragraphs 1 and 2 of this Article, either Party may, (a) maintain laws and regulations requiring reports of currency transfer and imposing income taxes by such means as a withholding tax applicable to dividends or other transfers; and (b) protect the rights of creditors, or ensure the satisfaction of judgements in adjudicatory proceedings, through the equitable, non-discriminatory and good faith application of its law.	(1) Each Contracting Party shall allow without delay the investors of the other Contracting Party the transfer of payments in connection with the investment in a freely convertible currency, particularly of, (a) interests, dividends, profits and other returns; (b) repayments of loans related to the investment; (c) payments derived from rights enumerated in Article 1, paragraph (2), letter (d) of this Agreement; (d) the proceeds of the partial or total sale of the investment; (e) compensation for dispossession or loss described in Article 6 of this Agreement; (f) the earnings of foreign employees working in relation to an investment once the legal requirements have been fulfilled. (2) A transfer shall be deemed to have been made without delay if carried out within such period as is normally required for the completion of transfer formalities. The said period shall start on the day on which the relevant request has been submitted in due form and may in no case exceed two months. Transfers shall be made at the prevailing rate of exchange on the date of transfer. (3) Transfers concerning investments made under the Chilean Special Program of Foreign Debt Equity Swaps are subject to special regulations. (4) Equity capital can only be transferred one year after it has entered the territory of the Contracting Party unless its legislation provides for a more favourable treatment.

3. Protection provided

(a) *Type of currency*

The provision on the free transfer of funds usually specifies the type of currency in which transfer is guaranteed. Here again, two different approaches are common. One approach is to require that the transfer should be permitted in any freely convertible currency. This approach gives the investor the greatest protection. It is typical of BITs concluded by Finland, Sweden and the United States.[105] A second approach is to require that the host country should permit the transfer in the convertible currency in which the investment was made or in any convertible currency to which the parties agree. This approach is typical of BITs concluded by Denmark and the United Kingdom.

(b) *Timing of transfer*

Many BITs provide that transfers covered by the treaty shall be "free" or permitted "without delay". Such language is typical of BITs concluded, for example, by Chile with other Latin American countries and by France, Germany, Switzerland, the United Kingdom and the United States. Some BITs, such as those concluded by the Netherlands, Norway and Sweden, guarantee transfer without "undue delay". Treaties occasionally impose a precise limit on the period of permissible delay, such as one[106] or six months.[107] This provision does not preclude a host country from ensuring that transfers are consistent with local law ordinarily applicable to external currency transfers, such as those involving reporting requirements, tax payments or satisfaction of creditors.

Other BITs include an explicit qualification that the host State may delay transfer for the time normally necessary to complete formalities. These include in particular the BITs concluded by Germany, which generally require that formalities should be completed within two months.[108]

(c) *Exchange rate*

Many BITs also specify the rate of exchange at which transfers shall be allowed. This clause is intended to ensure that the value of the payments to be transferred is preserved during currency-exchange transactions.

There are considerable variations among BITs on this subject. One crucial distinction among the different formulations is the extent to which the exchange rate is subject to the control of the host country. For example, some BITs specify the official exchange rate, which may be more readily subject to host-country adjustment. Other BITs, however, link the exchange rate to factors less subject to the host country's control. In some cases, for example, BITs specify the market rate of exchange. In other cases, they specify a particular rate used by the IMF.[109] It is important that

---

[105] The BITs concluded by the United States use the phrase "freely usable currency" (defined by the IMF as being the United States dollar, the German mark, the French franc, the British pound and the Japanese yen).

[106] See, for example, the BIT between Denmark and Poland (article 6 (5)).

[107] See, for example, the BIT between Finland and Hungary (article 7 (1)).

[108] The BITs concluded by Chile specify that "without delay" means the normal time necessary to fulfill the formalities with respect to the transfer. This "normal time" should not exceed 30 days (e.g., in the BITs between Bolivia and Chile, Chile and Paraguay and Chile and Uruguay), 60 days (e.g., in the BIT between Chile and Ecuador), one month (e.g., in the BIT between Chile and Guatemala), two months (in, e.g., the BITs between Argentina and Chile and Chile and Venezuela), or six months (e.g., in the BIT between Brazil and Chile).

[109] See, for example, the BIT between Bangladesh and Germany (article 6).

the provision on exchange rates not penalize a country that moves from fixed exchange rates to those determined by the market. In such a situation, the value of a currency will usually drop. Investors, of course, prefer the rate of exchange that is more favourable to them.

Some BITs specify the date on which the exchange rate shall be determined. Most BITs concluded between countries in the western hemisphere (including the United States) and countries from other regions specify the exchange rate on the date of transfer, which is presumably the rate that would be used in the absence of an explicit provision to the contrary.

4. Exceptions

As noted, some developing countries with limited foreign currency reserves are concerned that they will not have sufficient foreign currency to permit a transfer requested by an investor or that foreign currency reserves needed for some other purpose will be depleted by an investor repatriating investment returns. The BIT between the Netherlands and the Philippines takes this contingency into account and allows the host country some relief in this situation (table III.12).

Many BITs allow exceptions to the obligation of free transfer only during periods when foreign currency reserves are at exceptionally low levels. Such clauses generally allow the transfer to be delayed for a temporary period. Sometimes they are subject to one or more other conditions. One condition may be that any delay must be on an MFN basis, that is, the host country may not allow investors from a third country to exchange local currency without also allowing covered investors similar treatment. Another condition that sometimes appears is that the host country must allow a certain percentage of the payment to be transferred each year until the full amount has been transferred. The treaty between Jamaica and the United Kingdom (article 7 (a) and (b)), for example, referring to the power to take exceptional measures to preserve its balance of payments, includes the following limitations:

> (a) such powers shall not however be used to impede the transfer of profits, interests, dividends, royalties or fees;

> (b) as regards investments and any other form of return transfer of a minimum of 20 % per year is guaranteed.[110]

Sometimes a BIT makes special provision for the repatriation of capital because of the size of the transfer. This is done by allowing the payment to be made in installments or over a period of a few years.[111] Significantly, article XII of the WTO General Agreement on Trade in Services (GATS) provides for restrictions to safeguard the balance of payments within certain defined limits with respect to trade in services. Developing countries can utilize this provision in negotiating BITs, although the general trend in developing countries is not to require phasing of payments over a period of time.

---

[110] Examples of exceptions due to balance-of-payments difficulties can be found in other BITs concluded by countries in the American continent, such as the BITs between El Salvador and Peru (article 8 (4)), Colombia and Peru (article 6 (3)) and Argentina and El Salvador (article 6 (4)).

[111] See, for example, article 7 (1) (b) of the BIT between Jamaica and the United Kingdom, which provides for a five year period, and article 5 (4) of the BIT between Jamaica and the Netherlands, which provides for three years. Since 1991, Jamaica has not consistently sought this phasing.

Yet another approach confers the right to make monetary transfers, but subject to the exchange-control laws of the host country.[112] The BIT between China and Japan (article 8) follows this approach and provides as follows:

(1)   Nationals and companies of either Contracting Party shall be guaranteed by the other Contracting Party freedom of payments, remittances, and transfers of financial instruments or funds including value of liquidation of an investment between the territories of the two Contracting Parties as well as between the territories of such other Contracting party and any third country.

(2) The provisions of paragraph 1 of the present Article shall not preclude either Contracting Party from imposing exchange restrictions in accordance with its applicable laws and regulations.

Some clauses add a condition that any delay be in accordance with the host country's obligation to exercise equitably and in good faith the powers conferred by its laws. The BIT between Malaysia and the United Arab Emirates is an example. The AALCC model A mentions "reasonable restrictions for temporary periods" (article 6 (i)).

As previously noted, some BITs guarantee the right to transfer only a fraction of the earnings or wages of nationals of the other contracting party to their home country. Examples of this approach are the BITs between the Netherlands and Thailand, and Norway and Indonesia, as well as the BITs signed by France with Jordan, Singapore and the Sudan. These treaties usually stipulate also that the repatriation of earnings is permitted only for nationals authorized to work in the host country by permits or licences or in relation to an agreed investment.

Some recent BITs have included a novel type of exception for countries with transitional economies. They provide for a limited period during which countries may make exceptions to the obligation of free transfer. Thus, the BIT between Lithuania and the Netherlands states that:

During a period of two years ... the Republic of Lithuania shall do its outmost to guarantee the free transfer of payments ... . After these two years the unrestricted transfer ... shall be in force.[113]

Exceptions such as those described here might be of little use to a country unless that country includes a similar exception in all of its BITs. If a BIT omits such an exception, then investors under that BIT could be entitled to free transfer and investors covered by all other BITs with an MFN clause would also be entitled to free transfer, despite the fact that those BITs have an exception clause.

Finally, another novel approach to addressing foreign exchange problems concerns the provisions that appear in the protocol to the BIT between Ecuador and the United States, which states that the terms of the article on transfers may be superseded by a debt-equity conversion agreement. This provision is intended to encourage debt-equity conversion agreements, which bring foreign exchange into the host country.

* * *

Traditionally, the imposition of foreign exchange controls – in the exercise of a country's monetary sovereignty – has been quite prevalent not only among developing countries but among developed countries as well. Policy differences in this respect are not so much the result of

---

[112] For example, all BITs concluded by Chile include a protocol which restricts the transfer of capital for a period of one year from the date the capital enters the country, pursuant to its exchange-control laws.

[113] See also the BIT between Poland and the United States (protocol, para. 4).

controversies on matters of principle but of the specific balance-of-payments constraints facing countries and their need to maintain foreign exchange in sufficient levels for essential purposes. For policy makers, a main issue to consider therefore is the type of qualifications and limitations to the freedom of transfer that can be reasonably imposed for coping with balance-of-payments crises without unduly restricting transfers under normal circumstances.

I. Other specific protection clauses

1. Performance requirements

Many capital importing countries allow FDI in the hope that it will create employment, increase exports, generate foreign exchange and improve the balance of payments. To ensure that FDI has the intended effect, some host countries have imposed performance requirements on foreign investors as a condition for investing in the territory of the host country. Other countries induce investors to accept performance requirements voluntarily by linking them to the granting of incentives.[114] Examples of such performance requirements include obligations to hire nationals of the host country, to use locally produced raw materials or inputs, and to export a portion of the finished product. However, invetors may object to performance requirements because they impede the management of their investment and may require the investor to conduct the business in ways that reduce its efficiency and hence profitability. It has been argued, moreover, that because they regulate imports and exports, certain performance requirements may also distort international trade.

Most BITs do not explicitly restrict performance requirements. If the performance requirements are imposed following the admission of an investment, they may violate a BIT's guarantee of national treatment. To the extent that they are imposed as a condition of the admission of investment, however, they may escape the national treatment restriction because in many BITs the right to national treatment applies to investment only after it has been admitted. To avoid this, some BITs do restrict performance requirements as a condition for admission. For example, the following provision appears in the 1984 United States model BIT (article II, para. 5):

> Neither party shall impose performance requirements as a condition of establishment, expansion or maintenance of investments, which require or enforce commitments to export goods produced, or which specify that goods or services must be purchased locally, or which impose similar requirements.

The vast majority of BITs signed by the United States include a prohibition on performance requirements as a condition of establishing, expanding or maintaining an investment project. More recently, a number of BITs signed by Canada have followed this approach as well, examples being the BIT between Canada and the Philippines (table III.13), as well as the BITs concluded by Canada with Trinidad and Tobago, Venezuela and Barbados. The BIT between the United States and Zaire (now the Democratic Republic of the Congo), on the other hand, changed the thrust of this provision; rather than prohibit the host country from imposing performance requirements on investments from the other contracting party, it requires the host country to use its "best efforts" to avoid imposing such requirements (table III.13). Some recent BITs between developing countries also address performance requirements, such as the BIT between Malaysia and the United Arab Emirates (table III.13).[115]

The prohibition of performance requirements would not seem to preclude a host country from offering an investor special incentives as an inducement to agree to abide by performance

---

[114] On the use of incentives, see UNCTAD (1996d).

[115] See also the BIT between El Salvador and Peru (article 5).

requirements. Any such incentives, however, may be subject to the MFN obligation and thus would have to be offered to other investors as well.

Because of their potential effects on trade, performance requirements were also discussed at the Uruguay Round of GATT negotiations,[116] where they were referred to as trade-related investment measures (TRIMs). The Agreement on Trade-related Investment Measures reached at

Table III.13. Examples of provisions on performance requirements in BITs

BIT between the United States and Zaire (1984)	BIT between Malaysia and the United Arab Emirates (1991)	BIT between Canada and the Philippines (1995)
Article II	Article 2	Articles V and VI
7. Within the context of its national economic policies and goals, each Party shall endeavor to avoid imposing on the investments of nationals or companies of the other Party conditions which require the export of goods produced or the purchase of goods or services locally. This provision shall not preclude the right of either Contracting Party to impose restrictions on the importation of goods and services into their respective territories.	9. Contracting States shall seek as far as practicable to avoid performance requirements as a condition of establishment, expansion or maintenance of investments, which require or enforce commitments to export goods produced or which specify that goods or services must be purchased locally or which impose any other similar requirements.	V. (2) Neither Contracting Party may impose any of the following requirements in connection with permitting the establishment or acquisition of an investment or enforce any of the following requirements in connection with the subsequent regulation of that investment: (a) to export a given level or percentage of goods; (b) to achieve a given level or percentage of domestic content; (c) to purchase, use or accord a preference to goods produced or services provided in its territory, or to purchase goods or services from persons in that territory; (d) to relate in any way the volume or value of imports to the volume or value of exports or to the amount of foreign exchange inflows associated with such investment; or (e) to transfer technology, a production process or other proprietary knowledge to a person in its territory unaffiliated with the transferor, except when the requirement is imposed or the commitment or undertaking is enforced by a court, administrative tribunal or competition authority, either to remedy an alleged violation of competition laws, or acting in manner not inconsistent with the provisions of this Agreement. * * * VI. (2) The provisions of Articles II, III, IV and V of this Agreement do not apply to: (a) procurement by a government or state enterprise; (b) subsidies or grants provided by a government or state enterprise, including government-supported loans, guarantees and insurance; (c) any current or future foreign aid program to promote economic development, whether under a bilateral agreement, or pursuant to a multilateral arrangement or agreement, such as the OECD Agreement on Export Credits.

---

[116] On the question of trade-related investment measures in bilateral investment treaties and the GATT, see Shenkin (1994).

the Uruguay Round prohibits performance requirements that are inconsistent with the GATT's obligation of national treatment or its obligation to eliminate quantitative restrictions.[117] In many BITs, the investor-to-State dispute settlement provision may be broad enough to permit the investor to enforce the TRIMs agreement through the arbitral mechanism created by that provision.[118]

2. Entry and sojourn of foreign nationals

Just as most countries retain the unqualified right to exclude foreign capital from certain industries, they also wish to retain an unqualified right to exclude foreign nationals from their territory. At the same time, foreign investors generally are reluctant to establish affiliates that they cannot control, and the desired control may require the presence of expatriate personnel at the site of the investment for extended periods of time. Further, the efficient operation of an investment may require the application of specialized knowledge possessed only by foreign nationals. For these reasons, host countries need to find a proper balance between their right to exclude aliens and their desire to provide a favourable investment climate, which may necessitate the admission of certain aliens.

In general, BITs provide little assistance for investors seeking to obtain the admission of particular individuals into the territory of the investment. A number of BITs, however, including those concluded by Canada, France, Germany and the United States, and some BITs between developing countries,[119] contain a provision on the question of the admission of individuals of one contracting party (and their employees) into the territory of the other contracting party in connection with an investment. Article II of the BIT between Romania and the United States is a typical example of the United States approach (table III.14). This clause, by including the words "subject to the laws relating to the entry and sojourn of aliens", makes it clear that the right of entry is subordinate to the domestic laws of the parties. Thus, an investor has a right of entry provided that such entry is not inconsistent with or prohibited by the laws of each party relating to entry, sojourn and employment of aliens.

The BITs concluded by France and Germany require each contracting party to give sympathetic consideration to applications for the entry and sojourn in its territory of persons of the other contracting party in connection with an investment. A typical example of this second approach is the protocol to the BIT between Dominica and Germany (table III.14).

---

[117] An illustrative list of TRIMs that are inconsistent with the obligation of national treatment was annexed to the TRIMs agreement. It includes measures that require an enterprise to use products from domestic sources or that limit an enterprise's imports by the volume or value of its exports. An illustrative list of TRIMs that are inconsistent with the obligation to eliminate quantitative restrictions was also annexed to the agreement. It includes measures that restrict imports of products to the volume or value of exports or that restrict access to foreign exchange to an amount related to the foreign exchange inflows attributable to the enterprise or that restrict exports by an enterprise. For a discussion of TRIMs, see UNCTC and UNCTAD (1991); for a discussion of the TRIMs agreement, see UNCTAD (1994).

[118] See below under "settlement of disputes" for a more in-depth discussion on this point. It should be noted that, in the case of parties to the WTO Agreement and a BIT, provisions on performance requirements must now be read subject to the TRIMS agreement.

[119] See, for example, the BIT between El Salvador and Peru (article 6 (1)).

Table III.14. Examples of provisions on entry and sojourn of foreign nationals in BITs

BIT between Romania and the United States (1992) Article II	BIT between Dominica and Germany (1984) Protocol
3. Subject to the laws relating to the entry and sojourn of aliens, nationals of either Party shall be permitted to enter and to remain in the territory of the other Party for the purpose of establishing, administering or advising on the operation of an investment to which they, or a company of the first Party that employs them, have committed or are in the process of committing a substantial amount of capital or other resources.	The Contracting Parties shall within the framework of their national legislation give sympathetic consideration to applications for the entry and sojourn of persons of either Contracting Party who wish to enter the territory of the other Contracting Party in connection with the making and carrying through of an investment; the same shall apply to nationals of either Contracting Party who in connection with an investment wish to enter the territory of the other Contracting Party and sojourn there to take up employment. Application for work permits shall also be given sympathetic consideration.

3. Hiring of local personnel

In order to promote economic development, host countries often have laws requiring foreign investors to hire local personnel. Such laws are intended to ensure that nationals of the host country receive technical training and managerial experience as well as employment, a matter of great importance for many developing countries that must build technological and managerial capabilities as part of their development strategies.

As noted in the preceding section, however, investors prefer to retain the right to control their investment, and that control generally includes the power to appoint at least certain managerial personnel. In line with this approach, the BITs concluded by the United States seek broad rights with respect to employment:

> Companies which are legally constituted under the applicable laws or regulations of one Party, and which are investments, shall be permitted to engage top managerial personnel of their choice, regardless of nationality.[120]

As regards developing countries, the BIT between El Salvador and Peru also includes a similar clause (article 7 (l)).

This provision, however, is not understood to prevail over the host country's immigration laws. Thus, the protection it affords is relatively weak because the host country can preclude the appointment of particular personnel simply by refusing them entry into its territory.[121]

---

[120] See, for example, the BITs concluded by the United States with Jamaica (article II (4)) and Romania (article II (4)). The BIT between Jamaica and the United States makes it clear that the right to hire top managerial staff is "subject to the laws of each party relating to entry, sojourn and employment of aliens".

[121] Regarding employment practices and BITs see also the Sumitomo Shoji, America Inc. v. Avagliano case (United States Supreme Court, 1982), in which United States female employees of Sumitomo sued their employer under the United States civil rights legislation on grounds that their employer had discriminated against them in promotion and had favoured Japanese male employees. The company defended itself on the grounds that it was free to do so under the FCN Treaty between Japan and the United States. Both, the United States and Japan, however, rejected the company's interpretation of the treaty provisions. In the end, the Court ruled in favour of the employees.

J. Transparency

One important feature of a favourable investment climate is the transparency of local laws and administrative practices: foreign investors are more likely to invest in a country if they believe that they can ascertain accurately the laws that will govern their investments. Most BITs, however, do not explicitly address this subject. The BIT concluded by Malaysia and the United Arab Emirates is unusual in this respect (table III.15). The term "make public" suggests that such laws must be available to investors, but does not necessarily require extensive distribution of the written materials in which such laws may be found. The treaties signed by the United States have a similar provision.

Table III.15. Examples of provisions on transparency in BITs

BIT between Malaysia and the United Arab Emirates (1991)	BIT between Canada and Hungary (1991)	BIT between China and Viet Nam (1992)
Article 2 (10) Each Contracting Party shall make public all laws, regulations, administrative practices and procedures that pertain to or affect investments.	Article X Upon request by either Contracting Party, the other Contracting Party shall agree to consultations on the interpretation or application of this Agreement. Upon request by either Contracting Party, information shall be exchanged on the impact that the laws, regulations, decisions, administrative practices or procedures, or policies of the other Contracting Party may have on investments covered by this Agreement.	Article 11 1. The representatives of the two Contracting States shall hold meetings from time to time for the purpose of: (a) reviewing the implementation of this Agreement; (b) exchanging legal information and investment opportunities; (c) resolving disputes arising out of investment; (d) forwarding proposals on promotion of investment; (e) studying other issues in connection with investments.

A separate provision may impose on each contracting party the obligation to provide information concerning investments to the other contracting party. The BIT between Canada and Hungary is an example of this approach (table III.15). Similarly, some early BITs concluded by the United States require each contracting party to "endeavor to establish appropriate procedures" for the provision of information concerning investments that is requested by the other contracting party. This obligation is subject to each contracting party's laws and due regard for business confidentiality.

Other means for promoting transparency are consultative mechanisms, such as the one in the treaty between China and Viet Nam, which requires the two parties to hold meetings from time to time for a number of treaty-related purposes, including exchanging information on host country laws (table III.15).[122]

* * *

The transparency of laws and other government measures has many facets, from simply disclosing and publicizing all government measures in accordance with a country's legal system, to specifically notifying and making available certain types of measures to an international body or to officials of another country. Efforts by developing countries to achieve greater transparency, including through appropriate clauses in BITs, demonstrate the credibility of their commitment to

---

[122] See also below under "Dispute resolution".

providing a favourable investment climate. Such efforts are therefore important in attracting FDI. Nevertheless, it is for the country concerned to decide the best manner in which such information should be made available.[123] While a system of formal publication of laws is a basic requirement, notification and special forms of publication may not be feasible, particularly for some developing countries, except for certain types of measures.

K. General treaty exceptions

In addition to exceptions to specific treaty provisions, BITs sometimes contain general treaty exceptions that permit a host country to take actions that would otherwise violate the BIT. The United States BITs, for example, permit measures necessary for the maintenance of public order, the fulfilment of the host country's obligations with respect to the maintenance or restoration of international peace or security,[124] or the protection of its own essential security interests. The BIT between Bolivia and Peru (article 3 (5)) contains the following general exceptions:

> Nothing in this Treaty shall prevent a Contracting Party from adopting measures, if not discriminatory, for reasons of internal and external national security, public or moral order.[125]

The inclusion of general treaty exceptions is unusual. Most BITs have no such general exceptions, although, as has been noted, specific clauses are sometimes subordinated to the contracting parties' national laws.[126]

L. Preservation of rights

A BIT is generally intended to establish a minimum standard of treatment to which an investment is entitled. Questions may arise concerning the effect that a BIT has on other laws or agreements that provide treatment more favourable than the minimum guaranteed by the BIT.

Nothing in BITs suggests that they prevail over more favourable laws or agreements. To conclude that they did so would be inconsistent with the purpose of BITs, which is to enhance rather than reduce the protection afforded to investment. Nevertheless, to avoid any misinterpretation, some BITs expressly state that other laws or agreements providing investment with more favourable treatment shall prevail. Such provisions differ among themselves in the types of laws or agreements to which they apply. They may generally apply to any of three different types of laws or agreements: provisions of international law; provisions of the host country's domestic law; and agreements between the investor and the host country. Many such provisions apply to the first two categories, that is, international and domestic law that provides for more favourable treatment. Typical of this group are the BITs concluded by Finland, Germany, Sweden and the United Kingdom.[127] More

---

[123] For example, the World Bank Guidelines on the Treatment of Foreign Direct Investment (UNCTAD, 1996b) suggest that States prepare an investment handbook, that is, a compendium where all laws, regulations, and other relevant provisions pertaining to foreign investment can be found.

[124] This second exception is intended to exempt from treaty obligations actions taken in fulfilment of a country's obligations under the Charter of the United Nations. The United States has taken the position that the determination of whether a measure is necessary for the protection of a country's essential security interests is a matter exclusively within its competence, not subject to review by any international tribunal. The International Court of Justice questioned this argument, however, with respect to a similar clause in an FCN treaty between Nicaragua and the United States (International Court of Justice, 1986), in a case concerning certain activities in Nicaragua. For a critique of the United States position, see Vandevelde (1993a).

[125] A similar clause also appears in the BIT between Paraguay and Peru.

[126] Some BITs contain general "cultural" exceptions.

[127] See, for example, the treaty between Chile and Finland (article 10 (2)).

specifically, the agreements concluded by Sweden with China, Pakistan and Yugoslavia provide that they will not prejudice "any rights or benefits accruing under national or international law to interests of a national or a company of one Contracting State in the territory of the other Contracting State" (BIT between Sweden and Pakistan, article 9).

Some provisions apply only to the third category, that is, agreements between the investor and the host country; examples of such provisions can be found in several BITs concluded by Switzerland.[128] The provision in the BITs concluded by the United States applies to all three categories.[129]

The AALCC model agreements contain an umbrella clause in brackets, indicating that there were differences of opinion with respect to this clause among the experts.

The provision on preservation of rights should be distinguished from the "stabilization clause". The latter requires that, if there is a change in the law after the admission of an investor protected under a BIT, and the new law is less favourable to the investor, the pre-existing, more favourable norms remain applicable to that investor. Such a clause is intended to protect investors from changes in legislation after their admission.[130] An example of a stabilization clause can be found in the treaty between France and Yugoslavia.

M. Dispute resolution

1. Introduction

Provisions for the settlement of investment disputes play a critical role in BITs as they provide the means of ensuring that the standards of treatment and protection granted by a treaty are effectively implemented and enforced. Experience shows that problems regarding the interpretation and implementation of BITs are likely to arise and, while some of these might be resolved by the parties themselves, others might require more formal means of resolution. The presence of effective mechanisms for the resolution of disputes is thus the ultimate guarantee of protection for foreign investors.

Investment disputes under BITs may involve disputes between private investors, between one State and investors of the other State, or between the States parties to a treaty. Disputes between private parties are normally resolved through recourse to the courts of the State that has jurisdiction under private international law rules, or to commercial arbitration (these types of disputes are not reviewed in this study).

Disputes between one State and investors of the other State should also normally be submitted to the competent national courts or authorities. (The question of identifying the competent national courts involves complex legal rules of public and private international law which are not discussed here.) These disputes may also be submitted to a mutually agreed third-party dispute-settlement mechanism, which is presently the common practice with respect to BITs (the relevant provisions on investor-to-State dispute settlement are examined in section 4 below). The methods for resolving disputes between States parties to BITs involving the application or

---

[128] See, for example, the treaty between Ghana and Switzerland (article 10).

[129] See, for example, the treaty between Romania and the United States (article 14).

[130] Some have questioned whether such a clause in a contract can achieve the effect of pre-empting the legislative sovereignty of a State for a lengthy period of time (see, Kuwait v. American Independent Oil Company (1982)). On the effects of stabilization clauses in general, see Sornarajah (1994).

interprctation of the treaty are typically spelled out in a number of provisions in BITs (these are examined in section 5 below).

2. Consultations

Many BITs include a provision requiring that the contracting parties should consult each other concerning a treaty matter at the request of either contracting party. Among the countries that have included consultations provisions in their BITs are China, Denmark, Finland, the Netherlands, Norway and the United States. Some BITs specify that the parties shall consult periodically to review the implementation of the treaty and to discuss matters involving investment.[131]

It could be argued that a consultations provision is superfluous because customary international law imposes on countries, as part of their obligation to seek a peaceful resolution of disputes, the duty to negotiate in good faith.[132] In addition, the State-to-State dispute provision of most BITs explicitly requires the contracting parties to attempt to resolve any disputes through negotiations before submitting them to arbitration.

The inclusion of a consultations provision nevertheless serves several useful purposes. First, it creates an obligation to consult on any matters involving the treaty, including matters that may not yet be properly classifiable as a dispute. Indeed, timely consultations concerning proposed courses of action could prevent a situation from evolving into a dispute. Second, a consultations provision serves to emphasize the general importance that the contracting parties place on the amicable resolution of all differences involving the treaty, a matter that is a strong cultural preference for some countries. Third, in some BITs the consultations provision is designed as a method of monitoring the implementation of the BIT.[133]

3. Subrogation on insurance claims

As noted in the introduction, a number of countries have created programmes under which they insure the foreign investments of their nationals and companies against certain political risks, such as expropriation or currency exchange controls. Under these programmes, first, investors pay a fee to a government agency in return for which they are compensated for any losses covered by the insurance agreement. Second, the agency thereafter seeks reimbursement of the amount paid to the investors from the host country that caused the loss. Third, should investors obtain compensation from the host country, they will be required by the insurance agreement to pay any such compensation to the insuring agency.

Most BITs, including those between developing countries, have a provision on subrogation, the exception being those concluded by the United States.[134] The provision typically states that where the investor's home country has paid compensation for a loss under such an insurance agreement, the host country shall recognize that the investor's home country has become subrogated to any rights that the investor has against the host country arising out of the loss.

The subrogation provisions generally contain minor variations. Some BITs include language stating that the investor's home country may assert any right or claim to the same extent

---

[131]   See, for example, the BIT between China and Viet Nam (article 11) (table III.15).

[132]   See, for example, the North Sea Continental Shelf Cases (Federal Republic of Germany v. Denmark, Federal Republic of Germany v. Netherlands) (International Court of Justice, 1969).

[133]   See, for example, the BITs between Denmark and Poland (article 13); China and Viet Nam (article 11) and Kenya and the Netherlands (article 13).

[134]   The United States treaties do not contain a subrogation clause because questions linked to investment insurance by the Overseas Private Investment Corporation are covered by investment guarantee agreements that contain a detailed subrogation clause.

as the investor. This may be found, for example, in BITs concluded by Germany, Norway and the United Kingdom. Other BITs include language stating that any compensation received by the investor's home country in non-convertible currency as a result of subrogation shall be freely available for purposes of meeting expenditures incurred in the territory of the host country. This provision generally appears, for example, in BITs concluded by the United Kingdom.[135]

The question that may arise following the investor's receipt of payment under the insurance programme is whether the host country's responsibility is reduced by the amount of the payment received. A large number of BITs include clauses that explicitly address this question. In general, they provide that the host country shall not assert in mitigation of its responsibility that the investor has received compensation pursuant to any insurance agreement. An example of this type of clause is found in the BIT between Australia and the Lao People's Democratic Republic (table III.16).

The rationale for this clause is that the compensation received by an investor does not come from the host country, but from an insurance fund created by the fees paid by investors. To reduce the host country's responsibility by the amount of the insurance policy proceeds would permit the host country to escape the consequences of its acts just because the investor was prudent enough to purchase insurance.

4. Investor-to-State disputes

(a) *Purpose of the provision*

As noted, in the absence of a treaty with specific dispute-settlement provisions, an investor whose investment is injured because of unfair (or unlawful) treatment would have only two remedies. Frequently, however, neither would be effective, for two main reasons.

First, investors could bring a claim against the host country in a domestic court. However, the investors might not be comfortable with the host country's courts or the speed with which they function. Further, jurisdiction over the claim may be barred by the doctrine of sovereign immunity.

Second, investors could request that their home country espouse the claim against the host country, a process also known as exercising diplomatic protection. Diplomatic protection, as noted, is a doctrine of international law under which a State may assert a claim against another State based on an injury to one of its nationals caused by the latter State. Diplomatic protection may not always be effective, however. First, no country is required by international or domestic law to espouse a claim. Further, if it chooses to espouse a claim, a country will usually seek to resolve the claim through diplomatic negotiations, which could continue for years without any resolution. The espousing country is entitled to settle the claim on any terms that it wishes and, in theory, may retain any compensation paid by the other country. Sometimes, as in the case of lump-sum agreements, the settlement may be considerably less than full compensation. The customary rule, moreover, is that a country may not espouse a claim unless the injured private party has exhausted the remedies available under the local law of the country with which the dispute exists.[136] The exhaustion requirement is intended to ensure that a dispute is not elevated to the international plane unless the country that is alleged to have committed a wrongful act has had an opportunity to resolve the dispute through its own legal system.

---

[135] An example of this language can be found in the BIT between Nigeria and the United Kingdom (article 10).

[136] For a discussion on this point see the Interhandel Case (Switzerland v. United States) (International Court of Justice, 1959).

The earliest BITs addressed these situations to some extent by the inclusion of a State-to-State dispute provision that enabled the investor's home country to submit any claims against the host country to binding international arbitration. Thus, where espousal occurred, the home country would have some remedy other than negotiations. A similar provision still appears in most BITs. Although preferable to no dispute-settlement provision at all, such a provision gives the foreign investor less control over the handling of the dispute. To address such difficulties, most BITs today include provisions on investor-to-State settlement of disputes.

(b)   *Disputes to which the provision applies*

The first clause of an investor-to-State dispute-settlement provision typically defines the types of disputes to which the provision applies. Only disputes falling within the definition may be submitted to arbitration under the investor-to-State dispute-settlement provision.[137]

The most common approach requires only that the dispute should involve an investment issue in some way. The treaties following this approach use different formulations, among which there is little substantive difference. For example, a BIT may provide that the investor-to-State dispute provision applies to disputes "in connection with" investment, "related to" investment, "with respect to" investment, "regarding" investment, or "concerning" an investment. This approach has been used by many different countries, including Denmark, Finland, France, Germany, the Netherlands, Norway, Sweden, Switzerland and the United Kingdom. A specific example of this approach is the BIT between Lithuania and the Netherlands (table III.16). These formulations are sufficiently broad to include disputes that do not involve an alleged violation of the BIT. For example, a dispute over whether an investor has violated the domestic laws of the host country could be within the scope of the investor-to-State dispute provision, even if there is no allegation that enforcement of these laws violates the BIT.

A second approach requires that a dispute should involve a provision of the BIT. Some BITs, for example, apply the investor-to-State dispute provision to any dispute concerning the "interpretation or application" of the BIT[138] or concerning the obligations of the host country under the BIT.[139] This is obviously a much narrower provision than the first type discussed above.

A variation on this second approach is to limit the application of the investor-to-State dispute-settlement provision to disputes involving only certain provisions of a BIT. A few BITs, such as the BIT between China and Viet Nam (table III.16), limit the provision to disputes involving expropriation. This approach reflects a desire to treat arbitration with foreign nationals as an exceptional remedy, for relatively rare occasions.

A third approach, which is characteristic of the United States BITs, falls between these extremes. It applies the investor-to-State dispute-settlement provision to disputes relating to the breach of a BIT obligation or an obligation under an investment agreement or authorization. This approach, unlike the first, requires that the dispute should be related to a particular class of legal

---

[137] Note that once an agreement is reached in principle to submit investor-to-State disputes to international arbitration, it also includes disputes brought by a host country as a claimant against an investor. There is at least one example of such a case having been brought before the ICSID.

[138] See, for example, the BIT between the Czech and Slovak Federal Republic and Sweden (article 8 (1)).

[139] See, for example, the BITs between Belize and the United Kingdom (article 8 (1)) Panama and the United Kingdom (article 79) and Haiti and the United Kingdom (article 8 (1)).

Table III.16. Examples of provisions on investor-to-State dispute settlement in BITs

BIT between China and Viet Nam (1992)	BIT between Lithuania and the Netherlands (1994)	BIT between Australia and the Lao People's Democratic Republic (1994)
Article 8	Article 9	Article 12
1. Any dispute between an investor of one Contracting State and the other Contracting State in connection with an investment in the territory of the other Contracting State shall, as far as possible, be settled amicably through negotiations between the parties to the dispute. 2. If the dispute cannot be settled through negotiations within six months, either party to the dispute shall be entitled to submit the dispute to the competent court of the Contracting State accepting the investment. 3. If a dispute involving the amount of compensation cannot be settled within six months after resort to negotiations as specified in paragraph 1 of this Article, it may be submitted at the request of either party to an ad hoc arbitral tribunal. The provisions of this paragraph shall not apply if the investor concerned has resorted to the procedure specified in the paragraph 2 of this Article. 4. Such an arbitral tribunal can be constituted for each individual case in the following way: each party to the dispute shall appoint an arbitrator, and these two shall select a national of a third State which has diplomatic relations with the two contracting States as Chairman. The first two arbitrators shall be appointed within the next two months of the written notice for arbitration by either party to the dispute to the other, and the Chairman be selected within four months. If within the period specified above, the tribunal has not been constituted, either party to the dispute may invite the Secretary General of the International Centre under the Convention on the Settlement of Investment Disputes between Nationals of Other States opened for signature in Washington on 18 March 1965 to make the necessary appointments.	Each Contracting Party hereby consents to submit any legal dispute arising between that Contracting Party and an investor of the other Contracting Party concerning an investment of that investor in the territory of the former Contracting Party to the International Centre for the Settlement of Investment Disputes between States and nationals of other States opened for s i g n a t u r e a t Washington on 18 March 1965. A legal person which is an investor of one Contracting Party and which before such a dispute arises is controlled by investors of the other Contracting Party shall in accordance with Article 25 (2) (b) of the Convention for the purpose of the Convention be treated as an investor of the other Contracting Party.	(1) In the event of of a dispute between a Contracting Party and a national of the other Contracting Party relating to an investment, the parties to the dispute shall initially seek to resolve the dispute by consultations and negotiations. (2) If the dispute in question cannot be resolved through consultations and negotiations, either party to the dispute may: (a) in accordance with the law of the Contracting Party which has admitted the investment, initiate proceedings before that Contracting Party's competent judicial or administrative bodies; (b) if both Contracting Parties are at the time party to the 1965 Convention on the Settlement of Investment Disputes between States and Nationals of other States ("the Convention"), refer the dispute to the International Centre for the Settlement of Investment Disputes ("the Centre") for conciliation or arbitration pursuant to Articles 28 or 36 of the Convention; (c) if both Contracting Parties are not at the time party to the Convention, refer the dispute to an Arbitral Tribunal constituted in accordance with Annex B of this Agreement, or by agreement, to any other arbitral authority. (3) Where a dispute is referred to the Centre pursuant to sub-paragraph (2)(b) of this Article: (a) where that action is taken by a national of one Contracting Party, the other Contracting Party shall consent in writing to the submission of the dispute to the Centre within thirty days of receiving such a request from the national. (b) if the parties to the dispute cannot agree whether conciliation or arbitration is the more appropriate procedure, the national affected shall have the right to choose;

(Table III.16, continued)

BIT between China and Viet Nam (1992)		BIT between Australia and the Lao People's Democratic Republic (1994)
Article 8 (continued) 5. The tribunal shall determine its own procedure. However, the tribunal may, in the course of determination of procedure, take as guidance the Arbitration Rules of the International Centre for Settlement of Investment Disputes. 6. The tribunal shall reach its decision by a majority of votes. Such decision shall be final and binding on both parties to the dispute. Both Contracting States shall commit themselves to the enforcement of the decision in accordance with their respective domestic law. 7. The tribunal shall adjudicate in accordance with the law of the Contracting State to the dispute accepting the investment including its rules on the conflict of laws, the provisions of this Agreement as well as the generally recognized principle of international law accepted by both Contracting Parties. 8. Each party to the dispute shall bear the cost of its appointed member and its representation in the proceedings. The cost of the appointed Chairman and the remaining costs shall be borne in equal parts by the parties to the dispute.		Article 12 (continued) (c) a company which is constituted or incorporated under the law in force in the territory of one Contracting Party and in which before the dispute arises the majority of the shares are owned by nationals of the other Contracting Party shall, in accordance with Article 25(2)(b) of the Convention, be treated for the purposes of the Convention as a company of the other Contracting Party. (4) Once an action referred to in paragraph (2) of this Article has been taken, neither Contracting Party shall pursue the dispute through diplomatic channels unless: (a) the relevant judicial or administrative body, the Secretary General of the Centre, the arbitral authority or tribunal or the conciliation commission, as the case may be, has decided that it has no jurisdiction in relation to the dispute in question; or (b) the other Contracting Party has failed to abide by or comply with any judgement, award, order or other determination made by the body in question. (5) In any proceeding involving a dispute relating to an investment, a Contracting Party shall not assert, as a defence, counter-claim, right of set-off or otherwise, that the national concerned has received or will receive, pursuant to an insurance or guarantee contract, indemnification or other compensation for all or part of any alleged loss.

obligations, but, unlike the second, does not limit that class to obligations created or codified by the BIT. Rather, it permits the investor to use the investor-to-State dispute-settlement mechanism to enforce investment agreements with the host country.[140]

(c) *The duty to negotiate*

Bilateral investment treaties are largely uniform in requiring that the investor and the host country should attempt to resolve a dispute amicably, that is, through negotiations, before submitting it to arbitration. A typical example is the BIT between China and Viet Nam (table III.16).

---

[140] Many BITs concluded by the United States also contain an exception not found in other BITs. The exception excludes from BIT coverage disputes arising under export credit or insurance programmes administered by the Export–Import Bank or the Overseas Private Investment Corporation. These programmes are generally covered by other agreements that have their own dispute-settlement provisions, which the drafters of these BITs did not wish to displace.

In most cases, treaties require that a specified minimum amount of time must elapse between the origin of a dispute and its submission to arbitration. The time specified most commonly is six months,[141] but it is not unusual for a BIT to specify another period of time.[142]

(d)   *Exhaustion of local remedies*

As has been noted, under customary international law, a home country generally may not espouse a private investor's claim against a host State unless the private investor has first exhausted any local remedies. The question arises as to whether an investor must also exhaust local remedies before invoking a BIT's investor-to-State dispute-settlement mechanism and proceeding against the host country directly. BITs have answered this question in several different ways. Particularly in the early years of BITs, a number of them required that the investor should first invoke local remedies by submitting the dispute to the courts or administrative tribunals of the host country.[143]

Some BITs that prescribe recourse to local remedies allow the investor to submit a dispute to arbitration under the investor-to-State dispute-settlement mechanism after the dispute has been before the local courts or administrative tribunals for some fixed period of time, even if the local courts or administrative tribunals have not concluded their proceedings. This fixed period has varied from as little as three months to as much as two years.[144] In a few cases, BITs provide that arbitration is available only if the result reached through local proceedings is unjust. Implicit in this provision is the principle that proceedings before a local tribunal are to be suspended at such a time as the dispute is referred to international arbitration. Indeed, article 26 of the Convention on the Settlement of Disputes between States and nationals of Other States expressly provides that consent to ICSID arbitration, unless otherwise stated, is deemed consent to the exclusion of any other remedy (UNCTAD, 1996b, Vol I, p. 25).

A quite different approach is to state explicitly that the exhaustion requirement is waived by virtue of the host country's consent to arbitration. Alternatively, some BITs state simply that an investor's invocation of local remedies extinguishes the right to arbitration.[145] This alternative not only implies that exhaustion is not required, but may actually discourage the investor from pursuing local remedies.

Another group of BITs seeks neither to require nor to discourage exhaustion. These BITs merely specify submission of the dispute to local remedies as one of the choices available to the investor. The BIT between Australia and the Lao People's Democratic Republic is an example of this approach (table III.16).[146] Sometimes these BITs do not preclude an investor who has invoked local remedies from later resorting to international arbitration if the result reached locally is unsatisfactory to the investor. Many recent BITs do not even mention the exhaustion of local remedies.[147]

---

[141]   See, for example, the BIT between Chile and Sweden (article 7 (2)).

[142]   For example, in the BIT between Indonesia and the Republic of Korea (article 9 (2)) the time prescribed is twelve months, and in the BIT between Denmark and Lithuania (article 8 (2)) it is three months.

[143]   See, for example, the BIT between Malaysia and the Netherlands (article XII). In the first years of BIT negotiations, Jamaica sought provision for the exhaustion of local remedies. Thus, article 9 of the BIT between Jamaica and the United States provides for ICSID arbitration following the failure to reach settlement "through pursuit of local remedies in accordance with international law"; article 9 (3) of the BIT between Jamaica and the Netherlands is similar. Significantly, Jamaica no longer insists on the exhaustion of local remedies.

[144]   Article 7 of the BIT between Romania and Sri Lanka, for example, provides for a time-limit of six months.

[145]   See, for example, the BIT between Romania and the United States (article VI (3) (a)).

[146]   See also the BIT between Chile and Sweden (article 7 (2)).

[147]   See, for example, the BIT between Germany and Swaziland (article 11). In the 1989 case of Elettronica Sicula S.p.A. (ELSI) (United States v. Italy), the International Court of Justice faced the question of the need to exhaust local remedies in a bilateral treaty that provided for international arbitration between the two States, but made no mention of the need to exhaust local remedies. The Court held in the context of an arbitration between two States that the principle of exhaustion of local remedies was such an important principle of international law that it

(e)   The ICSID clause[148]

In 1965, the Convention on the Settlement of Investment Disputes between States and Nationals of Other States was opened for signature.[149] The Convention created the International Centre for Settlement of Investment Disputes (ICSID), an affiliate agency of the World Bank. The purpose of ICSID is to provide a facility for the conciliation or arbitration of investment disputes between a private investor and a host country. According to article 25 (1) of the Convention, ICSID's jurisdiction exists where both the home and host countries are parties to the Convention, and the host country and the investor have consented to ICSID's jurisdiction.[150]

An advantage of ICSID arbitration from the investors' perspective is that it allows the investors to control the presentation of their claims. Investors do not need to persuade their home countries to espouse a claim or surrender control over the claim to the home country in order for the claim to be resolved. The advantage of this means of dispute-settlement from the perspective of both the host country and the home country is that it takes the investment dispute outside the political realm; the dispute becomes a matter for resolution between the investor and the host country in an international legal forum, rather than a matter of contention between two countries.

In 1968, Indonesia and the Netherlands concluded the first BIT to include a provision for ICSID arbitration in investment disputes (Dolzer and Stevens, 1995). Over the next decade, countries negotiating BITs began to include in their agreements investor-to-State dispute provisions expressing various forms of consent of each contracting party to arbitration before ICSID.[151] Such a provision, with numerous variations, appears in a large number of BITs (table III.16).[152]

In some BITs, the contracting parties give less than full consent to ICSID arbitration. A number of BITs, for example, provide that the host country "shall consent" to ICSID arbitration.[153] This language presumably means that ICSID has no jurisdiction until consent is given, but refusal to consent would violate the BIT, giving rise to an enforcement proceeding under the State-to-State dispute provision. A few BITs provide that consent is subject to agreement between the host country and the investor, which means essentially that the host country has not consented and perhaps might not consent.[154] Treaties occasionally provide merely that the host country shall give sympathetic consideration to an investor's request that the dispute should be submitted to ICSID arbitration.[155] The majority of the recent treaties, however, include provisions setting forth the contracting parties' irrevocable consent.

Even where consent is given, it would be illusory if both contracting parties are not parties to the Convention on the Settlement of Investment Disputes between States and Nationals of Other States. In some BITs, the contracting parties consent to ICSID arbitration even though one, or

---

would not be held to have been tacitly dispensed with in the absence of specific words indicating a clear intention to do so.

[148]   For an analysis of the types of arbitration articles in BITs, see Broches (1982 and 1991).

[149]   The text of the Convention appears in UNCTAD, 1996b, Vol. I, pp. 25-45.

[150]   As at June 1997, 127 countries were parties to the Convention.

[151]   It should be noted that ICSID has jurisdiction only if both contracting parties have adhered to the Convention on the Settlement of Investment Disputes between States and Nationals of Other States and if the respondent contracting party has consented to ICSID jurisdiction over the claim.

[152]   For a discussion of dispute settlement provisions in BITs, see Brewer (1995).

[153]   See, for example, the BITs between the Netherlands and the Philippines (article 9 (1), Japan and Sri Lanka (article 11) and Egypt and Japan (article 11).

[154]   See, for example, the BIT between Malaysia and Sweden (article 6).

[155]   See, for example, the BIT between Kenya and the Netherlands (article XI).

neither, of them is a party to the Convention. Such consent would be ineffective until both contracting parties adhered to the Convention. To address this problem, ICSID established in 1978 the "Additional Facility" as an alternative mechanism that has jurisdiction to arbitrate or conciliate certain types of disputes that are outside ICSID's jurisdiction.[156] The Additional Facility is available only if the host country or the home country of the investor, but not both, is a party to the Convention.[157]

Some BITs concluded since 1978 have included a provision under which both contracting parties consent to arbitration of disputes before the Additional Facility in the event that ICSID lacks jurisdiction. The great majority of BITs, however, do not contain an explicit reference to the Additional Facility.

(f) *Choice of mechanisms*

The earliest investor-to-State dispute provisions contained each contracting party's consent only to ICSID arbitration. The recent trend is to give investors a choice of mechanisms. One choice authorized by some BITs is arbitration through some institution other than ICSID or the affiliated Additional Facility. Other institutions include the International Chamber of Commerce or the Stockholm Chamber of Commerce.

Another choice is ad hoc arbitration, that is, arbitration before a single individual appointed, or a tribunal specially constituted, for a particular dispute. If ad hoc arbitration is to be effective, the BIT must prescribe the rules that will govern the selection of the arbitrator (or arbitrators). Most BITs accomplish this by specifying that some existing set of rules governs the arbitration, including the formation of the tribunal. The rules most commonly specified are the arbitration rules promulgated by the United Nations Commission on International Trade Law (UNCITRAL) (UNCTAD, 1996b, Vol. I, p. 71). Some BITs specify that the procedure prescribed in the State-to-State dispute resolution provision is to be used.

The principal advantage of ad hoc arbitration is that it allows parties the flexibility to structure the arbitration in the way that they prefer. Indeed, those BITs that provide for ad hoc arbitration using the UNCITRAL rules often specify that the parties may modify the rules by agreement. The disadvantage of *ad hoc* arbitration, however, is that the parties do not have the benefit of the assistance provided by arbitral institutions such as ICSID. These institutions may be able to provide lists of arbitrators or detailed rules of procedure, and may even assist in the selection of arbitrators.

BITs create a choice by setting forth the contracting parties' consent to arbitration of disputes covered by any of these mechanisms. Thus, the BIT between Moldova and the United States states:

> Each Party hereby consents to the submission of any investment dispute for settlement by binding arbitration in accordance with the choice specified in the written consent of the national or company under paragraph 3 (article VI (4)).

The decision to provide alternatives to ICSID arbitration is the result of a number of considerations. First, there was concern at one point that ICSID awards might be particularly

---

[156] The rules of the Additional Facility are set out in ICSID (1982).

[157] Additional Facility Rules, article 26 (4) (a) (ii).

vulnerable to annulment.[158] Second, the successful use of the UNCITRAL rules by the Iran–United States Claims Tribunal seemed to suggest that these rules were especially adaptable to investor-to-State dispute-settlement. Third, some States developed preferences for particular arbitral institutions for reasons that had to do with the particularities of those institutions.

Where a BIT contains the contracting parties' consent to more than one mechanism, it often states that the investor is entitled to choose the mechanism to which the dispute is to be submitted. Even where a BIT is silent on how the choice is to be made (or provides that either disputant may choose to submit the dispute to arbitration), as a practical matter the investor will probably have the sole power to control the choice of dispute-settlement mechanism. This is because a BIT is an agreement between two countries and only the countries are bound by it; although the BIT may contain the contracting parties' consent to arbitration, it generally does not contain the consent of the investor. The host country thus cannot invoke the investor-to-State dispute provision without some act of consent by the investor. For this reason, the investor can control the choice of mechanism simply by a selective withholding of consent.

Some BITs, such as the BIT between Australia and the Lao People's Democratic Republic (table III.16), provide for conciliation or arbitration before ICSID.[159] For the reasons just discussed, an investor will generally have the power, explicitly or implicitly, to choose between these alternatives as well.

A number of BITs include among the mechanisms that the investor may select, submission of the dispute to local remedies, that is, the courts or administrative tribunals of the host country. An example of this approach is the BIT between Lithuania and the Netherlands (table III.16).[160] As noted, one issue that should be resolved by a BIT is whether the investor's decision to invoke local remedies precludes the subsequent submission of the dispute to international arbitration.

(g)   *Governing law*

International tribunals generally give effect to agreements between disputants concerning the law that is to govern the dispute. An investor and a host country may include in an investment agreement a clause specifying the law applicable to disputes involving an investment. Alternatively, some BITs include a choice-of-law clause in the investor-to-State dispute provision. This is done, for example, in the BIT between China and Viet Nam (table III.16) and the one between the Belgium–Luxembourg Economic Union and Cyprus (article 10 (5)).

In the absence of such a choice-of-law clause, an arbitrator or arbitral tribunal may use national or international law, or both, to decide the case. The arbitration of investment disputes has at times been governed by international law and at other times by national law. When ICSID arbitration is selected, the arbitration is subject to article 42 of the ICSID convention, which

---

[158] Two ICSID awards have been annulled through internal procedures, thereby indicating that the procedure could be lengthy and cumbersome. For a debate on this issue, see, among others, Reisman (1989) and Broches (1991).

[159] It should be noted, however, that BITs do not normally require the investor and the host country to attempt conciliation before going to arbitration, or even mention conciliation as an option. It is interesting to recall in this respect that the first ICSID conciliation case, which was based on a contract between Tesoro Petroleum and the Government of Trinidad and Tobago, required an attempt at conciliation prior to arbitration and the conciliation was successful (Nurick and Schnobly, 1986).

[160] Other examples of BITs with host-country courts or tribunals as a method of settlement are article IV (2) (a) of the BIT between Jamaica and the United States, article 8 (2) of the BIT between Jamaica and China, and the BIT between Argentina and Jamaica.

provides that, in the absence of agreement between the parties with respect to the choice of law, the tribunal will apply the law of the host State and such rules of international law as may be applicable.

Investors may prefer to have international law applied to any investment dispute, either because international law sometimes provides greater protection than national law, or because the host country can change its own law to the disadvantage of the investor. In fact, the very act that gives rise to the dispute may modify national law in such a way as to extinguish any claim by the investor under national law. For the same reasons, the host country generally prefers that its own laws apply.

Some BITs, such as the BIT between China and Viet Nam (table III.16) provide that both international law and national law apply. This leaves the tribunal with the task of deciding which law shall govern each issue raised by a dispute. BITs typically do not specify that only national law applies, although specific provisions of a BIT are sometimes made subject to the host country's national law.

A BIT may specify the choice of law indirectly. Some provide, for example, that the treatment accorded to investment shall in no case be less than that required by international law. Such a clause does not preclude the application of national law, as long as the application of national law does not result in treatment inconsistent with international law.

(h)   *Enforcement of an arbitral award*

Many BITs include clauses that are intended to facilitate enforcement of an award of the arbitral tribunal in local courts. A number of international agreements require the contracting parties to enforce arbitral awards in their courts under certain conditions. The BIT clauses discussed here attempt to ensure that any award issued under the investor-to-State dispute provision satisfies these conditions and that, accordingly, enforcement of an award will be required under one or more of these international agreements.

One of the most important such agreements is the Convention on the Settlement of Investment Disputes between States and Nationals of Other States, which requires all parties to it to enforce any award issued by an ICSID tribunal.[161] Thus, if an investor chooses ICSID arbitration, the resulting award should be enforceable in the territory of any State that is party to the Convention.[162] If an investor chooses any other form of dispute-settlement, the Convention does not require enforcement of the resulting award.

Another important agreement for this purpose is the United Nations Convention on the Recognition and Enforcement of Foreign Arbitral Awards (UNCTAD, 1996b, Vol. I, p. 15), often referred to as the New York Convention. It applies to foreign arbitral awards generally and thus can be used to enforce arbitral awards not issued by ICSID.

The New York Convention, however, permits parties to make certain declarations that limit its applicability (article I (1)). One such declaration, made by a majority of the countries that have adhered to the Convention, is that the party will enforce an arbitral award only if made in the territory of a country that is also a party to the New York Convention. To ensure that this

---

[161] Article 54 of the Convention on the Settlement of Investment Disputes between States and Nationals of Other States.

[162] If countries utilize the Convention, they must make sure that they have adopted the necessary legislation or other measures to give effect to article 42 of the Convention, requiring enforcement of ICSID awards in their national system.

declaration does not preclude enforcement under the New York Convention of awards issued through the investor-to-State dispute-settlement mechanism, some BITs (e.g. the BIT between the Russian Federation and the United States, in article VI (3) (d)) provide that such awards must be made in a country that is a party to the New York Convention. The Additional Facility Arbitration Rules similarly require that Additional Facility proceedings should take place in a country that is a party to the New York Convention.

A critical issue as regards enforcement, whether under the ICSID convention or the New York Convention, is whether enforcement is precluded by the sovereign immunity defence and the act-of-State doctrine. On one or the other ground, awards have been refused enforcement by United States and other courts.

If a country is not bound by an agreement such as the ICSID convention or the New York Convention, it is under no obligation to enforce an arbitral award. Thus, it could happen that an award issued under the investor-to-State dispute-settlement provision would not be enforceable in the territory of either of the contracting parties, although the same award might be enforceable in the territory of third countries under the New York Convention or another agreement. To ensure that an award issued under the investor-to-State dispute-settlement provision is enforceable at least in the territory of the contracting parties, some BITs, such as the treaty beween the Russian Federation and the United States (article VI (3) (e)), provide that each party shall enforce the award in its territory or that each party shall provide for enforcement of the award in its territory.

A variation on this clause provides that each party shall enforce the award in its territory in accordance with its laws. This is found, for example, in the BITs between China and Viet Nam (table III.16) and between Lithuania and Sweden (article 7 (5)). This language would seem to mean that an award is not enforceable if the contracting party's local law does not provide for enforcement. Thus, the subordination of the enforceability clause to local law deprives it of much of its force.

(i) *Effect and finality of awards*

Some BITs, such as the one between Chile and Norway (article 8 (4)), provide that any awards issued under the investor-to-State dispute-settlement mechanism shall be final and binding. The effect of this provision is that an investor cannot choose one of the arbitral mechanisms and then, if dissatisfied with the result, resubmit the dispute to a different mechanism.

(j) *Corporate nationality*

The ICSID convention applies to disputes between a State and an investor from another State. Where a host country takes wrongful action against a company that is incorporated under local law but owned by nationals of the other contracting party, the company could potentially be regarded as having the nationality of the host country and thus the company could not redress the wrongful action through ICSID arbitration.

To avoid this problem, article 25 (2) of the ICSID convention provides that two States may agree that, for the purposes of ICSID arbitration, a company shall be treated as a company of a State if, immediately prior to the action giving rise to the dispute, nationals of that State owned or controlled it.[163] A large number of BITs contain a provision setting forth just such a proposition (table III.16).

---

[163] The leading interpretations of article 25 (2) are found in Amco Asia Corporation (et al.) v. Indonesia (ICSID, 1985) and Vacuum Salts Products Ltd. v. Ghana (ICSID, 1992).

This provision thus allows a company incorporated under the laws of a host country to submit a dispute with the host country to investor-to-State arbitration, provided that, immediately prior to the dispute, the company was owned or controlled by nationals of the other BIT contracting party. Ownership and control are measured immediately prior to the event giving rise to the dispute so that, if the dispute arises out of the host country's expropriation of the local company, the local company will not be treated by virtue of the expropriation as a national of the host country.

(k) *Espousal of disputes submitted to investor-to-State arbitration*

Because BITs that contain an investor-to-State dispute-settlement provision almost always include a State-to-State dispute-settlement provision as well, some countries have been concerned that a dispute submitted to arbitration by the investor may be subsequently submitted to arbitration by the investor's home country. To prevent this situation, some BITs contain a clause stating that a dispute submitted for arbitration under the investor-to-State dispute-settlement provision may not also be submitted to arbitration under the State-to-State dispute-settlement provision. The ICSID convention also provides that, where a dispute is submitted to ICSID arbitration, the same dispute may not be the subject of a subsequent claim by the investor's home country unless the host country fails to comply with the arbitral award.[164]

The clause typically contains one or two exceptions. One exception, found, for example, in the BIT between Australia and the Lao People's Democratic Republic (table III.16), applies where the tribunal formed under an investor-to-State dispute-settlement provision does not have jurisdiction over the dispute. A more common exception applies where the host country does not comply with the award issued by the tribunal.[165]

5. State-to-State dispute resolution

Virtually all BITs include a provision for binding third-party arbitration of disputes between the contracting parties. These provisions have become remarkably uniform among BITs, despite the large number of new countries that have begun to conclude BITs in recent years.

(a) *Disputes to which the provision applies*

The standard language used in most BITs provides that the State-to-State dispute settlement provision applies to disputes between the contracting parties concerning the interpretation or application of the BIT. In many BITs, as discussed above, the investor-to-State dispute-settlement mechanism applies to all investment disputes, even if they do not involve the interpretation or application of the BIT. Thus, in these BITs, the State-to-State dispute-settlement mechanism has a narrower range of applicability than the investor-to-State dispute settlement mechanism. It also deals with different problems and has different functions.

As was also noted above, there is a provision in some BITs stating that a dispute submitted for resolution under the investor-to-State dispute-settlement provision may not also be submitted for resolution under the State-to-State dispute-settlement provision, with certain exceptions.

---

[164] Article 27 (i) of the Convention on Settlement of Disputes between States and Nationals of Other States.

[165] See, for example, the BIT between Estonia and Switzerland (article 9 (5)).

(b) Duty to negotiate

A State-to-State dispute-settlement provision generally begins with a statement that disputes should be settled by negotiation, if possible. For example, the BIT between Lithuania and Norway provides that:

> Disputes between the Contracting Parties concerning the interpretation or application of this agreement should, as far as possible, be settled through negotiations between the Contracting Party. (article X (1))

As in the investor-to-State dispute-settlement provision, it is common to stipulate that a certain minimum amount of time must elapse between the date on which a dispute arises and the date on which it may be submitted to arbitration.[166] The period usually prescribed is six months, but it can be as little as three months or as much as a year. The time period is not always quantified.[167] Some BITs, such as the BIT between Lithuania and the Netherlands (article 13 (1)) require that a "reasonable time" should have elapsed.

(c) Selection of arbitrators

State-to-State dispute-settlement provisions almost always provide for arbitration by a tribunal specifically constituted for the dispute involved, rather than arbitration before an existing institution. Most BITs use the same procedure for constituting a tribunal.

The usual procedure is that each contracting party selects one arbitrator, following which the two party-appointed arbitrators jointly select a third arbitrator, who serves as the chair of the tribunal. It is often specified that the third arbitrator may not be a national of either of the two contracting parties. Thus the BIT between Austria and the Republic of Korea states that:

> Each Contracting Party shall appoint one member and these two members shall agree upon a national of a third State as their chairman. (article 9 (3))

Some BITs require that the third arbitrator should be approved by both contracting parties.[168] Other BITs include no such requirement, perhaps on the assumption that the party-appointed arbitrators will not agree on anyone who would be unacceptable to the contracting parties.

The process of selecting arbitrators generally is governed by a series of deadlines. The most common approach is to allow each contracting party two months to appoint an arbitrator and then to allow the two party-appointed arbitrators an additional two months to select the chair. Some BITs lengthen one or both of these periods to three or six months, and less time is occasionally permitted.

The process of constituting the tribunal may fail in either of two situations: where a contracting party declines to appoint an arbitrator or where the party-appointed arbitrators fail to agree on a chair. To prevent either of these situations from defeating the operation of the State-to-State dispute-settlement mechanism, BITs provide that, in the event that an arbitrator is not named in the specified period, either contracting party may request that a neutral official, referred to as the appointing authority, should make the appointment. For example, the BIT between Austria and the Republic of Korea states that:

---

[166] See, for example, the BIT between Lithuania and Norway (article X (2)).

[167] See, for example, the BITs between the United Kingdom and Uzbekistan (article 9 (2)) and between Indonesia and the Republic of Korea (article 12 (2)).

[168] See, for example, the BITs between Lithuania and Norway (article X (3)) and between the United Kingdom and Uzbekistan (article 9 (3)).

If the periods specified have not been observed, either Contracting Party may, in the absence of other relevant arrangement, invite the President of the International Court of Justice to make the necessary appointments. (article 10 (4))

Treaties vary, however, their choice of appointing authority. By far the most commonly designated appointing authority is the President of the International Court of Justice. Some BITs designate the Secretary-General of the United Nations. Other officials designated include the Secretary-General of ICSID, the Secretary-General of the Permanent Court of Arbitration, and the President of the Arbitration Institute of the Stockholm Chamber of Commerce.

Some BITs designate an alternate appointing authority, who shall make the appointment in one of the following situations: where the official initially designated as the appointing authority is unable for some reason to make the appointment; or where the official initially designated is a national of one of the two contracting parties. For example, many of the BITs that designate the President of the International Court of Justice as the appointing authority state that in one or both of these situations the appointing authority shall be the Vice-President of the International Court. These BITs may also provide that, if the Vice-President is unable to make the appointment, the most senior member of the Court able to make the appointment shall be the appointing authority. Thus, for example, the BIT between Austria and the Republic of Korea (quoted above) goes on to provide that:

If the President is a national of either of the Contracting Parties or if he is otherwise prevented from discharging the said function, the Vice-President or in case of his inability the member of the International Court of Justice next in seniority shall be invited under the same conditions to make the necessary appointments.

(d) *Tribunal procedure*

Many BITs explicitly authorize the tribunal to determine its own procedure. The tribunal may thus draft its own rules or may adopt an existing set of rules, such as the UNCITRAL rules, perhaps with some modifications. Some BITs specify that a particular set of rules is to be used. The BITs concluded by the United States, for example, initially required use of the Model Rules on Arbitral Procedure adopted by the International Law Commission unless the parties otherwise agreed, but since 1987 have required use of the UNCITRAL rules, again subject to the right of the parties to select other rules.

The authorization for the tribunal to determine its own procedure is generally subject to the requirement that any decisions must be made by majority vote. This requirement ensures that the tribunal will not be paralysed by the insistence of any one arbitrator that unanimity is required even to decide that future decisions shall be by majority vote. In some cases, the tribunal's power to determine its own procedure is subject to the agreement of the contracting parties.[169]

Under customary international law, international arbitral tribunals have inherent authority to determine their own rules of procedure. Thus, the provision that the tribunal is authorized to determine its own procedure is not strictly necessary. For the reason explained, inclusion of a requirement that the tribunal should proceed by majority vote is desirable.

Very few BITs specify the law that is to be applied by a tribunal. Some, however, do include a provision stating that the tribunal is to apply the provisions of the treaty and the principles of international law. These include BITs concluded by Denmark, Norway and the United States.

---

[169] See, for example, the BITs between Chile and Denmark (article 10 (6)) and between Ghana and Switzerland (article 13 (6)).

Many BITs provide that the treatment accorded to investment is to be consistent with that required by international law, which implicitly requires the tribunal to apply international law to disputes involving the treatment of an investment.

A few BITs have a different choice-of-law clause. For example, some of the BITs concluded by the Netherlands authorize the tribunal to decide *ex aequo et bono* if the parties so agree. A BIT may also call for the law of the host State to be taken into account.[170]

A choice-of-law provision is omitted from many BITs on the assumption that international law governs arbitration between States unless the parties agree otherwise. As noted, many BITs that address the choice-of-law question do provide for the application of international law. At the same time, as also previously noted, some BITs specify that any tribunal formed under the investor-to-State dispute provision is to apply the law of the host country as well as international law. Arguably, the result could be that, in these BITs, a different body of law could be applied depending on whether a dispute is referred to State-to-State or investor-to-State arbitration. Where international law is likely to be more favourable to an investor, this could create an incentive for an investor to request the home country to refer a dispute to State-to-State arbitration, rather than pursuing the claim through investor-to-State arbitration.

The clause on tribunal procedures also usually specifies that all awards made by a tribunal are final and binding. In this respect, the State-to-State dispute-settlement provision is similar to the investor-to-State dispute-settlement provision.

(e) *Costs of arbitration*

Most State-to-State dispute-settlement provisions explicitly address the manner in which the costs of arbitration are to be divided among the contracting parties. The most common approach is to state that each contracting party shall bear the costs of its own representation before the tribunal and of the arbitrator whom it appoints. The remaining costs of the tribunal are to be divided equally among the contracting parties. For example, the BIT between Germany and Swaziland, provides that:

> Each Contracting Party shall bear the cost of its own member and of its representatives in the arbitration proceedings; the cost of the Chairman and the remaining costs shall be borne in equal parts by the Contracting Parties. (article 10 (5))

An alternative is to state that each contracting party shall bear the costs of its own representation, but that all costs of the tribunal (including the costs of the party-appointed arbitrators) are to be divided equally among the contracting parties. An example is the BIT between Tunisia and Turkey, which provides that:

> Expenses incurred by the Chairman, the other arbitrators and other costs of the proceeding shall be paid ... equally by the parties. (article VIII (6))

The difference between these two approaches thus is that under one approach each contracting party pays the costs of the arbitrator it appoints while under the other approach such costs are divided equally.[171]

---

[170] See, for example, the BITs between Germany and Israel (article 10 (6)) and between China and the Netherlands (article 13 (8)).

[171] The theory of arbitration, of course, is that all arbitrators are neutral. This would seem consistent with having the costs of all arbitrators borne equally by the contracting parties. The reality, however, is that party-appointed arbitrators often favour the party that appointed them and may even be in communication with that party

Many BITs treat the apportionment of costs described above merely as a presumptive arrangement and allow the tribunal to decide on the apportionment of the costs between the contracting parties according to some other formula. Thus, the BIT between Tunisia and Turkey quoted above goes on to state:

> The tribunal may, however, at its discretion, direct that a higher proportion of the costs be paid by one of the Parties.

These BITs rarely specify the grounds that might justify such a reapportionment. This provision would allow the tribunal, for example, to place a greater share of the costs on a contracting party that had raised frivolous arguments or acted in some other way to hinder or increase the cost of the arbitration.

6. Judicial access

Investors may find at times that they wish to submit a dispute for resolution to the local courts of the host country either because the dispute falls outside the scope of the investor-to-State or the State-to-State dispute-settlement provisions or, because the investor chooses to submit it to the local courts for political or other reasons, even though the dispute is within the scope of one of the BIT's dispute resolution mechanisms.

No BIT precludes an investor from submitting an investment dispute to the local courts of the host country. As noted, a few BITs even require that this should be done prior to invoking the investor-to-State dispute-settlement provision. At the same time, few BITs provide much assistance to the investor who either must, or chooses to, submit a dispute to the local courts. The BITs concluded by the United States do require that each contracting party should provide investors with "effective means of asserting claims and enforcing rights with respect to investment, investment agreements and investment authorizations".[172] Some early BITs concluded by the United States also guarantee investors MFN and national treatment with respect to access to the courts of justice and the right to employ the counsel of their choice to represent them.[173] This special provision for MFN and national treatment was omitted in later BITs as it duplicated the protection provided by the general MFN and national treatment provisions. In addition, as discussed elsewhere,[174] many BITs require that, in the event of an expropriation, the host country should provide the investor with a means for prompt judicial review of the legality of the expropriation and the adequacy of any compensation paid.

* * *

during the arbitration. This reality presumably underlies countries' tendency to assume that they should pay the costs of the arbitrator they appoint. The independence of the arbitrator, however, is more than a matter of theory. It is important to note that all arbitral rules require an arbitrator to be independent and that one of the parties can challenge and request the removal of an arbitrator who is not independent. Moreover, any resulting award would face the risk of challenge in the courts if the arbitrator fails to be independent.

The tendency for countries to pay the cost of the arbitrator they appoint may also be due to the fact that many BITs use ad hoc arbitral tribunals. In the case of ad hoc tribunals there is no fixed standard rate of payment for the work of the arbitrators. If the decision is left to agreement by the parties, the parties may not be able to agree on the appropriate honoraria and the process might be delayed for a long period of time.

[172] See, for example, the BIT between the Kyrgyz Republic and the United States (article II (6)).

[173] See, for example, the BIT between Egypt and the United States (article II (8)).

[174] See section on expropriation above.

The provision of alternative means of dispute settlement in BITs is generally considered as the single most important means of securing a reliable investment climate. BITs emphasize, first of all, that negotiation and conciliation are the more rapid, discreet, less costly and therefore more desirable means of dispute settlement. In addition, the possibility of resolving investor-to-State disputes through a neutral forum, authorized by many BITs, represents significant progress in the quest to "depoliticize" investment disputes (Shihata, 1986). Recourse to host country domestic courts remains, of course, a possibility, but these investment disputes demand specialized technical knowledge to deal with the complexities of certain types of investment issues and relations. Among the issues to negotiate regarding third-party international arbitration are the arbitration mechanism or facility, the rules of procedure, the substantive rules to be applied by the arbitrators, the implementation of arbitration awards and the relationship between BIT mechanisms and other investment dispute procedures.

N. Some concluding remarks

As noted in the introduction, the manner in which BITs address development is mostly indirect. Nevertheless, the foregoing survey of BIT clauses show several ways through which the development dimension is given expression in the structure and contents of BITs:

• **By including development as one of the main objectives of the BIT.** The objective of promoting development thus provides the main guiding principle for the application and interpretation of the substantive standards of BITs.

• **By allowing national policies to operate through BITs.** Characteristically, most BITs refer the question of admission of foreign investment to the national laws of host countries. In this manner, BITs allow for the implementation of national development objectives relating to FDI, as expressed in national laws.

• **By allowing preferential treatment for developing countries.** Development considerations are more significant for some provisions such as admission, national treatment, expropriation and transfer of funds, than for others. Such provisions often introduce a number of qualifications, exemptions or derogations on account of the special development needs and objectives of the host country.

• **By actively promoting foreign investments.** BITs contain commitments to facilitate and encourage investment, although these do not normally involve concrete commitments from the home country.

• **By preventing major investment problems and resolving differences.** BITs put considerable emphasis on informal and formal means of dispute-settlement, so as to avoid major disruptions in investment relations that could have serious implications for the development process.

To ensure maximum developmental effects from BITs, the main challenge for developing countries is to find an appropriate balance between the formulation of provisions aimed at the protection of foreign investments and the formulation of provisions aimed at protecting their own interests, in situations where the former impinges on the latter. Whether this can be achieved within the structure and contents of BITs as described in this chapter, or whether it would require addressing issues in a different setting or including new issues, is, of course, a matter for the countries concerned to determine. (This matter is given some attention in the concluding chapter.)

Chapter IV

THE IMPACT ON FOREIGN DIRECT INVESTMENT

BITs are concluded by host countries to attract FDI. The objective of this chapter is to examine whether the conclusion of BITs does indeed contribute to an increase in FDI.[1] The reasons why the conclusion of BITs should have a positive effect on FDI were discussed in greater detail in chapter I; the most important reasons are that BITs strengthen the standards of protection and treatment of foreign investors, facilitate entry into a host country and establish mechanisms for dispute settlement.

Before moving to the statistical analysis, a number of caveats need to be made.

• FDI is a highly sophisticated international transaction, which involves (unlike, say, trade transactions) the engagement of often considerable assets abroad, a long-term commitment and all the usual requirements for a successful investment project (such as good prospects for sustainable profitability and acceptable risk/profitability ratios). No single determinant therefore explains FDI flows. Typically, many conditions and requirements must be met for an investment project to take place, and it is sometimes difficult to identify the conditions which play a decisive role.

• To make matters more complicated, the relative importance of these conditions (and thus the importance of FDI determinants, including BITs) differs according to the type of investment (e.g. natural resources-seeking or market-seeking), the type of investor (e.g. services or manufacturing transnational corporations (TNCs), small and medium-sized or large TNCs), and the perspective from which they are viewed (that of the home or host country). Nevertheless, the literature identifies a number of determinants as more important than others in influencing FDI flows (UNCTC, 1992). Some of these determinants will be included in the analysis that follows.

---

[1] The relationship could also work the other way around: existing FDI can stimulate BITs. Agencies responsible for international economic relations in developed countries report occasionally that they are encouraged by firms to conclude BITs with host countries in which they have already invested.

- The conclusion of BITs by host countries is only one element in a wide spectrum of policies dealing with FDI and, as such, is only one among many policy determinants. FDI, especially in developing countries, has often been governed by special investment codes. It is also influenced, in all countries, by internal regulations concerning the conduct of business, such as tax codes, subsidies and foreign exchange regulations. Indeed, many of the policy changes in recent years aimed at attracting FDI – such as the liberalization of FDI policies and the relaxation of performance requirements – have taken place alongside the growth of BITs. However, policies themselves, especially liberalization policies, though they are undoubtedly a necessary precondition for FDI (since without them, FDI projects could not be undertaken), have only little influence on investment flows (UNCTC, 1991, pp. 59–60).[2]

- The convergence of the FDI policies of host countries and the promotion of FDI, including through the conclusion of BITs, somewhat neutralizes the advantage that host countries with more liberalized policies and more advanced promotional efforts once enjoyed over other countries, thus reducing the importance of policies, including BITs, as FDI determinants and increasing the importance of other factors.

- Finally, the function of BITs can be fulfilled by other instruments, such as regional agreements.

A. Theoretical considerations: a two-stage analysis

The analysis that follows is based on the theoretical argument that, for the reasons outlined above, the conclusion of a BIT between two countries – a developed country and a developing country or a country in transition – may have an impact on FDI flows (or other measures of TNC investment) from a developed country (the home country) to a developing country or a country in transition (the host country) in the years following the conclusion of the BIT.

There is no commonly accepted theory of the response lag of investors to policy changes, including to the conclusion of BITs. Some studies (e.g. UNCTC, 1991) that have traced the response of investors to changes in government policy announcements suggest a quick response of one to two years. Others (e.g. Kreinin, Plummer and Abe, 1997) suggest a longer lag of up to five years. There is evidence from the trade area that firms may anticipate policy changes such as trade policy liberalization and increase their exports before the changes occur. For example, trade among member countries of the European Economic Community had accelerated even before the Treaty of Rome establishing it had come into force. To deal with this issue, different lags (including a zero lag and negative lags) will be examined to find the best statistical fit. To allow this, the behaviour of FDI flows will be examined during the five years before and the five years after the conclusion of a BIT.

As regards the choice between the two possible dates of the conclusion of a BIT – the date of signing and the date of ratification – the former has been selected as an independent variable for the analysis. As the great majority of BITs are ratified, it is reasonable to assume that, in the perception of investors, signing a BIT is the crucial action: once a BIT is signed, or expected to be signed, the market has absorbed it or begins to absorb it.

---

[2] It should be noted, however, that it is very difficult to measure policy changes in the area of FDI, including changes in the degree of liberalization and degree of openness to FDI. Therefore, analyses of the impact of liberalization and other policy changes on FDI flows are not very precise.

This theoretical argument and the resulting selection of variables is obviously based on certain simplifying assumptions and, therefore, is not necessarily watertight. For example:

- It cannot be ruled out that a BIT continues to have an impact on FDI flows as long as it is in force, and not just during the five years after its conclusion.[3] BITs may also prevent declines in FDI, by keeping existing investors in the host country.

- The argument treats all BITs as equal, but in fact they may differ in scope and force, and thus in their importance to investors.

- BITs with identical clauses may have a different "enforcement value" for TNCs from different home countries, depending on the strength of a corporation's home Government (Conklin and Lecraw, 1997).

The hypothesis examines the relationship between BITs and FDI flows in the most direct way, by examining the FDI flows between the countries concerned. It will be tested in two stages:

(1) In *stage one* of the analysis, the relationship is tested by using FDI data covering 11 years for individual BITs. Such data are available for 200 BITs signed between 14 home and 72 host countries, and make it possible to draw meaningful conclusions about the relationship, even though over 1,100 BITs and many participating countries are excluded from the analysis.

(2) In order to expand the coverage of BITs and countries, additional analysis is undertaken in *stage two* on the basis of data on total FDI flows and stocks of host countries and, for some dependent variables, on the total number of BITs. As these two variables are more easily available than information on bilateral FDI flows, the number of host countries covered rises to 133, with a corresponding increase in the number of BITs covered.

The modification of variables, by introducing total FDI stocks and flows and a cumulative number of BITs, also modifies the theoretical argument. For example, a possible relationship between the total number of BITs and total stock of FDI is based on the assumption that countries with a greater number of BITs receive more bilateral flows from home countries with which they have concluded these BITs than countries with a smaller number of BITs and that, consequently, these higher flows lead to larger stocks, either in absolute terms or relative to the size of their economies. By the same token, if total flows of FDI are taken as the dependent variable, the assumption is that countries with a greater number of BITs signed during the period under consideration receive more bilateral flows and that this is reflected in their total flows (in absolute or relative terms).

In stage two, an additional question is raised, namely: if the effect of BITs on FDI is weak, or non-existent, what other variables have a greater influence on FDI? These variables might include host countries' market size and growth, country-risk indices, changes in exchange rates, inflation rates, and capital investment. Moreover, by relating total stock of FDI to the total number of BITs of host countries, stage two avoids one of the weaknesses of stage one, whereby consideration of the impact is limited to a period of 11 years.

---

[3] This may happen for a number of reasons. For example, a host country signing a BIT may not yet be able to offer the other locational advantages that are necessary to attract FDI; once it is able to offer these advantages, FDI may rise. Also, in a number of former centrally planned economies which already had BITs with home countries, the flow of FDI only became noticeable when these countries began the transition process.

B. Stage one: analysis of time-series data for individual bilateral investment treaties

1. Data and methodology

In this stage of the analysis, the focus is on changes in FDI flows between pairs of countries as a result of the signing of BITs. The analysis of FDI flows between pairs of countries over several years provides a time-based perspective that the subsequent, cross-country analysis in stage two cannot give. As already mentioned, obtaining bilateral FDI data in connection with individual BITs is not easy. The 200 observations that were collected refer to the bilateral flows between 72 FDI-recipient countries and 14 home countries during the period 1971–1994. They were obtained from a variety of sources, including UNCTAD's FDI/TNC database, the Organisation for Economic Co-operation and Development and the Governments or central banks of some developed countries.

Four FDI indicators will be used as dependent variables:

(1)   *FDI*: FDI flows between the pair of countries that have signed BITs (in millions of dollars).

(2)   *FDI/gross domestic product (GDP)*: the ratio of FDI over GDP of the host country. The FDI/GDP ratio corrects the imbalance created by large countries in a data set. It supplements an FDI growth index based on absolute figures by relating it to a host country's economic growth.

(3)   *FDI/inflow*: the share of a home-country partner to a BIT in a host country's total FDI inflow. For example, if Zambia and Japan sign a BIT and Japan's share in Zambia's FDI inflows increases, one can suggest that the BIT is associated with Japan's increased share of FDI in Zambia.

(4)   *FDI/outflow*: the share of a particular host country in a home country's total FDI outflows. For example, if Mali and France sign a BIT and Mali's share in France's total FDI outflow increases, one can suggest that the BIT is associated with Mali's increased share in France's FDI outflows.

Since FDI flows have been increasing generally for most countries over time, especially in the past decade, it may be argued that higher absolute FDI figures in the years following a BIT may only reflect the general rising trend, and not specifically the impact of a BIT. The addition of the two share variables (which are based on relative rather than absolute figures) is intended to correct this bias. If either of these increases follows the signing of a BIT, and is statistically significant, then one is on firmer ground in asserting that it is the BIT that is associated with the increase, rather than the general increase in FDI.

For each pair of BIT countries, the data on these four variables were recorded for five years before and five years after the BIT was signed. For each pair, Year 0 is called the BIT year; the data go from Year –5 to Year +5, as follows:

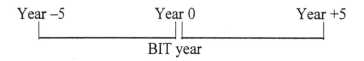

As the data for a single pair of countries generate a set of observations which is too small to allow for statistical testing, testing has to be done for the entire set of observations and for groups of countries. For each before/after BIT comparison, a T-test of differences in group means was conducted to test for significant differences. While simple, this is a robust technique (even given a moderate amount of missing data). Since the hypothesis is that BITs increase FDI, a one-tailed T- test is appropriate.

The main objective is to determine how the mean values of FDI in the years before a BIT was signed compare with the mean values of FDI in the years after the BIT was signed. However, as mentioned earlier, it is not known exactly when investors begin to react to the signing of a BIT: hence, to determine also any lags (or advance reactions) in the effects of BITs, the mean values of dependent variables for 200 BITs were grouped in various combinations of two time periods, each resulting from different possible splits of the 11 years covered by the analysis. This included not only combinations of data for the years before and after the BIT year (thus using the BIT year as a cut-off date) but also combinations using other cut-off years, comparing, for example, the period between Year –4 and Year +1 with the period between Year +2 and Year +5. The comparisons thus involve periods of varying length before and after the cut-off year, with a minimum of two and a maximum of five years on either side. A total of 54 pairs of time periods (before and after combinations, using different cut-off points) were tested on the basis of the 200 observations. The 200 observations were also divided up by region (Africa; Central and Eastern Europe; South, East and South-East Asia; Latin America and the Caribbean; and West Asia) to examine any regional effect. Similar tests were done for each region.

Thus, for each set of tests, and for each of the four dependent variables indicated above, there is a maximum of 54 comparisons of group means. Two salient questions were asked in these tests: How many of the 54 tests in each category were statistically significant? And what time-lag for investors' reaction to the signing of BITs can be deduced from the pattern of statistically significant results?

2. Results

(a) *The overall pattern of significant T-tests*

The results of the tests examining the association between the signing of a BIT and FDI flows, presented in table IV.1 and, in greater detail, in annex table IV.1, can be summarized as follows:

- The results are not strong,[4] but are consistent enough over all four variables (FDI, FDI/GDP, FDI/inflow, and FDI/outflow) to suggest that BITs have an effect on FDI. Of the four variables, FDI/inflow and FDI/outflow registered the largest number of statistically significant results. This suggests that BITs may serve, at the margin, to redirect the share of FDI from /to BIT signatories.

- When all countries are taken together, the strongest results are obtained in the FDI/inflow category, where 37 of the 54 tests were significant (table IV.1 and annex table IV.3). The negative sign for the difference appears because, as was expected, the FDI share before a BIT was lower than the FDI share after it. The consistent negative sign in this category (and indeed in virtually all the results in other annex tables containing the results of stage two) indicates a noticeable, if weak, effect.

---

[4] One could argue that significance between the 0.05 and 0.10 level is somewhat weak. However, its use is common for many similar studies. Moreover, T-tests of differences in group means are a robust and unambiguous enough technique that a significance level of 0.10 or over is acceptable.

Table IV.1. Comparison of means for the FDI/inflow variable[a]

Test number	Mean FDI share for period	Mean FDI share for period	Difference	P[b]
1	2 years before BIT to 1 year before BIT	BIT year to 1 year after BIT	-7720.2	.033*
2	2 years before BIT to 1 year before BIT	BIT year to 2 years after BIT	-10992.5	.029*
3	2 years before BIT to 1 year before BIT	BIT year to 3 years after BIT	-13483.3	.050*
4	2 years before BIT to 1 year before BIT	1 year after BIT to 2 years	-15413.1	.041*
5	2 years before BIT to 1 year before BIT	1 year after BIT to 3 years	-17639.4	.065*
6	2 years before BIT to 1 year before BIT	1 year after BIT to 4 years	-12680.6	.054*
7	2 years before BIT to 1 year before BIT	2 years after BIT to 3 years	-21609.4	.061*
8	2 years before BIT to 1 year before BIT	2 years after BIT to 4 years	-14304.8	.057*
9	2 years before BIT to 1 year before BIT	2 years after BIT to 5 years	-9152.2	.083*
10	3 years before BIT to 1 year before BIT	BIT year to 1 year after BIT	-1830.7	.073*
11	3 years before BIT to 1 year before BIT	BIT year to 2 years after BIT	-8101.6	.048*
12	3 years before BIT to 1 year before BIT	BIT year to 3 years after BIT	-10600.5	.080*
13	3 years before BIT to 1 year before BIT	1 year after BIT to 2 years	-12345.4	.064*
14	3 years before BIT to 1 year before BIT	1 year after BIT to 3 years	-14627.9	.093*
15	3 years before BIT to 1 year before BIT	1 year after BIT to 4 years	-9761.5	.095*
16	3 years before BIT to 1 year before BIT	2 years after BIT to 3 years	-18054.9	.083*
17	3 years before BIT to 1 year before BIT	2 years after BIT to 4 years	-10928.4	.097*
18	4 years before BIT to 1 year before BIT	BIT year to 1 year after BIT	-8812.8	.041*
19	4 years before BIT to 1 year before BIT	BIT year to 2 years after BIT	-11814.9	.024*
20	4 years before BIT to 1 year before BIT	BIT year to 3 years after BIT	-14205.5	.042*
21	4 years before BIT to 1 year before BIT	1 year after BIT to 2 years	-16240.7	.033*
22	4 years before BIT to 1 year before BIT	1 year after BIT to 3 years	-18380.3	.055*
23	4 years before BIT to 1 year before BIT	1 year after BIT to 4 years	-13556.0	.049*
24	4 years before BIT to 1 year before BIT	2 years after BIT to 3 years	-22335.6	.047*
25	4 years before BIT to 1 year before BIT	2 years after BIT to 4 years	-15254.9	.049*
26	4 years before BIT to 1 year before BIT	2 years after BIT to 5 years	-10250.8	.097*
27	2 years before BIT to BIT year	1 year after BIT to 3 years	-49261.3	.095*
28	2 years before BIT to BIT year	2 years after BIT to 3 years	-19323.1	.046*
29	2 years before BIT to BIT year	2 years after BIT to 4 years	-13094.7	.042*
30	2 years before BIT to BIT year	2 years after BIT to 5 years	-8684.9	.073*
31	3 years before BIT to BIT year	2 years after BIT to 3 years	-17985.2	.055*
32	3 years before BIT to BIT year	2 years after BIT to 4 years	-11819.9	.060*
33	4 years before BIT to BIT year	1 year after BIT to 2 years	-49583.2	.094*
34	4 years before BIT to BIT year	1 year after BIT to 3 years	-50635.2	.087*
35	4 years before BIT to BIT year	2 years after BIT to 3 years	-21321.0	.033*
36	4 years before BIT to BIT year	2 years after BIT to 4 years	-15152.2	.032*
37	4 years before BIT to BIT year	2 years after BIT to 5 years	-10775.1	.065*

[a] 37 out of 54 comparisons were significant as shown in annex table IV.3.
[b] * Significant at the 0.10 level (one-tailed T-test); **Significant at the 0.05 level (one-tailed T-test).

- The fact that FDI/inflow and FDI/outflow produced more significant results than FDI alone or the FDI/GDP ratio is gratifying, since the share measures are better measures of the role of BITs than the other two variables.

- In terms of specific regions, BITs signed by African countries appear to have more effect than BITs in other regions. In particular, the share of FDI inflows from a particular home country is more likely to be affected by the conclusion of BITs when the host country is an African country (annex table IV.1). This suggests that BITs are relatively more significant in redirecting FDI flows when the host countries are least developed or perceived by investors as environments with a higher risk. However, this is only a hypothesis, and would need to be tested further.

- Central and Eastern Europe is another region where BITs appear to have an influence, as measured by some variables. In particular, when FDI is used as the dependent variable (annex table IV.6), half of the comparisons are significant, especially those with a greater lagged response. This is further discussed below.

- In the case of South, East and South-East Asia, BITs may be instrumental in redirecting the share of FDI outflows from home countries (annex table IV.1).

(b) Time-lag effects

By examining for which time periods comparisons are significant, one may deduce the lag response between BIT signing (Year 0) and FDI response. The data for the FDI/inflow variable for all countries reveal no clear pattern in the various significant results (table IV.1 and annex table IV.3). On the other hand, the test on the FDI variable for all countries (annex table IV.2) shows significant results only in Year +2. In the case of Africa, the FDI/GDP variable exhibits a similar pattern (annex table IV.4): comparisons involving the period starting in Year +2 are the main ones that show significance. However, in the case of the FDI/inflow variable, again for Africa, the significant entries are in Year +1 or Year 0. Finally, in Central and Eastern Europe (annex table IV.6), the pattern of significant entries is again found in comparisons starting in Year +2.

As the results are rather mixed, only a tentative conclusion can be drawn, namely, that the response lag after the signing of a BIT may be as little as zero, but is more likely to be two years.

C. Stage two: cross-sectional analysis

In this stage, a cross-sectional analysis of the determinants of FDI, including BITs as an explanatory variable, was performed for 133 host countries (annex table IV.7). As most BITs were signed in the 1990s, the analysis was based on total FDI flows and stocks for the year 1995, with data for explanatory variables going back three years (1993 to 1995). As mentioned earlier, the objective is two-fold. First, it is to test anew the relationship between BITs and FDI flows based on a larger sample of countries and BITs than it was possible to assemble for stage one. To the extent that some of the regressions will test the relationship between the total number of BITs signed by host countries and their total stock of FDI, this will give a maximum possible coverage of the BITs tested, at the cost, however, of using a less perfect dependent variable than bilateral FDI flows. The second objective is to introduce other explanatory variables pertaining to the characteristics of host countries. Moreover, in relating total FDI flows in 1995 to the BITs signed between 1993 and 1995, one can double check the time-lag effects.[5]

1. Selection of explanatory variables

The effect of BITs on FDI did not turn out to be very significant in the stage-one analysis. Even if it had been significant, BITs may have a weaker influence on FDI flows than other FDI determinants; hence the need to introduce other independent variables. The literature on FDI determinants divides them broadly into firm-level determinants (see, for example, Pygal, 1981) and country-specific determinants (see, for example, Lunn, 1983). The literature on country-specific determinants, in turn, is divided into explanations of patterns of outward FDI from one home country (see, for example, Scaperlanda and Balough, 1983) and cross-sectional analyses comparing inward FDI flows from all sources across a sample of host countries. The analysis here focuses on the latter type of variables, using host-country-specific variables commonly found in the literature to explain inflows of FDI to host countries, such as market size and growth, exchange rate changes, inflation, capital formation and country risk.

(a)   *Market size*

The size of the host-country market is one of the most frequently used variables in the literature. It was found significant as an explanatory variable in a number of empirical studies (Kravis and Lipsey, 1982; Scaperlanda and Balough, 1983; UNCTC, 1991; UNCTAD, 1993; and Kreinin, Plummer and Abe, 1997). A large market permits firms, including foreign firms, to achieve scale and scope economies; simply, it can accommodate more firms and more investments than small markets. The notion that FDI and market size should correlate positively is not automatic. If a country with a large market restricts or excludes FDI, as was until recently the case with large markets of the former centrally planned economies, it would be futile to test the FDI/market size correlation. Second, the argument of market size applies only to FDI oriented towards the local market, and not to extractive, or export-platform-motivated investments intended for markets other than the country in question. Third, operationalizing the market-size measure with GDP or equivalent measures (as most studies do) leaves the analysis open to all the limitations of GDP as a surrogate for market size. Nevertheless, despite such caveats, market size is considered one of the most prominent determinants of FDI inflows in the literature.

(b)   *Market growth*

Apart from market size per se, change in market size, typically measured by change in GDP, is another explanatory variable used in several studies (Lunn, 1983; Julius, 1990; Kreinin, Plummer and Abe, 1997). As growth is a magnet for firms, including TNCs, a high growth rate in a host country tends to stimulate investment by both domestic and foreign producers. Thus, FDI flows are hypothesized to respond to economic growth. Conversely, a slowdown in economic growth (or a decrease in GDP) is expected to slow down or reduce investment, including FDI. It has to be noted that the GDP growth variable has not always produced consistent results.

---

[5] The results for another year (such as 1994) would be roughly comparable, as far as the overall conclusions are concerned.

(c)   *Change in the exchange rate*

In pure theory, with exchange rates indexed to purchasing power parity, the exchange rate variable should have no effect on FDI-flow motivations. However, persistent deviations of actual exchange rates from purchasing power parity are well known. More pertinently, a sharp devaluation creates an opportunity for foreign investors to buy assets in the country cheaply. On this argument alone, a devaluation should be followed by a subsequent rise in FDI inflows into the country. However, the true picture is much more complicated, because a local currency devaluation also affects the future expected profit stream of foreign investors, as measured in their own currencies, in ways that are by no means uniform. Export-oriented investments benefit (but only so long as the currency remains relatively undervalued). The profits of local-market-oriented investments, as measured in the foreign investor's currency, may suffer for a temporary or prolonged period, until price increases can be passed on to local customers, but this depends on relative inflation, macroeconomic demand conditions accompanying the devaluation, and the price elasticity for the product in question. Hence a uniform hypothesis, applicable to all countries, is not advisable. Moreover, sharp devaluations are sporadic: there is therefore no a priori reason to expect a change in the exchange rate variable to show up as significant, especially in a cross-sectional study covering one year at a time. Nevertheless, since some studies (e.g. Froot and Stein, 1991) have found devaluations to be significant in explaining FDI flows, it was felt worthwhile to include this variable in this study.

(d)   *Inflation*

Once again, assuming the theory of purchasing power parity is working – that is, that relative inflation is reflected in continuous adjustments in the exchange rate – the inflation variable ought not, in theory, to be a significant explanation for FDI flows. However, high inflation may be perceived as reflecting macroeconomic instability resulting from mismanagement; moreover, by heightening economic uncertainty, it can by itself be a deterrent to investors. For this reason, a negative relationship can be hypothesized between inflation and FDI.

(e)   *Rate of capital formation*

The rate of domestic capital formation can be used to explain FDI flows (UNCTAD, 1993). There should be a complementary relationship between FDI inflows and the rate of domestic investment as a proportion of GDP: "the hypothesis is that economies or regions that invest a high proportion of their GNP in plant and equipment are likely to be attractive markets for foreign investors seeking to increase their participation through the acquisition of existing firms or the establishment of greenfield operations" (UNCTAD, 1993, p. 10). Thus, this variable is an extension of the arguments on market size and growth. On the other hand, one could also think that FDI projects might be a substitute for domestic investment projects on the grounds of their higher efficiency – a substitution more likely to take place in smaller economies. Therefore, a negative association between the two may be expected.

(f)   *Country risk*

Both a priori reasoning, as well as the results of previous studies (e.g. Green and Cunningham, 1975; Schneider and Frey, 1985) indicate that, all other things being equal, the higher the perceived risk associated with a country, the lower the FDI flows to that country. Risk scores for a country are based on political, economic or financial criteria that rating agencies try to apply uniformly across countries. Instead of the word "risk" (which can be misleading), such scores are often better regarded as indexes of the quality of a country's investment climate. The operationalization of the country-risk variable remains rather varied, depending on the agency that compiles the comparative data on the risk profiles of countries. Examples of agencies that supply such ratings include the Economist Intelligence Unit, Frost and Sullivan, the PRS Group and Moody's. Typically, risk scores for countries are calibrated on a 0 to 100 scale, although some agencies use a letter format (A, B, C, etc.). In general, the hypothesis in previous studies is that country risk is negatively associated with FDI.

(g)   Other variables

A few additional variables have been used occasionally in other studies, such as comparative labour rates, human capital (skills) and infrastructure development. For the most part, these variables are more relevant to certain industries, or to particular types of investments such as export-oriented FDI, and not to a study such as this one, encompassing large numbers of countries and all sectors combined. On infrastructure, which is coming under increasing scrutiny as a possible bottleneck to FDI, there is unfortunately no large-scale comparative index that can be applied across a large group of host countries. However, some risk-rating agencies attempt to include infrastructure in their assessment of a country's "economic" risk score.

(h)   Summary of hypotheses

For each of the explanatory variables discussed above, a positive or negative sign in the parenthesis indicates its hypothesized relationship to FDI (box IV.1).

FDI is expected to be positively associated with BITs, market size, market growth and exchange rate devaluation; it is expected to be negatively associated with inflation and political risk.[6] The relationship between FDI and capital investment is hypothesized to be bi-directional.

Box IV.1.   Summary of variables and their expected impact on FDI

FDI = **f** [BITs (+); market size (+); market growth (+); devaluation of exchange rate (+); inflation (–); capital formation (?); country risk (–)]

The relationship between FDI and these variables is hypothesized to be stronger with a lag of one to two years (following the results of UNCTC, 1991), although other studies propose longer lags. Thus, for example, the values of independent variables in 1994 would be expected to have the strongest relationship with FDI in 1995.

2.   Definitions of variables

(a)   Dependent variables

Data on FDI have been operationalized in terms of FDI flows and FDI stocks. In addition to the absolute value of FDI flows and stocks, both variables were normalized by population and GDP. This was done to correct for the effect of large countries, and to see how BITs affect not just

---

[6] However, note that some rating agencies (such as the PRS Group) invert the scale, using a minimum of 1 for the most "risky" nation and a maximum of 100 points for the least "risky" country. In effect, the scale then is one describing a favourable investment climate.

FDI, but FDI per unit of GDP (or FDI per capita) across countries. Finally, the dependent variable is expressed in terms of its growth rate to see if the growth rate is affected by BITs or other variables.

Each of the dependent variables (table IV.2) is regressed (one at a time) against the explanatory variables (table IV.3).

Table IV.2. List of dependent variables

	Variable (and abbreviation)	Unit
A.	*FDI flows into host country*	
	Absolute flow (Flow)	Millions of dollars
	Flow per capita (Fper)	Dollars
	Flow per $1 000 GDP (Fgdp$)	Dollars
	Flows growth (Fgrow)	Change over previous year (percentage)
B.	*FDI stock in host country*	
	Absolute stock (Stock)	Millions of dollars
	Stock per capita (Sper)	Dollars
	Stock per $1 000 GDP (Sgdp$)	Dollars
	Stock growth (Sgrow)	Change over previous year (percentage)

(b)   *Independent variables*

The principal explanation for FDI that is being tested is its link with BITs. These treaties are measured in four different ways: the number of BITs signed by a host country in a particular year; the total number a host country has signed up to and including that year; BITs per million of population; and BITs per billion dollars of GDP. Tests will reveal which of these measures are best able to explain FDI flows from a statistical point of view.

Table IV.3. List of independent variables

Explanatory variables (FDI host country)	Description
BITs	Number of BITs signed in a particular year by a host country
Cumulative BITs	Total number of BITs signed up to and including that year
BITs per capita	BITs per million of population
BITs as a ratio of GDP	BITs per billion of GDP in dollars
GDP in dollars	GDP in local currency/exchange rate, in millions of dollars
GDP growth	Change over previous year, as a percentage
GDP per capita in dollars	GDP/population
Population	Population, in millions
Capital investment	Value of gross fixed capital formation, in billions of dollars
Exchange rate	Amount of local currency per dollar, average annual rate
Change in the exchange rate	Change over previous year, as a percentage. Exchange rates in local currency units per dollar
Inflation rate	Annual change in consumer prices, as a percentage
Political rating for country	100 = best investment rating; 1 = worst
Economic rating	100 = best investment rating; 1 = worst
Financial rating	100 = best investment rating; 1 = worst
Composite country rating	100 = best investment rating; 1 = worst

At the same time, other explanatory variables will be tested, in case the BIT variables fail to provide an adequate explanation. These variables include population and various GDP measures such as indexes of market size and growth. Measures for the GDP variable that will be used, one at a time, include the absolute size of GDP, GDP growth and GDP per capita. Other FDI determinants include capital investment measured by the value of gross fixed capital formation in a host country and the inflation rate measured by the consumer price index. Finally, investors' perceptions of a country's investment environment (or, in other words, the risk rating for FDI) are shown on a scale ranging from 1 (worst environment or highest risk) to 100 (best environment or lowest risk), broken down for economic, political and financial ratings, and also presented as a composite score combining these three criteria. (For details on the criteria used to construct these country ratings, see annex table IV.9.) In the statistical analysis, these indicators of investment risk are not used simultaneously, but as alternatives.

3. Methodology

(a) Multivariate regression

Given that the hypotheses postulate a relationship between a dependent variable and multiple independent variables across countries, multiple linear regression was considered an appropriate statistical technique to use. Each of the dependent variables (table IV.2) was individually regressed against the independent variables (table IV.3).

For all independent variables loaded at once – using the stringent criterion that an entire row of data is eliminated if any entry for a country is missing – only 17 countries are left in the data pool. This is too small for any meaningful statistical analysis. To address this problem, statistical software packages have "missing value substitution" procedures[7]. These procedures may involve, for example, replacing missing data with the mean value for a variable. However, this kind of substitution lowers the confidence one can place in the results of a study.

An often better alternative to the problem of missing data is to use stepwise multiple regression, where independent variables are loaded in steps, or one at a time, starting for instance, with the independent variable that has the strongest explanatory significance, followed by the independent variable that has the second-strongest explanatory significance, and so on. The statistical routine then stops at a point where only a subset of the most powerful of the explanatory variables are entered, and the rest are left out. Stepwise multiple regression, in a situation such as the one in this analysis, has three virtues:

(1)   Because not all the independent variables are entered, the problem of the missing data is reduced, and more cases are included in the analysis.

(2)   The technique serves to identify the subset of explanatory variables that is best able to explain statistically the dependent variable. In this analysis, it can serve to identify which of the nine or more explanatory variables were best in explaining FDI flows (table IV.3).

(3)   Most importantly for the purposes of this study, a stepwise regression that loaded the strongest independent variable first would tell whether BITs – as opposed to other FDI determinants – are the better explanation. That is to say, if the BIT variable is loaded first, this would indicate that, of all the variables, the BIT variable was the most statistically

---

[7] For this analysis, the Statistical Package for the Social Sciences was used.

important.[8] On the other hand, if the BIT variable is selected for entry in later steps, that would diminish its importance in relation to other FDI determinants, and if the BIT variable was not selected at all, then BITs could not be said to play an explanatory role for that particular regression run.

It should be emphasized that even without using the stepwise regression technique there are several independent variables that should not, a priori, be entered together. That is to say, some of the variables in table IV.3 are redundant, and may be used as alternatives to each other, but not together. As one example, country investment ratings are broken into several sub-categories, such as "political", "economic" and "financial." Scores were obtained for each country on each of these sub-variables. However, both in theory and in practice, it is difficult to disentangle political, financial and economic risks. Such distinctions may provide some value to investors who wish to track a country's performance over time, but in a study involving over a hundred countries, they may not be meaningful. Moreover, the sub-categories are often strongly correlated. Hence they may be used as alternatives to each other, one at a time.

Additional variations to the regressions involved the removal of three countries shown to be egregious outliers (China, Singapore, and Hong Kong Special Administrative Region of China)[9] and log transformation of independent variables (in case some exhibited a non-normal distribution). (Annex table IV.10 contains a breakdown of the 192 regressions performed (24 X 8).) Other variables, such as independent variables with mean value substitution, and regression runs on a regional basis (as shown in annex table IV. 11) raised the total number of regression runs to 264.

(b) Euclidean distance

In addition to the regression technique, n-dimensional Euclidean distance or "pattern analysis" was used to test for the relationship between FDI and the profile of countries in terms of these independent variables. This technique involves identifying a small top percentile of the countries in terms of FDI (or outcome variables) and determining the profile of this desired group in terms of the mean values of the independent variables. Once the desired profile is determined, then for each of the remaining countries (the sample countries) a distance measure is computed that measures the distance of each of these countries from the ideal profile in a multidimensional space. If the distance from the ideal profile is greater, then it is hypothesized that FDI will be lower; in other words, the correlation between distance and FDI is supposed to be negative and significant.

Distance is computed as a squared Euclidean distance. However, given the differences in the scales being used to measure the several independent variables (for instance, one variable could be in billions of dollars, while another is a percentage, or another a ratio), another measure, the Mahalanobis distance, is more appropriate. The Mahalanobis procedure first standardizes each variable by subtracting its mean and dividing it by its standard deviation, which reduces each variable to a comparable scale.

---

[8] However, this is a tentative deduction, since interaction effects combined with other variables and multicollinearity may sometimes cause a variable to be loaded in an early step even though it is weaker than the rest.

[9] Statistical practice often recommends removal of clear outliers in order to improve the statistics and thus the significance of remaining variables. This requires no a priori theory. However, *ex post*, one knows from similar FDI studies that China often stands out as a gross outlier. Hong Kong Special Administrative Region of China and Singapore also stand out in some studies because of the relatively small size of their populations.

```
┌─────────────────────────────────────────────────────────────────────┐
│                    Box IV.2.  Mahalanobis distance                    │
│                                                                       │
│                     n                                                 │
│       Distance =    Σ   ( x_sk - x̄_ik )/s.d._ik                       │
│                    k=1                                                │
│       where,  k = variable                                            │
│               n = number of variables                                 │
│               s = sample group, and i = ideal group                  │
│               s.d. = standard deviation and  x̄ = mean                 │
│                                                                       │
└─────────────────────────────────────────────────────────────────────┘
```

$$\text{Distance} = \sum_{k=1}^{n} (x_{sk} - \bar{x}_{ik})/\text{s.d.}_{ik}$$

4. Results

(a) Multivariate regression

For this stage of the analysis, eight different dependent variables referring to FDI in 1995 (table IV.2) were computed and regressed with independent variables for three years: 1995, 1994 and 1993 (table IV.3). This permitted a total of 192 regression runs, using a variety of techniques such as log-transformed variables, and the removal of outlier countries.

The salient results covering the stepwise regression method for all countries and untransformed variables on a normal basis are shown in table IV.4, while the 192 combinations and their methodological details are summarized in annex table IV.10. As discussed above, stepwise regression with forward inclusion is a technique that helps to identify the subset of explanatory variables that have the strongest significance, that is, explanatory power vis-à-vis the dependent variable. The technique enters variables one at a time, starting with the strongest until the adjusted R^2 stops growing or until minimum loading criteria can no longer be fulfilled to justify the loading of the rest. The subset of variables thus entered comprises the resultant regression equation. Table IV.4 shows the results for only three of the eight dependent variables – FDI flow, FDI stock and FDI/GDP ratio – because the results for the other five dependent variables were patchy (they are summarized in annex table IV.10).

In table IV.4, the order of loading of the independent variables is from left to right. The overall conclusion is that indexes of a host country's market size, such as population and GDP, are the leading determinants of FDI. It was only in equation 9 in table IV.4 that the BIT variable was loaded first. Overall, the BIT variable appears only twice in table IV.4. In general, these results suggest that BITs play only a secondary, and minor, role in cross-sectional analysis comparing a large number of countries with each other.

Looking at individual dependent variables, FDI flow (equations 1, 2 and 3) is consistently a function of population, GDP measured in dollars and capital investment. When regressed with lagged variables, the BIT variable for 1993 partially explains FDI flow with a two-year lag.

FDI stock (equations 4, 5 and 6) is also consistently a function of population, GDP measured in dollars and capital investment. Political risk in a country also seems to explain FDI stock in some contexts.

Results for Fgdp$ (FDI flow per $1,000 of GDP of the recipient country, in equations 7, 8 and 9) are not as strong. The equations' adjusted R^2 is lower, albeit highly significant. However in equation 9, BIT (93) is highly significant and by itself explains 50 per cent of the variation of Fgdp$, a higher score than the population independent variable.

Table IV.4. Regression results[a]

1. FDI flow (95) =	- 18.91	+ 25.16 Population (95)	+ 0.02 GDP$ (95)	- 45.89 Capital (95)	
	(-0.08)	(27.42)**	(5.53)**	(-3.94)**	
Adj. R² = 0.99	F = 651.87	P = 0.00			
2. FDI flow (95) =	- 0.63	+ 27.18 Population (94)	+ 0.02 GDP$ (94)	- 56.32 Capital (94)	
	(-0.003)	(28.87)**	(5.31)**	(-3.78)**	
Adj. R² = 0.99	F = 651.87	P = 0.00			
3. FDI flow (95) =	- 493.58	+ 25.63 Population (93)	+ 0.022 GDP$ (93)	- 52.53 Capital (93)	+ 162.74 Bit
	(-1.58)	(24.97)**	((5.97)**	(-3.88**)	(2.32)*
Adj. R² = 0.99	F = 661.53	P = 0.00			
4. FDI stock (95) =	52544.74	+ 0.43 GDP$ (95)	- 963.01 Capital (95)	- 868.54 Political rating (95)	
	(1.99)	(10.91)**	(- 6.79)**	(- 2.20)*	
Adj. R² = 0.95	F = 92.55	P = 0.00			
5. FDI stock (95) =	-4527.93	+ 0.50 GDP$ (94)	- 1230.34 Capital (94)	+ 49.98 Population (94)	
	(-1.61)	(10.32)**	(-7.17)**	(4.61)**	
Adj. R² = 0.95	F = 99.87	P = 0.00			
6. FDI Stock (95) =	- 3362.03	+ 0.49 GDP$ (93)	- 1187.80 Capital (93)	+ 34.90 Population (93)	
	(-1.38)	(11.20)**	(-7.26)**	(3.26)**	
Adj. R² = 0.96	F = 128.71	P = 0.00			
7. Fgdp$ (95) =	57,69	- 0.02 Population (95)	-1.16 Economic risk (95)		
	(2.94)*	(3.46)**	(-2.15)*		
Adj. R² = 0.55	F = 10.66	P = 0.002			
8. Fgdp$ (95) =	50.21	+ 0.03 Population (94)	-1.10 Economic risk (94)	+ 1.40 Bit (94)	
	(2.89)**	(3.32)**	(-2.44)*	(2.37)*	
Adj. R² = 0.72	F = 14.68	P = 0.002			
9. Fgdp$ (95) =	44.74	+ 1.86 Bit (93)	-0.94 Financial risk (93)	+ 0.02 Population (93)	
	(3.90)**	(2.81)*	(-3.21)**	(2.95)*	
Adj. R² = 0.75	F = 16.55	P = 0.001			

[a] The results represent stepwise regression and the variables are ordered in the sequence of highest contribution. In each regression result, the second row with numbers in parenthesis represents "t" values for the coefficients. Significance levels ** are at better than 0.01; * are at better than 0.05. Regressions were tried with each of the eight dependent variables for three years (1995, 1994 and 1993) and only these nine regressions had large enough R^2 and P values. All coefficients of independent variables are significant at the 0.05 level. For key to abbreviations of variables, see table IV.2.

Population and GDP, two indicators of market size, are positively and significantly associated with FDI flow and stock, as hypothesized. Capital investment is consistently, negatively and significantly associated with FDI flow and stock. Two alternative hypotheses regarding this variable have been put forward, as the literature is silent or ambivalent on this issue. One hypothesis (UNCTAD, 1993, p.10) suggests that a high rate of capital formation in a country – defined as gross fixed capital formation in billions of dollars for a particular year (table IV. 3) – taken as an indicator of economic activity and investment, could attract FDI to a country. That is to say, FDI and capital formation are complementary and positively associated. The alternative hypothesis is that FDI is a substitute for domestic capital formation, which suggests a negative association between the variables. The findings lend some credence to the latter hypothesis.

Political risk, while significant, is negatively correlated. Given the fact that the political risk factor was in increasing order of favourable conditions (a score of 1 being high risk and a score of 100 being low risk), the negative result does not support the hypothesis.

The BIT variable is significant in two of the nine regression equations, indicating than an increase in BITs is associated with an increase in FDI flows, but with a lag of two years. As regards the magnitude of its effect on the dependent variable in question, in equation 3 (which is for many countries grouped together), each BIT in 1993 can be said to be associated with an incremental $162 million in FDI flows in 1995. However, this is a statistical abstraction, in the sense of a fitted regression trend line for many countries, and not a policy conclusion. In the same vein, in equation 9, each BIT can be said to be associated with increasing the ratio of FDI to $1,000 of GDP of the host country by a factor of three. However, to reiterate the larger picture, BITs had a discernible effect in only two of the nine equations. In the other seven equations, the BIT variable failed to be loaded for lack of statistical significance – that is to say, BITs remain a very minor consideration overall.

Foreign direct investment, and especially FDI flows, can fluctuate from year to year, and thus distort calculations based on flow data for one year. To make up for this, an additional 27 regressions were made with dependent variables going back to 1993 and independent variables going back to 1991 (table IV.5). The only meaningful dependent variables turned out to be FDI flow, FDI stock and FDI/GDP. Other relative dependent variables did not produce meaningful relationships. As regards independent variables, the pattern of relationships that was revealed earlier for the dependent variables for 1995, was confirmed by these additional regressions for 1993 and 1994. GDP, population and capital were the most dominant variables. A weak relationship was also revealed between political, economic and financial risk and the BIT variable.

As the extension of the dependent variables to two additional years has not made a difference for the results, further analysis was based, again, on the 1995 data for dependent variables and 1993-1995 data for independent variables. The data were divided into five regions: Africa; Central and Eastern Europe; East and South-East Asia; Latin America and the Caribbean; and West Asia. Additional regression runs were performed on each region separately to see if there were any regional variations regarding the significance of BITs (annex table IV.11). BIT-related independent variables were frequently included in runs involving only one dependent variable, Flow (95), for all regions except West Asia. Moreover, because the division of data into regions resulted in incomplete data, a mean value substitution procedure had to be followed (since without one, no statistically significant results would have been obtained). However, not too much reliance can be placed in these results.

The overall conclusion from tables IV.4 and IV.5 (and annex tables IV.10 and IV.11) is that BITs play a minor and secondary role in a cross-country comparison of FDI determinants. In keeping with other studies (such as Scaperlanda and Balough, 1983; UNCTC, 1991; Kreinin, Plummer and Abe, 1997), market size appears to be the leading determinant of FDI flows.

(b)   N-dimensional pattern analysis

Pattern analysis measures the n-dimensional Euclidean distance for standardized variables, to a desired or ideal point. In this analysis, it measures the "distance" between a country and a desired subset of countries that exhibits high FDI flows. From this analysis one can deduce whether BITs are associated with high FDI flows.

Table IV.5.   Additional regression results [a]

1. FDI Flow (95) =	- 9310.21	+ 30.12 Population (92)	+ 158.73 Political risk (92)		
	(-3.51)**	(19.79)**	(3.88)**		
Adj. R^2 = 0.937	F = 195.86	P = 0.000			
2. FDI Flow (95) =	246.82	+ 27.75 Population (91)	+ 0.006813 GDP$ (91)		
	(0.680)	(17.207)**	(2.436)*		
Adj. R^2 = 0.947	F = 240.12	P = 0.000			
3. FDI Flow (94) =	- 1380.06	+ 14.95 Population (94)	+ 111.15 Bit (94)		
	(-1.824)*	(6.459)**	(3.251)**		
Adj. R^2 = 0.631	F = 36.09	P = 0.000			
4. FDI Flow (94) =	- 646.73	+ 89.34 Capital (93)	+ 9.28 Population (93)		
	(-0.94)	(4.99)**	(3.64)**		
Adj. R^2 = 0.720	F = 39.54	P = 0.000			
5. FDI Flow (94) =	- 621.40	+ 25.84 Population (92)	+ 0.16 GDP per capita (92)	+ 0.00658 GDP$ (92)	
	(-1.38)	(12.99)**	(2.30)*	(2.07)*	
Adj. R^2 = 0.932	F = 119.04	P = 0.000			
6. FDI Flow (94) =	- 280.25	+ 24.74 Population (91)	+ 0.01099 GDP$ (91)		
	(-0.76)	(15.12)**	(3.87)**		
Adj. R^2 = 0.940	F = 211.845	P = 0.000			
7. FDI Flow (93) =	- 620.08	+ 0.02084 GDP$ (93)	+ 8.20 Population (93)		
	(-1.19)	(5.80)**	(4.45)**		
Adj. R^2 = 0.773	F = 52.16	P = 0.000			
8. FDI Flow (93) =	- 6845.03	+ 22.14 Population (92)	+ 112.26 Political risk (92)	+ 0.02192 GDP$ (92)	- 64.99 Capital (92)
	(-2.92)**	(12.50)**	(2.99)**	(3.11)**	(-2.32)*
Adj. R^2 = 0.934	F = 92.49	P = 0.000			
9. FDI Flow (93) =	- 3460.99	+ 21.26 Population (91)	+ 0.03181 GDP$ (91)	- 87.02 Capital (91)	+ 56.10 Composite risk (91)
	(-2.39)*	(16.10)**	(4.66)**	(-3.41)**	(2.32)*
Adj. R^2 = 0.950	F = 129.166	P = 0.000			
10. FDI Stock (95) =	586.14	+ 0.16 GDP$ (92)	+ 41.38 Population (92)		
	(0.16)	(6.23)**	(2.49)*		
Adj. R^2 = 0.773	F = 45.23	P = 0.000			
11. FDI Stock (95) =	- 1715.11	+ 0.18 GDP$ (91)	+ 48.39 Population (91)		
	(-0.51)	(6.90)**	(3.20)**		
Adj. R^2 = 0.804	F = 56.30	P = 0.000			
12. FDI Stock (94) =	- 848.82	+ 0.12 GDP$ (94)			
	(-0.27)	(6.97)**			
Adj. R^2 = 0.537	F = 48.54	P = 0.000			
13. FDI Stock (94) =	- 43527.4	+ 0.37 GDP$ (93)	- 845.17 Capital (93)	+ 1244.82 Economic risk (93)	
	(-2.91)**	(6.18)**	(-3.83)**	(2.84)**	
Adj. R^2 = 0.794	F = 39.64	P = 0.000			
14. FDI Stock (94) =	- 12.27	+ 0.17 GDP$ (92)			
	(-0.00)	(8.41)**			
Adj. R^2 = 0.729	F = 70.79	P = 0.000			
15. FDI Stock (94) =	- 2249.36	+ 0.19 GDP$ (91)			
	(-0.69)	(8.98)**			
Adj. R^2 = 0.747	F = 80.64	P = 0.000			
16. FDI Stock (93) =	- 31993.9	+ 0.37 GDP$ (93)	- 909.82 Capital (93)	+ 1067.66 Economic risk (93)	- 1659.86 Bit (93)
	(-2.45)*	(7.36)**	(-4.97)**	(2.89)**	(-2.30)*
Adj. R^2 = 0.799	F = 30.85	P = 0.000			
17. FDI Stock (93) =	598.95	+ 0.14 GDP$ (92)			
	(0.18)	(7.35)**			
Adj. R^2 = 0.671	F = 54.07	P = 0.000			
18. FDI Stock (93) =	- 1624.61	+ 0.16 GDP$ (91)			
	(-0.55)	(8.21)**			
Adj. R^2 = 0.711	F = 67.41	P = 0.000			

[a]   Same as in table IV.4.

The pattern analysis results do not consistently support the hypothesis that a deviation from an ideal BIT profile will necessarily result in lower FDI levels. The results are not only mixed in direction, but also not very strong. This could be due to the fact that some of the variables are correlated among themselves.

Table IV.6. Pattern analysis correlation

Variable	Distance measure with 1994 variables[a]	Distance measure with 1995 variables[a]
Flow (95)	0.39*	0.58**
Stock (95)	0.48*	0.46*
Flow/GDP$ (95)	−0.14	−0.38*
Fgdp$ (95)	−0.28	−0.42*
Growth (95)	−0.05	0.38*

[a]   * Correlation significant at the 0.05 level (one-tailed). ** Correlation significant at the 0.01 level (one-tailed).

D. Conclusions

The time-series data analysis, based on bilateral FDI flows between the BIT signatory countries, shows that the influence of BITs on FDI is weak, especially in redirecting the share of FDI flowing from or to BIT signatory countries. In other words, following the signing of a BIT, it is more likely than not that the host country will marginally increase its share in the outward FDI of the home country; the same applies to the share of the home country in the FDI inflows of the host country. The effect, however, is usually small.

On the question of the time lag – that is, how long it takes for the effect, if any, of signing a BIT to materialize – the analysis can only supply a very tentative conclusion, namely, that, the response of foreign investors may be immediate but is more likely to occur in the three years following the signature of the BIT.

In the cross-country comparison of FDI determinants, the overall conclusion is that BITs appear to play a minor and secondary role in influencing FDI flows.[10] Other determinants of FDI flows, especially the size of a host country's market, are more important; this finding supports the results of several previous studies. Moreover, since some two-thirds of BITs have been concluded in the 1990s, the distinctive influence of a BIT, as a competitive signal to attract investment, may have been eroded. Rather, BITs are increasingly regarded by foreign investors as a normal feature of the institutional structure introduced in the past decade.

---

[10] To quote a paper prepared by the Government of Germany: "BITs definitely are not the condition sine qua non for foreign investors' decision" (Germany, 1997, p. 1). The same paper observes (on p. 3): "As many investors, however, postpone their investments until their establishment is protected by a BIT, the business community seems to be aware of additional benefits through these agreements." Similiarly, according to an expert from China: "We are often consulted by foreign investors and our own overseas investors on BITs, especially when a large amount of investment and investment in some sensitive sectors such as natural resources, public utilitities, are to be made" (China, 1997, pp. 5-6).

Annex tables to chapter IV

Annex table IV.1. Overview of stage one results[a]

	(1) FDI	(2) FDI/GDP	(3) FDI/inflow	(4) FDI/outflow
I. Global analysis: 72 host countries				
1. Full data set (200 observations)				
1.1 No adjustment (stringent criterion)	*(1)	*(1)	*(21)	*(6) **(3)
1.2 Missing value adjustment (non-stringent)	*(12) **(3)		*(21) **(16)	*(1)
1.3 Missing adjustment and replace ' - ' with ' 0 '	*(12) **(20) <1 year	*(3)	*(24)	
II. Regional analysis				
1. Africa				
1.1 No adjustment	*(5)	*(8) **(9)	*(2)	*(10) **(4)
1.2 Missing value adjustment	*(7)	*(5) , **(12)	*(26) **(3)	*(9)
1.3 Missing adjustment and replace ' - ' with ' 0 '			*(25) **(7)	*(8) **(1)
2. Central and Eastern Europe				
2.1 No adjustment	**(2)		*(3) **(1)	*(9) **(9)
2.2 Missing value adjustment	*(18) **(9)		*(15)	*(9)
2.3 Missing adjustment and replace ' - ' with ' 0 '	*(1) **(53)	*(2) **(51)		
3. South, East and South-East Asia				
3.1 No adjustment	*(9) **(1)	*(3) **(7)	*(3)	*(4) **(2)
3.2 Missing value adjustment	*(8)	*(2)		*(14)
3.3 Missing adjustment and replace ' - ' with ' 0 '	*(8)	*(2)		*(27) **(1)
4. Latin America and the Caribbean				
4.1 No adjustment	*(1)	*(2) **(2)		*(7) **(3)
4.2 Missing value adjustment	*(1)	*(1)		*(14) **(4)
4.3 Missing adjustment and replace ' - ' with ' 0 '				
5. West Asia				
5.1 No adjustment	*(1)	*(2)	*(1)	*(7) **(1)
5.2 Missing value adjustment				*(8)
5.3 Missing adjustment and replace ' - ' with ' 0 '				*(12)

[a] The shaded portions summarize information in annex tables IV.2, IV.3, IV.4, IV.5 and IV.6. Numbers in parentheses indicate the number of significant T-tests in each cell (out of a maximum number of 54 tests in each cell). * significant at the 0.1 level (one-tailed); ** significant at the 0.05 level (one-tailed). See also "General note" on following page.

(Annex table IV.1, cont'd)

General note:

   Missing data. The analysis in stage one is based on FDI-flow data for 200 BITs covering 11 years for each BIT. However, complete data covering the entire 11 year period do not exist for all 200 BITs. The missing data were not extensive, but the gaps were scattered throughout the data. To have used only data that were complete in every entry would have meant a large reduction in the number of observations, from 200 to less than 50. To avoid this, a special programme was used which supplies a mean value in lieu of the missing data. Since the extent of the missing data was not large (albeit pervasive), this substitution is acceptable, especially for as robust a test as a comparison of group means. The line "Missing value adjustment" refers to this situation. "No adjustment" refers to a situation in which the data are unadjusted, and a calculation is removed by the computer if a value is missing. This is a stringent approach and sometimes voids statistical results even if underlying patterns exist.

   In addition, in the OECD data set used, several entries are reported as a dash, which can indicate either a zero value or a missing entry. In most cases it is likely that the reason an entry is missing is because FDI flows were in fact zero, or near zero. In order to try and include a greater number of observations in the analysis, another set of calculations was made replacing the dash with a zero, referred to in the table as "Missing adjustment and replace '-' with '0'". Because of this uncertainty, results, if different, must be considered with caution.

   Numbers in parentheses. Each cell of the matrix for parts I and II of the table summarizes the results of 54 t-tests. The numbers in parentheses report how many of the 54 T-tests were significant. For example, the cell in row II.1.2 (on Africa) under column FDI/GDP shows that eight T-tests reached a 0.1 level of significance, and nine T-tests reached a 0.05 level of significance, giving a somewhat low total of 17 T-tests out of a maximum of 54. (This is a summary of information in annex table IV.4, which actually shows the statistics.) On the other hand, also for Africa, the FDI/inflow share variable shows as many as 29 tests out of 54 as being significant. (This summarizes information in annex table IV.5.) For all countries, the cell in row I.1.2 under the column for the FDI/inflow share variable shows that as many as 37 tests out of 54 were significant. (This summarizes information in annex table IV.3 and in table IV.1.)

Annex table IV.2. Global analysis: detailed results for dependent variable FDI

Comparison, number	Variable[a]	Means of first period	Means of second period	Difference[b]	P
1	b2b1 - 0a1	18.1	12.8	5.2	0.24
2	b2b1 - 0a2	17.6	14.2	3.3	0.33
3	b2b1 - 0a3	17.4	17.7	-0.3	0.48
4	b2b1 - a1a2	17.5	14.7	2.8	0.39
5	b2b1 - a1a3	17.2	20.5	-3.3	0.36
6	b2b1 - a1a4	17.1	21.3	-4.2	0.30
7	b2b1 - a2a3	19.6	27.5	-7.9	0.25
8	b2b1 - a2a4	19.3	27.1	-7.8	0.23
9	b2b1 - a2a5	19.0	29.2	-10.2	0.15
10	b3b1 - 0a1	15.9	12.7	3.3	0.32
11	b3b1 - 0a2	15.4	14.0	1.5	0.42
12	b3b1 - 0a3	15.3	17.4	-2.0	0.39
13	b3b1 - a1a2	15.0	14.5	0.6	0.48
14	b3b1 - a1a3	14.8	20.2	-5.5	0.28
15	b3b1 - a1a4	14.7	21.0	-6.3	0.23
16	b3b1 - a2a3	16.7	27.1	-10.4	0.19
17	b3b1 - a2a4	16.4	26.7	-10.2	0.17
18	b3b1 - a2a5	16.1	28.7	-12.5	0.11
19	b4b1 - 0a1	13.6	12.7	1.0	0.44
20	b4b1 - 0a2	13.1	14.0	-0.8	0.45
21	b4b1 - 0a3	13.1	17.3	-4.3	0.27
22	b4b1 - a1a2	14.0	14.6	-0.6	0.47
23	b4b1 - a1a3	13.8	20.3	-6.5	0.23
24	b4b1 - a1a4	13.7	21.1	-7.4	0.18
25	b4b1 - a2a3	15.6	27.0	-11.5	0.15
26	b4b1 - a2a4	15.3	26.6	-11.3	0.14
27	b4b1 - a2a5	15.1	28.5	-13.4	0.088*
28	b20 - a1a2	14.5	14.4	6.7	0.50
29	b20 - a1a3	14.3	19.7	-5.4	0.22
30	b20 - a1a4	14.2	20.4	-6.3	0.15
31	b20 - a2a3	15.4	25.4	-10.1	0.13
32	b20 - a2a4	15.2	25.2	-10.0	0.10
33	b20 - a2a5	14.9	26.8	-4.8	.055*
34	b30 - a1a2	13.2	14.3	-1.1	0.45
35	b30 - a1a3	13.1	19.6	-6.5	0.19
36	b30 - a1a4	13.0	20.3	-7.3	0.13
37	b30 - a2a3	14.0	25.3	-11.3	0.12
38	b30 - a2a4	13.8	25.0	-11.2	0.093*
39	b30 - a2a5	13.6	26.6	-13.0	0.054*
40	b40 - a1a2	12.6	14.2	-1.6	0.42
41	b40 - a1a3	12.4	19.4	-7.0	0.17
42	b40 - a1a4	12.4	20.2	-7.8	0.12
43	b40 - a2a3	13.4	25.1	-11.6	0.11
44	b40 - a2a4	13.3	24.8	-11.6	0.085*
45	b40 - a2a5	13.1	26.3	-13.2	0.052*
46	b2a1 - a2a3	14.2	24.5	-10.3	0.092*
47	b2a1 - a2a4	14.1	24.7	-10.6	0.057*
48	b2a1 - a2a5	13.9	26.5	-12.6	0.023**
49	b3a1 - a2a3	13.3	24.3	-11.0	0.090*
50	b3a1 - a2a4	13.2	24.5	-11.3	0.059*
51	b3a1 - a2a5	13.0	26.3	-13.4	0.027**
52	b4a1 - a2a3	12.9	24.2	-11.3	0.083*
53	b4a1 - a2a4	12.7	24.3	-11.6	0.057*
54	b4a1 - a2a5	12.6	26.1	-13.5	0.029**

* significant at the 0.10 level (one-tailed); ** significant at the 0.05 level (one-tailed).
[a] "b" refers to the years before, and "a" to the years after the signing of a BIT.
[b] Figures in this table have been rounded; the difference was calculated before rounding.

Annex table IV.3. Global analysis: detailed results for dependent variable FDI/inflows

Comparison, number	Variable[a]	Means of first period	Means of second period	Difference[b]	P
1	b2b1 - 0a1	-2573.0	5147.2	-7720.2	0.033**
2	b2b1 - 0a2	-2471.7	8510.7	-10992.5	0.029**
3	b2b1 - 0a3	-2430.0	11053.3	-13483.3	0.05**
4	b2b1 - a1a2	-2631.0	12782.0	-15413.1	0.041**
5	b2b1 - a1a3	-2554.2	15085.2	-17639.4	0.065*
6	b2b1 - a1a4	-2535.7	10144.9	-12680.6	0.054*
7	b2b1 - a2a3	-2965.5	18643.9	-21609.4	0.061*
8	b2b1 - a2a4	-2916.1	11388.7	-14304.8	0.057*
9	b2b1 - a2a5	-2868.3	6284.0	-9152.2	0.083*
10	b3b1 - 0a1	241.9	5072.6	-1830.7	0.073*
11	b3b1 - 0a2	231.9	8333.4	-8101.6	0.048**
12	b3b1 - 0a3	227.1	10827.7	-10600.5	0.080*
13	b3b1 - a1a2	247.3	12592.7	-12345.4	0.064*
14	b3b1 - a1a3	240.2	14868.1	-14627.9	0.093*
15	b3b1 - a1a4	238.5	10000.0	-9761.5	0.095*
16	b3b1 - a2a3	278.3	18333.2	-18054.9	0.083*
17	b3b1 - a2a4	273.7	11202.0	-10928.4	0.097*
18	b3b1 - a2a5	269.2	6182.6	-5913.4	0.19
19	b4b1 - 0a1	-3776.7	5036.1	-8812.8	0.041**
20	b4b1 - 0a2	-3595.6	8219.3	-11814.9	0.024**
21	b4b1 - 0a3	-3523.2	10682.3	-14205.5	0.042**
22	b4b1 - a1a2	-3831.8	12408.8	-16240.7	0.033**
23	b4b1 - a1a3	-3723.1	14657.2	-18380.3	0.055*
24	b4b1 - a1a4	-3696.9	9859.1	-13556.0	0.049**
25	b4b1 - a2a3	-4303.0	18032.6	-22335.6	0.047**
26	b4b1 - a2a4	-4233.6	11021.3	-15254.9	0.049**
27	b4b1 - a2a5	-4166.3	6084.5	-10250.8	0.097*
28	b20 - a1a2	-3030.0	45130.0	-4.8	0.10
29	b20 - a1a3	-2953.2	46308.0	-49261.3	0.095*
30	b20 - a1a4	-2934.7	41823.9	-44758.6	0.11
31	b20 - a2a3	-3381.3	15941.9	-19323.1	0.046**
32	b20 - a2a4	-3333.0	9761.8	-13094.7	0.042**
33	b20 - a2a5	-3286.0	5398.9	-8684.9	0.073*
34	b30 - a1a2	-1935.2	44838.8	-46774.0	0.11
35	b30 - a1a3	-1886.5	46016.8	-47903.3	0.10
36	b30 - a1a4	-1874.7	41562.5	-43437.2	0.12
37	b30 - a2a3	-2158.0	15827.2	-17985.2	0.055*
38	b30 - a2a4	-2127.4	9692.5	-11819.9	0.060*
39	b30 - a2a5	-2097.6	5361.2	-7458.8	0.12
40	b40 - a1a2	-5031.8	44551.4	-49583.2	0.094*
41	b40 - a1a3	-4906.2	45729.2	-50635.2	0.087*
42	b40 - a1a4	-4875.6	41304.3	-46179.9	0.10
43	b40 - a2a3	-5606.9	15714.1	-21321.0	0.033**
44	b40 - a2a4	-5527.9	9624.3	-15152.2	0.032**
45	b40 - a2a5	-5451.1	5323.9	-10775.1	0.065*
46	b2a1 - a2a3	35714.6	14965.8	20748.8	0.28
47	b2a1 - a2a4	35235.2	9172.1	26063.1	0.22
48	b2a1 - a2a5	34768.5	5077.1	29691.4	0.19
49	b3a1 - a2a3	35957.5	14864.7	21092.8	0.23
50	b3a1 - a2a4	35478.1	9111.0	26367.1	0.22
51	b3a1 - a2a5	35011.2	5043.7	29967.5	0.18
52	b4a1 - a2a3	32819.0	14765.0	18054.1	0.30
53	b4a1 - a2a4	32384.3	9050.6	23333.7	0.25
54	b4a1 - a2a5	31961.0	5010.8	26950.3	0.21

* significant at the 0.10 level (one-tailed); ** significant at the 0.05 level (one-tailed).
[a] "b" refers to the years before, and "a" to the years after the signing of a BIT.
[b] Figures in this table have been rounded; the difference was calculated before rounding.

Annex table IV.4. African region: detailed results for dependent variable FDI/GDP

Comparison, number	Variable[a]	Means of first period	Means of second period	Difference[b]	P
1	b2b1 - 0a1	0.03	-0.2	0.2	0.41
2	b2b1 - 0a2	0.03	-0.5	0.5	0.39
3	b2b1 - 0a3	0.03	0.4	-0.4	0.39
4	b2b1 - a1a2	0.04	-1.0	1.0	0.40
5	b2b1 - a1a3	0.04	0.4	-0.5	0.44
6	b2b1 - a1a4	0.04	1.6	-1.7	0.12
7	b2b1 - a2a3	-0.1	0.7	-0.8	0.39
8	b2b1 - a2a4	-0.1	2.6	-2.6	0.052*
9	b2b1 - a2a5	-0.1	1.7	-1.7	0.093*
10	b3b1 - 0a1	-0.2	-0.2	-0.1	0.46
11	b3b1 - 0a2	-0.2	-0.4	0.2	0.44
12	b3b1 - 0a3	-0.2	0.3	-0.6	0.33
13	b3b1 - a1a2	-0.3	-0.9	0.6	0.43
14	b3b1 - a1a3	-0.3	0.4	-0.6	0.40
15	b3b1 - a1a4	-0.3	1.4	-1.7	0.082*
16	b3b1 - a2a3	-0.3	0.6	-0.9	0.35
17	b3b1 - a2a4	-0.3	2.2	-2.5	0.036**
18	b3b1 - a2a5	-0.3	1.4	-1.7	0.063*
19	b4b1 - 0a1	-0.2	-0.2	0.0	0.47
20	b4b1 - 0a2	-0.2	-0.4	0.2	0.44
21	b4b1 - 0a3	-0.2	0.4	-0.6	0.32
22	b4b1 - a1a2	-0.2	-0.8	0.5	0.43
23	b4b1 - a1a3	-0.2	0.4	-0.6	0.39
24	b4b1 - a1a4	-0.2	1.4	-1.6	0.072*
25	b4b1 - a2a3	-0.2	0.7	-0.9	0.34
26	b4b1 - a2a4	-0.2	2.1	-2.4	0.032**
27	b4b1 - a2a5	-0.2	1.7	-2.0	0.030**
28	b20 - a1a2	0.7	-0.8	1.5	0.37
29	b20 - a1a3	0.7	0.4	0.2	0.47
30	b20 - a1a4	0.6	1.4	-0.8	0.30
31	b20 - a2a3	0.7	0.7	0.0	0.50
32	b20 - a2a4	0.6	2.2	-1.5	0.060*
33	b20 - a2a5	0.6	1.5	-0.8	0.27
34	b30 - a1a2	0.5	-0.7	1.2	0.38
35	b30 - a1a3	0.5	0.4	0.1	0.49
36	b30 - a1a4	0.5	1.3	-0.9	0.27
37	b30 - a2a3	0.5	0.6	-0.1	0.48
38	b30 - a2a4	0.5	2.0	-1.5	0.074*
39	b30 - a2a5	0.5	1.3	-0.9	0.24
40	b40 - a1a2	0.5	-0.7	1.2	0.38
41	b40 - a1a3	0.5	0.4	0.1	0.49
42	b40 - a1a4	0.5	1.3	-0.8	0.27
43	b40 - a2a3	0.5	0.6	-0.1	0.48
44	b40 - a2a4	0.5	2.0	-1.5	0.074*
45	b40 - a2a5	0.5	1.6	-1.2	0.17
46	b2a1 - a2a3	0.02	0.7	-0.7	0.37
47	b2a1 - a2a4	0.02	2.0	-2.1	0.029**
48	b2a1 - a2a5	0.02	1.4	-1.4	0.047**
49	b3a1 - a2a3	-0.1	0.6	-0.8	0.35
50	b3a1 - a2a4	-0.1	1.9	-2.1	0.025**
51	b3a1 - a2a5	-0.1	1.3	-1.5	0.038**
52	b4a1 - a2a3	-0.2	0.6	-0.8	0.35
53	b4a1 - a2a4	-0.1	1.9	-2.1	0.024**
54	b4a1 - a2a5	-0.1	1.6	-1.7	0.020**

* significant at the 0.10 level (one-tailed); ** significant at the 0.05 level (one-tailed).
[a] "b" refers to the years before, and "a" to the years after the signing of a BIT.
[b] Figures in this table have been rounded; the difference was calculated before rounding.

Annex table IV.5.   African region: detailed results for dependent variable FDI/inflows

Comparison, number	Variable[a]	Means of first period	Means of second period	Difference[b]	P
1	b2b1 - 0a1	-10605.5	16666.8	-27272.3	0.052*
2	b2b1 - 0a2	-10605.5	27272.8	-37878.3	0.051*
3	b2b1 - 0a3	-10605.5	39141.5	-49747.1	0.077*
4	b2b1 - a1a2	-11666.1	46666.7	-58332.8	0.064*
5	b2b1 - a1a3	-11666.1	58889.0	-70555.1	0.090*
6	b2b1 - a1a4	-11289.8	38709.8	-49999.6	0.076*
7	b2b1 - a2a3	-12068.4	55172.6	-67241.0	0.10
8	b2b1 - a2a4	-11666.1	35555.7	-47221.8	0.089*
9	b2b1 - a2a5	-11666.1	26666.7	-38332.8	0.078*
10	b3b1 - 0a1	-6060.3	16666.8	-22727.0	0.048**
11	b3b1 - 0a2	-5882.0	26470.6	-32352.6	0.058*
12	b3b1 - 0a3	-5882.0	37990.3	-43872.3	0.091*
13	b3b1 - a1a2	-6451.2	45161.4	-51612.6	0.073*
14	b3b1 - a1a3	-6451.2	56989.4	-63440.6	0.10
15	b3b1 - a1a4	-6249.6	37500.1	-43749.7	0.091*
16	b3b1 - a2a3	-6666.3	53333.5	-59999.8	0.12
17	b3b1 - a2a4	-6451.2	34408.7	-40859.9	0.11
18	b3b1 - a2a5	-6451.2	25806.5	-32257.7	0.10
19	b4b1 - 0a1	-9558.3	16176.6	-25734.8	0.031**
20	b4b1 - 0a2	-9285.2	25714.3	-34999.5	0.043**
21	b4b1 - 0a3	-9285.2	36904.9	-46190.0	0.075*
22	b4b1 - a1a2	-10155.7	43750.1	-53905.7	0.060*
23	b4b1 - a1a3	-10155.7	55208.5	-65364.1	0.089*
24	b4b1 - a1a4	-9847.9	36363.7	-46211.6	0.074*
25	b4b1 - a2a3	-10483.3	51613.0	-62096.3	0.11
26	b4b1 - a2a4	-10155.7	33333.4	-43489.1	0.091*
27	b4b1 - a2a5	-10155.7	25000.1	-35155.7	0.079*
28	b20 - a1a2	-2019.9	42424.3	4404.0	0.072*
29	b20 - a1a3	-2019.9	53535.5	-55555.3	0.10
30	b20 - a1a4	-1960.4	35294.2	-37254.6	0.090*
31	b20 - a2a3	-2083.0	50000.1	-52083.1	0.12
32	b20 - a2a4	-2019.9	32323.3	-34343.2	0.11
33	b20 - a2a5	-2019.9	24242.5	-26262.3	0.10
34	b30 - a1a2	-1470.3	41176.5	-42646.9	0.078*
35	b30 - a1a3	-1470.3	51960.9	-53431.2	0.11
36	b30 - a1a4	-1428.3	34285.8	-35714.1	0.098*
37	b30 - a2a3	-1514.9	48485.0	-49999.9	0.13
38	b30 - a2a4	-1470.3	31372.6	-32843.0	0.12
39	b30 - a2a5	-1470.3	23529.5	-24999.8	0.12
40	b40 - a1a2	-5440.7	41176.5	-46617.3	0.064*
41	b40 - a1a3	-5440.7	51960.9	-57401.6	0.096*
42	b40 - a1a4	-5285.3	34285.8	-39571.1	0.081*
43	b40 - a2a3	-5605.6	48485.0	-54090.6	0.11
44	b40 - a2a4	-5440.7	31372.6	-36813.4	0.10
45	b40 - a2a5	-5440.7	23529.5	-28970.2	0.090*
46	b2a1 - a2a3	5303.3	48485.0	-43181.6	0.16
47	b2a1 - a2a4	5147.4	31372.6	-26225.3	0.17
48	b2a1 - a2a5	5147.4	23529.5	-18382.1	0.18
49	b3a1 - a2a3	3578.7	47058.9	-43480.3	0.16
50	b3a1 - a2a4	3476.4	30476.3	-26999.8	0.16
51	b3a1 - a2a5	3476.4	22857.2	-19380.8	0.17
52	b4a1 - a2a3	-783.9	47058.9	-47842.9	0.14
53	b4a1 - a2a4	-761.5	30476.3	-31237.8	0.13
54	b4a1 - a2a5	-761.5	22857.2	-23618.7	0.13

* significant at the 0.10 level (one-tailed); ** significant at the 0.05 level (one-tailed).
[a] "b" refers to the years before, and "a" to the years after the signing of a BIT.
[b] Figures in this table have been rounded; the difference was calculated before rounding.

Annex table IV.6. Central and Eastern European region: detailed results for dependent variable FDI

Comparison, number	Variable[a]	Means of first period	Means of second period	Difference[b]	P
1	b2b1 - 0a1	15.3	8.8	6.5	0.19
2	b2b1 - 0a2	13.5	10.4	3.1	0.29
3	b2b1 - 0a3	13.5	10.2	3.3	0.27
4	b2b1 - a1a2	4.2	5.4	-1.2	0.37
5	b2b1 - a1a3	4.2	5.1	-0.9	0.40
6	b2b1 - a1a4	4.2	5.4	-1.2	0.37
7	b2b1 - a2a3	4.2	5.9	-1.7	0.32
8	b2b1 - a2a4	4.2	6.0	-1.8	0.31
9	b2b1 - a2a5	4.2	8.4	-4.2	0.19
10	b3b1 - 0a1	15.3	8.8	6.5	0.19
11	b3b1 - 0a2	13.5	10.4	3.1	0.29
12	b3b1 - 0a3	13.5	10.2	3.3	0.27
13	b3b1 - a1a2	4.2	5.4	-1.2	0.37
14	b3b1 - a1a3	4.2	5.1	-0.9	0.40
15	b3b1 - a1a4	4.2	5.4	-1.2	0.37
16	b3b1 - a2a3	4.2	5.9	-1.7	0.32
17	b3b1 - a2a4	4.2	6.0	-1.8	0.31
18	b3b1 - a2a5	4.2	8.4	-4.2	0.19
19	b4b1 - 0a1	15.8	8.8	7.0	0.17
20	b4b1 - 0a2	13.8	10.4	3.4	0.27
21	b4b1 - 0a3	13.8	10.2	3.6	0.25
22	b4b1 - a1a2	4.6	5.4	-0.8	0.41
23	b4b1 - a1a3	4.6	5.1	-0.5	0.44
24	b4b1 - a1a4	4.6	5.4	-0.8	0.41
25	b4b1 - a2a3	4.6	5.9	-1.3	0.36
26	b4b1 - a2a4	4.6	6.0	-1.4	0.35
27	b4b1 - a2a5	4.6	8.4	-3.8	0.22
28	b20 - a1a2	3.5	16.6	-13.1	0.064*
29	b20 - a1a3	3.5	17.0	-13.5	0.057*
30	b20 - a1a4	3.5	17.1	-13.6	0.056*
31	b20 - a2a3	3.3	15.4	-12.1	0.070*
32	b20 - a2a4	3.3	15.2	-11.8	0.074*
33	b20 - a2a5	3.3	16.1	-12.8	0.060*
34	b30 - a1a2	3.5	16.6	-13.1	0.064*
35	b30 - a1a3	3.5	17.0	-13.5	0.057*
36	b30 - a1a4	3.5	17.1	-13.6	0.056*
37	b30 - a2a3	3.3	15.4	-12.1	0.070*
38	b30 - a2a4	3.3	15.2	-11.9	0.074*
39	b30 - a2a5	3.3	16.1	-12.8	0.060*
40	b40 - a1a2	3.6	16.6	-13.0	0.065*
41	b40 - a1a3	3.6	17.0	-13.4	0.059*
42	b40 - a1a4	3.6	17.1	-13.5	0.057*
43	b40 - a2a3	3.4	15.4	-12.0	0.071*
44	b40 - a2a4	3.4	15.2	-11.8	0.076*
45	b40 - a2a5	3.4	16.1	-12.7	0.061*
46	b2a1 - a2a3	5.7	15.2	-9.5	0.020**
47	b2a1 - a2a4	5.7	17.8	-12.0	0.040**
48	b2a1 - a2a5	5.7	20.7	-14.9	0.049**
49	b3a1 - a2a3	5.7	15.2	-9.5	0.020**
50	b3a1 - a2a4	5.7	17.8	-12.0	0.040**
51	b3a1 - a2a5	5.7	20.7	-15.0	0.049**
52	b4a1 - a2a3	5.8	15.2	-9.4	0.021**
53	b4a1 - a2a4	5.8	17.8	-12.0	0.041**
54	b4a1 - a2a5	5.8	20.7	-14.9	0.049**

* significant at the 0.10 level (one-tailed); ** significant at the 0.05 level (one-tailed).

[a] "b" refers to the years before, and "a" to the years after the signing of a BIT.

[b] Figures in this table have been rounded; the difference was calculated before rounding.

Annex table IV.7.   List of host economies included in the analysis in stage two

Albania	Indonesia	Spain
Algeria	Iran, Islamic Republic of	Sri Lanka
Antigua and Barbuda	Iraq	Sudan
Argentina	Israel	Swaziland
Armenia	Jamaica	Syrian Arab Republic
Bahrain	Jordan	Taiwan Province of China
Bangladesh	Kazakhstan	Tajikistan
Barbados	Kenya	Thailand
Belarus	Kuwait	Togo
Belize	Kyrgyzstan	Trinidad and Tobago
Benin	Lao, People's Democratic Republic	Tunisia
Bolivia	Latvia	Turkey
Brazil	Lebanon	Uganda
Bulgaria	Lesotho	Ukraine
Burkina Faso	Liberia	United Arab Emirates
Burundi	Macedonia	United Republic of Tanzania
Cambodia	Madagascar	Uruguay
Cameroon	Malawi	Uzbekistan
Cape Verde	Malaysia	Venezuela
Central African Republic	Mali	Viet Nam
Chad	Malta	Yemen
Chile	Mauritania	Zambia
China	Mauritius	Zimbabwe
Colombia	Mexico	
Congo	Moldova, Republic of	
Costa Rica	Mongolia	
Cote d'Ivoire	Morocco	
Croatia	Namibia	
Cuba	Nepal	
Cyprus	New Zealand	
Czech Republic	Nicaragua	
Democratic Republic of the Congo	Niger	
Dominica	Nigeria	
Dominican Republic	Oman	
Ecuador	Pakistan	
Egypt	Panama	
El Salvador	Papua New Guinea	
Equatorial Guinea	Paraguay	
Estonia	Peru	
Ethiopia	Philippines	
Gabon	Poland	
Gambia	Portugal	
Ghana	Romania	
Greece	Russian Federation	
Grenada	Rwanda	
Guinea	Saint Lucia	
Guinea-Bissau	Saint Vincent and the Grenadines	
Guyana	Saudi Arabia	
Haiti	Senegal	
Honduras	Sierra Leone	
Hong Kong, China	Singapore	
Hungary	Slovakia	
Iceland	Slovenia	
India	South Africa	

Annex table IV.8. List of home countries and the number of BITs signed by them

Country	Number of BITs
Germany	103
United Kingdom	85
Switzerland	75
France	73
Netherlands	56
Italy	45
Belgium and Luxembourg	39
United States	37
Denmark	36
Sweden	33
Finland	29
Austria	18
Norway	15
Australia	14
Canada	10
Japan	4

Annex table IV.9. Criteria underlying indicators of country investment risk

Components	Indicators of country investment climate and risk
Political	Economic expectations and economic reality; economic planning failures; political leadership; external conflict; corruption in Government; military in politics; organized religion in politics; tradition of law and order; racial and national tensions; political terrorism; civil war; development of political parties; quality of the bureaucracy
Financial	Loan default or unfavourable loan restructuring; delayed payment of suppliers' credits; repudiation of contracts by Governments; losses from exchange controls; expropriation of private investments
Economic	Inflation; debt service as a percentage of exports of goods and services; international liquidity ratios; experience of foreign trade collection; current account balance as a percentage of goods and services; parallel foreign exchange rate market indicators
Composite rating	Determined by combining the political, financial and economic risk ratings

Source: PRS Group.

Annex table IV.10. Summary of independent variables loaded in 192 regression runs for eight dependent variables

	Flow (95)	Fper (95)	Fgdp$ (95)	Fgrow (95)	Stock (95)	Sper (95)	Sgdp$ (95)	Sgrow (95)
I. Total / All / Normal								
1. Independent variable (95)	13				1,3,8	3,8,13		
2. Independent variable (94)	3,6,8,11.	3,8,9,10,11	9,11,13	1,2,4,8,9,1	3,8			
3. Independent variable (93)	13				3,8			
II. Total / Without / Normal								
1. Independent variable (95)					2,3,8			
2. Independent variable (94)	11	3,9,10,11	9,11	7,9,10,11,12,13				
3. Independent variable (93)			1,2,3,6,9,10,11,12,13		3,8			
III. Total / All / Log								
1. Independent variable (95)								
2. Independent variable (94)								
3. Independent variable (93)								
IV. Total / Without / Log								
1. Independent variable (95)								
2. Independent variable (94)								
3. Independent variable (93)								
V. Stepwise / All / Normal								
1. Independent variable (95)	3,8,13	10	5,13		3,8,12	1		1
2. Independent variable (94)	3,8,13	10	1,5,13		3,8,13	10		10
3. Independent variable (93)	1,3,8,13	10	1,7,13		3,8,13	10		10
VI. Stepwise / Without / Normal								
1. Independent variable (95)	3,8	10	10		3,8	1		1
2. Independent variable (94)	1,3,8,10	10	1,8		3,8	3,8		
3. Independent variable (93)	3,8	1.0	11		3,8	3,8		
VII. Stepwise / All / Log								
1. Independent variable (95)	2	6,13		6	6,7,8,11	2,10	1,4	2
2. Independent variable (94)		10	1		6,8	2,10	3	2
3. Independent variable (93)		1.0				1,10		2
VIII. Stepwise / Without / Log								
1. Independent variable (95)	2	6,13		6	6,7,8,11	2,10	1,4	2
2. Independent variable (94)		10	1		6,8	2,10	3	2
3. Independent variable (93)		10			6,8	1,10		2

Note: This table lists variables whose probability value is better than 0.05 (one-tailed). Shaded boxes correspond to table IV.11.

[a] Independent variables

1. Number of BITs in a year
2. Total number of BITs
3. Capital investment
4. Composite country rating
5. Economic rating
6. Change in exchange rate
7. Financial rating
8. GDP in dollars
9. GDP growth in local currency
10. GDP per capita
11. Inflation
12. Political rating
13. Population

Key to dependent variables

Flow = FDI flow   Fper = FDI flow per capita   Fgdp$ = FDI flow per $1,000 GDP   Fgrow = FDI flow growth

Stock = FDI stock   Sper = FDI stock per capita   Sgdp$ = FDI stock per $1,000 GDP   Sgrow = FDI stock growth

Annex table IV.11. Summary of independent variables loaded in 60 stepwise regressions for separate regions[a]

Region	Flow (95)	Fper (95)	Fgdp$ (95)	Fgrow (95)
I. Africa				
1. Independent variables (95)	1, 11, 13	1, 10		
2. Independent variables (94)	2, 3, 6, 13	8, 10		
3. Independent variables (93)	4, 8, 13	8, 10		
II. Central & Eastern Europe				
1. Independent variables (95)	2, 7, 8	7,		
2. Independent variables (94)	2, 8, 12	7,		
3. Independent variables (93)	1, 8, 13	4, 13		
III. East & Southeast Asia				
1. Independent variables (95)	1, 2, 13	3, 10	10	6, 11, 13
2. Independent variables (94)	2, 4, 8, 13	10	10	6
3. Independent variables (93)	1, 7	3, 12	12	3, 10, 12
IV. Latin America & Caribbean				
1. Independent variables (95)	1, 3, 8, 11, 13		12	
2. Independent variables (94)	2, 5, 6, 13			
3. Independent variables (93)	8			
V. West Asia				
1. Independent variables (95)	3	10		
2. Independent variables (94)	8, 13	10		
3. Independent variables (93)	8, 9			

Note: This table lists variables whose probability value is less than 0.05 (one tailed). The mean-value substitution procedure was used in the calculations.

[a] Independent variables

1.	Number of BITs in a year	6.	Change in exchange rate	11.	Inflation
2.	Total number of BITs	7.	Financial rating	12.	Political rating
3.	Capital investment	8.	GDP in dollars	13.	Population
4.	Composite country rating	9.	GDP growth in local currency		
5.	Economic rating	10.	GDP per capita		

Key to dependent variables   Flow = FDI flow   Fper = FDI flow per capita

Fgdp$ = FDI flow per $1,000 GDP   Fgrow = FDI flow growth

**Annex tables IV.10 and IV.11: general note on the details on regression runs
carried out in cross-sectional stage-two analysis**

Chapter IV shows only nine of the most significant regression equations using the stepwise forward inclusion technique being the Statistical Package for the Social Sciences for three dependent variables, each for three years (table IV.4). However, a total of 264 regression runs were undertaken in a comprehensive search for determinants of FDI, including BITs. The results for 192 regressions are summarized in annex table IV.10. The results for a further 60 regressions are summarized in annex table IV.11. The remaining 12 are not shown.

The 192 regressions in annex table IV.10 result from the combination of:

- eight dependent variables (Flow (95), Fper (95), Fgdp$ (95), Fgrow (95), Stock (95), Sper (95), Sgdp$ (95) and Sgrow(95)); see the key to dependent variables in the footnote to annex table IV.10);
- two loading methods (Total = all independent variables entered together; Stepwise = stepwise forward inclusion);
- three years (1995, 1994 and 1993);
- countries excluded/included (All = all 133 countries; Without = without China, Singapore and Hong Kong Special Administrative Region of China; and
- transformation of independent variables (Normal = untransformed; Log = log transformed).

Annex table IV.10 does not show the actual statistics relating to each equation, but only summarizes which independent variable achieved at least a 0.05 significance level. In this way, an overall picture or pattern emerges as to which of the independent variables, including BITs, emerge as possible determinants of FDI. In many of the regression runs, indicated by blanks, not even one of the independent variables achieved significance; this was particularly so in the case of log transformed variables (apparently, the data did not need transformation in the first place). For reasons explained in the main text, the reader should focus on section V (Stepwise/All/Normal) in annex table IV.10 where all variables, on a normal untransformed basis, are entered stepwise. This procedure yielded the best results. Detailed statistics for the equations in the shaded boxes in annex table IV.10 are shown in table IV.4 in the main text.

The 60 regressions in annex table IV.11 resulted from a combination of:

- four dependent variables (Flow (95), Fper (95), Fgdp$ (95), Fgrow (95));
- five regions (Africa; Central and Eastern Europe; East and South-East Asia; Latin America and the Caribbean; and West Asia); and
- three years (1993, 1994 and 1995).

BIT-related independent variables (the number of BITs in a year and the economic rating) were frequently included in runs involving the dependent variable Flow (95) for all regions, except West Asia. Because the division of data into regions resulted in few complete data sets, a mean-value substitution procedure was followed, without which no statistically significant results would have been obtained. However, this means that one cannot rely too much on the results.

Chapter V

CONCLUSIONS[1]

The BIT network that has emerged after nearly 40 years of negotiating and concluding BITs, has several particularly striking characteristics. Foremost is the number and diversity of countries that have concluded BITs. As noted in the introduction, BITs have been concluded by 162 countries and territories in every region of the world. Increasingly, the negotiation and conclusion of BITs is a universal phenomenon. Although BITs were originally agreements concluded between a developed and a developing country, in the 1990s BITs between developing countries or between developing countries and countries with economies in transition have become more and more common. Today, less than two-thirds of the total number of BITs are between developed and developing countries.

A. Similarities and differences between treaties

An important characteristic of the new generation of BIT is the considerable uniformity in the broad principles underlying the agreements, coupled with numerous variations in the specific formulations employed. As this study's survey of BIT provisions has suggested, there is a core of provisions that is common to a large number of BITs, namely:

- The definition of investment is broad and open-ended so that it can accommodate new forms of foreign investment; it includes tangible and intangible assets and generally applies to existing as well as new investments;

---

[1] This chapter takes into account the main points made in UNCTAD's Expert Meeting on Existing Agreements on Investment and Their Development Dimensions, held in Geneva in May 1997. For more details on the discussions of the Expert Meeting, see (UNCTAD, 1997b).

- The entry and establishment of investment is encouraged, although it is typically subject to national laws and regulations (most BITs do not grant a right of establishment);[2]
- Investment promotion is weak and is based mainly on the creation of a favourable investment climate for investment through the conclusion of a BIT;
- Most treaties provide for fair and equitable treatment, often qualified by more specific standards, such as those prohibiting arbitrary or discriminatory measures or prescribing a duty to observe commitments concerning investment;
- Most treaties specify that when various agreements apply to an investment, the most favourable provisions amongst them apply;
- Most treaties now grant national treatment, the principle also being often subject to qualifications (to take into account the different characteristics between national and foreign firms) and exceptions (relating mainly to specific industries or economic activities, or to policy measures such as incentives and taxation);
- A guarantee of MFN treatment, subject to some standardized exceptions, is virtually universal;
- Virtually all BITs subject the right of the host country to expropriate to the condition that it should be for a public purpose, non-discriminatory, in accordance with due process and accompanied by compensation, while the standards for determining compensation are often described in terms that could result in similar outcomes;
- A guarantee of the free transfer of payments related to an investment is common to virtually all BITs, although it is often qualified by exceptions applicable to periods when foreign currency reserves are at low levels;
- A State-to-State dispute-settlement provision is also virtually universal;
- An investor-to-State dispute-settlement provision has become a standard practice, with a growing number of BITs providing the investor with a choice of mechanisms.

In addition, some BITs include one or several of the following:

- A requirement that the host country should ensure that investors have access to information on national laws;
- A prohibition on the imposition of performance requirements, such as local content, export conditions and employment requirements, as a condition for the entry or operation of an investment;
- A commitment to permit or facilitate the entry and sojourn of foreign personnel in connection with the establishment and operation of an investment;
- A guarantee of national and MFN treatment on entry and establishment.

The analysis in chapter III confirms that there are also a number of issues that are generally not addressed in BITs but are nevertheless relevant for investment relations.[3] These include:

- Obligations regarding progressive liberalization;
- The treatment of foreign investment during privatization;
- Control of restrictive business practices;
- Private management practices that restrain investment and trade;
- Consumer protection;
- Environmental protection;
- Taxation of foreign affiliates;

---

[2] Some countries have emphasized that addressing the right of establishment in international investment agreements is still a sensitive issue for countries that have not yet liberalized their economy (Peru, 1997).

[3] On this point see UNCTAD (1997b) and the Philippines (1997).

- Avoidance of illicit payments;
- Protection against violations of intellectual property rights;
- Labour standards;
- Provisions concerning the transfer of technology;
- Specific commitments by home countries to promote investments;
- Social responsibilities of foreign investors in host countries;
- Obligations of subnational authorities.

At the same time, despite the apparent uniformity among many BIT provisions, there are many significant differences in the formulation of individual provisions. Some of the variations among BITs reflect the fact that they were negotiated at different periods of time. Treaties have tended to become somewhat more complex and sophisticated over time, so that any one country's early BITs may differ noticeably from its later agreements. Also, because countries have monitored each other's BIT practice, innovations introduced by one country tend to find their way into the BITs subsequently negotiated by other countries. For example, for most of the 1960s, no BIT had an investor-to-State dispute-settlement provision. After the first one appeared in 1968, many countries introduced such provisions into their treaties, so that they now are virtually universal. More recently, a few countries began to give investors a choice of investor-to-State dispute-settlement mechanisms, and it has now become increasingly common to offer investors a choice between at least two mechanisms. Hence, BIT programmes are in a constant state of evolution, while they are generally moving in the same direction.

Nevertheless, despite the growing convergence of FDI policies and approaches worldwide, there continue to be significant variations in recently signed BITs, even in those signed by the same countries. This may be due in part to the differences in the prototype treaties proposed by countries, which reveal preferences on what individual countries would consider to be an ideal BIT. For instance, the model proposed by the United States goes well beyond the models proposed by European countries with respect to granting investors rights of entry and with respect to performance requirements. Differences in approach are also apparent among the BITs proposed by European countries. For example, Germany attaches great significance to the granting of national treatment, while Sweden, until recently, did not include national treatment in its BITs. To take another example, the BITs concluded by Singapore show the following variations in the formula for compensation upon expropriation: "just" compensation is used in its treaties with Germany and the Netherlands, while in its treaty with France the standard is "the commercial value of the assets on the day of the expropriation" and in its BITs with Switzerland and the United Kingdom, the standard of "prompt, adequate and effective" compensation is used.

With respect to the BITs concluded between developing countries, the picture is even more mixed, partly because, as noted, many of these countries have drawn on a variety of models for their formulation. Of course, in each case the relative bargaining position of the BIT partners and their underlying strategies play an important role in the formulation of the agreement as well.

Overall, the main differences among the most common substantive provisions of BITs – apart from the differences regarding the inclusion of certain issues noted above – are found in the formulations on admission of investment, promotion of investment, general standards of treatment (especially with respect to the degree of detail of these provisions), the scope and range of qualifications and exceptions to the standards of national and MFN treatment, standards for compensation upon nationalization, balance-of-payments exceptions regarding the transfer of funds, and the requirement of exhaustion of local remedies, in the case of investor-to-State dispute settlement.[4]

Looking at individual clauses, however, offers little guidance for comparing the relative strength of the protection granted by an agreement as a whole. BITs often represent a package of mutual advantages in which acceptance of one provision is balanced with concessions on another provision. It is therefore uncommon to find two BITs that are identical in every respect.

B. Experience with the application of bilateral investment treaties

As far as home countries are concerned, BITs are principally concluded to provide legal protection to foreign investment and thus reduce non-commercial risks. Host countries conclude BITs primarily with a view towards improving their investment climate and thus attracting more FDI.

With respect to the objective of protection, little is known about how individual protection standards have been applied in practice, and there are few judicial or arbitral authorities to shed light on this aspect. Indeed, invocations of the investor-to-State dispute-settlement provisions have been rare. As at April 1998, 14 cases had been brought to ICSID involving BITs,[5] and only two awards (ICSID, 1990 and 1997) and two settlements[6] had been issued. Cases involving the treaties between the Belgium–Luxembourg Economic Union and Burundi, the Netherlands and Venezuela, Argentina and France, the Czeck Republic and the Slovak Republic, the United States and Argentina, Argentina and Spain, the United States and Ukraine, Chile and Spain were pending before ICSID as at that date. It does not appear that the State-to-State dispute-settlement provision of any BIT has ever been invoked.

At the same time, BIT obligations have been cited during informal discussions on the treatment of particular investments. Some of these treaties, therefore, may well have provided a basis for the resolution of potential disputes through consultations. In the end, the measure of the success of a BIT lies as much in its ability to prevent an investment dispute from arising or escalating as in its ability to provide a basis for resolving a dispute once it has arisen. In the kind of investment climate that a BIT is intended to promote, investors and the host country will seek to operate on the basis of cooperation rather than confrontation.

---

[4] Regarding the main differences in the formulation of BIT provisions, see, for example, Cuba (1997) and Turkey (1997). According to some countries (Philippines, 1997), these provisions are also among the most difficult to negotiate.

[5] Asian Agricultural Products Limited v. Democratic Socialist Republic of Sri Lanka (registered in 1987; award issued); American Manufacturing & Trading, Inc. v. Republic of Zaire (registered in 1993; award issued); Philippe Gruslin v. Government of Malaysia (registered in 1994; amicable settlement); Tradex Hellas S.A. v. Republic of Albania (registered in 1994; pending); Leaf Tobacco A. Michaelides S.A. and Greek-Albanian Leaf Tobacco & Co. S.A. v. Republic of Albania (1995; pending); Antoine Goetz and others v. Republic of Burundi (registered in 1995; pending); Fedax N.V. v. Republic of Venezuela (registered in 1996; pending); Compañía General de Aguas del Aconquija S.A. and Companie Générale des Eaux S.A. v. Republic of Argentina (registered in 1996; pending); Ceskoslovenska Obchodni Banka, A.S. v. Slovak Republic (registered in 1997; pending); Lanco International, Inc. v. Republic of Argentina (registered in 1997; pending); Emilio Agustín Maffezini v. Kingdom of Spain (registered in 1997; pending); Joseph C. Lemire v. Ukraine (registered in 1998; pending); Houston Industries Energy, Inc. and others v. Republic of Argentina (registered in 1998; pending); Victor Pey Casado and another v. Republic of Chile (registered in 1998; pending) (ICSID, 1998).

[6] In the cases of Philippe Gruslin v. Government of Malaysia and Leaf Tobacco A. Michaelides S.A. and Greek- Albania Leaf Tobacco & Co. S.A. v. Republic of Albania (ICSID, 1998). Owing to the fact that these cases were amicably settled, the facts and legal arguments are not available to the public.

Beyond that, foreign investors have found that the existence of a BIT facilitates investment because, in case of problems, investors can much more easily approach their home-country authorities for assistance, since there are both agreed standards and established consultative and arbitral mechanisms applicable to the situation. Thus, having treatment standards embodied in a treaty does promote favourable treatment.[7]

It is nevertheless remarkable that, after nearly 40 years of BIT practice, information on the experience with the application of BITs still remains rather sketchy and anecdotal. This may be explained by the fact that, unlike in the case of regional and multilateral agreements, there is no systematic independent follow-up and monitoring of the implementation of BITs. It is very much up to individual partners to decide how they wish to monitor their BITs, and this may vary considerably from country to country and from case to case, depending on the underlying diplomatic and economic relations. In the absence of systematic follow-up, a number of open questions remain, such as, for example, whether BIT provisions are interpreted and applied in a consistent manner, both within the same treaty and across treaties and countries. As one author has put it, "so far as the literature discloses, BITs have not yet been put to the test so that we do not know how much they enhance the security of foreign investment" (Vagts, 1990, p. 112).[8]

With respect to the objective of the promotion of FDI flows – another important function of BITs – it is generally recognized that investment decisions, and thus FDI flows, are determined by a variety of economic, institutional and political factors, including the size and growth rate of the host-country market, the availability of raw materials or labour, the nature of the physical and legal infrastructure, and political and economic stability (UNCTAD, 1998). It would therefore be unreasonable to expect that any individual factor, let alone a BIT, could be isolated and "credited" with a decisive impact on the size or increase of FDI flows. Even such important locational determinants as large and growing markets or oil deposits, typically found in econometric and other studies as significant drivers of FDI, do not work alone as FDI determinants, but only in tandem with other factors.

The importance of other FDI determinants as compared with BITs is clear without further analysis: there are many examples of countries with large FDI inflows and few, if any, BITs. Examples of countries that have concluded numerous BITs and have received modest inflows also abound. Given this, the results of the econometric analysis of time-series data on bilateral FDI flows for 200 BITs[9] in the years before and after their signing, reported in chapter IV, are rather surprising in that they show, in some circumstances, a very weak association between the signing of BITs and absolute or relative changes in FDI flows. However, this association almost disappears altogether in the cross-sectional analysis of 133 host countries, investigating the relationship between their total FDI flows and stocks and the number of BITs and other independent variables such as market growth and size, exchange rates and country risks. When the other independent variables are added to the analysis, they become important as FDI determinants (market size is especially important), and BITs lose almost all significance. The overall conclusion is that BITs appear to play, at best, a minor and secondary role in influencing increases in FDI flows and explaining differences in their

---

[7] Insurers and financiers of FDI too have an interest in monitoring compliance since they are affected by the protection standards granted by BITs, as shown by the fact that access to many insurance and financing programmes are made easier by the existence of a BIT. Some countries have noted that they, as well as investors, quite frequently ask for the text of BITs (China, 1997; Turkey, 1997) and are interested in the interpretation of relevant provisions given by the respective Government (Cuba, 1997). Issues most often the subject of consultations appear to include registration, authorization and admission procedures (Germany, 1997).

[8] Cited in Sornarajah (1994), p. 276.

[9] These 200 BITs were concluded between developed countries (the home countries) and developing countries and countries in transition (the host countries).

size among countries. Thus, it would be misleading to suggest that the greater the number of BITs a host country concludes, the higher FDI flows it can expect.

Yet, it would be incorrect to conclude, without further analysis based on much more comprehensive data than are currently available, that BITs have no influence at all on the size of FDI stocks or flows of countries. They may not increase FDI flows or explain inter-country differences in the size of FDI flows or stocks, but they may support the existing level of investment or prevent it from declining. It is also possible that two countries may decide to sign a BIT in order to solidify rising FDI by giving better protection to the existing investment; there is some evidence that foreign investors encourage Governments of home countries to conclude BITs with host countries where they already have FDI. This type of impact would not lead to larger FDI flows, but would keep the existing projects going, and thus would not show up as "an impact" in an analysis aimed at capturing increases, as much of the analysis in chapter IV attempts to do. Furthermore, BITs may matter as a protecting tool for small projects undertaken by small and medium-sized enterprises, where the amounts involved are too small to affect the total or even bilateral flows of a host country.[10] Moreover, while it may be quite reasonable to expect that a BIT will have an impact on FDI flows close to or soon after its conclusion (as most of the analysis in chapter IV does), it cannot be ruled out that the impact may occur only many years later. This may happen if important determinants of FDI are not yet in place in a host country, or in a home country (in the case of a BIT between two developing countries), at the time of a BIT's conclusion; in other words, the impact may take place when these other determinants improve.[11] Finally, as mentioned several times in this study, the usefulness of BITs for countries and investors can go beyond the promotion of FDI. For example, as regards investors, BITs can facilitate the purchase of political risk insurance from public investment insurance agencies and reduce premiums for this insurance. In an even broader sense, BITs are increasingly seen as simply a normal component of a good investment climate – which makes it all the more difficult to identify their distinctive impact, if there is one.

C. Bilateral investment treaties and general investment rules

From the perspective of their role in shaping international rules, the substantive provisions of BITs fall into two categories: provisions that reflect rules and principles of customary international law; and provisions that, at the time of their inclusion in a BIT, do not reflect customary international law.

A reading of the practice in international economic relations and jurisprudence suggests that some BIT provisions reflect traditional principles of customary international law regarding the treatment of foreign property. These include, for example, provisions reflecting the right of States to control the entry of foreign investors and their investments into their territories, the principle of fair and equitable treatment (which might be extended to include non-discrimination and protection under the law) and some of the legal requirements for expropriation of foreign property. With respect to other BIT provisions, for example, certain standards for compensation upon nationalization, the question of whether they reflect customary international law rules applying to foreign investment relations, as noted in the introduction, has been surrounded by controversy. Moreover, given the rather vague and general nature of many of these principles, differences of opinion concerning the meaning and significance to be attached to such principles cannot be excluded.

---

[10] See, for example, Japan (1997), in which it is noted that the expansion of small and medium-sized firms in the electronic and automobile-parts industries to unfamiliar host countries could be positively affected by the legal and institutional protection afforded by BITs.

[11] In general, the more distant a hypothetical impact is from the date of a BIT conclusion, the more difficult it is to link it to the BIT.

The second category of BIT provisions that stipulate new investment rules, includes those relating to the resolution of investment disputes between a State and investors from another State. They tend to substitute recourse both to diplomatic protection and to international arbitration for the jurisdiction of national tribunals of the host country.[12]

The question that arises therefore is what role BITs play in the development of customary international rules on FDI.[13] More specifically, can it be said that provisions in BITs that reflect new principles, or principles whose status as customary international law has been challenged by some members of the international community of States, have become part of customary international law by virtue of the fact that they appear in a large number of BITs?

The question of how customary international law develops has received much attention in the legal literature.[14] It is generally acknowledged that the formation of a rule of customary international law involves a quantitative element as well as a qualitative element. The quantitative element is the "corpus" of the rule – what the International Court of Justice referred to as "State practice ... both extensive and virtually uniform ..." (International Court of Justice, 1969, p. 176); the qualitative element is the "animus" of the rule, the *opinio juris sive necesitatis*, the general recognition that a rule of law or legal obligation is involved.

A number of authors (e.g. Mann, 1991), have emphasized the number of BITs and the striking similarities between them in support of the view that BITs are contributing to the creation of customary international law. Those who are sceptical of the custom-forming role of BITs (e.g. Dolzer, 1981; Schachter, 1984) have noted that, as a matter of principle, the repetition of the same provisions in bilateral treaties does not create an inference that those clauses express customary law binding on third States. For the provisions to have that effect, it would have to be established that, quite independently of the treaties, they were accepted as a general rule of law (*opinio juris*) by the parties. Indeed, in the words of the International Court of Justice, for State practice to become general customary international law:

> Not only must the acts concerned amount to a settled practice, but they must also be such ... as to be evidence of a belief that this practice is rendered obligatory by the existence of a rule of law requiring it .... The States concerned must therefore feel that they are conforming to what amounts to a legal obligation. (International Court of Justice, 1969, p. 44, para. 77)

In this respect, it has been pointed out that the acceptance of certain clauses in BITs as *lex specialis* does not necessarily imply that the country concerned would find the same rules acceptable as part of general customary international law, keeping in mind that, for many host countries, the conclusion of BITs is dictated by the practical need to attract foreign investment from individual countries, which often involves making compromises and taking into account other considerations which affect the relationship of the countries concerned.[15]

At the same time, in recent years the increasing number of countries from all regions that have concluded BITs and, in particular, the growing number of BITs between developing countries, both suggest that there is a certain convergence of approaches on the treatment and protection of investment. While the divergences in the standards and principles stated in the treaties may be such

---

[12] See Portugal (1997).

[13] See Kishoian (1994).

[14] On the various views see, for example, Baxter (1968 and 1970). However, scholars and jurists have not paid as much attention to the question of how a rule of customary international law, once formed, becomes dislodged or displaced over a period of time (for views on this question see, for example, Dolzer (1981) and Fatouros (1980)). It may be that a rule loses its force and vitality once its constituent elements disapear (for a more elaborate discussion of these issues, see Robinson (1986) from which this section draws substantially).

[15] For a discussion of the effects of pressure on *opinio juris* see Dolzer (1981), p. 561.

that they cannot be regarded as supporting definite positions on important aspects of customary international law on foreign investment, these treaties have contributed to the development of international law (Sornarajah, 1994). For example, through these treaties there is recognition that intangible assets (such as intellectual property rights) are perceived as an important aspect of the definition of investment for the purpose of international law protection. Similarly, concepts such as MFN treatment, which were primarily developed in the context of trade in goods, have now become a standard feature of BITs and, through these treaties, their meaning and significance in the area of investment have been tested; and, as jurisprudence on BITs develops, it contributes to clarify them. Thus, the principle of "complete and full protection" under the law that appears often in BITs was interpreted by an arbitral tribunal as constituting an obligation of the host country to observe "due diligence".[16] It would, however, be premature to speak about a major infusion of BIT concepts into customary international law at this stage.

More clear is the influence of BITs in recent regional investment agreements, as demonstrated by the investment provisions of the Energy Charter Treaty, NAFTA, MERCOSUR, the Association of South-East Asian Nations (ASEAN) and the Unified Agreement for Investment of Arab Capital in the Arab States, to mention a few. They all bear the stamp of the BIT framework. In the case of NAFTA, for example, the wording of the United States model BIT is reflected in several provisions, notably on the establishment of investments, performance requirements and the entry and sojourn of foreign nationals. Conversely, regional investment agreements have also influenced BITs. Canada's BITs signed after the negotiation of NAFTA reveal close similarities between these texts, whereas the provisions in the BIT between El Salvador and Peru dealing with performance requirements and the entry and sojourn of foreign personnel bears a resemblance to both the United States BITs and NAFTA. All this suggests that the elaboration of international investment rules is proceeding simultaneously at various levels through processes that feed into each other. As a result, there is a growing similarity between recent investment instruments at all levels.

Last but not least, in discussing the relationship between BITs and other investment agreements, the implications of the MFN clauses of the treaties need to be taken into account, insofar as the presence of an MFN clause may oblige a country to extend to its treaty partners any benefits or privileges that it grants to any other country in any future agreement dealing with investment. This is known as the "free rider" phenomenon, whereby any more favourable conditions granted to investors under a BIT are automatically extended (at least in principle) to third countries, not only through other BITs, but also through regional and multilateral agreements signed by any of the partners.

Given the various instruments available to countries for the development of frameworks for the treatment of foreign investment, the question may be raised as to what the advantages and disadvantages are of concluding BITs vis-à-vis regional and multilateral instruments.[17] Some of the BITs' advantages are that they can be tailored to the specific circumstances of the two parties more easily than other types of agreements, and they are relatively easy to conclude, and therefore can be realized more quickly than regional and, in particular, multilateral agreements. Some of the disadvantages of BITs relate to, among other things, the fact that a bilateral negotiation between parties with unequal bargaining power may disproportionately favour one party's interests. Also, the proliferation of BITs may lead to a complex web of inconsistent provisions that are difficult to apply and may distort investment flows. The settlement of investment disputes could also be made

---

[16] See, Asian Agricultural Products Ltd. (AAPL) v. Republic of Sri Lanka (ICSID, 1990, p. 577) regarding the BIT between Sri Lanka and the United Kingdom; see also the case concerning Elettronica Sicula S.p.a. (ELSI) (International Court of Justice, 1989) concerning the FCN treaty between Italy and the United States, and Portugal (1997).

[17] For a more detailed discussion of the advantages and disadvantages of BITs in relation to regional and multilateral agreements, see UNCTAD (1996c and 1997b).

easier.[18] Still, BITs may have a contribution to make to the elaboration of regional and multilateral rules if the two types of agreement can be seen as mutually reinforcing.[19]

Finally, regarding the interaction between BITs and national law, the matter could be presented as a dialectic between material sources and formal sources of law. To begin with, BIT negotiators are inspired by their own national laws and, in that sense, a BIT can be seen as a compromise between two national laws. However, as a BIT is a compromise, it also differs from each of the national laws concerned. Consequently, the countries commit to adapt their national laws to make them consistent with the BIT, but only, of course, insofar as the two parties to the BIT are concerned, not in relation to third countries. The means by which this adaptation takes place may vary from country to country. In this sense, conventional international law (i.e. BITs) directly affects national legislation.[20] At the same time, even though BITs are *lex specialis*, their provisions may indirectly inspire general investment laws.[21] In fact, most recent BITs provide standards of treatment and legal protection that are typically available under the national laws of host countries that were enacted to create a favourable investment climate.

D. The development dimension

As noted in the introduction, the goal of developing countries in signing BITs is to attract FDI as a means of fostering economic growth and development. In fact, the increasing interest of developing countries and transitional economies in concluding BITs has resulted from the recognition of the positive role that both inward and outward FDI can play in economic growth and development. The conclusion of BITs is typically one of many steps developing countries and countries in transition take to attract FDI, increase its quality and maximize its contribution to development. (The actual usefulness of BITs in attracting FDI flows has been discussed earlier.) However, given the many determinants that influence decisions on investment location, the effectiveness of BITs as tools to attract investment for development could be enhanced further by strengthening the promotion provisions of BITs (as discussed in chapter III) with commitments by home countries to undertake appropriate practical measures to encourage investments in their developing-country BIT partners.

Even if BITs fulfil well their main functions from the point of view of a developing country, they can only do so much to serve the development objectives of developing countries. The main task of furthering a country's development objectives through FDI remains with individual Governments. This, in turn, needs to be given effect through appropriate national policy instruments. The contribution of BITs to development can thus be assessed in terms of whether they provide sufficient flexibility to enable host countries to pursue their development policies. In this respect, a characteristic of most BITs is that they subordinate the admission of investment to the host country's domestic law. The admission clauses in BITs therefore provide developing countries with the opportunity to give expression to their development strategies with respect to foreign investment. At the same time, the conditions that define the development friendliness of international investment agreements need to be explored further.[22]

---

[18] This point was emphasized in Japan (1997).

[19] On this point, see Germany (1997); on the advantages and disadvantages of BITs in relation to other types of international investment agreements, see China (1997).

[20] On this point, see Portugal (1997).

[21] This influence is particularly noticeable in the national investment regimes of countries that have undergone important national legislative changes aimed at facilitating FDI after signing BITs, or where the two processes have proceeded simultaneously. On this point, see, for example, Cuba (1997).

[22] The UNCTAD secretariat is exploring the issue of development friendliness elements of international investment agreements in the context of its work on a possible multilateral framework on investment.

In terms of their individual structure and contents, BITs can be considered as useful developmental tools inasmuch as they can be tailored to the specific developmental concerns of individual developing countries. As noted in chapter III, this has been achieved so far mainly through the use of exceptions, exemptions, temporal derogations or similar mechanisms that allow developing countries to adapt BIT commitments to their development needs. Thus, for example, to address the balance-of-payments concerns of host developing countries, many BITs provide for the suspension of financial transfers abroad in case of balance-of-payments difficulties. Similarly, many BITs introduce qualifications or exceptions to their national treatment provision on account of the inherent weaknesses of firms from developing countries.

Still, the question arises as to whether BITs could do more to support the development efforts of developing countries. In this respect, it is worth recalling that these treaties characteristically define duties for host countries, while leaving it to host countries to regulate the investor's operations through local law (subject to any limitations placed on it by the treaties).[23] Moreover, BITs oblige countries to accord a certain standard of treatment to investors, but they do not normally mention any obligations on the part of home countries. These features of BITs are further compounded by the fact that, while the treaties are reciprocal in form (i.e. they establish identical rights and duties for both sides), capital often flows mainly in one direction, at least for a period of time.

It is true that the pattern of the global distribution of FDI flows is changing; the number of TNCs headquartered in developing countries is growing and more TNCs are seeking to expand abroad, which strengthens, at least in principle, the bargaining position of host countries vis-à-vis individual investors. In addition, a number of the traditional home countries are also important recipients of foreign investment and are themselves grappling with issues of sovereignty and control over such investment. However, even if there is an underlying balance of interests, it could be argued that greater efforts by home countries – be they formalized or not – to promote investment flows to developing countries (in particular the kind of investment the developing countries wish to attract) would contribute to better investment relations.

In conclusion, as new BITs are being negotiated and existing BITs may be revised or amended in the future, and since BITs can influence the structure and contents of other international investment agreements, the opportunities for strengthening the development dimensions of these treaties should be considered.

* * * *

---

[23] Some commentators have stressed that this is the desirable way of dealing with investors obligations and reflects international principles. See, for example, Germany (1997).

References

Akinsanya, Adeoye (1987). "International protection of foreign direct investment in the third world", *International and Comparative Law Quarterly*, vol. 36 (January), pp. 58–75.

Amerasinghe, C.F. (1964). *State Responsibility for Injuries to Aliens* (Oxford: Clarendon Press).

_____ (1992). "Issues of compensation for the taking of alien property in the light of recent cases and practice", *International and Comparative Law Quarterly*, vol. 41, pp. 22–65.

Baxter, R.R. (1968). "Multilateral treaties as evidence of customary international law", *The British Yearbook of International Law 1965–1966* (London, Oxford University Press), pp. 275–300.

_____ (1970). "Treaty and custom", *Recueil des Cours* (The Hague: Academy of International Law), vol. 129, pp. 24–105.

Bergmann, M.S. (1983). "Bilateral investment treaties: an examination of the evolution and the significance of the United States prototype treaty", *New York University Journal of International Law and Politics*, vol. 16, pp. 1–43.

Borchard, Edwin M. (1915). *The Diplomatic Protection of Citizens Abroad or the Law of International Claims* (New York: Banks Law Publishing Company).

Brewer, Thomas (1995). "International dispute settlement provisions: the evolving regime for foreign direct investment", *Law and Policy in International Business*, vol. 26 (Spring), pp. 633–672.

Brierly, J. (1963). *The Law of Nations: An Introduction to the International Law of Peace*, 6th ed. (Oxford: Clarendon Press).

"British Petroleum Exploration (Libya) Limited v. Government of the Lybian Arab Republic" (International Arbitration, 1974), *International Law Reports* (Cambridge: Grotious Publications), vol. 53 (1979), pp. 297–388.

Broches, Aron (1982). "Bilateral investment protection treaties and arbitration of investment disputes", in J. C. Schultsz and A. J. Van den Berg, eds., *The Art of Arbitration: Liber Amicorum Pieter Sanders* (Deventer: Kluwer), pp. 63–72.

_____ (1991). "Observations on the enforceability of ICSID arbitration", *ICSID Review: Foreign Investment Law Journal*, vol. 6 (Fall), pp. 321–379.

Brownlie, Ian (1991). *Principles of Public International Law, 4th ed.* (Oxford: Clarendon Press).

Calvo, Carlos (1868). *Le Droit International Théorique et Pratique, 5th ed.* (Paris: A. Rousseau).

China (1997). "Paper submitted by the expert from China to the Expert Meeting on Existing Agreements on Investment and Their Development Dimensions, Geneva, 28–30 May 1997" (Geneva: UNCTAD), mimeo.

Conklin, David and Donald Lecraw (1997). "Restrictions on foreign ownership during 1984–1994: developments and alternative policies", *Transnational Corporations,* 6, 1 (April), pp.1–30.

Cuba (1997). "Paper submitted by the expert from Cuba to the Expert Meeting on Existing Agreements on Investment and Their Development Dimensions", Geneva, 28–30 May 1997 (Geneva: UNCTAD), mimeo.

Czech Republic (1997). "Paper submitted by the expert from the Czech Republic to the Expert Meeting on Existing Agreements on Investment and Their Development Dimensions", Geneva, 28–30 May 1997 (Geneva: UNCTAD), mimeo.

Denza, Eileen and Shelagh Brooks (1987). "Investment protection treaties: United Kingdom experience", *International and Comparative Law*, vol. 36 (Fall), pp. 908–923.

Diez de Velasco (1978). *Instituciones de Derecho Público,* vol. I (Madrid: Editorial Technicos).

Dolzer, Rudolf (1981). "New foundations of the law of expropriation of alien property", *American Journal of International Law*, vol. 75, pp. 553–589.

_____ (1986). "Indirect expropriation of alien property", *ICSID Review: Foreign Investment Law Journal*, vol. 1, pp. 41–65.

_____ and Margrete Stevens (1995). *Bilateral Investment Treaties* (The Hague: Kluwer).

Dunn, F. (1932). *The Protection of Nationals: A Study in the Application of International Law* (Baltimore: Johns Hopkins Press).

Fatouros, Argyrios A. (1962). *Government Guarantees to Foreign Investors* (New York and London: Columbia University Press).

_____ (1980). "International law and the internationalized contract", *American Journal of International Law*, vol. 74, pp. 134–274.

Foighel, Isi (1957). *Nationalization: A Study in the Protection of Alien Property in International Law* (London: Stevens).

_____ (1964). *Nationalization and Compensation* (London: Stevens).

Freeman, A.V. (1938). *The International Responsibility of States for the Denial of Justice* (London: Longmans, Green and Company).

Friedman, S. (1953). *Expropriation in International Law* (London: Stevens).

Froot, K.A. and J.C. Stein (1991). "Exchange rates and foreign direct investment: an imperfect capital markets approach", *Quarterly Journal of Economics,* 106, 4, pp. 1191–1217.

Gabon (1997). "Paper Submitted by the expert from Gabon to the Expert Meeting on Existing Agreements on Investment and their Development Dimensions, Geneva, 28–30 May 1997 (Geneva: UNCTAD), mimeo.

Gann, Pamela B. (1985). "The US bilateral investment treaty program", *Stanford Journal of International Law*, vol. 21, pp. 373–459.

Garcia Amador, Francisco V. (1958). "State responsibility: some new problems", *Recueil des Cours* (The Hague Academy of International Law), pp. 365–487.

_____ (1984). *The Changing Law of International Claims* (New York: Oceana).

Germany (1997). "Paper Submitted by the expert from Germany to the Expert Meeting on Existing Agreements on Investment and their Development Dimensions, Geneva, 28–30 May 1997 (Geneva: UNCTAD), mimeo.

Green, R.T. and W. Cunningham (1975). "The determinants of US foreign investment: an empirical examination", *Management International Review,* 15, pp. 113–120.

Gudgeon, Scott K. (1986). "United States bilateral investment treaties: comments on their origin, purposes and general treatment standards", *International Tax and Business Lawyer*, vol. 4, pp.105–135.

Habeeb, William Mark (1988). *Power and Tactics in International Negotiations: How Weak Nations Bargain with Strong Nations* (Baltimore: John Hopkins University Press).

Hamrak, K. (1992). "The ELSI case: towards an international definition of arbitrary conduct", *Texas International Law Journal*, vol. 27, pp. 837–844.

Hashem, Hala Z. (1984) "Legal treatment of foreign investment in Egypt: a comparative study of international law and bilateral investment treaties", *Revue Égyptienne de Droit International*, vol. 40, pp. 133–166.

Hawkins, H. (1951). *Commercial Treaties and Agreements: Principles and Practice* (New York: Rinehart).

Huu-Tru, Nguyen (1988). "Le réseau suisse d'accords bilatéraux d'encouragement et de protection des investissements", *Revue Générale du Droit International Public*, vol. 92, pp. 577–671.

_____ (1990). "La validité internationale des mobiles d'expropriation", *Revue Belge de Droit International*, vol. 23, pp. 441–463.

International Centre for Settlement of Investment Disputes (ICSID) (1972 -), *Investment Treaties* (Dobbs Ferry, NY: Oceana).

_____ (1982). "ICSID Additional Facility", *International Legal Materials*, vol. 21, pp. 1443–1472.

_____ (1985). "Amco Asia Corporation (et al.) v. Indonesia", *International Legal Materials*, vol. 24, pp. 1022–1039.

_____ (1990). "Asian Agricultural Products Ltd. (AAPL) v. Republic of Sri Lanka", *International Legal Materials*, vol. 30, pp. 577–655.

_____ (1992). "Vacuum Salt Products Ltd. v. Ghana", *ICSID Review: Foreign Law Journal*, vol. 9 (Spring), pp. 71–101.

_____ (1997). "American Manufacturing & Trading, Inc. v. Republic of Zaire", *International Legal Materials*, vol. 36, pp. 1534–1561.

_____ (1998). *ICSID Cases* (Document ICSID/16/Rev.5, November 30, 1996, updated in March 1998).

International Court of Justice (1955). "Nottebohm Case (Liechtenstein v. Guatemala), Judgement", *International Court of Justice Reports*, 1955 Report, pp. 4–65.

_____ (1959). "Interhandel Case (Switzerland v. United States), Judgement", *International Court of Justice Reports*, 1959 Report, pp. 6–125.

_____ (1969). "North Sea Continental Shelf Cases (Federal Republic of Germany v. Denmark, Federal Republic of Germany v. Netherlands), Judgement", *International Court of Justice Reports*, 1969 Report, pp. 3–257.

_____ (1970). Barcelona Traction Light and Power Company Limited (Belgium v. Spain), Judgement", *International Court of Justice Reports*, 1970 Report, pp. 3–357.

_____ (1986). "Military and Paramilitary Activities in and against Nicaragua (Nicaragua v. the United States), Merits Judgement", *International Court of Justice Reports*, 1986 Report, pp. 14–546.

_____ (1989). "Elettronica Sicula S.p.A. (ELSI) (United States of America v. Italy), Judgement, *International Court of Justice Reports*, 1989 Report, pp. 15–121.

International Monetary Fund (IMF) (1945). "Articles of Agreement of the International Monetary Fund", *United Nations Treaty Series*, vol. 2, pp. 39–133.

Iran (1997). "Paper submitted by the expert from Iran to the Expert Meeting on Existing Agreements on Investment and Their Development Dimensions, Geneva, 28–30 May 1997" (Geneva: UNCTAD), mimeo.

Japan (1997). "Paper submitted by the expert from Japan to the Expert Meeting on Existing Agreements on Investment and Their Development Dimensions, Geneva, 28-30 May 1997" (Geneva: UNCTAD), mimeo.

Juillard, Patrick (1979). "Les conventions bilatérales d'investissement conclues par la France", *Journal du Droit International*, vol. 106, pp. 274–321.

Julius, D. (1990). *Global Companies and Public Policy: The Growing Challenge of Foreign Direct Investment* (New York: Council of Foreign Relations).

Karl, Joachim (1996). "The promotion and protection of German foreign investment abroad", *ICSID Review: Foreign Investment Law Journal*, vol. II, no. 1 (Spring), pp. 1–36.

Katzarov, K. (1964). *The Theory of Nationalization* (The Hague: Nijhoff).

Khalil, Mohamed I. (1992). "Treatment of foreign investment in bilateral investment treaties", *ICSID Review: Foreign Investment Law Journal*, vol. 8, (Fall), pp. 339–427.

Khan, Rahmatullah (1990). *The Iran–United States Claims Tribunal: Controversies, Cases and Contribution* (Dordrecht: Nijhoff).

Kishoian, Bernard (1994). "The utility of bilateral investment treaties in the formulation of customary international law", *Northwestern Journal of International Law and Business*, vol. 14 (Winter), pp. 327–375.

Klebes, H. (1983). "Encouragement et protection des investissements privés dans les pays en développement: les traités bilatéraux de la République Fédérale d'Allemagne dans leur contexte" (Strasbourg), unpublished thesis.

Kline, John M. and Rodney D. Ludema (1997). "Building a multilateral framework for investment: comparing the development of trade and investment accords", *Transnational Corporations*, vol. 6, no. 3 (December 1997), pp. 1-31.

Kohona, Palitha T.B. (1987a). "Investment protection agreements: an Australian perspective", *Journal of World Trade Law*, vol. 21, no. 2, pp. 79–103.

_____ (1987b). "Some major provisions in modern investment protection agreements. The application of law and development theory: some case studies", *Third World Legal Studies*, Annual (1987), pp. 151–180.

Kravis, I., and R. Lipsey (1982). "The location of overseas production for export by US multinational firms", *Journal of International Economics*, 12, pp. 201–223.

Kreinin, M., M. Plummer and S. Abe. (forthcoming). "The trade-investment nexus", in F.J. Contractor ed., *Economic Transformation in Emerging Countries: The Role of Investment, Trade and Finance* (London: Elsevier).

Kunzer, Kathleen (1983). "Developing a model bilateral investment treaty", *Law and Policy in International Business*, vol. 15, pp. 273–301.

"Kuwait v. American Independent Oil Company", Arbitration case (1982), *International Legal Materials*, vol. 21, pp. 976–1053.

Laviec, Jean-Pierre (1985). *Protection et Promotion des Investissements: Études de Droit International Économiques* (Paris: Presses Universitaires de France).

Lebanon (1997). "Paper submitted by the expert from Lebanon to the Expert Meeting on Existing Agreements on Investment and Their Development Dimensions, Geneva, 28–30 May 1997" (Geneva: UNCTAD), mimeo.

Lillich, Richard B. (1972, 1973, 1975, 1987). *The Valuation of Nationalized Property in International Law*, 4 vols. (Charlottesville: University of Virginia Press).

_____ ed. (1983). *International Law and State Responsibility for Injuries to Aliens* (Charlottesville: University of Virginia Press).

Lunn, J.L. (1983). "Determinants of US direct investment in the EEC revisited again", *European Economic Review*, 21 (May), pp. 391–395.

Mann, F.A. (1981). "British treaties for the promotion and protection of investments", *British Yearbook of International Law*, vol. 52, pp. 241–264.

Matsui, Yoshiro (1989). "Japan's international legal policy for the protection of foreign investment", *Japanese Annual of International Law*, 32, pp. 1–17.

Mouri, Allahyar (1994). *The International Law of Expropriation as Reflected in the Work of the Iran–US Claims Tribunal* (Dordrecht: Nijhoff).

Muller, M.H. (1981). "Compensation for nationalization: a North–South dialogue", *Columbia Journal of Transnational Law*, vol. 19, pp. 35–78.

Murphy, Sean D. (1991). "The ELSI case: an investment dispute at the International Court of Justice", *Yale Journal of International Law*, vol. 16, pp. 391–452.

Nurick, Lester and Stephen J. Schnably (1986). "The first ICSID conciliation: Teoro Petroleum Corporation v. Trinidad and Tobago", *ICSID Review: Foreign Investment Law Journal*, vol. 1, pp. 340–353.

Ocran, T. Modibo (1987). "Bilateral investment protection treaties: a comparative study", *New York Law School Journal of International and Comparative Law*, vol. 8 (Fall), pp. 401–429.

Oppenheim, L. (1992). *International Law,* 9th ed. (Harlow: Longman), (Jennings, Sir Robert, and Watts A. eds.).

Organisation for Economic Co-operation and Development (OECD) (1968). "Council Resolution of 12 October 1967 on the Draft Convention on the Protection of Foreign Property", *International Legal Materials*, vol. 7, pp. 117–143.

_____ (1985). *Intergovernmental Agreements Relating to Investment in Developing Countries* (Paris, OECD).

Organization of American States (OAS), Trade Unit (1997). *Investment Agreements in the Western Hemisphere: A Compendium* (Washington, DC: OAS, Trade Unit).

Parra, Antonio R. (1995). "The scope of new investment laws and international instruments", *Transnational Corporations*, vol. 4, no. 3 (December), pp. 27–48.

Paterson, Robert K. (1991). "Canadian investment promotion and protection treaties", *Canadian Yearbook of International Law*, vol. 29, pp. 373–396.

Permanent Court of International Justice (1924). "Mavrommatis Palestine Concessions Case (Greece v. the United Kingdom)", *Permanent Court of International Justice Reports*, Series A, no. 2, p. 6–88.

Peru (1997). "Paper submitted by the expert from Peru to the Expert Meeting on Existing Agreements on Investment and Their Development Dimensions, Geneva, 28–30 May 1997 (Geneva: UNCTAD), mimeo.

Philippines (1997). "Paper submited by the expert from the Philippines to the Expert Meeting on Existing Agreements on Investment and their Development Dimensions, Geneva, 28–30 May 1997" (Geneva: UNCTAD), mimeo.

Portugal (1997). "Paper submitted by the expert from Portugal to the Expert Meeting on Existing Agreements on Investment and Their Development Dimensions, Geneva, 28–30 May 1997" (Geneva: UNCTAD), mimeo.

Pygal, T.A. (1981). "The determinants of foreign direct investment: analysis of US manufacturing industries", *Managerial and Decision Economics,* 2 (December), pp. 220–228.

Reading, Michael R. (1992). "The bilateral investment treaty in ASEAN: a comparative analysis", *Duke Law Journal*, vol. 42, pp. 679–705.

Reisman, W. Michael (1989). "The breakdown of the control mechanism in ICSID arbitration", *Duke Law Journal*, (September), pp. 739–807.

Robinson, Patrick (1986). *The Question of a Reference to International Law in the United Nations Code of Conduct on Transnational Corporations* (Current Studies Series A, no. 4) (New York: United Nations), United Nations publication, sales no. E.86.II.A.5.

_____ (1993). "Treaty negotiations, drafting, ratification and accession by CARICOM States", *West Indian Law Journal*, vol. 18, no. 2, pp. 1–24.

Roffe, Pedro (1984). "Calvo y su vigencia en América Latina" *Revista de Derecho Industrial*, 6, no. 17, (May–August) 1984, pp. 353–384.

Romania (1997). "Paper submitted by the expert from Romania to the Expert Meeting on Existing Agreements on Investment and Their Development Dimensions, Geneva, 28–30 May 1997" (Geneva: UNCTAD), mimeo.

Salacuse, Jeswald W. (1990). "BIT by BIT: the growth of bilateral investment treaties and their impact on foreign investment in developing countries", *The International Lawyer*, vol. 24, pp. 655–675.

Salem, Mahmoud (1986). "Le développement de la protection conventionelle des investissements étrangers", *Journal du Droit International*, vol. 113, pp. 579–626.

Sauvant, Karl P. and Victoria Aranda (1993). "The international legal framework for transnational corporations", in A.A. Fatouros, ed., *Transnational Corporations: The International Legal Framework. United Nations Library on Transnational Corporations*, vol. 20 (London, Routledge), pp. 83–115.

Scaperlanda, A. and Balough, R. (1983). "Determinants of US direct investment in the EEC revisited", *European Economic Review,* 21, pp. 381–390.

Schachter, Oscar (1984). "Compensation for expropriation", *American Journal of International Law*, vol. 78, pp. 121–130.

Schneider, F. and B. Frey. (1985). "Economic and political determinants of foreign direct investment", *World Development*, 13 (February), pp. 161–175.

Schwarzenberger, Georg (1969). *Foreign Investments and International Law* (London: Stevens).

Sharma, Surya P. (1992). "Interpretation of bilateral investment treaties: the case of Asian Agricultural Products Ltd.", *Asia Pacific Law Review*, vol. 1, pp. 123–133.

Shawcross, Lord (1961). "The problems of foreign investment in international law", *Recueil des Cours* (The Hague Academy of International Law), vol. 102, pp. 335–363.

Shenkin, Todd S. (1994). "Trade-related investment measures in bilateral investment treaties and the GATT: moving toward a multilateral investment treaty", *University of Pittsburg Law Review*, vol. 55, pp. 541–606.

Shihata, Ibrahim F. (1996). "Recent trends relating to entry of foreign investment", *ICSID Review: Foreign Investment Law Journal*, vol. 9 (Spring), pp. 47–70.

Shishi, Li (1988). "Bilateral investment promotion and protection agreements: practice of the People's Republic of China", in Paul de Waart, Paul Peters and Eric Denters, eds., *International Law and Development*, (The Hague: Nijhoff) pp. 163–184.

Sornarajah, M. (1986). "State responsibility and bilateral investment treaties", *Journal of World Trade Law*, vol. 20, 1, pp. 79–98.

_____ (1994). *The International Law on Foreign Investment* (Cambridge: Cambridge University Press).

Turkey (1997). "Paper submitted by the expert from Turkey to the Expert Meeting on Existing Agreements on Investment and Their Development Dimensions, Geneva, 28–30 May 1997" (Geneva: UNCTAD), mimeo.

United Nations (1945). *Charter of the United Nations and Statute of the International Court of Justice* (New York: United Nations).

_____ (1987). "Vienna Convention on the Law of Treaties", United Nations document A/CONF.39/27 (23 May 1969), *United Nations Treaty Series*, vol. 1155, pp. 331–353.

United Nations Centre on Transnational Corporations (UNCTC) (1988). *Bilateral Investment Treaties* (New York: United Nations), United Nations publication, sales no. E.88.II.A.1.

_____ (1990). *Key Concepts in International Investment Arrangments and Their Relevance to Negotiations on International Transactions in Services* (Current Studies Series A, no. 13) (New York: United Nations), United Nations publication, sales no. E.90.II.A.3.

_____ (1991). *Government Policies and Foreign Direct Investment* (New York: United Nations), United Nations publication, sales no. E.91.II.A.20.

_____ (1992). *The Determinants of Foreign Direct Investment: A Survey of the Evidence* (New York: United Nations), United Nations publication, sales no. E.92.II.A.2.

_____- International Chamber of Commerce (ICC) (1992). *Bilateral Investment Treaties, 1959–1991* (New York: United Nations), United Nations publication, sales no. E.92.II.A.16.

UNCTC and UNCTAD (1991). *The Impact of Trade-related Investment Measures on Trade and Development* (New York: United Nations), United Nations publication, sales no. E.91.II.A.19.

United Nations, Transnational Corporations and Management Division (1992). *World Investment Report 1992: Transnational Corporations as Engines of Growth* (New York and Geneva, United Nations), United Nations publication, sales no. E.92.II.A.19.

United Nations, Transnational Corporations and Management Division (1993). *Foreign Direct Investment and Intellectual Property Rights* (New York: United Nations), United Nations publication, sales no.E.93.II.A.10.

United Nations Conference on Trade and Development (UNCTAD) (1993). *Explaining and Forecasting Regional Flows of Foreign Direct Investment* (New York and Geneva: United Nations), United Nations publication, sales no. E.93.II.A.15.

_____ (1994). *World Investment Report 1994: Transnational Corporations, Employment and the Workplace* (Geneva and New York: United Nations), United Nations publication, sales no. E.94.II.A.14.

_____ (1995). *World Investment Report 1995: Transnational Corporations and Competitiveness* (Geneva and New York: United Nations), United Nations publication, sales no. E.95.II.A.9.

_____ (1996a). "Report of the United Nations Conference on Trade and Development on its Ninth Session, held in Midrand, South Africa, from 27 April to 11 May 1996", UNCTAD document TD/378.

_____ (1996b). *International Investment Agreements: A Compendium. Volume I: Multilateral Instruments, Volume II: Regional Instruments, Volume III: Regional Integration, Bilateral and Non-governmental Instruments* (Geneva: United Nations), United Nations publications, sales nos. E.96.II.A.9, 10 and 11, respectively.

_____ (1996c). *World Investment Report 1996: Investment, Trade and International Policy Arrangements* (New York and Geneva: United Nations), United Nations Publication, sales no. E.96.II.A.14.

_____ (1996d). *Incentives and Foreign Direct Investment* (Geneva: United Nations), United Nations publication, sales no. E.96.II.A.6.

_____ (1997a). *World Investment Report 1997: Transnational Corporations, Market Structure and Competition Policy* (Geneva: United Nations), United Nations publication, sales no. E.97.II.D.10.

_____ (1997b). "Report of the Expert Meeting on Existing Agreements on Investment and Their Development Dimensions", UNCTAD document TD/B/COM.2/5 -TD/B/COM.2/EM.1/3.

United States Supreme Court (1982). "Sumitomo Shoji, America, Inc. v. Avagliano", *Supreme Court Reports* (Saint Paul, MN: West), vol. 102, pp. 2374–2382.

Vagts, Detlev F. (1986). *The Question of a Reference to International Obligations in the United Nations Code of Conduct on Transnational Corporations: A Different View* (UNCTC Current Studies Series A, No. 2) (New York: United Nations), United Nations publication, sales no. E.86.II.A.11.

_____ (1990). "Protecting foreign direct investment: an international law perspective" in C. Wallace, ed., *Foreign Direct Investment in the 1990s: A New Climate in the Third World* (Dordrecht: Nijhoff), pp. 102–118.

Vandevelde, Kenneth J. (1988). "The bilateral treaty program of the United States", *Cornell International Law Journal*, vol. 21, pp. 201–276.

_____ (1992). *United States Investment Treaties: Policy and Practice* (Deventer: Kluwer).

_____ (1993a). "United States bilateral investment treaties: the second wave", *Michigan Journal of International Law*, vol. 14, pp. 621–704.

_____ (1993b). "Of politics and markets: the shifting ideology of BITs", *International Tax and Business Lawyer*, vol. 11, pp. 159–186.

Vascianne, Stephen C. (1992). "Bilateral investment treaties and civil strife: the AAPL/Sri Lanka Arbitration", *Netherlands International Law Review*, vol. 39, no. 3, pp. 332–354.

Voss, Jürgen (1981). "The protection and promotion of European private investment in developing countries: an approach towards a concept for a European policy on foreign investments. A German contribution", *Common Market Law Review*, vol. 18, pp. 363–374.

Waelde, T. and G. Ndi (1996). "Stabilizing international investment commitments: international law versus contract interpretation", *Texas International Law Journal*, vol. 31 (Spring), pp. 216–267.

Walker, Herman Jr. (1956). "Treaties for the encouragement and protection of foreign investment: present United States practice", *American Journal of Comparative Law*, vol. 5, pp. 229–247.

_____ (1958). "Modern treaties of friendship, commerce and navigation", *Minnesota Law Review*, vol. 42 (April), pp. 805–824.

Weston, Burns H. (1975). "'Constructive takings' under international law", *Virginia Journal of International Law*, vol. 16, pp. 103–174.

White, Gillian (1961). *Nationalization of Foreign Property* (London: Stevens).

Wiesner, E. (1993). "ANCOM: a new attitude towards foreign investment?", *Inter-American Law Review*, vol. 24 (Spring/Summer), pp. 435–465.

Wilson, Robert. R. (1949). "Postwar commercial treaties of the United States", *American Journal of International Law*, vol. 43, pp. 262–287.

_____ (1951). "Property protection provisions in the United States commercial treaties", *American Journal of Comparative Law*, vol. 45, pp. 83–107.

_____ (1953). *The International Law Standard in the Treaties of the United States* (Cambridge, MA: Harvard University Press).

_____ (1956). "A decade of new commercial treaties", *American Journal of International Law*, vol. 50, pp. 927–933.

_____ (1960). *United States Commercial Treaties and International Law* (New Orleans: Hauser Press).

World Bank (1992). *Legal Framework for the Treatment of Foreign Investment: Survey of Existing Instruments*, vol. I (Washington, DC: World Bank).

Wortley, B.A. (1959). *Expropriation in Public International Law* (Cambridge: Cambridge University Press).

ANNEXES

Annex I. List of bilateral investment treaties
concluded up to 31 December 1996

Country/territory	*Date of signature*	*Date of entry into force*
Albania		
Greece	1 August 1991	4 January 1995
Italy	12 September 1991	-
Germany	31 October 1991	18 August 1995
Turkey	1 June 1992	-
Switzerland	22 September 1992	30 April 1993
China	13 February 1993	-
Poland	5 March 1993	9 August 1993
Austria	18 March 1993	-
Croatia	10 May 1993	-
Egypt	22 May 1993	6 April 1994
Tunisia	30 October 1993	-
United Kingdom	30 March 1994	30 August 1995
Netherlands	15 April 1994	1 September 1995
Bulgaria	27 April 1994	28 January 1996
Czech Republic	27 June 1994	7 July 1995
United States	10 January 1995	-
Malaysia	18 January 1995	-
Sweden	31 March 1995	1 April 1996
Russian Federation	11 April 1995	-
Romania	11 May 1995	-
France	13 June 1995	-
Denmark	5 September 1995	-
Hungary	24 January 1996	-
Israel	29 January 1996	-
Algeria		
Belgium/Luxembourg	24 April 1991	-
Italy	18 May 1991	-
France	13 February 1993	-
Romania	22 October 1994	-
Spain	23 December 1994	-

Note: While every effort has been made to assure the accuracy of the information in the list, it would be appreciated if readers would bring any errors or omissions to the attention of UNCTAD (at the address on p. 302).

This list has been prepared on the basis of information supplied by governments, and most of the information has been confirmed by both parties to each treaty. However, if one party did not respond to requests for information, the information supplied by the other party has been used. Any discrepancies in the information supplied by the two parties were resolved by contacting the parties or consulting independent sources.

Country/territory	*Date of signature*	*Date of entry into force*
Germany	11 March 1996	-
Mali	11 July 1996	-
Jordan	1 August 1996	-
China	17 October 1996	-
Viet Nam	21 October 1996	-
Qatar	24 October 1996	-

Antigua and Barbuda

United Kingdom	12 June 1987	12 June 1987

Argentina

Italy	22 May 1990	14 October 1993
Belgium/Luxembourg	28 June 1990	20 May 1994
United Kingdom	11 December 1990	19 February 1993
Germany	9 April 1991	8 November 1993
Switzerland	12 April 1991	6 November 1992
France	3 July 1991	3 March 1993
Poland	31 July 1991	1 September 1992
Chile	2 August 1991	1 January 1995
Spain	3 October 1991	28 September 1992
Canada	5 November 1991	29 April 1993
United States	14 November 1991	20 October 1994
Sweden	22 November 1991	28 September 1992
Turkey	8 May 1992	1 May 1995
Egypt	11 May 1992	3 December 1993
Tunisia	17 June 1992	23 January 1995
Austria	7 August 1992	1 January 1995
Netherlands	20 October 1992	1 October 1994
China	5 November 1992	1 August 1994
Denmark	6 November 1992	2 February 1995
Hungary	5 February 1993	-
Senegal	6 April 1993	-
Armenia	16 April 1993	20 December 1994
Romania	29 July 1993	1 May 1995
Bulgaria	21 September 1993	-
Finland	5 November 1993	3 May 1996
Venezuela	16 November 1993	1 July 1995
Jamaica	8 February 1994	1 December 1995
Ecuador	20 February 1994	-
Bolivia	17 March 1994	-
Republic of Korea	17 May 1994	-
Malaysia	6 September 1994	-
Portugal	6 October 1994	-
Peru	10 November 1994	-
Croatia	2 December 1994	-
Israel	23 July 1995	-
Ukraine	9 August 1995	-
Australia	23 August 1995	-
Indonesia	7 November 1995	-
Cuba	30 November 1995	-
Lithuania	14 March 1996	-
Panama	10 May 1996	-
Morrocco	13 June 1996	-

Country/territory	*Date of signature*	*Date of entry into force*
Czech Republic	27 September 1996	-
Mexico	13 November 1996	-

Armenia [a]

China	4 July 1992	-
United States	23 September 1992	29 March 1996
Viet Nam	February 1993	-
Argentina	16 April 1993	20 December 1994
United Kingdom	22 May 1993	-
Greece	25 May 1993	28 April 1995
Kyrgyzstan	4 July 1994	27 October 1995
Romania	20 September 1994	24 December 1995
Lebanon	1 January 1995	-
Egypt	9 January 1995	-
Cyprus	18 January 1995	-
Bulgaria	10 April 1995	-
Iran, Islamic Republic of	6 May 1995	-
France	4 November 1995	-
Germany	21 December 1995	-
Georgia	1 June 1996	-

Australia

China	11 July 1988	11 July 1988
Papua New Guinea	3 September 1990	20 October 1991
Viet Nam	5 March 1991	11 September 1991
Poland	7 May 1991	27 March 1992
Czechoslovakia (former)	29 July 1991	-
Hungary	15 August 1991	10 May 1992
Indonesia	17 November 1992	29 July 1993
Romania	21 June 1993	22 April 1994
Hong Kong, China	15 September 1993	15 October 1993
Czech Republic	30 September 1993	29 June 1994
Lao People's Democratic Republic	6 April 1994	8 April 1995
Philippines	25 January 1995	8 December 1995
Argentina	23 August 1995	-
Peru	7 December 1995	-
Chile	9 July 1996	-

Austria

Romania	30 September 1976	8 November 1977
Bulgaria	15 May 1981	-
Malaysia	12 April 1985	1 January 1987
China	12 September 1985	11 October 1986
Hungary	26 May 1988	1 September 1989
Turkey	16 September 1988	1 January 1992
Poland	24 November 1988	1 November 1989
Yugoslavia	25 October 1989	1 June 1991
USSR (former)	8 February 1990	1 September 1991
Czechoslovakia (former)	15 October 1990	1 October 1991
Republic of Korea	14 March 1991	1 November 1991
Cape Verde	3 September 1991	1 April 1993

Country/territory	Date of signature	Date of entry into force
Argentina	7 August 1992	1 January 1995
Morocco	2 November 1992	-
Albania	18 March 1993	-
Paraguay	13 August 1993	-
Estonia	16 May 1994	8 February 1995
Latvia	17 November 1994	1 May 1996
Viet Nam	27 March 1995	-
Tunisia	1 June 1995	-
Romania	15 May 1996	-
Lithuania	28 June 1996	-
Hong Kong, China	11 October 1996	-
Ukraine	8 November 1996	-
Kuwait	16 November 1996	-
South Africa	28 November 1996	-

Azerbaijan [a]

Turkey	9 February 1994	-
China	8 March 1994	1 April 1995
Germany	22 December 1995	-
United Kingdom	4 January 1996	-
Georgia	1 March 1996	-
Uzbekistan	27 May 1996	-
Kazakhstan	16 September 1996	-

Bahrain

United Kingdom	30 October 1991	30 October 1991

Bangladesh

United Kingdom	19 June 1980	19 June 1980
Germany	6 May 1981	14 September 1986
Belgium/Luxembourg	22 May 1981	14 September 1987
France	10 September 1985	3 October 1986
United States	12 March 1986	25 July 1989
Republic of Korea	18 June 1986	6 October 1988
Romania	13 March 1987	31 October 1987
Turkey	12 November 1987	21 June 1990
Thailand	13 March 1988	-
Italy	20 March 1990	13 August 1994
Malaysia	12 October 1994	-
Netherlands	1 November 1994	-
China	12 September 1996	-

Barbados

United Kingdom	7 April 1993	7 April 1993
Venezuela	15 July 1994	31 October 1995
Germany	2 December 1994	-
Switzerland	29 March 1995	22 December 1995
Italy	25 October 1995	-
Cuba	19 February 1996	-
Canada	29 May 1996	-

Country/territory	Date of signature	Date of entry into force
Belarus [a]		
Poland	24 April 1992	18 January 1993
Viet Nam	8 July 1992	-
Finland	28 October 1992	21 March 1993
China	11 January 1993	14 January 1995
Germany	2 April 1993	-
Switzerland	28 May 1993	13 July 1994
France	28 October 1993	-
United States	15 January 1994	-
United Kingdom	1 March 1994	-
Sweden	20 December 1994	-
Netherlands	11 April 1995	-
Romania	31 May 1995	-
Iran (Islamic Republic of)	14 July 1995	-
Italy	25 July 1995	-
Turkey	8 August 1995	-
Ukraine	14 December 1995	-
Bulgaria	21 February 1996	-
Yugoslavia	6 March 1996	-
Czech Republic	14 October 1996	-
Belgium/Luxembourg		
Tunisia	15 July 1964	9 March 1966
Morocco	28 April 1965	18 October 1967
Indonesia [b]	15 January 1970	17 June 1972
Republic of Korea	20 December 1974	3 September 1976
Democratic Republic of Congo [b]	28 March 1976	1 January 1977
Egypt	28 February 1977	20 September 1978
Romania [j]	8 May 1978	1 May 1980
Singapore	17 November 1978	27 November 1980
Malaysia	22 November 1979	8 February 1982
Cameroon	27 March 1980	1 November 1981
Bangladesh	22 May 1981	14 September 1987
Sri Lanka	5 April 1982	26 April 1984
Rwanda	2 November 1983	1 August 1985
Mauritania	23 November 1983	-
China	4 June 1984	5 October 1986
Liberia	5 June 1985	-
Thailand	19 March 1986	-
Hungary	14 May 1986	23 September 1988
Turkey	27 August 1986	4 May 1990
Malta	5 March 1987	21 May 1990
Poland [c]	19 May 1987	2 August 1991
Bulgaria	25 October 1988	29 May 1991
USSR (former) [c]	9 February 1989	13 October 1991
Burundi	13 April 1989	-
Czechoslovakia (former) [e]	24 April 1989	13 February 1992
Bolivia	25 April 1990	-
Argentina	28 June 1990	20 May 1994
Viet Nam	24 January 1991	-
Cyprus	26 February 1991	-
Algeria	24 April 1991	13 February 1992
Uruguay	4 November 1991	-

Country/territory	Date of signature	Date of entry into force
Mongolia	3 March 1992	-
Chile	15 July 1992	-
Paraguay	6 October 1992	-
Georgia	23 June 1993	-
Ukraine	20 May 1995	-
Estonia	24 January 1996	-
Romania	4 March 1996	-
Latvia	27 March 1996	-
Hong Kong, China	7 October 1996	-

Belize

United Kingdom	30 April 1982	30 April 1982

Benin

Switzerland	20 April 1966	6 October 1973
Germany	29 June 1978	18 July 1985
United Kingdom	27 November 1987	27 November 1987

Bolivia

Germany	23 March 1987	9 November 1990
Switzerland	6 November 1987	13 May 1991
United Kingdom	24 May 1988	16 February 1990
France	25 October 1989	-
Spain	24 April 1990	12 May 1992
Belgium/Luxembourg	25 April 1990	-
Italy	30 April 1990	22 February 1992
Sweden	20 September 1990	3 July 1992
Netherlands	10 March 1992	1 November 1994
China	8 May 1992	-
Peru	30 July 1993	19 March 1995
Argentina	17 March 1994	-
Chile	22 September 1994	-
Denmark	12 March 1995	-
Cuba	6 May 1995	-
Ecuador	25 May 1995	-
Romania	9 October 1995	-
Republic of Korea	1 April 1996	

Bosnia and Herzegovina

Malaysia	16 December 1994	27 May 1995
Croatia	26 February 1996	-
Iran, Islamic Republic of	27 June 1996	-

Brazil

Portugal	9 February 1994	-
Chile	22 March 1994	-
United Kingdom	19 July 1994	-
Switzerland	11 November 1994	-
France	21 March 1995	-
Finland	28 March 1995	-

Country/territory	*Date of signature*	*Date of entry into force*
Italy	3 April 1995	-
Denmark	4 May 1995	-
Venezuela	4 July 1995	-
Republic of Korea	1 September 1995	-
Germany	21 September 1995	-

Bulgaria

Austria	15 May 1981	-
Finland	16 February 1984	16 July 1985
Malta	12 June 1984	7 February 1985
Germany	12 April 1986	10 March 1988
Cyprus	12 November 1987	18 May 1988
Netherlands	8 March 1988	24 May 1990
Belgium/Luxembourg	25 October 1988	29 May 1991
Italy	5 December 1988	27 December 1990
France	5 April 1989	1 May 1990
China	27 June 1989	21 August 1994
Ghana	20 October 1989	-
Switzerland	28 October 1991	26 October 1993
United States	23 September 1992	2 June 1994
Greece	12 March 1993	29 April 1995
Denmark	14 April 1993	20 May 1995
Portugal	27 May 1993	-
Russian Federation	8 June 1993	-
Argentina	21 September 1993	-
Israel	6 December 1993	-
Poland	11 April 1994	9 March 1995
Sweden	19 April 1994	1 April 1995
Albania	27 April 1994	28 January 1996
Romania	1 June 1994	23 May 1995
Hungary	8 June 1994	7 September 1995
Turkey	6 July 1994	-
Slovakia	18 August 1994	9 March 1995
Ukraine	8 December 1994	10 December 1995
Georgia	19 January 1995	-
Armenia	10 April 1995	-
Spain	5 September 1995	-
United Kingdom	11 December 1995	-
Yugoslavia	13 February 1996	-
Belarus	21 February 1996	-
Republic of Moldova	17 April 1996	-
Morocco	22 May 1996	-
Croatia	25 June 1996	-
Viet Nam	19 September 1996	-

Burkina Faso

Switzerland	6 May 1969	15 September 1969
Tunisia	7 January 1993	-
Germany	22 October 1996	-

Burundi

Germany	10 September 1984	9 December 1987

Country/territory	Date of signature	Date of entry into force
Belgium/Luxembourg	13 April 1989	-
United Kingdom	13 September 1990	13 September 1990

Cambodia

Thailand	29 March 1995	-
China	19 July 1996	-
Switzerland	12 October 1996	-

Cameroon

Germany	29 June 1962	21 November 1963
Switzerland	28 January 1963	6 April 1964
Netherlands	6 July 1965	7 May 1966
Belgium/Luxembourg	27 March 1980	1 November 1981
Romania	30 August 1980	16 December 1981
United Kingdom	4 June 1982	7 June 1985
United States	26 February 1986	6 April 1989

Canada [d]

USSR (former)	20 November 1989	27 June 1991
Poland	26 October 1990	22 November 1990
Czechoslovakia (former)	15 November 1990	9 March 1992
Uruguay	16 May 1991	-
Hungary	3 October 1991	21 November 1993
Argentina	5 November 1991	29 April 1993
Ukraine	24 October 1994	-
Latvia	26 April 1995	27 July 1995
Trinidad and Tobago	11 September 1995	8 July 1996
Philippines	10 November 1995	-
South Africa	27 November 1995	-
Romania	17 April 1996	-
Ecuador	29 April 1996	-
Barbados	29 May 1996	17 January 1997
Venezuela	1 July 1996	-
Panama	12 September 1996	-
Egypt	13 November 1996	-

Cape Verde

Germany	18 January 1990	15 December 1993
Portugal	26 October 1990	4 October 1991
Austria	3 September 1991	1 April 1993
Switzerland	28 October 1991	6 May 1992
Netherlands	11 November 1991	25 November 1992

Central African Republic

France	13 August 1960	-
Germany	23 August 1965	21 January 1968
Switzerland	28 February 1973	4 July 1973

Chad

France	13 August 1960	-

Country/territory	Date of signature	Date of entry into force
Switzerland	21 February 1967	31 October 1967
Germany	11 April 1967	23 November 1968
Italy	11 June 1969	11 June 1969

Chile

Country/territory	Date of signature	Date of entry into force
Argentina	2 August 1991	1 January 1995
Spain	2 October 1991	28 March 1994
Germany	19 October 1991	-
Switzerland	11 November 1991	-
France	14 July 1992	13 July 1993
Belgium/Luxembourg	15 July 1992	-
Malaysia	11 November 1992	-
Italy	8 March 1993	-
Venezuela	2 April 1993	25 May 1995
Sweden	24 May 1993	30 December 1995
Finland	27 May 1993	1 May 1996
Denmark	28 May 1993	3 November 1995
Norway	1 June 1993	7 September 1994
Ecuador	27 October 1993	-
Brazil	22 March 1994	-
China	23 March 1994	-
Bolivia	22 September 1994	-
Croatia	28 November 1994	-
Czech Republic	24 April 1995	-
Portugal	28 April 1995	-
Romania	4 July 1995	-
Poland	5 July 1995	-
Paraguay	7 August 1995	-
Ukraine	30 October 1995	-
Philippines	20 November 1995	-
United Kingdom	8 January 1996	-
Cuba	10 January 1996	-
Australia	9 July 1996	-
Greece	10 July 1996	-
Costa Rica	11 July 1996	-
Republic of Korea	7 September 1996	-
Guatemala	8 November 1996	-
Nicaragua	10 November 1996	-
El Salvador	11 November 1996	-
Honduras	11 November 1996	-
Panama	18 November 1996	-

China

Country/territory	Date of signature	Date of entry into force
Sweden	29 March 1982	29 March 1982
Romania	10 February 1983	12 January 1984
Germany	7 October 1983	18 March 1985
France	30 May 1984	19 March 1985
Belgium/Luxembourg	4 June 1984	5 October 1986
Finland	4 September 1984	26 January 1986
Norway	21 November 1984	10 July 1985
Italy	28 January 1985	28 August 1987
Thailand	12 March 1985	13 December 1985
Denmark	29 April 1985	29 April 1985
Netherlands	17 June 1985	1 February 1987

Country/territory	Date of signature	Date of entry into force
Austria	12 September 1985	11 October 1986
Singapore	21 November 1985	7 February 1986
Kuwait	23 November 1985	24 December 1986
Sri Lanka	13 March 1986	25 March 1987
United Kingdom	15 May 1986	15 May 1986
Switzerland	12 November 1986	18 March 1987
Poland	7 June 1988	8 January 1989
Australia	11 July 1988	11 July 1988
Japan	27 August 1988	14 May 1989
Malaysia	21 November 1988	31 March 1990
New Zealand	22 November 1988	25 March 1989
Pakistan	12 February 1989	30 September 1990
Bulgaria	27 June 1989	21 August 1994
Ghana	12 October 1989	-
USSR (former)	21 July 1990	-
Turkey	13 November 1990	19 August 1994
Papua New Guinea	12 April 1991	12 February 1993
Hungary	29 May 1991	1 April 1993
Mongolia	26 August 1991	1 November 1993
Czechoslovakia (former)	4 December 1991	1 December 1992
Portugal	3 February 1992	1 December 1992
Spain	6 February 1992	1 May 1993
Uzbekistan	13 March 1992	14 April 1994
Bolivia	8 May 1992	-
Kyrgyzstan	14 May 1992	
Greece	25 June 1992	21 December 1993
Armenia	4 July 1992	-
Philippines	20 July 1992	-
Kazakhstan	10 August 1992	13 August 1994
Republic of Korea	30 September 1992	4 December 1992
Ukraine	31 October 1992	29 May 1993
Argentina	5 November 1992	1 August 1994
Republic of Moldova	7 November 1992	1 March 1995
Turkmenistan	21 November 1992	6 June 1995
Viet Nam	2 December 1992	1 September 1993
Belarus	11 January 1993	14 January 1995
Lao People's Democratic Republic	31 January 1993	1 June 1993
Albania	13 February 1993	-
Tajikistan	9 March 1993	20 January 1994
Georgia	3 June 1993	1 March 1995
Croatia	7 June 1993	1 July 1994
United Arab Emirates	1 July 1993	28 September 1994
Estonia	2 September 1993	1 June 1994
Slovenia	13 September 1993	1 January 1995
Lithuania	8 November 1993	1 June 1994
Uruguay	2 December 1993	-
Azerbaijan	8 March 1994	1 April 1995
Ecuador	21 March 1994	-
Chile	23 March 1994	-
Iceland	31 March 1994	-
Egypt	21 April 1994	-
Peru	9 June 1994	1 February 1995
Romania	12 July 1994	1 September 1995
Jamaica	26 October 1994	-

Country/territory	Date of signature	Date of entry into force
Indonesia	18 November 1994	1 April 1995
Oman	18 March 1995	-
Morocco	27 March 1995	-
Israel	10 April 1995	-
Cuba	24 April 1995	-
Yugoslavia	18 December 1995	-
Saudi Arabia	29 February 1996	-
Mauritius	4 May 1996	-
Zimbabwe	21 May 1996	-
Lebanon	13 June 1996	-
Zambia	21 June 1996	-
Cambodia	19 July 1996	-
Bangladesh	12 September 1996	-
Algeria	17 October 1996	-
Syrian Arab Republic	19 December 1996	-

Colombia

United Kingdom	9 March 1994	-
Peru	26 April 1994	-
Cuba	16 July 1994	-
Spain	9 June 1995	-

Congo

France	15 August 1960	-
Switzerland	18 October 1962	11 July 1964
Germany	13 September 1965	14 October 1967
United Kingdom	25 May 1989	9 November 1990
United States	12 February 1990	-
Italy	17 March 1994	-

Costa Rica

Switzerland	1 September 1965	18 August 1966
United Kingdom	7 September 1982	-
France	8 March 1984	-
Germany	13 September 1994	-
Chile	11 July 1996	

Côte d'Ivoire

Switzerland	26 June 1962	18 November 1962
Netherlands	26 April 1965	8 September 1966
Sweden	27 August 1965	3 November 1966
Germany	27 October 1966	10 June 1968
Denmark	23 November 1966	10 January 1968
Italy	23 July 1969	-
United Kingdom	8 June 1995	-

Croatia

Albania	10 May 1993	-
China	7 June 1993	1 July 1994

Country/territory	*Date of signature*	*Date of entry into force*
Romania	8 June 1994	-
The former Yugoslav Republic of Macedonia	6 July 1994	5 April 1995
Chile	28 November 1994	-
Argentina	2 December 1994	-
Malaysia	16 December 1994	-
Poland	21 February 1995	4 October 1995
Portugal	9 May 1995	-
Slovakia	12 February 1996	-
Turkey	12 February 1996	-
Bosnia and Herzegovina	26 February 1996	-
Czech Republic	5 March 1996	-
Bulgaria	25 June 1996	-
Switzerland	30 June 1996	-
United States	13 July 1996	-
Italy	5 November 1996	-

Cuba

Italy	7 May 1993	23 August 1995
Russian Federation	7 July 1993	-
Spain	27 May 1994	9 June 1995
Colombia	16 July 1994	-
United Kingdom	30 January 1995	11 May 1995
China	24 April 1995	-
Bolivia	6 May 1995	-
Ukraine	20 May 1995	19 February 1996
Viet Nam	12 October 1995	-
Argentina	30 November 1995	-
South Africa	8 December 1995	-
Lebanon	14 December 1995	-
Chile	10 January 1996	-
Romania	26 January 1996	-
Barbados	19 February 1996	-
Germany	30 April 1996	-
Greece	18 June 1996	-
Switzerland	28 June 1996	-
Venezuela	14 December 1996	-

Cyprus

Bulgaria	12 November 1987	18 May 1988
Hungary	24 May 1989	25 May 1990
Belgium/Luxembourg	26 February 1991	-
Romania	26 July 1991	10 July 1993
Greece	30 March 1992	26 February 1993
Poland	4 June 1992	1 July 1993
Armenia	18 January 1995	-

Czechoslovakia (former) [e]

Belgium/Luxembourg	24 April 1989	13 February 1992
United Kingdom	10 July 1990	26 October 1992
Italy	1 August 1990	-
France	13 September 1990	27 September 1991

Country/territory	_Date of signature_	_Date of entry into force_
Germany	2 October 1990	2 August 1992
Switzerland	5 October 1990	7 August 1991
Austria	15 October 1990	1 October 1991
Finland	6 November 1990	23 October 1991
Sweden	13 November 1990	23 September 1991
Canada	15 November 1990	9 March 1992
Spain	12 December 1990	28 November 1991
Denmark	6 March 1991	19 September 1992
Netherlands	29 April 1991	1 October 1992
Norway	21 May 1991	6 August 1992
Greece	3 June 1991	31 December 1992
Australia	29 July 1991	-
Thailand	26 August 1991	
United States	22 October 1991	19 December 1992
China	4 December 1991	1 December 1992
Republic of Korea	27 April 1992	16 March 1995
Turkey	30 April 1992	-

Czech Republic [e]

Slovakia	23 November 1992	-
Hungary	14 January 1993	25 May 1995
Slovenia	4 May 1993	21 May 1994
Egypt	29 May 1993	4 June 1994
Poland	16 July 1993	29 June 1994
Australia	30 September 1993	29 June 1994
Romania	8 November 1993	28 July 1994
Portugal	12 November 1993	3 August 1994
Tajikistan	11 February 1994	3 December 1995
Thailand	12 February 1994	4 May 1995
Peru	16 March 1994	6 March 1995
Ukraine	17 March 1994	2 November 1995
Russian Federation	5 April 1994	-
Albania	27 June 1994	7 July 1995
Estonia	24 October 1994	18 July 1995
Latvia	25 October 1994	1 August 1995
Lithuania	27 October 1994	12 July 1995
United Arab Emirates	23 November 1994	25 December 1995
Philippines	4 April 1995	-
Singapore	6 April 1995	7 October 1995
Chile	24 April 1995	-
Venezuela	27 April 1995	-
Kuwait	8 January 1996	-
Italy	22 January 1996	-
Croatia	5 March 1996	-
Malaysia	9 September 1996	-
Argentina	27 September 1996	-
India	1 October 1996	-
Kazakhstan	8 October 1996	-
Belarus	14 October 1996	-

Democratic Republic of the Congo

Germany	18 March 1969	22 July 1971
Switzerland	10 March 1972	10 May 1973
France	5 October 1972	1 March 1975
Belgium/Luxembourg	28 March 1976	1 January 1977

Country/territory	Date of signature	Date of entry into force
United States	3 August 1984	28 July 1989
Republic of Korea	19 July 1990	-
Greece	26 April 1991	-

Denmark [f]

Madagascar	10 December 1965	26 July 1967
Malawi	1 August 1966	1 August 1966
Côte d'Ivoire	23 November 1966	10 January 1968
Indonesia	30 January 1968	2 July 1968
Romania	12 November 1980	9 April 1981
China	29 April 1985	29 April 1985
Sri Lanka	4 June 1985	4 June 1985
Hungary	2 May 1988	1 October 1988
Republic of Korea	2 June 1988	2 June 1988
Turkey	7 February 1990	1 August 1992
Poland	1 May 1990	13 October 1990
USSR (former)	1 May 1990	-
Czechoslovakia (former)	6 March 1991	19 September 1992
Estonia	6 November 1991	24 February 1993
Malaysia	6 January 1992	18 September 1992
Ghana	13 January 1992	6 January 1995
Latvia	30 March 1992	18 November 1994
Lithuania	30 March 1992	8 January 1993
Ukraine	23 October 1992	29 April 1994
Argentina	6 November 1992	2 February 1995
Bulgaria	14 April 1993	20 May 1995
Paraguay	22 April 1993	-
Chile	28 May 1993	3 November 1995
Viet Nam	23 July 1993	7 August 1994
Uzbekistan	23 September 1993	-
Russian Federation	4 November 1993	-
Hong Kong, China	2 February 1994	4 March 1994
Romania	13 June 1994	24 August 1995
Peru	23 November 1994	17 February 1995
Venezuela	28 November 1994	-
Bolivia	12 March 1995	-
Nicaragua	12 March 1995	26 January 1996
Mongolia	13 March 1995	-
Brazil	4 May 1995	-
Albania	5 September 1995	-
India	6 September 1995	-
South Africa	22 February 1996	-
Tunisia	28 June 1996	-

Dominica

Germany	1 October 1984	11 May 1986
United Kingdom	23 January 1987	23 January 1987

Dominican Republic

Germany	16 December 1959	3 June 1960
Spain	16 March 1995	-

Country/territory	Date of signature	Date of entry into force
Ecuador		
Switzerland	2 May 1968	11 September 1969
Egypt	19 April 1992	-
United States	27 August 1993	-
Chile	27 October 1993	-
Venezuela	16 November 1993	1 February 1995
Paraguay	28 January 1994	-
Argentina	20 February 1994	-
China	21 March 1994	-
United Kingdom	10 May 1994	24 August 1995
El Salvador	16 May 1994	15 January 1996
France	7 September 1994	-
Bolivia	25 May 1995	-
Germany	21 March 1996	-
Romania	21 March 1996	-
Russian Federation	1 April 1996	-
Canada	29 April 1996	-
Spain	26 June 1996	-
Egypt		
Kuwait	2 May 1966	9 August 1966
Switzerland	25 July 1973	4 June 1974
Germany	5 July 1974	22 July 1978
France	22 December 1974	1 October 1975
United Kingdom	11 June 1975	24 February 1976
Morocco	3 June 1976	7 September 1978
Netherlands [j]	30 October 1976	1 January 1978
Japan	28 January 1977	14 January 1978
Belgium/Luxembourg	28 February 1977	20 September 1978
Sudan	28 May 1977	14 March 1978
Yugoslavia	3 June 1977	--
Sweden	15 July 1978	29 January 1979
Finland	5 May 1980	22 January 1982
Oman	28 April 1985	9 October 1985
United States	11 March 1986	27 June 1992
United Arab Emirates	19 June 1988	-
Yemen	19 October 1988	3 March 1990
Italy	2 March 1989	
Tunisia	8 December 1989	2 January 1991
Saudi Arabia	13 March 1990	15 September 1992
Libyan Arab Jamahiriya	3 December 1990	4 July 1991
Ecuador	19 April 1992	-
Argentina	11 May 1992	3 December 1993
Spain	3 November 1992	26 April 1994
Uzbekistan	16 December 1992	-
Ukraine	21 December 1992	10 October 1993
Kazakhstan	24 December 1992	-
Albania	22 May 1993	6 April 1994
Czech Republic	29 May 1993	5 June 1994
Greece	16 July 1993	6 April 1995
Indonesia	19 January 1994	5 August 1994
China	21 April 1994	-
Romania	24 November 1994	-

Country/territory	Date of signature	Date of entry into force
Armenia	9 January 1995	-
Hungary	23 May 1995	-
Turkmenistan	23 May 1995	-
Poland	1 July 1995	-
Uganda	4 November 1995	-
Netherlands	17 January 1996	-
Sri Lanka	11 March 1996	-
Republic of Korea	18 March 1996	-
Jordan	8 May 1996	-
Canada	13 November 1996	-

El Salvador

France	20 September 1978	12 December 1992
Ecuador	16 May 1994	15 January 1996
Switzerland	8 December 1994	-
Spain	14 February 1995	20 February 1996
Peru	13 June 1996	-
Chile	11 November 1996	-

Equatorial Guinea

France	3 March 1982	23 September 1983

Eritrea

Italy	6 February 1996	-

Estonia [a]

Denmark	6 November 1991	24 February 1993
Finland	13 February 1992	2 December 1992
Sweden	31 March 1992	20 May 1992
France	14 May 1992	17 February 1995
Norway	15 June 1992	15 June 1992
Netherlands	27 October 1992	1 September 1993
Germany	12 November 1992	Provisional application
Switzerland	21 December 1992	18 August 1993
Poland	6 May 1993	6 August 1993
China	2 September 1993	1 June 1994
Israel	14 March 1994	23 May 1995
United States	19 April 1994	-
United Kingdom	12 May 1994	16 December 1994
Austria	16 May 1994	8 February 1995
Czech Republic	24 October 1994	18 July 1995
Ukraine	15 February 1995	5 May 1995
Lithuania	7 September 1995	-
Belgium/Luxembourg	24 January 1996	-
Latvia	7 February 1996	-

Ethiopia

Germany	21 April 1964	--
Italy	23 December 1994	-
Kuwait	14 September 1996	-

Country/territory	Date of signature	Date of entry into force
Finland		
Egypt	5 May 1980	22 January 1982
Bulgaria	16 February 1984	16 July 1985
China	4 September 1984	26 January 1986
Malaysia	15 April 1985	3 January 1988
Sri Lanka	27 April 1985	25 October 1987
Hungary	6 June 1988	12 May 1989
USSR (former)	8 February 1989	15 August 1991
Poland	5 April 1990	21 February 1991
Czechoslovakia (former)	6 November 1990	23 October 1991
Estonia	13 February 1992	2 December 1992
Latvia	5 March 1992	7 December 1992
Romania	26 March 1992	6 January 1993
Ukraine	14 May 1992	30 January 1993
Lithuania	12 June 1992	8 January 1993
Kazakhstan	29 September 1992	-
Uzbekistan	1 October 1992	22 October 1993
Belarus	28 October 1992	21 March 1993
Turkey	13 May 1993	12 April 1995
Chile	27 May 1993	1 May 1996
Viet Nam	13 September 1993	2 May 1996
Republic of Korea	21 October 1993	11 May 1996
Argentina	5 November 1993	3 May 1996
Thailand	18 March 1994	-
Brazil	28 March 1995	-
Peru	2 May 1995	-
Republic of Moldova	25 August 1995	-
Kuwait	10 March 1996	-
United Arab Emirates	12 March 1996	-
Indonesia	13 March 1996	-
Poland	25 November 1996	-
France		
Chad	11 August 1960	-
Central African Republic	13 August 1960	-
Congo	15 August 1960	-
Tunisia	30 June 1972	30 June 1972
Democratic Republic of the Congo	5 October 1972	1 March 1975
Mauritius	22 March 1973	1 April 1974
Indonesia	14 June 1973	29 April 1975
Gabon	12 February 1974	-
Yugoslavia	28 March 1974	3 March 1975
Senegal	29 March 1974	-
Egypt	22 December 1974	1 October 1975
Malaysia	24 April 1975	1 September 1976
Morocco [j]	15 July 1975	13 December 1976
Singapore	8 September 1975	18 October 1976
Philippines	14 June 1976	1 July 1976
Malta	11 August 1976	1 January 1978
Romania [j]	16 December 1976	1 August 1978
Syrian Arab Republic	28 November 1977	1 March 1979
Republic of Korea	28 December 1977	1 March 1979

Country/territory	Date of signature	Date of entry into force
Jordan	23 February 1978	18 October 1979
Sudan	31 July 1978	5 July 1980
El Salvador	20 September 1978	12 December 1992
Paraguay	30 November 1978	11 December 1980
Liberia	23 March 1979	22 January 1982
Sri Lanka	10 April 1980	19 April 1982
Equatorial Guinea	3 March 1982	23 September 1983
Panama	5 November 1982	9 October 1985
Nepal	2 May 1983	13 June 1985
Pakistan	1 June 1983	14 December 1984
Israel	9 June 1983	11 January 1985
Costa Rica	8 March 1984	-
Yemen	27 April 1984	1 October 1991
Haiti	23 May 1984	25 March 1985
China	30 May 1984	19 March 1985
Bangladesh	10 September 1985	3 October 1986
Hungary	6 November 1986	30 September 1987
Poland	14 February 1989	10 February 1990
Bulgaria	5 April 1989	1 May 1990
USSR (former)	4 July 1989	18 July 1991
Kuwait	27 September 1989	16 May 1991
Bolivia	25 October 1989	-
Lao People's Democratic Republic	12 December 1989	8 March 1991
Nigeria	27 February 1990	19 August 1991
Czechoslovakia (former)	13 September 1990	27 September 1991
Argentina	3 July 1991	3 March 1993
United Arab Emirates	9 September 1991	18 December 1992
Mongolia	8 November 1991	22 December 1993
Lithuania	22 April 1992	17 February 1995
Estonia	14 May 1992	17 February 1995
Latvia	15 May 1992	1 October 1994
Viet Nam	26 May 1992	10 August 1994
Chile	14 July 1992	13 July 1993
Kazakhstan	25 September 1992	-
Jamaica	25 January 1993	15 September 1994
Algeria	13 February 1993	-
Peru	6 October 1993	30 May 1996
Uruguay	14 October 1993	-
Uzbekistan	27 October 1993	-
Belarus	28 October 1993	-
Trinidad and Tobago	28 October 1993	21 April 1996
Turkmenistan	28 April 1994	2 May 1996
Ukraine	3 May 1994	26 January 1996
Kyrgyzstan	2 June 1994	-
Ecuador	7 September 1994	-
Philippines	13 September 1994	-
Oman	17 October 1994	-
Brazil	21 March 1995	-
Romania	21 March 1995	-
Albania	13 June 1995	-
South Africa	11 October 1995	-
Armenia	4 November 1995	-
Hong Kong, China	30 November 1995	-
Morocco	13 January 1996	-

Country/territory	*Date of signature*	*Date of entry into force*
Qatar	8 July 1996	

Gabon

Italy	18 November 1968	--
Germany	16 May 1969	29 March 1971
Switzerland	28 January 1972	18 October 1972
France	12 February 1974	-
Morocco	13 January 1979	7 November 1979
Romania	11 April 1979	18 September 1982
Spain	2 March 1995	-

Gambia

Switzerland	22 November 1993	-

Georgia [a]

Turkey	31 July 1992	-
China	3 June 1993	1 March 1995
Belgium/Luxembourg	23 June 1993	-
Germany	25 June 1993	-
United States	7 March 1994	-
Greece	9 November 1994	-
Ukraine	1 January 1995	-
Bulgaria	19 January 1995	-
United Kingdom	15 February 1995	15 February 1995
Israel	19 June 1995	-
Uzbekistan	4 September 1995	-
Iran (Islamic Republic of)	27 September 1995	-
Azerbaijan	1 March 1996	-
Turkemenistan	20 March 1996	-
Armenia	1 June 1996	-
Kazakhstan	17 September 1996	-

Germany

Pakistan	25 November 1959	28 April 1962
Dominican Republic	16 December 1959	3 June 1960
Malaysia	22 December 1960	6 July 1963
Greece	27 March 1961	15 July 1963
Togo	16 May 1961	21 December 1964
Morocco	31 August 1961	21 January 1968
Liberia	12 December 1961	22 October 1967
Thailand	13 December 1961	10 April 1965
Guinea	19 April 1962	13 March 1965
Turkey	20 June 1962	16 December 1965
Cameroon	29 June 1962	21 November 1963
Madagascar	21 September 1962	21 March 1966
Sudan	7 February 1963	24 November 1967
Sri Lanka	8 November 1963	7 December 1966
Tunisia	20 December 1963	6 February 1966
Senegal	24 January 1964	16 January 1966
Republic of Korea	4 February 1964	15 January 1967
Ethiopia	21 April 1964	--

Country/territory	*Date of signature*	*Date of entry into force*
Niger	29 October 1964	10 January 1966
United Republic of Tanzania	30 January 1965	12 July 1968
Sierra Leone	8 April 1965	10 December 1966
Central African Republic	23 August 1965	21 January 1968
Congo	13 September 1965	14 October 1967
Iran (Islamic Republic of)	11 November 1965	6 April 1968
Côte d'Ivoire	27 October 1966	10 June 1968
Uganda	29 November 1966	19 August 1968
Zambia	10 December 1966	25 August 1972
Chad	11 April 1967	23 November 1968
Rwanda	18 May 1967	28 February 1969
Indonesia	8 November 1968	19 April 1971
Democratic Republic of the Congo	18 March 1969	22 July 1971
Gabon	16 May 1969	29 March 1971
Mauritius	25 May 1971	27 August 1973
Haiti	14 August 1973	1 December 1975
Singapore	3 October 1973	1 October 1975
Yemen	21 June 1974	19 December 1978
Egypt	5 July 1974	22 July 1978
Jordan	15 July 1974	10 October 1977
Malta	17 September 1974	14 December 1975
Israel	24 June 1976	Provisional application
Mali	28 July 1977	16 May 1980
Syrian Arab Republic	2 August 1977	20 April 1980
Benin	29 June 1978	18 July 1985
Saudi Arabia	2 February 1979	15 March 1980
Oman	25 June 1979	4 February 1986
Romania	12 October 1979	10 January 1981
Portugal	16 September 1980	23 April 1982
Papua New Guinea	12 November 1980	3 November 1983
Bangladesh	6 May 1981	14 September 1986
Somalia	27 November 1981	15 February 1985
Lesotho	11 November 1982	17 August 1985
Mauritania	8 December 1982	26 April 1986
China	7 October 1983	18 March 1985
Panama	2 November 1983	10 March 1989
Burundi	10 September 1984	9 December 1987
Dominica	1 October 1984	11 May 1986
Saint Lucia	16 March 1985	22 July 1987
Saint Vincent and the Grenadines	25 March 1986	8 January 1989
Bulgaria	12 April 1986	10 March 1988
Hungary	30 April 1986	7 November 1987
Nepal	20 October 1986	7 July 1988
Bolivia	23 March 1987	9 November 1990
Uruguay	4 May 1987	29 June 1990
USSR (former)	13 June 1989	5 August 1991
Yugoslavia	10 July 1989	26 October 1990
Poland	10 November 1989	24 February 1991
Guyana	6 December 1989	8 March 1994
Cape Verde	18 January 1990	15 December 1993
Swaziland	5 April 1990	7 August 1995
Czechoslovakia (former)	2 October 1990	2 August 1992
Argentina	9 April 1991	8 November 1993

Country/territory	*Date of signature*	*Date of entry into force*
Mongolia	26 June 1991	-
Chile	19 October 1991	-
Albania	31 October 1991	18 August 1995
Lithuania	28 February 1992	Provisional application
Kazakhstan	22 September 1992	10 May 1995
Jamaica	24 September 1992	-
Estonia	12 November 1992	-
Ukraine	15 February 1993	Provisional application
Belarus	2 April 1993	-
Viet Nam	3 April 1993	Provisional application
Latvia	20 April 1993	26 January 1996
Uzbekistan	28 April 1993	Provisional application
Georgia	25 June 1993	Provisional application
Paraguay	11 August 1993	-
Slovenia	28 October 1993	-
Namibia	21 January 1994	Provisional application
Republic of Moldova	28 February 1994	Provisional application
Kuwait	30 March 1994	-
Costa Rica	13 September 1994	-
Barbados	2 December 1994	-
Peru	30 January 1995	-
Ghana	24 February 1995	-
Honduras	21 March 1995	-
India	10 July 1995	-
South Africa	11 September 1995	-
Brazil	21 September 1995	-
Zimbabwe	29 September 1995	-
Armenia	21 December 1995	-
Azerbaijan	22 December 1995	-
Hong Kong, China	31 January 1996	-
Algeria	11 March 1996	-
Ecuador	21 March 1996	-
Cuba	30 April 1996	-
Kenya	3 May 1996	-
Nicaragua	6 May 1996	-
Venezuela	14 May 1996	-
Qatar	14 June 1996	-
Romania	25 June 1996	-
Lao People's Democratic Republic	9 August 1996	-
The former Yugoslav Republic of Macedonia	10 September 1996	-
Burkina Faso	22 October 1996	-
Saudi Arabia	29 October 1996	-

Ghana

United Kingdom	22 March 1989	25 October 1991
Netherlands	31 March 1989	1 July 1991
Romania	14 September 1989	-
China	12 October 1989	-
Bulgaria	20 October 1989	-
Switzerland	8 October 1991	16 June 1993
Denmark	13 January 1992	6 January 1995
Germany	24 February 1995	-

Country/territory	Date of signature	Date of entry into force
Malaysia	11 November 1996	-
Greece		
Germany	27 March 1961	15 July 1963
Hungary	26 May 1989	1 February 1992
Democratic Republic of the Congo	26 April 1991	-
Czechoslovakia (former)[e]	3 June 1991	31 December 1992
Albania	1 August 1991	4 January 1995
Romania	16 September 1991	21 October 1992
Cyprus	30 March 1992	26 February 1993
China	25 June 1992	21 December 1993
Poland	14 October 1992	20 February 1995
Tunisia	31 October 1992	21 April 1995
Bulgaria	12 March 1993	29 April 1995
Armenia	25 May 1993	28 April 1995
Russian Federation	30 June 1993	-
Egypt	16 July 1993	6 April 1995
Morocco	16 February 1994	-
Ukraine	1 September 1994	-
Georgia	9 November 1994	-
Republic of Korea	25 January 1995	4 November 1995
Latvia	20 July 1995	-
Cuba	18 June 1996	-
Chile	10 July 1996	-
Lithuania	19 July 1996	-
Grenada		
United States	2 May 1986	3 March 1989
United Kingdom	25 February 1988	25 February 1988
Guatemala		
Chile	8 November 1996	-
Guinea		
Germany	19 April 1962	13 March 1965
Switzerland	26 April 1962	29 July 1963
Italy	20 February 1964	20 February 1964
Tunisia	18 November 1990	-
Yugoslavia	22 October 1996	-
Malaysia	7 November 1996	-
Guinea-Bissau		
Portugal	24 June 1991	-
Guyana		
United Kingdom	27 October 1989	11 April 1990
Germany	6 December 1989	8 March 1994

Country/territory	*Date of signature*	*Date of entry into force*

Haiti

Germany	14 August 1973	1 December 1975
United States	13 December 1983	--
France	23 May 1984	25 March 1985
United Kingdom	18 March 1985	27 March 1995

Honduras

Switzerland	14 October 1993	-
United Kingdom	7 December 1993	8 March 1995
Spain	18 March 1994	-
Germany	21 March 1995	-
United States	1 July 1995	-
Chile	11 November 1996	

Hong Kong, China

Netherlands	19 November 1992	1 September 1993
Australia	15 September 1993	15 October 1993
Denmark	2 February 1994	4 March 1994
Sweden	27 May 1994	26 June 1994
Switzerland	22 September 1994	22 October 1994
New Zealand	6 July 1995	5 August 1995
Italy	28 November 1995	-
France	30 November 1995	-
Germany	31 January 1996	-
Belgium/Luxembourg	7 October 1996	-
Austria	11 October 1996	-

Hungary

Germany	30 April 1986	7 November 1987
Belgium/Luxembourg	14 May 1986	23 September 1988
France	6 November 1986	30 September 1987
Italy	17 February 1987	6 September 1989
United Kingdom	9 March 1987	28 August 1987
Sweden	21 April 1987	21 April 1987
Netherlands	2 September 1987	1 June 1988
Denmark	2 May 1988	1 October 1988
Austria	26 May 1988	1 September 1989
Finland	6 June 1988	12 May 1989
Switzerland	5 October 1988	16 May 1989
Republic of Korea	28 December 1988	1 January 1989
Cyprus	24 May 1989	25 May 1990
Greece	26 May 1989	1 February 1992
Uruguay	25 August 1989	1 July 1992
Kuwait	8 November 1989	1 March 1994
Spain	9 November 1989	1 August 1992
Norway	8 April 1991	4 December 1992
Israel	14 May 1991	14 September 1992
China	29 May 1991	1 April 1993
Australia	15 August 1991	10 May 1992
Canada	3 October 1991	21 November 1993
Thailand	18 October 1991	18 October 1991

Country/territory	Date of signature	Date of entry into force
Morocco	12 December 1991	-
Turkey	14 January 1992	22 February 1995
Portugal	28 February 1992	-
Indonesia	20 May 1992	13 February 1996
Poland	23 September 1992	16 June 1995
Czech Republic	14 January 1993	25 May 1995
Slovakia	15 January 1993	-
Argentina	5 February 1993	-
Malaysia	19 February 1993	8 July 1995
Paraguay	11 August 1993	1 April 1995
Romania	16 September 1993	-
Bulgaria	8 June 1994	7 September 1995
Viet Nam	26 August 1994	16 June 1995
Mongolia	13 September 1994	-
Ukraine	11 October 1994	-
Kazakhstan	7 December 1994	3 March 1996
Russian Federation	6 March 1995	-
Republic of Moldova	19 April 1995	-
Egypt	23 May 1995	-
Albania	24 January 1996	-

Iceland

China	31 March 1994	-

India

United Kingdom	14 March 1994	6 January 1995
Russian Federation	23 December 1994	-
Germany	10 July 1995	-
Malaysia	1 August 1995	-
Turkmenistan	1 September 1995	-
Denmark	6 September 1995	-
Italy	1 November 1995	-
Netherlands	6 November 1995	-
Tajikistan	1 December 1995	-
Israel	29 January 1996	-
Republic of Korea	26 February 1996	-
Czech Republic	1 October 1996	-
Poland	7 October 1996	-
Kazakhstan	9 December 1996	-

Indonesia

Denmark	30 January 1968	2 July 1968
Netherlands	7 July 1968	17 July 1971
Germany	8 November 1968	19 April 1971
Belgium/Luxembourg	15 January 1970	17 June 1972
France	14 June 1973	29 April 1975
Switzerland	6 February 1974	9 April 1976
United Kingdom	27 April 1976	24 March 1977
Singapore	28 August 1990	28 August 1990
Republic of Korea	16 February 1991	10 March 1994
Italy	25 April 1991	-
Viet Nam	25 October 1991	3 December 1993

Country/territory	Date of signature	Date of entry into force
Norway	26 November 1991	-
Tunisia	13 May 1992	12 September 1992
Hungary	20 May 1992	13 February 1996
Sweden	17 September 1992	18 February 1993
Poland	7 October 1992	1 July 1993
Australia	17 November 1992	29 July 1993
Egypt	19 January 1994	5 August 1994
Malaysia	22 January 1994	15 June 1994
Netherlands	6 April 1994	1 July 1995
Turkmenistan	2 June 1994	-
Slovakia	12 July 1994	1 March 1995
Lao People's Democratic Republic	18 October 1994	-
China	18 November 1994	1 April 1995
Pakistan	8 March 1995	3 December 1996
Ukraine	11 April 1995	-
Spain	30 May 1995	-
Kyrgyzstan	19 July 1995	-
Suriname	28 October 1995	-
Argentina	7 November 1995	-
Finland	13 March 1996	-
Ukraine	11 April 1996	-
Sri Lanka	10 June 1996	-
Uzbekistan	27 August 1996	-
Jordan	12 November 1996	-

Iran (Islamic Republic of)

Country/territory	Date of signature	Date of entry into force
Germany	11 November 1965	6 April 1968
Armenia	6 May 1995	-
Republic of Moldova	31 May 1995	-
Belarus	14 July 1995	-
Tajikistan	18 July 1995	-
Georgia	27 September 1995	-
Philippines	8 October 1995	-
Pakistan	8 November 1995	-
Kazakhstan	16 January 1996	-
Turkmenistan	23 January 1996	-
Yemen	29 February 1996	-
Ukraine	21 May 1996	-
Bosnia and Herzegovina	27 July 1996	-
Kyrgyzstan	31 July 1996	-
Turkey	21 December 1996	-

Iraq

Country/territory	Date of signature	Date of entry into force
Kuwait	25 October 1964	7 June 1966
Morocco	18 July 1990	-

Israel

Country/territory	Date of signature	Date of entry into force
Germany	24 June 1976	Provisional application
France	9 June 1983	11 January 1985
Hungary	14 May 1991	14 September 1992
Poland	22 May 1991	6 April 1992
Romania	2 September 1991	26 August 1992

Country/territory	Date of signature	Date of entry into force
Bulgaria	6 December 1993	-
Latvia	27 February 1994	9 May 1995
Estonia	14 March 1994	23 May 1995
Lithuania	2 October 1994	-
China	10 April 1995	-
Turkmenistan	24 May 1995	-
Georgia	19 June 1995	-
Argentina	23 July 1995	-
Kazakhstan	27 December 1995	-
Albania	29 January 1996	-
India	29 January 1996	-
Turkey	14 March 1996	-

Italy

Country/territory	Date of signature	Date of entry into force
Guinea	20 February 1964	20 February 1964
Malta	28 July 1967	15 October 1973
Gabon	18 November 1968	--
Chad	11 June 1969	11 June 1969
Côte d'Ivoire	23 July 1969	--
China	28 January 1985	28 August 1987
Tunisia	17 October 1985	24 June 1989
Hungary	17 February 1987	6 September 1989
Sri Lanka	25 March 1987	20 March 1990
Kuwait	17 December 1987	21 May 1990
Malaysia	4 January 1988	25 October 1990
Philippines	17 June 1988	4 November 1993
Bulgaria	5 December 1988	27 December 1990
Republic of Korea	10 January 1989	26 June 1992
Egypt	2 March 1989	-
Poland	10 May 1989	9 January 1992
USSR (former)	30 November 1989	8 July 1991
Czechoslovakia (former)	1 August 1990	-
Uruguay	21 February 1990	-
Bangladesh	20 March 1990	-
Bolivia	30 April 1990	22 February 1992
Viet Nam	18 May 1990	-
Argentina	22 May 1990	14 October 1993
Venezuela	4 June 1990	-
Morocco	18 July 1990	-
Romania	6 December 1990	14 October 1993
Indonesia	25 April 1991	-
Algeria	18 May 1991	-
Albania	12 September 1991	-
Mongolia	15 January 1993	-
Chile	8 March 1993	-
Cuba	7 May 1993	23 August 1995
Oman	23 June 1993	-
Jamaica	29 September 1993	5 November 1995
Congo	17 March 1994	-
Peru	5 May 1994	18 October 1995
Kazakhstan	22 September 1994	-
Lithuania	1 December 1994	-
Ethiopia	23 December 1994	-
United Arab Emirates	22 January 1995	-

Country/territory	*Date of signature*	*Date of entry into force*
Turkey	23 March 1995	-
Brazil	3 April 1995	-
Ukraine	2 May 1995	-
Belarus	25 July 1995	-
Barbados	25 October 1995	-
India	1 November 1995	-
Hong Kong, China	28 November 1995	-
Czech Republic	22 January 1996	-
Eritrea	6 February 1996	-
Jordan	21 July 1996	-
Kenya	10 September 1996	-
Saudi Arabia	10 September 1996	-
Croatia	5 November 1996	-

Jamaica

United Kingdom	20 January 1987	14 May 1987
Switzerland	11 December 1990	21 November 1991
Netherlands	18 April 1991	1 August 1992
Germany	24 September 1992	-
France	25 January 1993	15 September 1994
Italy	29 September 1993	5 November 1995
United States	4 February 1994	-
Argentina	8 February 1994	1 December 1995
China	26 October 1994	-

Japan

Egypt	28 January 1977	14 January 1978
Sri Lanka	1 March 1982	7 August 1982
China	27 August 1988	14 May 1989
Turkey	12 February 1992	12 March 1993

Jordan

Germany	15 July 1974	10 October 1977
Switzerland	11 November 1976	2 March 1977
France	23 February 1978	18 October 1979
United Kingdom	10 October 1979	24 April 1980
Romania	2 July 1992	-
Turkey	2 August 1993	-
Malaysia	2 October 1994	-
Tunisia	27 April 1995	-
Yemen	18 June 1995	-
Egypt	8 May 1996	-
Italy	21 July 1996	-
Algeria	1 August 1996	-
Indonesia	12 November 1996	-

Kazakhstan [a]

Turkey	1 May 1992	10 August 1995
United States	19 May 1992	12 January 1994
China	10 August 1992	13 August 1994
Germany	22 September 1992	10 May 1995

Country/territory	Date of signature	Date of entry into force
France	25 September 1992	-
Finland	29 September 1992	-
Egypt	24 December 1992	-
Spain	23 March 1994	-
Switzerland	12 May 1994	-
Lithuania	15 September 1994	-
Poland	21 September 1994	25 May 1995
Italy	22 September 1994	-
Mongolia	1 December 1994	-
Hungary	7 December 1994	3 March 1996
United Kingdom	23 November 1995	23 November 1995
Israel	27 December 1995	-
Iran (Islamic Republic of)	16 January 1996	-
Republic of Korea	20 March 1996	-
Romania	25 April 1996	-
Malaysia	27 May 1996	-
Azerbaijan	16 September 1996	-
Georgia	17 September 1996	-
Czech Republic	8 October 1996	-
India	9 December 1996	-

Kenya

Netherlands	11 September 1970	11 June 1979
Germany	3 May 1996	-
Italy	10 September 1996	-

Kuwait

Iraq	25 October 1964	7 June 1966
United Arab Emirates	12 February 1966	-
Egypt	2 May 1966	9 August 1966
Tunisia	14 September 1973	--
Morocco	3 April 1980	--
Pakistan	17 March 1983	15 March 1986
China	23 November 1985	24 December 1986
Italy	17 December 1987	21 May 1990
Turkey	27 October 1988	25 April 1992
France	27 September 1989	16 May 1991
Hungary	8 November 1989	1 March 1994
Poland	5 March 1990	18 December 1993
Romania	21 May 1991	26 July 1992
Republic of Moldova	4 February 1993	-
Germany	30 March 1994	-
Russian Federation	21 November 1994	-
Tajikistan	18 April 1995	-
Malta	19 April 1995	-
Czech Republic	8 January 1996	-
Finland	10 March 1996	-
Ethiopia	14 September 1996	-
Austria	16 November 1996	-

Kyrgyzstan [a]

Turkey	28 April 1992	-

Country/territory	*Date of signature*	*Date of entry into force*
China	14 May 1992	-
United States	19 January 1993	11 January 1994
Ukraine	23 February 1993	-
France	2 June 1994	-
Armenia	4 July 1994	27 October 1995
United Kingdom	8 December 1994	-
Indonesia	18 July 1995	-
Malaysia	20 July 1995	-
Pakistan	26 August 1995	-
Iran	31 July 1996	-
Uzbekistan	24 December 1996	-

Lao People's Democratic Republic

France	12 December 1989	8 March 1991
Thailand	22 August 1990	7 December 1990
Malaysia	8 December 1992	-
China	31 January 1993	1 June 1993
Mongolia	3 March 1994	-
Australia	6 April 1994	8 April 1995
Indonesia	18 October 1994	-
United Kingdom	1 June 1995	1 June 1995
Viet Nam	14 January 1996	23 June 1996
Republic of Korea	15 May 1996	14 June 1996
Germany	9 August 1996	9 August 1996
Sweden	29 August 1996	1 January 1997
Switzerland	4 December 1996	-
Russian Federation	6 December 1996	-

Latvia [a]

Finland	5 March 1992	7 December 1992
Sweden	10 March 1992	6 November 1992
Denmark	30 March 1992	18 November 1994
France	15 May 1992	1 October 1994
Norway	16 June 1992	1 December 1992
Taiwan Province of China	17 September 1992	8 October 1993
Switzerland	22 December 1992	16 April 1993
Germany	20 April 1993	26 January 1996
Poland	26 April 1993	19 July 1993
United Kingdom	24 January 1994	15 February 1995
Israel	27 February 1994	9 May 1995
Netherlands	14 March 1994	1 April 1995
Czech Republic	25 October 1994	1 August 1995
Austria	17 November 1994	1 May 1996
United States	13 January 1995	-
Canada	26 April 1995	27 July 1995
Greece	20 July 1995	-
Portugal	27 September 1995	-
Spain	26 October 1995	-
Viet Nam	6 November 1995	-
Estonia	7 February 1996	-
Lithuania	7 February 1996	-
Belgium/Luxembourg	27 March 1996	-
Uzbekistan	23 May 1996	-

Country/territory	Date of signature	Date of entry into force
Republic of Korea	23 October 1996	26 January 1997
Lebanon		
Romania	18 October 1994	-
Armenia	1 January 1995	-
Ukraine	25 March 1995	-
Cuba	14 December 1995	-
Spain	22 February 1996	-
China	13 June 1996	-
Lesotho		
United Kingdom	18 February 1981	18 February 1981
Germany	11 November 1982	17 August 1985
Liberia		
Germany	12 December 1961	22 October 1967
Switzerland	23 July 1963	22 September 1964
France	23 March 1979	22 January 1982
Belgium/Luxembourg	5 June 1985	--
Libyan Arab Jamahiriya		
Malta	8 February 1973	19 December 1973
Tunisia	6 June 1973	-
Morocco	25 January 1984	18 September 1993
Egypt	3 December 1990	4 July 1991
Lithuania [a]		
United States	28 October 1991	7 February 1992
Germany	28 February 1992	Provisional application
Sweden	17 March 1992	1 September 1992
Denmark	30 March 1992	8 January 1993
France	22 April 1992	17 February 1995
Finland	12 June 1992	8 January 1993
Norway	16 June 1992	19 December 1992
Poland	28 September 1992	6 August 1993
Switzerland	23 December 1992	13 May 1993
United Kingdom	17 May 1993	21 September 1993
Republic of Korea	24 September 1993	9 November 1993
Turkey	15 October 1993	-
China	8 November 1993	1 June 1994
Netherlands	26 January 1994	1 April 1995
Ukraine	8 February 1994	-
Romania	8 March 1994	15 December 1994
Spain	6 July 1994	22 December 1995
Kazakhstan	11 September 1994	-
Israel	2 October 1994	-
Czech Republic	27 October 1994	12 July 1995
Italy	1 December 1994	-
Venezuela	24 April 1995	-
Estonia	7 September 1995	-

Country/territory	Date of signature	Date of entry into force
Viet Nam	27 September 1995	-
Latvia	7 February 1996	-
Argentina	14 March 1996	-
Austria	28 June 1996	-
Greece	19 July 1996	-

Madagascar

Germany	21 September 1962	21 March 1966
Switzerland	17 March 1964	31 March 1966
Denmark	10 December 1965	26 July 1967
Sweden	2 April 1966	23 June 1967
Norway	13 May 1966	28 September 1967

Malawi

Denmark	1 August 1966	1 August 1966
Malaysia	5 September 1996	-

Malaysia

Germany	22 December 1960	6 July 1963
Netherlands	15 June 1971	13 September 1972
France	24 April 1975	1 September 1976
Switzerland	1 March 1978	9 June 1978
Sweden	3 March 1979	6 July 1979
Belgium/Luxembourg	22 November 1979	8 February 1982
United Kingdom	21 May 1981	21 October 1988
Sri Lanka	16 April 1982	31 October 1995
Romania	26 November 1982	20 June 1984
Norway	6 November 1984	7 January 1986
Austria	12 April 1985	1 January 1987
Finland	15 April 1985	3 January 1988
Italy	4 January 1988	25 October 1990
Republic of Korea	11 April 1988	31 March 1989
China	21 November 1988	31 March 1990
United Arab Emirates	11 October 1991	-
Denmark	6 January 1992	18 September 1992
Viet Nam	21 January 1992	-
Chile	11 November 1992	-
Lao People's Democratic Republic	8 December 1992	-
Hungary	19 February 1993	8 July 1995
Poland	21 April 1993	23 March 1994
Indonesia	22 January 1994	15 June 1994
Argentina	6 September 1994	-
Jordan	2 October 1994	-
Bangladesh	12 October 1994	-
Bosnia and Herzegovina	16 December 1994	27 May 1995
Croatia	16 December 1994	-
Albania	18 January 1995	-
Spain	4 April 1995	16 February 1996
Kyrgyzstan	20 July 1995	-
Mongolia	27 July 1995	-
India	1 August 1995	-

Country/territory	Date of signature	Date of entry into force
Peru	13 October 1995	25 December 1995
Kazakhstan	27 May 1996	-
Romania	25 June 1996	-
Malawi	5 September 1996	-
Czech Republic	9 September 1996	-
Guinea	7 November 1996	-
Ghana	11 November 1996	-

Mali

Germany	28 June 1977	16 May 1980
Switzerland	8 March 1978	8 December 1978
Tunisia	1 July 1986	-
Algeria	11 July 1996	-

Malta

Switzerland	20 January 1965	23 February 1965
Italy	28 July 1967	15 October 1973
Libyan Arab Jamahiriya	8 February 1973	19 December 1973
Germany	17 September 1974	14 December 1975
France	11 August 1976	1 January 1978
Bulgaria	12 June 1984	7 February 1985
Netherlands	10 September 1984	1 July 1985
United Kingdom	4 October 1986	4 October 1986
Belgium/Luxembourg	5 March 1987	21 May 1990
Kuwait	19 April 1995	-

Mauritania

Switzerland	9 September 1976	30 May 1978
Germany	8 December 1982	26 April 1986
Belgium/Luxembourg	23 November 1983	-
Tunisia	11 March 1986	-
Romania	14 March 1988	19 December 1989

Mauritius

Germany	25 May 1971	27 August 1973
France	22 March 1973	1 April 1974
United Kingdom	20 May 1986	13 October 1986
China	4 May 1996	-

Mexico

Spain	23 June 1995	-
Switzerland	10 July 1995	14 March 1996
Argentina	13 November 1996	-

Mongolia

Republic of Korea	28 March 1991	30 April 1991
Germany	26 June 1991	-
China	26 August 1991	1 November 1993
United Kingdom	4 October 1991	4 October 1991

Country/territory	Date of signature	Date of entry into force
France	8 November 1991	22 December 1993
Belgium/Luxembourg	3 March 1992	-
Ukraine	5 November 1992	5 November 1992
Italy	15 January 1993	-
Lao People's Democratic Republic	3 March 1994	-
Hungary	13 September 1994	-
United States	6 October 1994	-
Kazakhstan	1 December 1994	-
Netherlands	9 March 1995	-
Denmark	13 March 1995	-
Singapore	24 July 1995	-
Malaysia	27 July 1995	14 January 1996
Poland	8 November 1995	21 March 1996
Russian Federation	29 November 1995	-
Romania	6 December 1995	-

Morocco

Germany	31 August 1961	21 January 1968
Belgium/Luxembourg	28 April 1965	18 October 1967
Netherlands	23 December 1971	27 July 1978
France [j]	15 July 1975	13 December 1976
Egypt	3 June 1976	7 September 1978
Gabon	13 January 1979	7 November 1979
Kuwait	3 April 1980	--
Romania	11 September 1981	-
United Arab Emirates	16 June 1982	-
Libyan Arab Jamahiriya	25 January 1984	18 September 1993
United States	22 July 1985	29 May 1991
Switzerland	17 December 1985	12 April 1991
Portugal	18 October 1988	13 February 1990
Spain	27 September 1989	15 January 1992
Iraq	18 July 1990	-
Italy	18 July 1990	
Sweden	26 September 1990	Provisional application
United Kingdom	30 October 1990	Provisional application
Hungary	12 December 1991	-
Austria	2 November 1992	-
Romania	28 January 1994	-
Tunisia	28 January 1994	-
Greece	16 February 1994	-
Poland	24 October 1994	29 May 1995
China	27 March 1995	-
France	13 January 1996	-
Argentina	13 March 1996	-
Bulgaria	22 May 1996	-

Mozambique

Mauritius	14 February 1997	-

Namibia

Germany	21 January 1994	Provisional application

Country/territory	*Date of signature*	*Date of entry into force*
Switzerland	1 August 1994	-

Nepal

France	2 May 1983	13 June 1985
Germany	20 October 1986	7 July 1988
United Kingdom	2 March 1993	2 March 1993

Netherlands [g]

Tunisia	23 May 1963	19 December 1964
Côte d'Ivoire	26 April 1965	8 September 1966
Cameroon	6 July 1965	7 May 1966
Indonesia	7 July 1968	17 July 1971
United Republic of Tanzania	14 April 1970	28 July 1972
Uganda	24 April 1970	-
Sudan	22 August 1970	27 March 1972
Kenya	11 September 1970	11 June 1979
Malaysia	15 June 1971	13 September 1972
Morocco	23 December 1971	27 July 1978
Singapore	16 May 1972	7 September 1973
Thailand	6 June 1972	3 March 1973
Republic of Korea	16 October 1974	1 June 1975
Yugoslavia	16 February 1976	1 April 1977
Egypt [j]	30 October 1976	1 January 1978
Senegal	3 August 1979	5 May 1981
Sri Lanka	26 April 1984	1 May 1985
Malta	10 September 1984	1 July 1985
Philippines	27 February 1985	1 October 1987
Yemen	18 March 1985	1 September 1986
China	17 June 1985	1 February 1987
Turkey	27 March 1986	1 November 1989
Hungary	2 September 1987	1 June 1988
Oman	19 September 1987	1 February 1989
Bulgaria	8 March 1988	24 May 1990
Uruguay	22 September 1988	1 August 1991
Pakistan	4 October 1988	1 October 1989
Ghana	31 March 1989	1 July 1991
USSR (former)	5 October 1989	20 July 1991
Jamaica	18 April 1991	1 August 1992
Czechoslovakia (former)	29 April 1991	1 October 1992
Venezuela	22 October 1991	1 November 1993
Cape Verde	11 November 1991	25 November 1992
Bolivia	10 March 1992	1 November 1994
Poland	7 September 1992	1 February 1994
Argentina	20 October 1992	1 October 1994
Estonia	27 October 1992	1 September 1993
Paraguay	29 October 1992	1 August 1994
Nigeria	2 November 1992	1 February 1994
Hong Kong, China	19 November 1992	1 September 1993
Lithuania	26 January 1994	1 April 1995
Viet Nam	10 March 1994	1 February 1995
Latvia	14 March 1994	1 April 1995
Indonesia	6 April 1994	1 July 1995

Country/territory	Date of signature	Date of entry into force
Albania	15 April 1994	1 September 1995
Romania	19 April 1994	1 February 1995
Ukraine	14 July 1994	-
Bangladesh	1 November 1994	
Peru	27 December 1994	1 February 1996
Mongolia	9 March 1995	-
Belarus	11 April 1995	-
South Africa	9 May 1995	-
Republic of Moldova	26 September 1995	1 June 1996
India	6 November 1995	-
Egypt	17 January 1996	-
Uzbekistan	14 March 1996	-
Slovenia	24 September 1996	-
Zimbabwe	10 December 1996	-

New Zealand

China	22 November 1988	25 March 1989
Hong Kong, China	6 July 1995	5 August 1995

Nicaragua

Taiwan Province of China	29 July 1992	-
Spain	16 March 1994	28 March 1995
Denmark	12 March 1995	26 January 1996
United States	1 July 1995	-
Germany	6 May 1996	-
Chile	10 November 1996	-
United Kingdom	4 December 1996	-

Niger

Switzerland	28 March 1962	17 November 1962
Germany	29 October 1964	10 January 1966
Tunisia	5 June 1992	-

Nigeria

France	27 February 1990	19 August 1991
United Kingdom	11 December 1990	11 December 1990
Netherlands	2 November 1992	1 February 1994

Norway

Madagascar	13 May 1966	28 September 1967
Malaysia	6 November 1984	7 January 1986
China	21 November 1984	10 July 1985
Sri Lanka	13 June 1985	13 June 1985
Poland	5 June 1990	24 October 1990
Hungary	8 April 1991	4 December 1992
Czechoslovakia (former) [k]	21 May 1991	6 August 1992
Romania	11 June 1991	23 March 1992
Indonesia	26 November 1991	-
Estonia	15 June 1992	15 June 1992
Latvia	16 June 1992	1 December 1992

Country/territory	Date of signature	Date of entry into force
Lithuania	16 June 1992	19 December 1992
Chile	1 June 1993	7 September 1994
Peru	10 March 1995	5 May 1995
Russian Federation	4 October 1995	-

Oman

Germany	25 June 1979	4 February 1986
Egypt	28 April 1985	9 October 1985
Netherlands	19 September 1987	1 February 1989
Tunisia	19 October 1991	-
Italy	23 June 1993	-
France	17 October 1994	-
China	18 March 1995	-
Sweden	15 July 1995	-
United Kingdom	25 November 1995	-

Pakistan

Germany	25 November 1959	28 April 1962
Romania [j]	21 January 1978	26 June 1979
Sweden	12 March 1981	14 June 1981
Kuwait	17 March 1983	15 March 1986
France	1 June 1983	14 December 1984
Republic of Korea	24 May 1988	15 April 1990
Netherlands	4 October 1988	1 October 1989
China	12 February 1989	30 September 1990
Tajikistan	31 March 1994	-
Spain	15 September 1994	-
Turkmenistan	26 October 1994	-
United Kingdom	30 November 1994	30 November 1994
Indonesia	8 March 1995	3 December 1996
Singapore	8 March 1995	4 May 1995
Turkey	16 March 1995	-
Romania	10 July 1995	-
Switzerland	11 July 1995	-
Kyrgyzstan	26 August 1995	-
Iran (Islamic Republic of)	8 November 1995	-
Tunisia	18 April 1996	-

Panama

United States	27 October 1982	30 May 1991
France	5 November 1982	9 October 1985
United Kingdom	7 October 1983	7 November 1983
Switzerland	19 October 1983	22 August 1985
Germany	2 November 1983	10 March 1989
Argentina	10 May 1996	-
Canada	12 September 1996	-
Chile	18 November 1996	-

Papua New Guinea

Germany	12 November 1980	3 November 1983
United Kingdom	14 May 1981	22 December 1981

Country/territory	Date of signature	Date of entry into force
Australia	3 September 1990	20 October 1991
China	12 April 1991	12 February 1993

Paraguay

France	30 November 1978	11 December 1980
United Kingdom	4 June 1981	23 April 1992
Switzerland	31 January 1992	28 September 1992
Taiwan Province of China	6 April 1992	-
Belgium/Luxembourg	6 October 1992	-
Netherlands	29 October 1992	1 August 1994
Republic of Korea	22 December 1992	25 July 1993
Denmark	22 April 1993	-
Germany	11 August 1993	-
Hungary	11 August 1993	1 April 1995
Austria	13 August 1993	-
Spain	11 October 1993	-
Ecuador	28 January 1994	-
Peru	31 January 1994	18 December 1994
Romania	24 May 1994	-
Chile	7 August 1995	-
Venezuela	5 September 1996	-

Peru

Thailand	15 November 1991	15 November 1991
Switzerland	22 November 1991	23 November 1993
Republic of Korea	3 June 1993	20 April 1994
Bolivia	30 July 1993	19 March 1995
United Kingdom	4 October 1993	21 April 1994
France	6 October 1993	30 May 1996
Paraguay	31 January 1994	18 December 1994
Czech Republic	16 March 1994	6 March 1995
Colombia	26 April 1994	-
Sweden	3 May 1994	1 August 1994
Italy	5 May 1994	18 October 1995
Romania	16 May 1994	1 January 1995
China	9 June 1994	1 February 1995
Argentina	10 November 1994	-
Spain	17 November 1994	17 February 1996
Portugal	22 November 1994	18 October 1995
Denmark	23 November 1994	17 February 1995
Netherlands	27 December 1994	1 February 1996
Germany	30 January 1995	-
Norway	10 March 1995	5 May 1995
Finland	2 May 1995	-
Malaysia	13 October 1995	25 December 1995
Australia	7 December 1995	-
Venezuela	12 January 1996	-
El Salvador	13 June 1996	-

Philippines

France	14 June 1976	1 July 1976
United Kingdom	3 December 1980	2 January 1981

Country/territory	_Date of signature_	_Date of entry into force_
Netherlands	27 February 1985	1 October 1987
Italy	17 June 1988	4 November 1993
Viet Nam	27 February 1992	-
China	20 July 1992	-
Spain	19 October 1993	21 September 1994
Republic of Korea	7 April 1994	-
Romania	18 May 1994	-
France	13 September 1994	-
Australia	25 January 1995	8 December 1995
Czech Republic	4 April 1995	-
Thailand	30 September 1995	-
Iran (Islamic Republic of)	8 October 1995	-
Canada	10 November 1995	-
Chile	20 November 1995	-

Poland

Belgium/Luxembourg	19 May 1987	2 August 1991
United Kingdom	8 December 1987	14 April 1988
China	7 June 1988	8 January 1989
Austria	24 November 1988	1 November 1989
France	14 February 1989	10 February 1990
Italy	10 May 1989	9 January 1992
Sweden	13 October 1989	4 January 1990
Republic of Korea	1 November 1989	2 February 1990
Switzerland	8 November 1989	17 April 1990
Germany	10 November 1989	24 February 1991
Kuwait	5 March 1990	18 December 1993
United States	21 March 1990	6 August 1994
Finland	5 April 1990	21 February 1991
Canada	6 April 1990	22 November 1990
Denmark	1 May 1990	13 October 1990
Norway	5 June 1990	24 October 1990
Australia	7 May 1991	27 March 1992
Israel	22 May 1991	6 April 1992
Argentina	31 July 1991	1 September 1992
Uruguay	2 August 1991	21 October 1994
Turkey	21 August 1991	19 August 1994
Belarus	24 April 1992	18 January 1993
Cyprus	4 June 1992	1 July 1993
Spain	30 July 1992	1 May 1993
Netherlands	7 September 1992	1 February 1994
Hungary	23 September 1992	16 June 1995
Lithuania	28 September 1992	6 August 1993
Russian Federation	2 October 1992	-
Indonesia	6 October 1992	1 July 1993
Greece	14 October 1992	20 February 1995
Thailand	18 December 1992	10 August 1993
Ukraine	12 January 1993	14 September 1993
United Arab Emirates	31 January 1993	9 April 1994
Albania	5 March 1993	9 August 1993
Portugal	11 March 1993	9 October 1993
Tunisia	29 March 1993	22 September 1993
Malaysia	21 April 1993	23 March 1994
Latvia	26 April 1993	19 July 1993

Country/territory	Date of signature	Date of entry into force
Estonia	6 May 1993	6 August 1993
Singapore	3 June 1993	29 December 1993
Czech Republic	16 July 1993	29 June 1994
Bulgaria	11 April 1994	9 March 1995
Romania	23 June 1994	30 December 1995
Slovakia	18 August 1994	-
Viet Nam	31 August 1994	24 November 1994
Kazakhstan	21 September 1994	25 May 1995
Morocco	24 October 1994	29 May 1995
Republic of Moldova	16 November 1994	27 July 1995
Uzbekistan	11 January 1995	29 April 1995
Croatia	21 February 1995	4 October 1995
Egypt	1 July 1995	-
Chile	5 July 1995	-
Mongolia	8 November 1995	-
Slovenia	28 June 1996	-
Yugoslavia	3 September 1996	-
India	7 October 1996	-
Finland	25 November 1996	-
The former Yugoslav Republic of Macedonia	28 November 1996	-

Portugal

Country/territory	Date of signature	Date of entry into force
Germany	16 September 1980	23 April 1982
Morocco	18 October 1988	13 February 1990
Cape Verde	26 October 1990	4 October 1991
Guinea-Bissau	24 June 1991	-
China	3 February 1992	1 December 1992
Hungary	28 February 1992	-
Tunisia	11 May 1992	-
Poland	11 March 1993	9 October 1993
Bulgaria	27 May 1993	-
Czech Republic	12 November 1993	-
Romania	17 November 1993	-
Brazil	9 February 1994	-
Zimbabwe	5 May 1994	-
Venezuela	17 June 1994	7 October 1995
Russian Federation	21 July 1994	-
Argentina	6 October 1994	-
Peru	22 November 1994	18 October 1995
Chile	28 April 1995	-
Republic of Korea	3 May 1995	-
Croatia	9 May 1995	-
Slovakia	10 July 1995	-
Latvia	27 September 1995	-

Qatar

Country/territory	Date of signature	Date of entry into force
Tunisia	28 May 1996	-
Romania	6 June 1996	-
Germany	14 June 1996	-
France	8 July 1996	-
Algeria	24 October 1996	-

Country/territory	Date of signature	Date of entry into force
Republic of Korea		
Germany	4 February 1964	15 January 1967
Switzerland	7 April 1971	7 April 1971
Netherlands	16 October 1974	1 June 1975
Belgium/Luxembourg	20 December 1974	3 September 1976
Tunisia	23 May 1975	28 November 1975
United Kingdom	4 March 1976	4 March 1976
France	28 December 1977	1 March 1979
Sri Lanka	28 March 1980	15 July 1980
Senegal	12 July 1984	2 September 1985
Bangladesh	18 June 1986	6 October 1988
Malaysia	11 April 1988	31 March 1989
Pakistan	24 May 1988	15 April 1990
Denmark	2 June 1988	2 June 1988
Hungary	28 December 1988	1 January 1989
Italy	10 January 1989	26 June 1992
Thailand	24 March 1989	30 September 1989
Poland	1 November 1989	2 February 1990
Democratic Republic of the Congo	19 July 1990	-
Romania	7 August 1990	30 December 1994
USSR (former)	14 December 1990	10 July 1991
Indonesia	16 February 1991	10 March 1994
Austria	14 March 1991	1 November 1991
Mongolia	28 March 1991	30 April 1991
Turkey	14 May 1991	4 June 1994
Czechoslovakia (former)	27 April 1992	16 March 1995
Uzbekistan	17 June 1992	20 November 1992
China	30 September 1992	4 December 1992
Paraguay	22 December 1992	6 August 1993
Viet Nam	13 May 1993	4 September 1993
Peru	3 June 1993	20 April 1994
Lithuania	24 September 1993	9 November 1993
Finland	21 October 1993	11 May 1996
Spain	17 January 1994	19 July 1994
Philippines	7 April 1994	-
Argentina	17 May 1994	-
Greece	25 January 1995	4 November 1995
Portugal	3 May 1995	-
South Africa	7 July 1995	-
Tajikistan	14 July 1995	13 August 1995
Sweden	30 August 1995	-
Brazil	1 September 1995	-
India	26 February 1996	-
Egypt	18 March 1996	-
Kazakhstan	20 March 1996	-
Bolivia	1 April 1996	-
Lao People's Democratic Republic	15 May 1996	-
Chile	7 September 1996	-
Latvia	23 October 1996	-
Ukraine	16 December 1996	-

Country/territory	Date of signature	Date of entry into force
Republic of Moldova [a]		
Romania	14 August 1992	10 April 1996
China	7 November 1992	1 March 1995
Kuwait	4 February 1993	-
United States	21 April 1993	25 November 1994
Turkey	14 February 1994	-
Germany	28 February 1994	Provisional application
Poland	16 November 1994	27 July 1995
Hungary	19 April 1995	-
Iran (Islamic Republic of)	31 May 1995	-
Finland	25 August 1995	-
Ukraine	29 August 1995	-
Netherlands	26 September 1995	1 June 1996
Uzbekistan	21 November 1995	-
Switzerland	30 November 1995	-
United Kingdom	19 March 1996	-
Bulgaria	17 April 1996	
Romania		
United Kingdom [j]	19 March 1976	22 November 1976
Austria	30 September 1976	8 November 1977
France [j]	16 December 1976	1 August 1978
Pakistan [j]	21 January 1978	26 June 1979
Belgium/Luxembourg [j]	8 May 1978	1 May 1980
Sudan	8 December 1978	5 December 1979
Gabon	11 April 1979	18 September 1982
Germany	12 October 1979	10 January 1981
Senegal	19 June 1980	20 May 1984
Cameroon	30 August 1980	16 December 1981
Denmark	12 November 1980	9 April 1981
Sri Lanka	9 February 1981	3 June 1982
Morocco	11 September 1981	-
Malaysia	26 November 1982	20 June 1984
China	10 February 1983	12 January 1984
Bangladesh	13 March 1987	31 October 1987
Tunisia [j]	23 September 1987	4 February 1989
Mauritania	14 March 1988	19 December 1989
Ghana	14 September 1989	-
Republic of Korea	7 August 1990	30 December 1994
Uruguay	23 November 1990	29 August 1993
Italy	6 December 1990	-
Turkey	24 January 1991	17 April 1996
Kuwait	21 May 1991	26 July 1992
Norway	11 June 1991	23 March 1992
Cyprus	26 July 1991	10 July 1993
Israel	2 September 1991	26 August 1992
Greece	16 September 1991	21 October 1992
Finland	26 March 1992	6 January 1993
United States	28 May 1992	15 January 1994
Jordan	2 July 1992	-
Republic of Moldova	14 August 1992	10 April 1996
United Arab Emirates	11 April 1993	7 April 1996
Thailand	30 April 1993	20 August 1994

Country/territory	Date of signature	Date of entry into force
Australia	21 June 1993	22 April 1994
Argentina	29 July 1993	1 May 1995
Hungary	16 September 1993	-
Russian Federation	29 September 1993	-
Switzerland	25 October 1993	30 July 1994
Czech Republic	8 November 1993	28 July 1994
Portugal	17 November 1993	-
Morocco	28 January 1994	-
Slovakia	3 March 1994	7 March 1996
Lithuania	8 March 1994	15 December 1994
Netherlands	19 April 1994	1 February 1995
Peru	16 May 1994	1 January 1995
Philippines	18 May 1994	-
Paraguay	24 May 1994	-
Bulgaria	1 June 1994	23 May 1995
Croatia	8 June 1994	-
Denmark	14 June 1994	24 August 1995
Poland	23 June 1994	30 December 1995
China	12 July 1994	1 September 1995
Viet Nam	1 September 1994	16 August 1995
Armenia	20 September 1994	24 December 1995
Lebanon	18 October 1994	-
Algeria	22 October 1994	-
Turkmenistan	16 November 1994	-
Egypt	24 November 1994	-
Spain	25 January 1995	7 December 1995
Ukraine	23 February 1995	-
France	21 March 1995	-
Albania	11 May 1995	-
Belarus	31 May 1995	-
Chile	4 July 1995	-
Pakistan	10 July 1995	-
United Kingdom	13 July 1995	-
Bolivia	9 October 1995	-
Tunisia	16 October 1995	-
Yugoslavia	28 November 1995	-
Mongolia	6 December 1995	-
Slovenia	24 January 1996	-
Cuba	26 January 1996	-
Belgium/Luxembourg	4 March 1996	-
Ecuador	21 March 1996	-
Canada	17 April 1996	-
Kazakhstan	25 April 1996	-
Austria	15 May 1996	-
Qatar	6 June 1996	-
Uzbekistan	6 June 1996	-
Germany	25 June 1996	-
Malaysia	25 June 1996	-

Russian Federation [a]

United States	17 June 1992	-
Poland	2 October 1992	-
Bulgaria	8 June 1993	-
Greece	30 June 1993	-

Country/territory	Date of signature	Date of entry into force
Cuba	7 July 1993	-
Romania	29 September 1993	-
Denmark	4 November 1993	-
Slovakia	30 November 1993	-
Czech Republic	5 April 1994	-
Viet Nam	16 June 1994	-
Portugal	21 July 1994	-
Kuwait	21 November 1994	-
India	23 December 1994	-
Hungary	6 March 1995	-
Albania	11 April 1995	-
Sweden	19 April 1995	-
Norway	4 October 1995	-
Yugoslavia	11 October 1995	-
Mongolia	29 November 1995	-
Ecuador	1 April 1996	-
Lao People's Democratic Republic	6 December 1996	-

Rwanda

Switzerland	15 October 1963	15 October 1963
Germany	18 May 1967	28 February 1969
Belgium/Luxembourg	2 November 1983	1 August 1985

Saint Lucia

United Kingdom	18 January 1983	18 January 1983
Germany	16 March 1985	22 July 1987

Saint Vincent and the Grenadines

Germany	25 March 1986	8 January 1989

Saudi Arabia

Germany	2 February 1979	15 March 1980
Egypt	13 March 1990	15 September 1992
China	29 February 1996	-
Italy	10 September 1996	-
Germany	29 October 1996	-

Senegal

Switzerland	16 August 1962	13 August 1964
Germany	24 January 1964	16 January 1966
Sweden	24 February 1967	23 February 1968
France	29 March 1974	-
Netherlands	3 August 1979	5 May 1981
United Kingdom	7 May 1980	9 February 1984
Romania	19 June 1980	20 May 1984
United States	6 December 1983	25 October 1990
Tunisia	17 May 1984	-
Republic of Korea	12 July 1984	2 September 1985
Argentina	6 April 1993	-

Country/territory	*Date of signature*	*Date of entry into force*
Sierra Leone		
Germany	8 April 1965	10 December 1966
United Kingdom	8 December 1981	--
Singapore		
Netherlands	16 May 1972	7 September 1973
Germany	3 October 1973	1 October 1975
United Kingdom	22 July 1975	22 July 1975
France	8 September 1975	18 October 1976
Switzerland	6 March 1978	3 May 1978
Belgium/Luxembourg	17 November 1978	27 November 1980
Sri Lanka	9 May 1980	30 September 1980
China	21 November 1985	7 February 1986
Taiwan Province of China	9 April 1990	9 April 1990
Indonesia	28 August 1990	28 August 1990
Viet Nam	29 October 1992	25 December 1992
Poland	3 June 1993	29 December 1993
Pakistan	8 March 1995	4 May 1995
Czech Republic	6 April 1995	7 October 1995
Mongolia	24 July 1995	-
Slovakia [e]		
Czech Republic	23 November 1992	-
Hungary	15 January 1993	-
Slovenia	28 July 1993	-
Russian Federation	30 November 1993	-
Tajikistan	14 February 1994	-
Romania	3 March 1994	7 March 1996
Ukraine	22 June 1994	-
Indonesia	12 July 1994	1 March 1995
Bulgaria	18 August 1994	9 March 1995
Poland	18 August 1994	-
Uzbekistan	16 May 1995	-
Portugal	10 July 1995	-
Turkmenistan	17 November 1995	-
Yugoslavia	7 February 1996	-
Croatia	12 February 1996	-
Slovenia		
Sweden	10 November 1978	21 November 1979
Czech Republic	4 May 1993	21 May 1994
Slovakia	28 July 1993	-
China	13 September 1993	1 January 1995
Germany	28 October 1993	-
Switzerland	9 November 1995	-
Romania	24 January 1996	-
The former Yugoslav Republic of Macedonia	5 June 1996	-
Poland	28 June 1996	-

Country/territory	Date of signature	Date of entry into force
United Kingdom	3 July 1996	-
Netherlands	24 September 1996	-

Somalia

Germany	27 November 1981	15 February 1985

South Africa

United Kingdom	20 September 1994	-
Netherlands	9 May 1995	-
Switzerland	27 June 1995	-
Republic of Korea	7 July 1995	-
Germany	11 September 1995	-
France	11 October 1995	-
Canada	27 November 1995	-
Cuba	8 December 1995	-
Denmark	22 February 1996	-
Austria	28 November 1996	-

Spain

Morocco	27 September 1989	15 January 1992
Hungary	9 November 1989	1 August 1992
Bolivia	24 April 1990	12 May 1992
USSR (former) [e]	26 October 1990	28 November 1991
Czechoslovakia (former) [e]	12 December 1990	28 November 1991
Tunisia	28 May 1991	20 June 1994
Chile	2 October 1991	28 March 1994
Argentina	3 October 1991	28 September 1992
China	6 February 1992	1 May 1994
Uruguay	7 April 1992	6 May 1994
Poland	30 July 1992	1 May 1993
Egypt	3 November 1992	26 April 1994
Paraguay	11 October 1993	-
Philippines	19 October 1993	21 September 1994
Republic of Korea	17 January 1994	19 July 1994
Nicaragua	16 March 1994	28 March 1995
Honduras	18 March 1994	-
Kazakhstan	23 March 1994	-
Cuba	27 May 1994	9 June 1995
Lithuania	6 July 1994	22 December 1995
Pakistan	15 September 1994	-
Peru	17 November 1994	17 February 1996
Algeria	23 December 1994	-
Romania	25 January 1995	7 December 1995
El Salvador	14 February 1995	20 February 1996
Turkey	15 February 1995	-
Gabon	2 March 1995	-
Dominican Republic	16 March 1995	-
Malaysia	4 April 1995	16 February 1996
Indonesia	30 May 1995	-
Colombia	9 June 1995	-
Mexico	23 June 1995	-
Bulgaria	5 September 1995	-

Country/territory	*Date of signature*	*Date of entry into force*
Latvia	26 October 1995	-
Venezuela	2 November 1995	-
Lebanon	22 February 1996	-
Ecuador	26 June 1996	-

Sri Lanka

Germany	8 November 1963	7 December 1966
United Kingdom	13 February 1980	18 December 1980
Republic of Korea	28 March 1980	15 July 1980
France	10 April 1980	19 April 1982
Singapore	9 May 1980	30 September 1980
Romania	9 February 1981	3 June 1982
Switzerland	23 September 1981	12 February 1982
Japan	1 March 1982	7 August 1982
Belgium/Luxembourg	5 April 1982	26 April 1984
Malaysia	16 April 1982	31 October 1995
Sweden	30 April 1982	30 April 1982
Netherlands	26 April 1984	1 May 1985
Finland	27 April 1985	25 October 1987
Denmark	4 June 1985	4 June 1985
Norway	13 June 1985	13 June 1985
China	13 March 1986	25 March 1987
Italy	25 March 1987	20 March 1990
United States	20 September 1991	1 May 1993
Thailand	3 January 1996	-
Egypt	11 March 1996	-
Indonesia	10 June 1996	-

Sudan

Germany	7 February 1963	24 November 1967
Netherlands	22 August 1970	27 March 1972
Switzerland	17 February 1974	14 December 1974
Egypt	28 May 1977	14 March 1978
France	31 July 1978	5 July 1980
Romania	8 December 1978	5 December 1979

Suriname

Indonesia	28 October 1995	-

Swaziland

Germany	5 April 1990	7 August 1995
United Kingdom	5 May 1995	5 May 1995

Sweden [g]

Côte d'Ivoire	27 August 1965	3 November 1966
Madagascar	2 April 1966	23 June 1967
Senegal	24 February 1967	23 February 1968
Egypt	15 July 1978	29 January 1979
Slovenia	10 November 1978	21 November 1979
Yugoslavia	10 November 1978	21 November 1979

Country/territory	_Date of signature_	_Date of entry into force_
Malaysia	3 March 1979	6 July 1979
Pakistan	12 March 1981	14 June 1981
China	29 March 1982	29 March 1982
Sri Lanka	30 April 1982	30 April 1982
Yemen	29 October 1983	23 February 1984
Tunisia	15 September 1984	13 May 1985
Hungary	21 April 1987	21 April 1987
Poland	13 October 1989	4 January 1990
Bolivia	20 September 1990	3 July 1992
Morocco	26 September 1990	Provisional application
Czechoslovakia (former)	13 November 1990	23 September 1991
Argentina	22 November 1991	28 September 1992
Latvia	10 March 1992	6 November 1992
Lithuania	17 March 1992	1 September 1992
Estonia	31 March 1992	20 May 1992
Indonesia	17 September 1992	18 February 1993
Chile	24 May 1993	30 December 1995
Viet Nam	8 September 1993	2 August 1994
Bulgaria	19 April 1994	1 April 1995
Peru	3 May 1994	1 August 1994
Hong Kong, China	27 May 1994	26 June 1994
Belarus	20 December 1994	-
Albania	31 March 1995	1 April 1996
Russian Federation	19 April 1995	-
Oman	15 July 1995	-
Ukraine	15 August 1995	1 March 1997
Republic of Korea	30 August 1995	-
Lao People's Democratic Republic	29 August 1996	1 January 1997
Venezuela	25 November 1996	-

Switzerland [h]

Tunisia	2 December 1961	19 January 1964
Niger*	28 March 1962	17 November 1962
Guinea*	26 April 1962	29 July 1963
Côte d'Ivoire*	26 June 1962	18 November 1962
Senegal*	16 August 1962	13 August 1964
Congo*	18 October 1962	11 July 1964
Cameroon*	28 January 1963	6 April 1964
Liberia*	23 July 1963	22 September 1964
Rwanda*	15 October 1963	15 October 1963
Togo*	17 January 1964	9 August 1966
Madagascar*	17 March 1964	31 March 1966
Malta*	20 January 1965	23 February 1965
United Republic of Tanzania	3 May 1965	16 September 1965
Costa Rica	1 September 1965	18 August 1966
Benin*	20 April 1966	6 October 1973
Chad*	21 February 1967	31 October 1967
Ecuador	2 May 1968	11 September 1969
Burkina Faso*	6 May 1969	15 September 1969
Republic of Korea	7 April 1971	7 April 1971
Uganda	23 August 1971	8 May 1972
Gabon*	28 January 1972	18 October 1972

Country/territory	_Date of signature_	_Date of entry into force_
Democratic Republic of		
the Congo	10 March 1972	10 May 1973
Central African Republic*	28 February 1973	4 July 1973
Egypt	25 July 1973	4 June 1974
Indonesia	6 February 1974	9 April 1976
Sudan	17 February 1974	14 December 1974
Mauritania*	9 September 1976	30 May 1978
Jordan	11 November 1976	2 March 1977
Syrian Arab Republic	22 June 1977	10 August 1978
Malaysia	1 March 1978	9 June 1978
Singapore	6 March 1978	3 May 1978
Mali	8 March 1978	8 December 1978
Sri Lanka	23 September 1981	12 February 1982
Panama	19 October 1983	22 August 1985
Morocco	17 December 1985	12 April 1991
China	12 November 1986	18 March 1987
Bolivia	6 November 1987	13 May 1991
Turkey	3 March 1988	21 February 1990
Hungary	5 October 1988	16 May 1989
Uruguay	7 October 1988	22 April 1989
Poland	8 November 1989	9 November 1995
Czechoslovakia (former)	5 October 1990	7 August 1991
USSR (former)	1 December 1990	26 August 1991
Jamaica	11 December 1990	21 November 1991
Argentina	12 April 1991	6 November 1992
Ghana	8 October 1991	16 June 1993
Bulgaria	28 October 1991	26 October 1993
Cape Verde	28 October 1991	6 May 1992
Chile	11 November 1991	-
Peru	22 November 1991	23 November 1993
Paraguay	31 January 1992	28 September 1992
Viet Nam	3 July 1992	3 December 1992
Albania	22 September 1992	30 April 1993
Estonia	21 December 1992	18 August 1993
Latvia	22 December 1992	16 April 1993
Lithuania	23 December 1992	13 May 1993
Uzbekistan	16 April 1993	5 November 1993
Belarus	28 May 1993	13 July 1994
Honduras	14 October 1993	-
Romania	25 October 1993	30 July 1994
Venezuela	18 November 1993	30 November 1994
Gambia	22 November 1993	-
Kazakhstan	12 May 1994	-
Namibia	1 August 1994	-
Zambia	3 August 1994	7 March 1995
Hong Kong, China	22 September 1994	22 October 1994
Brazil	11 November 1994	-
El Salvador	8 December 1994	-
Barbados	29 March 1995	22 December 1995
Ukraine	20 April 1995	-
South Africa	27 June 1995	-
Mexico	10 July 1995	14 March 1996
Pakistan	11 July 1995	-
Slovenia	9 November 1995	-
Republic of Moldova	30 November 1995	-

Country/territory	Date of signature	Date of entry into force
Cuba	28 June 1996	-
Zimbabwe	15 August 1996	-
The former Yugoslav Republic of Macedonia	26 September 1996	-
Cambodia	12 October 1996	-
Croatia	30 October 1996	-
Lao People's Democratic Republic	4 December 1996	-
Mongolia	29 January 1997	-

Syrian Arab Republic

Switzerland	22 June 1977	10 August 1978
Germany	2 August 1977	20 April 1980
France	28 November 1977	1 March 1979
China	19 December 1996	-

Taiwan Province of China

Singapore	9 April 1990	9 April 1990
Paraguay	6 April 1992	-
Nicaragua	29 July 1992	-
Latvia	17 September 1992	8 October 1993
Thailand	30 April 1996	

Tajikistan [a]

United States	25 June 1992	
China	9 March 1993	20 January 1994
Czech Republic	11 February 1994	3 December 1995
Slovakia	14 February 1994	-
Pakistan	31 March 1994	-
Kuwait	18 April 1995	-
Republic of Korea	14 July 1995	13 August 1995
Iran (Islamic Republic of)	18 July 1995	-
India	1 December 1995	-
United Arab Emirates	17 December 1995	-
Turkey	6 May 1996	-

Thailand

Germany	13 December 1961	10 April 1965
Netherlands	6 June 1972	3 March 1973
United Kingdom	28 November 1978	11 August 1979
China	12 March 1985	13 December 1985
Belgium/Luxembourg	19 March 1986	--
Bangladesh	13 March 1988	-
Republic of Korea	24 March 1989	30 September 1989
Lao People's Democratic Republic	22 August 1990	7 December 1990
Czechoslovakia (former)	26 August 1991	-
Hungary	18 October 1991	18 October 1991
Viet Nam	30 October 1991	7 February 1992
Peru	15 November 1991	15 November 1991
Poland	18 December 1992	10 August 1993

Country/territory	Date of signature	Date of entry into force
Romania	30 April 1993	20 August 1994
Czech Republic	12 February 1994	4 May 1995
Finland	18 March 1994	-
Cambodia	29 March 1995	-
Philippines	30 September 1995	-
Sri Lanka	3 January 1996	-
Taiwan Province of China	30 April 1996	30 April 1996

The former Yugoslav Republic of Macedonia

Croatia	6 July 1994	5 April 1995
Turkey	9 September 1995	-
Slovenia	5 June 1996	-
Yugoslavia	4 September 1996	-
Germany	10 September 1996	-
Switzerland	26 September 1996	-
Poland	28 November 1996	-

Togo

Germany	16 May 1961	21 December 1964
Switzerland	17 January 1964	9 August 1966
Tunisia	13 September 1987	-

Trinidad and Tobago

United Kingdom	23 July 1993	8 October 1993
France	28 October 1993	21 April 1996
United States	26 September 1994	-
Canada	11 September 1995	8 July 1996

Tunisia

Switzerland	2 December 1961	19 January 1964
Netherlands	23 May 1963	19 December 1964
Germany	20 December 1963	6 February 1966
Belgium/Luxembourg	15 July 1964	9 March 1966
France	30 June 1972	30 June 1972
Libyan Arab Jamahiriya	6 June 1973	-
Kuwait	14 September 1973	--
Republic of Korea	23 May 1975	28 November 1975
Senegal	17 May 1984	-
Sweden	15 September 1984	13 May 1985
Italy	17 October 1985	24 June 1989
Mauritania	11 March 1986	-
Mali	1 July 1986	-
Togo	13 September 1987	-
Romania [j]	23 September 1987	4 February 1989
United Kingdom	14 March 1989	4 January 1990
Egypt	8 December 1989	2 January 1991
United States	15 May 1990	7 February 1993
Guinea	18 November 1990	-
Spain	28 May 1991	20 June 1994
Turkey	29 May 1991	7 February 1993
Oman	19 October 1991	-

Country/territory	Date of signature	Date of entry into force
Portugal	11 May 1992	-
Indonesia	13 May 1992	12 September 1992
Niger	5 June 1992	-
Argentina	17 June 1992	-
Greece	31 October 1992	21 April 1995
Burkina Faso	7 January 1993	-
Poland	29 March 1993	22 September 1993
Albania	30 October 1993	-
Morocco	28 January 1994	-
Jordan	27 April 1995	-
Austria	1 June 1995	-
Romania	16 October 1995	-
United Arab Emirates	10 April 1996	-
Pakistan	18 April 1996	-
Qatar	28 May 1996	-
Denmark	28 June 1996	-

Turkey

Country/territory	Date of signature	Date of entry into force
Germany	20 June 1962	16 December 1965
United States	3 December 1985	18 May 1990
Netherlands	27 March 1986	1 November 1989
Belgium/Luxembourg	27 August 1986	4 May 1990
Bangladesh	12 November 1987	21 June 1990
Switzerland	3 March 1988	21 February 1990
Austria	16 September 1988	1 January 1992
Kuwait	27 October 1988	25 April 1992
Denmark	7 February 1990	1 August 1992
China	13 November 1990	19 August 1994
USSR (former)	14 December 1990	-
Romania	24 January 1991	17 April 1996
United Kingdom	15 March 1991	-
Republic of Korea	14 May 1991	4 June 1994
Tunisia	29 May 1991	7 February 1993
Poland	21 August 1991	19 August 1994
Hungary	14 January 1992	22 February 1995
Japan	12 February 1992	12 March 1993
Kyrgyzstan	28 April 1992	-
Uzbekistan	28 April 1992	18 May 1995
Czechoslovakia (former)	30 April 1992	-
Kazakhstan	1 May 1992	10 August 1995
Turkmenistan	2 May 1992	-
Argentina	8 May 1992	1 May 1995
Albania	1 June 1992	-
Georgia	31 July 1992	-
Finland	13 May 1993	12 April 1995
Jordan	2 August 1993	-
Lithuania	15 October 1993	-
Azerbaijan	9 February 1994	-
Republic of Moldova	14 February 1994	-
Bulgaria	6 July 1994	-
Spain	15 February 1995	-
Pakistan	16 March 1995	-
Italy	22 March 1995	-
Belarus	8 August 1995	-

Country/territory	Date of signature	Date of entry into force
The former Yugoslav Republic of Macedonia	9 September 1995	-
Croatia	12 February 1996	-
Israel	14 March 1996	-
Tajikistan[a]	6 May 1996	-
Ukraine	27 November 1996	-
Iran, Islamic Republic of	21 December 1996	-

Turkmenistan [a]

Turkey	2 May 1992	-
China	21 November 1992	6 June 1995
France	28 April 1994	2 May 1996
Indonesia	2 June 1994	-
Pakistan	26 October 1994	-
Romania	16 November 1994	-
United Kingdom	9 February 1995	9 February 1995
Egypt	23 May 1995	-
Israel	24 May 1995	-
India	1 September 1995	-
Slovakia	17 November 1995	-
Uzbekistan	16 January 1996	-
Iran (Islamic Republic of)	23 January 1996	-
Georgia	20 March 1996	21 November 1996

Uganda

Germany	29 November 1966	19 August 1968
Netherlands	24 April 1970	--
Switzerland	23 August 1971	8 May 1972
Egypt	4 November 1995	-

Ukraine [a]

Finland	14 May 1992	30 January 1993
Denmark	23 October 1992	29 April 1994
China	31 October 1992	29 May 1993
Mongolia	5 November 1992	5 November 1992
Egypt	21 December 1992	10 October 1993
Poland	12 January 1993	14 September 1993
United Kingdom	10 February 1993	10 February 1993
Germany	15 February 1993	Provisional application
Kyrgyzstan	23 February 1993	-
Lithuania	8 February 1994	6 March 1995
United States	4 March 1994	-
Czech Republic	17 March 1994	2 November 1995
France	3 May 1994	26 January 1996
Slovakia	22 June 1994	-
Netherlands	14 July 1994	-
Greece	1 September 1994	-
Hungary	11 October 1994	-
Canada	24 October 1994	-
Bulgaria	8 December 1994	10 December 1995

Country/territory	Date of signature	Date of entry into force
Georgia	January 1995	-
Estonia	15 February 1995	5 May 1995
Romania	23 February 1995	-
Lebanon	25 March 1995	-
Indonesia	11 April 1995	-
Switzerland	20 April 1995	-
Italy	2 May 1995	-
Belgium/Luxembourg	20 May 1995	-
Cuba	20 May 1995	19 February 1996
Argentina	9 August 1995	-
Sweden	15 August 1995	-
Republic of Moldova	29 August 1995	-
Chile	30 October 1995	-
Belarus	14 December 1995	-
Viet Nam	27 March 1996	-
Indonesia	11 April 1996	-
Iran (Islamic Republic of)	21 May 1996	-
Austria	8 November 1996	-
Turkey	27 November 1996	-
Republic of Korea	16 December 1996	-

United Arab Emirates

Country/territory	Date of signature	Date of entry into force
Kuwait	12 February 1966	-
Morocco	16 June 1982	-
Egypt	19 June 1988	-
France	9 September 1991	18 December 1992
Malaysia	11 October 1991	-
United Kingdom	8 December 1992	13 December 1993
Poland	31 January 1993	9 April 1994
Romania	11 April 1993	7 April 1996
China	1 July 1993	28 September 1994
Czech Republic	23 November 1994	25 December 1995
Tajikistan	17 December 1995	-
Italy	22 January 1996	-
Finland	12 March 1996	-
Tunisia	10 April 1996	-

United Kingdom

Country/territory	Date of signature	Date of entry into force
Egypt	11 June 1975	24 February 1976
Singapore	22 July 1975	22 July 1975
Republic of Korea	4 March 1976	4 March 1976
Romania [j]	19 March 1976	22 November 1976
Indonesia	27 April 1976	24 March 1977
Thailand	28 November 1978	11 August 1979
Jordan	10 October 1979	24 April 1980
Sri Lanka	13 February 1980	18 December 1980
Senegal	7 May 1980	9 February 1984
Bangladesh	19 June 1980	19 June 1980
Philippines	3 December 1980	2 January 1981
Lesotho	18 February 1981	18 February 1981
Papua New Guinea	14 May 1981	22 December 1981
Malaysia	21 May 1981	21 October 1988
Paraguay	4 June 1981	23 April 1992

Country/territory	*Date of signature*	*Date of entry into force*
Sierra Leone	8 December 1981	-
Yemen	25 February 1982	11 November 1983
Belize	30 April 1982	30 April 1982
Cameroon	4 June 1982	7 June 1985
Costa Rica	7 September 1982	-
Saint Lucia	18 January 1983	18 January 1983
Panama	7 October 1983	7 November 1983
Haiti	18 March 1985	27 March 1995
China	15 May 1986	15 May 1986
Mauritius	20 May 1986	13 October 1986
Malta	4 October 1986	4 October 1986
Jamaica	20 January 1987	14 May 1987
Dominica	23 January 1987	23 January 1987
Hungary	9 March 1987	28 August 1987
Antigua and Barbuda	12 June 1987	12 June 1987
Benin	27 November 1987	27 November 1987
Poland	8 December 1987	14 April 1988
Grenada	25 February 1988	25 February 1988
Bolivia	24 May 1988	16 February 1990
Tunisia	14 March 1989	4 January 1990
Ghana	22 March 1989	25 October 1991
USSR (former)	6 April 1989	3 July 1991
Congo	25 May 1989	9 November 1990
Guyana	27 October 1989	11 April 1990
Czechoslovakia (former)	10 July 1990	26 October 1992
Burundi	13 September 1990	13 September 1990
Morocco	30 October 1990	Provisional application
Argentina	11 December 1990	19 February 1993
Nigeria	11 December 1990	11 December 1990
Turkey	15 March 1991	-
Mongolia	4 October 1991	4 October 1991
Uruguay	21 October 1991	-
Bahrain	30 October 1991	30 October 1991
United Arab Emirates	8 December 1992	13 December 1993
Ukraine	10 February 1993	10 February 1993
Nepal	2 March 1993	2 March 1993
Barbados	7 April 1993	7 April 1993
Lithuania	17 May 1993	21 September 1993
Armenia	22 May 1993	-
Trinidad and Tobago	23 July 1993	8 October 1993
Peru	4 October 1993	21 April 1994
Uzbekistan	24 November 1993	24 November 1993
Honduras	7 December 1993	8 March 1995
United Republic of Tanzania	7 January 1994	-
Latvia	24 January 1994	15 February 1995
Belarus	1 March 1994	28 December 1994
Colombia	9 March 1994	-
India	14 March 1994	6 January 1995
Albania	30 March 1994	30 August 1995
Ecuador	10 May 1994	24 August 1995
Estonia	12 May 1994	16 December 1994
Brazil	19 July 1994	-
South Africa	20 September 1994	-
Pakistan	30 November 1994	30 November 1994
Kyrgyzstan	8 December 1994	-

Country/territory	Date of signature	Date of entry into force
Cuba	30 January 1995	11 May 1995
Turkmenistan	9 February 1995	9 February 1995
Georgia	15 February 1995	15 February 1995
Zimbabwe	1 March 1995	-
Venezuela	15 March 1995	-
Swaziland	5 May 1995	5 May 1995
Lao People's Democratic Republic	1 June 1995	1 June 1995
Côte d'Ivoire	8 June 1995	-
Romania	13 July 1995	-
Kazakhstan	23 November 1995	23 November 1995
Oman	25 November 1995	-
Bulgaria	11 December 1995	-
Azerbaijan	4 January 1996	-
Chile	8 January 1996	-
Republic of Moldova	19 March 1996	-
Slovenia	3 July 1996	-
Nicaragua	4 December 1996	-

United Republic of Tanzania

Germany	30 January 1965	12 July 1968
Switzerland	3 May 1965	16 September 1965
Netherlands	14 April 1970	28 July 1972
United Kingdom	7 January 1994	-

United States

Panama [i]	27 October 1982	30 May 1991
Senegal	6 December 1983	25 October 1990
Haiti	13 December 1983	--
Democratic Republic of the Congo	3 August 1984	28 July 1989
Morocco	22 July 1985	29 May 1991
Turkey	3 December 1985	18 May 1990
Cameroon	26 February 1986	6 April 1989
Egypt	11 March 1986	27 June 1992
Bangladesh	12 March 1986	25 July 1989
Grenada	2 May 1986	3 March 1989
Congo	12 February 1990	13 August 1994
Poland	21 March 1990	6 August 1994
Tunisia	15 May 1990	7 February 1993
Sri Lanka	20 September 1991	1 May 1993
Czechoslovakia (former)	22 October 1991	19 December 1992
Lithuania	28 October 1991	7 February 1992
Argentina	14 November 1991	20 October 1994
Kazakhstan	19 May 1992	12 January 1994
Romania	28 May 1992	15 January 1994
Russian Federation	17 June 1992	-
Tajikistan	25 June 1992	-
Armenia	23 September 1992	29 March 1996
Bulgaria	23 September 1992	2 June 1994
Kyrgyzstan	19 January 1993	12 January 1994
Republic of Moldova	21 April 1993	25 November 1994
Ecuador	27 August 1993	-

Country/territory	Date of signature	Date of entry into force
Belarus	15 January 1994	-
Jamaica	4 February 1994	-
Ukraine	4 March 1994	-
Georgia	7 March 1994	-
Estonia	19 April 1994	-
Trinidad and Tobago	26 September 1994	-
Mongolia	6 October 1994	-
Uzbekistan	16 December 1994	-
Albania	10 January 1995	-
Latvia	13 January 1995	-
Honduras	1 July 1995	-
Nicaragua	1 July 1995	-
Croatia	13 July 1996	-

Uruguay

Germany	4 May 1987	29 June 1990
Netherlands	22 September 1988	1 August 1991
Switzerland	7 October 1988	22 April 1991
Hungary	25 August 1989	1 July 1992
Italy	21 February 1990	-
Romania	23 November 1990	29 August 1993
Canada	16 May 1991	-
Poland	2 August 1991	21 October 1994
United Kingdom	21 October 1991	-
Belgium/Luxembourg	4 November 1991	-
Spain	7 April 1992	6 May 1994
France	14 October 1993	-
China	2 December 1993	-

USSR (former) [a]

Finland	8 February 1989	15 August 1991
Belgium/Luxembourg	9 February 1989	13 October 1991
United Kingdom	6 April 1989	3 July 1991
Germany	13 June 1989	5 August 1991
France	4 July 1989	18 July 1991
Netherlands	5 October 1989	20 July 1991
Canada	20 November 1989	27 June 1991
Italy	30 November 1989	8 July 1991
Austria	8 February 1990	1 September 1991
Denmark	1 May 1990	-
China	21 July 1990	-
Spain	26 October 1990	28 November 1991
Switzerland	1 December 1990	26 August 1991
Republic of Korea	14 December 1990	10 July 1991
Turkey	14 December 1990	-

Uzbekistan [a]

China	13 March 1992	14 April 1994
Turkey	28 April 1992	18 May 1995
Republic of Korea	17 June 1992	20 November 1992
Finland	1 October 1992	22 October 1993
Egypt	16 December 1992	-

Country/territory	Date of signature	Date of entry into force
Switzerland	16 April 1993	5 November 1993
Germany	28 April 1993	Provisional application
Denmark	23 September 1993	-
France	27 October 1993	-
United Kingdom	24 November 1993	24 November 1993
United States	16 December 1994	-
Poland	11 January 1995	29 April 1995
Slovakia	16 May 1995	-
Georgia	4 September 1995	
Republic of Moldova	21 November 1995	-
Turkmenistan	16 January 1996	-
Netherlands	14 March 1996	-
Viet Nam	28 March 1996	-
Latvia	23 May 1996	-
Azerbaijan	27 May 1996	2 November 1996
Romania	6 June 1996	-
Indonesia	27 August 1996	27 January 1997
Kyrgyzstan	24 December 1996	-

Venezuela

Country/territory	Date of signature	Date of entry into force
Italy	4 June 1990	-
Netherlands	22 October 1991	1 November 1993
Chile	2 April 1993	25 May 1995
Argentina	16 November 1993	1 July 1995
Ecuador	18 November 1993	1 February 1995
Switzerland	18 November 1993	30 November 1994
Portugal	17 June 1994	7 October 1995
Barbados	15 July 1994	31 October 1995
Denmark	28 November 1994	-
United Kingdom	15 March 1995	-
Lithuania	24 April 1995	-
Czech Republic	27 April 1995	-
Brazil	4 July 1995	-
Spain	2 November 1995	-
Peru	12 January 1996	-
Germany	14 May 1996	-
Canada	1 July 1996	-
Paraguay	5 September 1996	-
Sweden	25 November 1996	-
Cuba	11 December 1996	-

Viet Nam

Country/territory	Date of signature	Date of entry into force
Italy	18 May 1990	-
Belgium/Luxembourg	24 January 1991	-
Australia	5 March 1991	11 September 1991
Indonesia	25 October 1991	3 December 1993
Thailand	30 October 1991	7 February 1991
Malaysia	21 January 1992	-
Philippines	27 February 1992	-
France	26 May 1992	10 August 1994
Switzerland	3 July 1992	3 December 1992
Belarus	8 July 1992	-
Singapore	29 October 1992	25 December 1992

Economy	*Date of signature*	*Date of entry into force*
China	2 December 1992	1 September 1993
Armenia	1 February 1993	-
Germany	3 April 1993	Provisional application
Republic of Korea	13 May 1993	4 September 1993
Denmark	23 July 1993	7 August 1994
Sweden	8 September 1993	2 August 1994
Finland	13 September 1993	2 May 1996
Netherlands	10 March 1994	1 February 1995
Russian Federation	16 June 1994	-
Hungary	26 August 1994	16 June 1995
Poland	31 August 1994	24 November 1994
Romania	1 September 1994	16 August 1995
Austria	27 March 1995	-
Lithuania	27 September 1995	-
Cuba	12 October 1995	-
Latvia	6 November 1995	-
Lao People's Democratic Republic	14 January 1996	-
Ukraine	27 March 1996	-
Uzbekistan	28 March 1996	-
Bulgaria	19 September 1996	-
Algeria	21 October 1996	-

Yemen

Germany	21 June 1974	19 December 1978
United Kingdom	25 February 1982	11 November 1983
Sweden	29 October 1983	23 February 1984
France	27 April 1984	1 October 1991
Netherlands	18 March 1985	1 September 1986
Egypt	19 October 1988	3 March 1990
Jordan	18 June 1995	-
Iran (Islamic Republic of)	29 February 1996	-

Yugoslavia

France	28 March 1974	3 March 1975
Netherlands	16 February 1976	1 April 1977
Egypt	3 June 1977	--
Sweden	10 November 1978	21 November 1979
Germany	10 July 1989	26 October 1990
Austria	25 October 1989	1 June 1991
Russian Federation	11 October 1995	-
Romania	28 November 1995	-
China	18 December 1995	-
Slovakia	7 February 1996	-
Bulgaria	13 February 1996	-
Belarus	6 March 1996	-
Poland	3 September 1996	25 January 1997
The former Yugoslav Republic of Macedonia	4 September 1996	-
Zimbabwe	19 September 1996	-
Guinea	22 October 1996	-

Country/territory	_Date of signature_	_Date of entry into force_
Zambia		
Germany	10 December 1966	25 August 1972
Switzerland	3 August 1994	7 March 1995
China	21 June 1996	-
Zimbabwe		
Portugal	5 May 1994	-
United Kingdom	1 March 1995	-
Germany	29 September 1995	-
China	21 May 1996	-
Switzerland	15 August 1996	-
Yugoslavia	19 September 1996	-
Netherlands	10 December 1996	-

Source: UNCTAD database on BITs.

Note: - means information not available.

a	Obligations from treaties up to 25 December 1991, concluded by the former Soviet Union, have been assumed by the successor States in accordance with the Alma Ata Declaration.
b	Signed by Belgium only.
c	Signed by Belgium and Luxembourg, but not as an economic union.
d	Canada has also signed 33 bilateral investment guarantee agreements.
e	Obligations from treaties concluded by Czechoslovakia have been assumed as from 1 January 1993 by both the Czech Republic and Slovakia.
f	Includes commercial agreements.
g	Includes economic cooperation agreements.
h	Includes agreements on commerce, investment protection and technical cooperation (these are marked with an asterisk).
i	See 1986 consolidated text (Senate Treaty Doc. 99-24) established following signature of the supplementary protocol.
j	Expires upon entry into force of a later treaty.
k	Separate agreements by protocols of 11 November 1993 and 16 September 1994, for Czech Republic and Slovakia, respectively.

Annex II. Samples of Model Bilateral Investment Treaties

ASIAN-AFRICAN LEGAL CONSULTATIVE COMMITTEE REVISED DRAFT OF MODEL AGREEMENTS
FOR PROMOTION AND PROTECTION OF INVESTMENTS[1]a/

Model A

AGREEMENT between the Government of _____

and

the Government of _____

for the Promotion, Encouragement and Reciprocal Protection of Investments.

The Government of _____ and the Government of
_____

Recognizing in particular the need to promote wider co-operation between the countries of the Asian-African region to accelerate their economic growth and to encourage investments by developing countries in other developing countries of the region;

Also recognizing that reciprocal protection of such investments will be conducive to the attainment of desired objectives in a spirit of partnership;

Desirous to create conditions in which the investments by each other and their nationals would be facilitated and thus stimulate the flow of capital and technology within the region;

Have agreed as follows:

Article 1
Definitions

For the purpose of this Agreement

(a) 'Investment'

(Alternative A)

'Investment' means every kind of asset and in particular, though not exclusively, includes:

    (i)   movable and immovable property and any other property rights such as mortgages, liens or pledges;

    (ii)   shares, stocks and debentures of companies or interests in the property of such companies;

    (iii)   claims to money or to any performance under contract having a financial value, and loans;

    (iv)   copyrights, know-how (goodwill) and industrial property rights such as patents for inventions, trade marks, industrial designs and trade names;

---

[1]Source: Asian-African Legal Consultative Committee (1985). *Models for Bilateral Agreements on Promotion and Protection of Investments: Report of the Committee* (Dehli: Asian-African Legal Consultative Committee) [Note added by the editor].

(v)   rights conferred by law or under contract, including licence to search for, cultivate, extract or exploit natural resources.

(Alternative B)

'Investment' includes every kind of asset such as:

(i)   shares and other types of holdings of companies;
(ii)   claims to any performance under contract having a financial value, claims to money, and loans;
(iii)   rights with respect to movable and immovable property;
(iv)   rights with regard to patents, trade marks and any other industrial property; and
(v)   contractual rights relating to exploration and exploitation of natural resources.

(Alternative C)

'Investment' means:

(i)   in respect of investment in the territory of
        (First Party) _____
(ii)   in respect of investment in the territory of
        (Second Party) _____

(b)   'National'

        (Alternative A)

        'National' in respect of each Contracting Party means a natural person who is a national or deemed to be a national of the Party under its Constitution or relevant law.

        (Alternative B)

        'National' in respect of (First Party) means _____ and in respect of (Second Party) means _____.

(c)   'Companies'

        (Alternative A)

        'Companies' means corporations, partnerships or associations incorporated, constituted or registered in a Contracting Party in accordance with its laws [and includes such entities in which nationals of a Contracting Party have substantial interest and majority shareholding].

        (Alternative B)

        'Companies' means in respect of the (First Party) _____ and in respect of the (Second Party) _____.

(d)   'State Entity' means a department of government, corporation, institution or undertaking wholly owned or controlled by government and engaged in activities of a commercial nature.

(e)   'Returns' includes profits, interests, capital gains, dividends, royalties or fees.

(f)   'Host State' means the country in whose territory the investment is made.

(g)   'Territory' means:

   (i)   In respect of the (First Party) _____;

   (ii)   In respect of the (Second Party) _____.

Article 2
Promotion and encouragement of investments

   (i)   Each Contracting Party shall take steps to promote investments in the territory of the other Contracting Party and encourage its nationals, companies and State entities to make such investments through offer of appropriate incentives, wherever possible, which may include such modalities as tax concessions and investment guarantees.

   (ii)   Each Contracting Party shall create favorable conditions to encourage the nationals, companies or State entities of the other Contracting Party to promote investment in its territory.

   (iii)   The Contracting Parties shall periodically consult among themselves concerning investment opportunities within the territory of each other in various sectors such as industry, mining, communications, agriculture and forestry to determine where investments from one Contracting Party into the other may be most beneficial in the interest of both the parties.

   (iv)   [Each Contracting Party shall duly honour all commitments made and obligations undertaken by it with regard to investments of nationals, companies or State entities of the other Contracting Party]. b/

Article 3
Reception of investments

   (i)   Each Contracting Party shall determine the mode and manner in which investments are to be received in its territory.

   (ii)   The Contracting Parties may determine that in a specified class of investments, a national, company or State entity of a Contracting Party intending to make investment in the territory of the other Contracting Party including collaboration arrangements on specific projects, shall submit its or his proposal to a designated authority of the Party where the investment is sought to be made. Such proposals shall be processed expeditiously and soon after the proposal is approved, a letter of authorization shall be issued and the investment shall be registered, where appropriate, with the designated authority of the host State. The investment shall be received subject to the terms and conditions specified in the letter of authorization.

   (iii)   The host State shall facilitate the implementation and operation of the investment projects through suitable administrative measures and in particular in the matter of expeditious clearance of authorizations or permits for importation of goods, employment of consultants and technicians of foreign nationality in accordance with its laws and regulations.

Article 4
Most-favoured-nation treatment

   (i)   Each Contracting Party shall accord in its territory to the investments or returns of nationals, companies or State entities of the other Contracting Party treatment that is not less favourable than that it accords to the investments or returns of nationals, companies or State entities of any third State.

(ii)   Each Contracting Party shall also ensure that the nationals, companies or State entities of the other Contracting Party are accorded treatment not less favourable than that it accords to the nationals or companies or State entities of any third State in regard to the management, use, enjoyment or disposal of their investments including management and control over business activities and other ancillary functions in respect of the investments.

Article 5 c/
National treatment

(i)   Each Contracting Party shall accord in its territory to the investments or returns of nationals, companies or State entities of the other Contracting Party treatment that is not less favourable than that it accords to the investments or returns of its own nationals, companies or State entities.

(ii)   Each of the Contracting Parties shall extend to the nationals, companies or State entities of the other Contracting Party, treatment that is not less favourable than it accords to its own nationals, companies or State entities in regard to management, control, use, enjoyment and disposal in relation to investments which have been received in its territory.

Article 6
Repatriation of capital and returns

(i)   Each Contracting Party shall ensure that the nationals, companies or State entities of the other Contracting Party are allowed full facilities in the matter of the right to repatriation of capital and returns on his or its investments subject, however, to any condition for re-investment and subject also to the right of the host State to impose reasonable restrictions for temporary periods in accordance with its laws to meet exceptional financial and economic situations [as determined in the light of guidelines generally applied by the IMF or such other criteria as may be agreed upon by the parties]. The capital and returns allowed to be repatriated shall include emoluments and earnings accruing from or in relation to the investment as also the proceeds arising out of sale of the assets in the event of liquidation or transfer.

(ii)   In the event of exceptional financial or economic situations as envisaged in paragraph (1) of this article, the host State shall exercise its powers to impose reasonable restrictions equitably and in good faith. Such restrictions shall not extend ordinarily beyond a period of _____ . As any restriction in operation thereafter shall not impede the transfer of profits, interests, dividends, royalties, fees, emoluments or earnings; as regards the capital invested or any other form of returns, transfer of a minimum of 20 per cent in each year shall be guaranteed.

(iii)   Repatriation shall be permitted ordinarily to the country from which the investment originated and in the same currency in which the capital was originally invested or in any other currency agreed upon by the investor and the host State at the rate of exchange applicable on the date of transfer upon such repatriation, unless otherwise agreed by the investor and the host State.

Article 7

Nationalization, expropriation and payment of compensation in respect thereof

(i)   Investments of nationals, companies or State entities of either Contracting Party shall not be nationalized, expropriated or subjected to measures having effect equivalent to nationalization or expropriation in the territory of the other Contracting Party except [for a public purpose] [in national interest] of that Party and against prompt, adequate and effective compensation, provided that such measures are taken on a non-discriminatory basis and in accordance with its laws.

(ii)   Such compensation shall be computed on the basis of the value of the investment immediately prior to the point of time when the proposal for expropriation had become public knowledge to be determined in accordance with recognized principles of valuation such as market value. Where the market value cannot be readily ascertained, the compensation shall be determined on equitable principles taking into account, *inter alia*, the capital invested, depreciation, capital already repatriated and other relevant factors. The compensation shall include interest at a normal commercial rate from the date of expropriation until the date of payment. The determination of the compensation, in the absence of agreement being reached between the investor and the host State, shall be referred to an independent judicial or administrative tribunal or authority competent under the laws of the expropriating State or to arbitration in accordance with the provisions of any agreement between the investor and the host State. The compensation as finally determined shall be promptly paid and allowed to be repatriated.

(iii)   Where a Contracting Party nationalizes or expropriates the assets of a company which is incorporated or constituted under the laws in force in its territory and in which nationals or companies or State entities of the other Contracting Party own shares, it shall ensure that prompt, adequate and effective compensation is received and allowed to be repatriated by the owners of the shares in the other contracting Party. Such compensation shall be determined on the basis of the recognized principles of valuation such as the market value of the shares immediately prior to the point of time when the proposal for nationalization or expropriation had become public knowledge. The compensation shall include interest at a normal commercial rate from the date of nationalization or expropriation until the date of payment. If any question arises regarding the determination of the compensation or its payment, such questions shall be referred to an independent judicial or administrative tribunal or authority competent under the laws of the expropriating State or to arbitration in accordance with the provisions of any agreement between the investor and the host State.

Article 8
Compensation for losses

[(i)   Nationals, companies or State entities of one Contracting Party whose material assets in the investments in the territory of the other Contracting Party suffer losses owing to war or other armed conflict, revolution, a state of national emergency, revolt, insurrection or riot in the territory of the latter Contracting Party, shall be accorded by that Contracting Party treatment regarding restitution, indemnification, compensation or other settlement, no less favourable than that it accords to (its own nationals, companies or State entities or to) nationals, companies or State entities of any third State]. d/

(ii)   Nationals, companies or State entities of one Contracting Party who suffer losses in the territory of the other contracting Party resulting from:

(a)   requisitioning of their property by its forces or authorities; or

(b)   destruction of their property by its forces or authorities which was not caused in combat action or was not required by the necessity of the situation;

shall be accorded restitution or adequate compensation and the resulting payments shall be allowed to be repatriated.

Article 9
Access to courts and tribunals

The nationals, companies or State entities of one Contracting Party shall have the right of access to the courts, tribunals both judicial and administrative, and other authorities competent under the laws of the other Contracting Party for redress of his or its grievances in relation to any matter concerning any investment including judicial review of measures relating to expropriation or nationalization, determination of compensation in the event of expropriation or nationalization, or losses suffered and any restrictions imposed on repatriation of capital or returns.

Article 10
Settlement of investment disputes

(i)   Each Contracting Party consents to submit any dispute or difference that may arise out of or in relation to investments made in its territory by a national, company or State entity of the other contracting Party for settlement through conciliation or arbitration in accordance with the provisions of this Article.

(ii)   If any dispute or difference should arise between a Contracting Party and a national, company or State entity of the other Contracting Party, which cannot be resolved within a period of _____ through negotiations, either party to the dispute may initiate proceedings for conciliation or arbitration unless the investor has chosen to avail himself or itself of local remedies.

(iii)   Unless the parties have reached agreement to refer the disputes to conciliation under the provisions of the International Convention for the Settlement of Investment Disputes between States and Nationals of other States 1965, conciliation shall take place under the UNCITRAL Conciliation Rules 1980 and the assistance of _____ may be enlisted in connection with the appointment of Conciliator(s).

(iv)   Where the conciliation proceedings have failed to resolve the dispute as also in the event of agreement having been reached to resort to arbitration, the dispute shall be referred to arbitration at the instance of either party to the dispute within a period of three months.

(v)   Any reference to arbitration shall be initiated under the provisions of the International Convention on the Settlement of Investment Disputes between States and Nationals of other States 1965 or "The Additional Facility Rules" of ICSID, whichever may be appropriate. In the event of neither of these procedures being applicable, the arbitration shall take place in accordance with the UNCITRAL Arbitration Rules 1976, and the appointing authority for the purposes of such rules shall be _____.

(vi)   Neither Contracting Party shall pursue through diplomatic channels any matter referred to arbitration until the proceedings have terminated and a Contracting Party has failed to abide by or to comply with the award rendered by the arbitral tribunal.

Article 11
Settlement of disputes between Contracting Parties

(i)   Disputes or differences between the Contracting Parties concerning interpretation or application of this agreement shall be settled through negotiations.

(ii)   If such disputes and differences cannot thus be settled, the same shall, upon the request of either Contracting Party be submitted to an arbitral tribunal.

(iii)   An arbitral tribunal shall be composed of three members. Each Contracting Party shall nominate one member on the tribunal within a period of two months of the receipt of the request for arbitration. The third member, who shall be the chairman of the tribunal, shall be appointed by agreement of the Contracting Parties. If a Contracting Party has failed to nominate its arbitrator or where agreement has not been reached in regard to appointment of the chairman of the tribunal within a period of three months, either Contracting Party may approach the President of the International Court of Justice to make the appointment. The chairman so appointed shall not be a national of either Contracting Party.

(iv)   The arbitral tribunal shall reach its decision by majority of votes. Such decision shall be binding on both the Contracting Parties. The tribunal shall determine its own procedure and give directions in regard to the costs of the proceedings.

Article 12
Subrogation

If either Contracting Party makes payment under an indemnity it has given in respect of an investment or any part thereof in the territory of the other Contracting Party. the latter Contracting Party shall recognize:

(a)   The assignment of any right or claim from the party indemnified to the former Contracting Party or its designated Agency; and

(b)   That the former Contracting Party or its designated Agency is entitled by virtue of subrogation to exercise the rights and enforce the claims of such a party.

Article 13
Exceptions

Neither Contracting Party shall be obliged to extend to the nationals or companies or State entities of the other, the benefit of any treatment, preference or privilege which may be accorded to any other State or its nationals by virtue of the formation of a customs union. a free trade area or any other regional arrangement on economic co-operation to which such a State may be a party.

Article 14
Application of the Agreement

The provisions of this Agreement shall apply to investments made after the coming into force of this Agreement [and the investments previously made which are approved and registered by the host State (in accordance with its laws) within a period of _____ from the date of entry into   force   of this Agreement]. e/

Article 15
Entry into force

[This Agreement shall enter into force on signature.]

or

[This Agreement shall enter into force as from _____.]

or

[This Agreement shall be ratified and shall enter into force on the exchange of instruments of ratification.] f/

Article 16
Duration and termination

This Agreement shall remain in force for a period of _____.   Thereafter it shall continue in force until the expiration of twelve months from any date on which either Contracting Party shall have given written notice of termination to the other.   [Provided that in respect of investments made whilst the Agreement is in force, its provisions shall continue in effect with respect to such investments for a period of _____ years after the date of termination.] g/

In WITNESS WHEREOF the undersigned. duly authorized thereto by their respective Governments. have signed this Agreement.

DONE in duplicate at _____. this _____ day of _____ 1980. (In the _____ and _____ languages. both texts being equally authoritative.)

For the Government of   For the Government of

_____   _____

*   *   *

Addendum to Model "A"

ASIAN-AFRICAN LEGAL CONSULTATIVE COMMITTEE (AALCC)

Models for Bilateral Agreements on Promotion and
Protection of Investments

as finally adopted at AALCC's Kathmandu session in February 1985.

SUGGESTIONS OF THE DELEGATION OF KUWAIT

1.   Article 2 (Promotion and encouragement of investments)

Paragraph (iv) should be expanded to read as follows (additions underlined):

"Each Contracting Party shall at all times ensure fair and equitable treatment to the investments of nationals. companies or State entities of the other Contracting Party. Each Contracting Party shall ensure that the management. maintenance. use. enjoyment or disposal of investments in its territory of nationals. companies or State entities of the other Contracting Party is not in any way impaired by unreasonable or discriminatory measures.

Each Contracting Party shall duly honour all commitments made and obligations undertaken by it with regard to investments of nationals. companies or State entities of the other Contracting Party."

2.   Article 6 (Repatriation of capital and returns)

It is proposed that the following paragraph be added to Article 6:

"(iv) The Contracting Parties undertake to accord to transfers referred to in paragraphs (i). (ii) and (iii) of this Article a treatment as favourable as that accorded to transfers originating from investments made by nationals. companies and State entities of any third Party."

3.   Article 11 (Settlement of disputes between Contracting Parties)

Paragraph (iii) of Article 11 should be expanded to read as follows:

... either Contracting Party may approach the President of the International Court of Justice to make the appointments. If the President is a national of either Contracting Party or if he is otherwise prevented from discharging the said function, the Vice-President shall be invited to make the necessary appointments. If the Vice-President is a national of either Contracting Party or if he too is prevented from discharging the said function, the member of the International Court of Justice next in seniority who is not a national of either Contracting Party shall be invited to make the necessary appointments.

4.   Suggested additional articles

There are two additional articles that should be incorporated into the agreement. They are related to the relations between governments and to the application of other rules.

Article
Relations between Governments

"The provisions of the present Agreement shall apply irrespective of the existence of diplomatic or consular relations between the Contracting Parties."

Article
Applications of other rules

"Notwithstanding the provisions of this Agreement, the relevant international agreements which bind both contracting parties may be applied with the consent of both parties."

*   *   *

Model B[2]

AGREEMENT between the Government of _____

and

the Government of _____ for Promotion, Encouragement and Reciprocal Protection of Investments.

The   Government   of   _____   and   the   Government   of _____,

Recognizing in particular the need to promote wider co-operation between the countries of the Asian-African region to accelerate their economic growth and to encourage investments by developing countries in other developing countries of the region;

Also recognizing that reciprocal protection of such investments will be conducive to the attainment of desired objectives in a spirit of partnership;

---

[2]The model agreement is intended to provide a possible negotiating text for consideration of Governments. It is merely a model and not an adhesive text. The possibility that the text would be modified or altered in the course of bilateral negotiations to suit the needs of the parties is clearly contemplated.

Desirous to create conditions in which investments by each other and their nationals would be facilitated and thus stimulate the flow of capital and technology within the region;

Have agreed as follows:

Article 1
Definitions

For the purpose of this Agreement

(a)   'Investment'

(Alternative A)

'Investment' means every kind of asset and in particular, though not exclusively, includes:

(i)   movable and immovable property and any other property rights such as mortgages, liens or pledges;

(ii)   shares, stocks and debentures of companies or interests in the property of such companies;

(iii)   claims to money or to any performance under contract having a financial value and loans;

(iv)   copyrights, know-how, [goodwill] and industrial property rights such as patents for inventions, trademarks, industrial designs and trade names;

(v)   rights conferred by law or under contract, including licence to search for, cultivate, extract or exploit natural resources.

(Alternative B)

'Investment' includes every kind of asset such as:

(i)   shares and other types of holdings of companies.

(ii)   claims to any performance under contract having a financial value, claims to money and loans;

(iii)   rights with respect to movable and immovable property,

(iv)   rights with regard to patents, trade marks, and any other industrial property; and

(v)   contractual rights relating to exploration and exploitation of natural resources.

(Alternative C)

'Investment' means:

(i)   in respect of investment in the territory of (First Party) _____ :

(ii)   in respect of investment in the territory of (Second Party)_____ .

228

(b)   'National'

(Alternative A)

'National' in respect of each Contracting Party means a natural person who is national or deemed to be a national of the Party under its Constitution or relevant law.

(Alternative B)

'National' in respect _____(First Party)_____
means _____ and in respect of (Second Party)
means _____.

(c)   'Companies'

(Alternative A)

'Companies' means corporations, partnerships or associations incorporated, constituted or registered in a Contracting Party in accordance with its laws [and includes such entities in which nationals of a Contracting Party have substantial interest and majority shareholding.]

(Alternative B)

'Companies' means in respect of the (First Party) _____ and in respect of the (Second Party) _____.

(d)   'State Entity' means a department of government, corporation, institution or undertaking wholly owned or controlled by government and engaged in activities of a commercial nature.

(e)   'Returns' includes profits, interest, capital gains, dividends, royalties or fees.

(f)   'Host State' means the country in whose territory the investment is made.

(g)   'Territory' means:

   (i)   in respect of the (First Party) _____;

   (ii)   in respect of the (Second Party) _____.

Article 2
Promotion and encouragement of investments

   (i)   Each Contracting Party shall take steps to promote investments in the territory of the other Contracting Party and encourage its nationals, companies and State entities to make such investments, through offer of appropriate incentives, wherever possible, which may include such modalities as tax concessions and investment guarantees.

   (ii)   Each Contracting Party shall create favourable conditions for the nationals, companies or State entities of the other Contracting Party to promote investment in its territory.

   (iii)   The Contracting Parties shall periodically consult among themselves concerning investment opportunities within the territory of each other in various sectors such as industry, mining, communications, agriculture and forestry to determine where investments from one Contracting Party into the other may be most beneficial in the interest of both the parties.

(iv)   [Each Contracting Party shall duly honour all commitments made and obligations undertaken by it with regard to investments of nationals, companies or State entities of the other Contracting Party.]

Article 3
Reception of investments

(i)   A national, company or State entity of a Contracting Party intending to make investment in the territory of the other Contracting Party including collaboration arrangements on specific projects, shall submit his or its proposal to a designated authority of the Party where the investment is sought to be made. Such proposals shall be examined expeditiously and so soon after the proposal is approved, a letter of authorization shall be issued and the investment shall be registered, where appropriate, with the designated authority of the host State.

(ii)   The investment shall be received subject to the terms and conditions specified in the letter of authorization. Such terms and conditions may include the obligation or requirement concerning employment of local personnel and labour in the investment projects, organisation of training programmes, transfer of technology and marketing arrangements for the products.

(iii)   The host State shall facilitate the performance of the contracts relatable to the investments through suitable administrative measures and in particular in the matter of expeditious clearance of authorization or permits for importation of goods, employment of consultants and technicians of foreign nationality in accordance with its laws and regulations.

(iv)   The Contracting Parties shall make every endeavour through appropriate means at their disposal to ensure that their nationals, companies or State entities comply with the laws and regulations of the host State and also carry out in good faith the obligations undertaken in respect of the investments made in accordance with the terms and conditions specified by the host State.

Article 4
Most-favoured-nation treatment

(i)   Each Contracting Party shall accord in its territory to the investments or returns of nationals, companies or State entities of the other Contracting Party treatment that is not less favourable than that it accords to the investments or returns of nationals, companies or State entities of any third State.

(ii)   Each Contracting Party shall also ensure that the nationals, companies or State entities of the other Contracting Party are accorded treatment not less favourable than that it accords to the nationals or companies or State entities of any third State in regard to the management, use, enjoyment or disposal of their investments including management and control over business activities and other ancilliary functions in respect of the investments.

Article 5
[1]National treatment

(i)   Each Contracting Party shall accord in its territory to the investments or returns of nationals, companies or State entities of the other Contracting Party treatment that is not less favourable than that it accords to the investments or returns of its own nationals, companies or State entities.

---

[1]There were some differences of view on the needs for inclusion of this clause.

[1]Some countries do not favour "national treatment" for foreign investments.

(ii)   Each of the Contracting Parties shall extend to the nationals. companies or State entities of the other Contracting Party, treatment that is not less favourable than that it accords to its own nationals, companies or State entities in regard to management. control. use, enjoyment and disposal in relation to investments which have been received in its territory.

Article 6
Repatriation of capital and returns

(i)   Each Contracting Party shall ensure that the nationals, companies or State entities of the other Contracting Party are allowed facilities in the matter of repatriation of capital and returns on his or its investments in accordance with the terms and conditions stipulated by the host State at the time of the reception of the investment.

(ii)   Such terms and conditions may specify:

(a)   the mode and manner of repatriation of profits and returns as also the requirement. if any, concerning re-investment;

(b)   the extent to which the capital invested may be allowed to be repatriated in each particular year;

(c)   any requirement concerning the currency in which repatriation is to be made and the place or places of such repatriation:

(d)   the nature of restrictions that may be imposed by the host State on repatriation of capital and returns in its national interest during any period of exceptional financial or economic situations.

(iii)   The stipulations concerning repatriation of capital and returns shall be set out in the letter of authorization referred to in Article 3. The terms and conditions so specified shall remain operative throughout the period of the investment and shall not be altered without the agreement of the parties.

Article 7
Nationalization, expropriation and payment of compensation in respect thereof

(i)   (Alternative 1)

A Contracting Party may exercise its sovereign rights in the matter of nationalization or expropriation in respect of investments made in its territory by nationals, companies or State entities of the other Contracting Party upon payment of appropriate compensation, subject however, to the provisions of its laws. The host State shall abide by and honour any commitments made or assurances given both in regard to nationalization or expropriation and the principles for determination of appropriate compensation including the mode and manner of payment thereof.

(Alternative 2)

Investments of nationals, companies or State entities of either Contracting Party shall not be nationalized, expropriated or subjected to measures having effect equivalent to nationalization or expropriation in the territory of the other Contracting Party except [for a public purpose] [in national interest] of that party and against prompt payment of appropriate compensation.

(ii)   (Alternative 1)

[1][Unless stipulations are made to the contrary at the time of the reception of the investment. the expression "appropriate compensation" shall mean compensation calculated on the basis of recognized principles of valuation.]

(Alternative 2)

Unless stipulations are made to the contrary at the time of the reception of the investment, the expression "appropriate compensation" shall mean compensation determined in accordance with equitable principles taking into account the capital invested, depreciation, capital already repatriated and other relevant factors.

Article 8
Compensation for losses

The nationals, companies or State entities of one Contracting Party who suffer losses in the territory of the other Contracting Party resulting from:

(a)   Requisitioning of their property by its forces or authorities; or

(b)   Destruction of their property by its forces or authorities which was not caused in combat actions or was not required by the necessity of the situation;

shall be accorded restitution or adequate compensation [and the resulting payments shall be allowed to be repatriated.]

Article 9
Access to courts and tribunals

(Alternative 1)

The nationals, companies or State entities of one Contracting Party shall have the right of access to the courts, tribunals, both judicial and administrative, and other authorities competent under the laws of the other Contracting Party for redress of his or its grievances in relation to any matter concerning an investment including judicial review of measures relating to nationalization or expropriation, determination of compensation in the event of nationalization or expropriation or losses suffered and any restrictions imposed on repatriation of capital or returns. The local remedies shall be exhausted before any other step or proceeding is contemplated.

[1][(Alternative 2)

Any difference or dispute between the investor and the host State in relation to any matter concerning an investment including those relating to nationalization or expropriation, determination of compensation in the event of nationalization or expropriation or losses suffered and any restrictions imposed on repatriation of capital and returns shall be settled through recourse to appropriate courts and tribunals, judicial or administrative and other authorities competent under the local laws of the host State. Neither Contracting Party shall pursue through diplomatic channel any such matter until the local remedies have been exhausted.]

---

[1]Some delegations had reservations on this provision.

[1]Several participants considered this provision to be inappropriate.

Article 10
Settlement of investment disputes

(i)   Each Contracting Party consents to submit any dispute or difference that may arise out of or in relation to investments made in its territory by a national, company or State entity of the other Contracting Party for settlement through conciliation or arbitration in accordance with the provisions of this Article.

(ii)   If any dispute or difference should arise between a Contracting Party and a national, company or State entity of the other Contracting Party, which cannot be resolved within a period of _____ through negotiations, either party to the dispute may initiate proceedings for conciliation or arbitration after the local remedies have been exhausted.

(iii)   Conciliation shall take place under the UNCITRAL Conciliation Rules 1980 unless the parties have reached agreement to refer the dispute to conciliation under the provisions of the International Convention for the Settlement of Investment Disputes between States and Nationals of other States 1965.

(iv)   Where the conciliation proceedings have failed to resolve the dispute, it shall be referred to arbitration at the instance of either party to the dispute within a period of three months.

(v)   Any reference to arbitration shall be initiated under the provisions of the International Convention for the Settlement of Investment Disputes between States and Nationals of other States 1965 or "The Additional Facility Rules" of ICSID, whichever may be appropriate. In the event of neither of these procedures being applicable, the arbitration shall take place in accordance with the UNCITRAL Arbitration Rules of 1976, and the appointing authority for the purposes of such rules shall be _____

(vi)   Neither Contracting Party shall pursue through diplomatic channel any matter referred to arbitration until the proceedings have terminated and a Contracting Party has failed to abide by or to comply with the award rendered by the arbitral tribunal.

Article 11
Settlement of disputes between Contracting Parties

(i)   Disputes or differences between the Contracting Parties concerning interpretation or application of this agreement shall be settled through negotiations.

(ii)   If such disputes and differences cannot thus be settled, the same shall upon the request of either Contracting Party be submitted to an arbitral tribunal.

(iii)   An arbitral tribunal shall be composed of three members. Each Contracting Party shall nominate one member on the tribunal within a period of two months of the receipt of the request for arbitration. The third member, who shall be the chairman of the tribunal, shall be appointed by agreement of the Contracting Parties. If a Contracting Party has failed to nominate its arbitrator or where agreement has not been reached in regard to the appointment of the chairman of the tribunal, within a period of three months, either Contracting Party may approach the President of the International Court of Justice to make the appointment.

(iv)   The arbitral tribunal shall reach its decision by majority of votes. Such decision shall be binding on both the Contracting Parties. The tribunal shall determine its own procedure and give direction in regard to the costs of the proceedings.

Article 12
Subrogation

If either Contracting Party makes payment under an indemnity it has given in respect of an investment or any part thereof in the territory of the other Contracting Party, the latter Contracting Party shall recognize:

(a)   The assignment of any right or claim from the party indemnified to the former Contracting Party or its designated Agency; and

(b)   That the former Contracting Party or its designated Agency is entitled by virtue of subrogation to exercise the rights and enforce the claims of such a party.

Article 13
Exceptions

Neither Contracting Party shall be obliged to extend to the nationals or companies or State entities of the other, the benefit of any treatment, preference or privilege which may be accorded to any other State or its nationals by virtue of the formation of a customs union, a free trade area or any other regional arrangement on economic co-operation to which such a State may be a party.

Article 14
Application of the Agreement

The provisions of this Agreement shall apply to investments made after the coming into force of this Agreement.

Article 15
Entry into force

[1][This Agreement shall enter into force on signature.]

or

[1][This Agreement shall enter into force as from _____.]

or

*[This Agreement shall be ratified and shall enter into force on the exchange of instruments of ratification].

Article 16
Duration and termination

This agreement shall remain in force for a period of _____ years. Thereafter it shall continue in force until the expiration of twelve months from any date on which either Contracting Party shall have

---

[1]Alternative provisions.

[1]Alternative provisions.

given written notice of termination to the other. [Provided that in respect of investments made whilst the agreement is in force, its provisions shall continue in effect with respect to such investments for a period of _____ years after the date of termination.]

In witness whereof the undersigned. duly authorized thereto by their respective Governments, have signed this Agreement.

Done in duplicate at _____ this _____ day of _____ 198__
[In the _____ and _____ languages, both texts being equally authoritative.]

For the Government of   For the Government of

_____   _____

*   *   *

Model C

Note: The provisions for incorporation in the text of this model draft would be identical with the provisions set out in Model A, with the exception of the definition of "Investment" in article 1 (a) and the text of article 14. The suggested texts for these provisions are as follows:

Article 1
Definitions

(a)   "Investment" means:

Capital and technology employed in projects or industries in specified sectors of national importance as set out in the schedule to this Agreement and includes the following in relation thereto:

(i)   shares and other types of holdings of companies;

(ii)   claims to any performance under contract having a financial value. claims to money and loans;

(iii)   rights with regard to patents, trademarks and any other industrial property; and

(iv)   contractual rights relating to exploration and exploitation of natural resources.

Article 14
Application of the Agreement

The provisions of this Agreement shall apply to investments made after the coming into force of this Agreement where the investment has been made in specified sectors set out in the schedule to this Agreement.

Explanatory notes to the provisions of the model agreement (Model C)

This Model Agreement has been prepared with a view to serve as a possible negotiating text for those States which prefer to conclude investment protection treaties relatable only to investments in specific sectors of national interest of the host State. The practice followed by these States generally reveals the position that with regard to investments covered under a treaty they would be prepared to accord full freedom in the matter of repatriation of capital and return as also market value as compensation in the event of nationalization or expropriation of the investment.

Model C accordingly contemplates that all the provisions contained in Model A should be incorporated in the text subject to only two variations, namely the definition of "investment" and the provision on application of the Agreement. These provisions are so drafted as to conform to the position that the investments covered under the treaty are those investments which are of national importance and related to those specified sectors as set out in the Schedule to the Agreement.

*   *   *

Notes

a/   The model agreements are intended to provide possible negotiating texts for consideration of Governments. They are merely models and not adhesive texts. The possibility that the texts would be modified or altered in the course of bilateral negotiations to suit the needs of the parties is clearly contemplated.

The AALCC has prepared three draft models which are described as follows: Model A: Draft of a bilateral agreement basically on similar pattern as the agreements entered into between some of the countries of the region with industrialized States with certain changes and improvements particularly in the matter of promotion of investments. Model B: draft of an agreement whose provisions are somewhat more restrictive in the matter of protection of investments and contemplate a degree of flexibility in regard to reception and protection of investments. Model C: draft of an agreement on the pattern of Model A but applicable to specific classes of investments only as determined by the host State.

b/   There were some differences of views on the need for inclusion of this clause.

c/   Some countries do not favour "National Treatment" for foreign investments.

d/   Several participants had reservations on the provisions of this paragraph.

e/   There were some differences of view about the past investments being covered.

f/   Alternative provisions.

g/   There were some differences of views whether past investments should be covered.

*   *   *

CARICOM Guidelines for use in the Negotiation of Bilateral Treaties[*]

Contribution Expected by CARICOM States from BITs

(i)   BITs should provide real opportunities for the promotion of the economic and social development of CARICOM countries, individually and collectively, through the enhancement of their production base in accordance with each country's particular criteria, goals and development strategy;

(ii)   CARICOM States, in the conclusion and implementation of BITs, should ensure the preservation and strengthening of the CARICOM Integration Movement.

Type of Agreement Desired

The preamble of the BIT should include:

(i)   a provision which reflects the objective of increasing capital flows from the USA to the CARICOM States to build up their productive base and hence enhance their economic and social development;

(ii)   a provision which reflects the undertaking of the USA to establish incentives and institutional arrangements to encourage the flow of investments from the USA to CARICOM States.

Most Favoured Nation Treatment

Subject to exceptions, preferential treatment should be given to investments in the following order:

(i)   nationals of country;

(ii)   nationals of other CARICOM countries;

(iii)   nationals of developing countries with whom there are arrangements;

(iv)   nationals of developed countries with whom there are arrangements;

(v)   nationals of other countries.

Performance Obligations

(i)   CARICOM countries should not accept any restrictions on their freedom to impose performance obligations;

(ii)   performance obligations, which should include but not limited to, export performance, employment, conformity with national laws and with trade union practices, and transfer of technology, should be linked to the benefits to be derived and in this context provision should be made for such obligations to be reviewed periodically.

---

[*]Source: Caribbean Community Secretariat (1984). "Guidelines for use in the Negotiation of Bilateral Treaties", mimeo. [Note added by the editor].

Exclusion Areas

CARICOM countries should, as part of their development plans and strategies, determine the terms on which foreign investment may enter their economies; the areas of their economies from which foreign investment would be prohibited or in which it would be permitted only under special conditions and the circumstances and criteria which will occasion restriction of foreign investment from any sector or activity.

Where no determination of such areas, circumstances or criteria has been made in advance of the negotiations, the BIT should incorporate an elaboration of the policy and/or criteria governing foreign investment.

Nationalisation and Compensation

(i)   CARICOM host countries should ensure that in any bilateral investment treaty they maintain the right to nationalise foreign-owned property, subject to fair and just compensation or other provisions as contained in national law;

(ii)   CARICOM host countries should ensure that in any bilateral investment treaty they maintain the right to determine at the time of the nationalisation the quantum of compensation and the terms of payment;

(iii)   in the event of any dispute, local remedies should be exhausted before recourse to any international remedy.

Dispute Settlement

(i)   In the case of disputes between the investor and the host country, resort to arbitration would only be permitted after all national remedies have been exhausted;

(ii)   In the case of disputes between the parties, or where there is resort to arbitration as provided for at (i) above, the following should be the proposed approach:

    (a)   *ad hoc* arbitration tribunal;

    (b)   arbitration takes place in the host country;

    (c)   the dispute be determined by national law and, where appropriate, rules of international law;

    (d)   to use the UNCITRAL Rules which are favoured by developing countries.

Retroactive Applicability and Duration of Treaty

The Treaty should apply to new investments. In this connection, Article IX, paragraph (i) of the US Draft Proposals should be amended by the deletion of 1(a) and (b) and the redrafting of (c) in such a way as to ensure that there was no automatic right of an existing investment to more favourable terms which might be in the Treaty.

Monitoring

(i)   The US Government should undertake to do all in its power to ensure that US-based investors be good corporate citizens in CARICOM host countries;

(ii)   The US Government should guarantee that machinery established under the CBI to promote capital transfer to CARICOM countries be effective.

Transfers

(i)   Transfers must be subject to the national law of the host country;

(ii)   A distinction should be made between the following types of transfers;

    (a)   capital transfer, however realised; and

    (b)   current transfer;

(iii)   In view of possible size of capital transfers and the possible impact on the balance of payments, integrity of the currency, etc. capital transfers should be restricted; (Several existing reciprocal and investment promotion and protection agreements provide for this);

(iv)   Free transfer of current account transactions is a desirable goal, subject to balance of payments and other economic considerations.

* * *

AGREEMENT

BETWEEN

THE GOVERNMENT OF THE REPUBLIC OF CHILE

AND

THE GOVERNMENT OF _____

ON THE RECIPROCAL PROMOTION AND PROTECTION OF INVESTMENTS[*]

The Government of the Republic of Chile and the Government of _____, hereinafter the "Contracting Parties",

Desiring to intensify economic cooperation to the mutual benefit of both countries;

With the intention to create and maintain favourable conditions for investments by investors of one Contracting Party which implies the transfer of capital in the territory of the other Contracting Party;

Recognizing that the reciprocal promotion and protection of such foreign investments favour the economic prosperity of both countries;

Have agreed as follows:

Article 1
Definitions

For the purpose of this Agreement:

(1)   "investor" means the following subjects which have made an investment in the territory of the other Contracting Party in accordance with the present Agreement:

    (a)   natural persons who, according to the law of that Contracting Party, are considered to be its nationals;

    (b)   a legal entity, including companies, corporations, business associations and other legally recognized entities, which are constituted or otherwise duly organised under the law of that Contracting Party and have their seat together with effective economic activities in the territory of that same Contracting Party.

(2)   "investment" means any kind of asset, provided that the investment has been admitted in accordance with the laws and regulations of the other Contracting Party, and shall include in particular, though not exclusively:

    (a)   movable and immovable property and any other property rights such as mortgages, liens or pledges;

    (b)   shares, debentures or any other kinds of participation in companies;

    (c)   a loan or other claim to money or to any performance having an economic value;

---

[*]Source: Government of the Republic of Chile (1994) [Note added by the editor].

(d)   intellectual and industrial property rights, including copyright, patents, trademarks, trade names, technical processes, know-how and goodwill;

(e)   concessions conferred by law or under contract, including concessions to search for, cultivate, extract or exploit natural resources.

(3)   "territory" means in respect of each Contracting Party the territory under its sovereignty, including the exclusive economic zone and the continental shelf where that Contracting Party exercises, in conformity with international law, sovereign rights or jurisdiction.

Article 2
Scope of application

This Agreement shall apply to investments in the territory of one Contracting Party made in accordance with its legislation, prior to or after the entry into force of the Agreement, by investors of the other Contacting Party. It shall however not be applicable to disputes which arose prior to its entry into force or to disputes directly related to events which occurred prior to its entry into force.

Article 3
Promotion and Protection of investments

(1)   Each Contracting Party shall, subject to its general policy in the field of foreign investments, promote investments by investors of the other Contracting Party.

(2)   Each Contracting Party shall protect within its territory investments made in accordance with its laws and regulations by investors of the other Contracting Party and shall not impair by unreasonable or discriminatory measures the management, maintenance, use, enjoyment, extension, sale and liquidation of such investments.

Article 4
Treatment of investments

(1)   Each Contracting Party shall extend fair and equitable treatment to investments made by investors of the other Contracting Party on its territory and shall ensure that the exercise of the right thus recognized shall not be hindered in practice.

(2)   A Contracting Party shall accord investments of the investors of one Contracting Party in its territory a treatment which is no less favourable than that accorded to investments made by its own investors or by investors of any third country, whichever is the most favourable.

(3)   If a Contracting Party accords special advantages to investors of any third country by virtue of an agreement establishing a free trade area, a customs union, a common market, an economic union or any other form of regional economic organization to which the Party belongs or through the provisions of an agreement relating wholly or mainly to taxation, it shall not be obliged to accord such advantages to investors of the other Contracting Party.

Article 5
Free transfer

(1)   Each Contracting Party shall allow without delay the investors of the other Contracting Party the transfer of funds in connection with an investment in a freely convertible currency, particularly of:

(a)   interests, dividends, profits and other returns;

(b)   repayments of a loan agreement related to the investment;

(c)   any capital or proceeds from the sale or partial sale or liquidation of the investment; and

(d)   compensation for expropriation or loss described in Article 6 of this Agreement.

(2)   Transfers shall be made at the exchange rate applying on the date of transfer in accordance with the law of the Contracting Party which has admitted the investment.

Article 6
Expropriation and compensation

(1)   Neither Contracting party shall take any measures depriving, directly or indirectly, an investor of the other Contracting Party of an investment unless the following conditions are complied with:

(a)   the measures are taken in the public or national interest and in accordance with the law;

(b)   the measures are not discriminatory;

(c)   the measures are accompanied by provisions for the payment of prompt, adequate and effective compensation.

(2)   The compensation shall be based on the market value of the investments affected immediately before the measure became public knowledge. Where that value cannot be readily ascertained, the compensation may be determined in accordance with generally recognised equitable principles of valuation taking into account the capital invested, depreciation, capital already repatriated, replacement value and other relevant factors. This compensation shall carry an interest at the appropriate market rate of interest from the date of expropriation or loss until the date of payment.

(3)   The investor affected shall have a right to access, under the law of the Contracting Party making the expropriation, to the judicial authority of that Party, in order to review the amount of compensation and the legality of any such expropriation or comparable measure.

(4)   The investors of one Contracting Party whose investments have suffered losses due to a war or any other armed conflict, revolution, state of emergency or rebellion, which took place in the territory of the other Contracting Party shall be accorded by the latter Contracting Party treatment as regard restitution, indemnification, compensation or other valuable consideration, no less favourable than that which that Contracting Party accords to its domestic investors or to investors of any third country, whichever is more favourable to the investors concerned.

Article 7
Subrogation

(1)   Where one Contracting Party or an agency authorized by the Contracting Party has granted a contract of insurance or any form of financial guarantee against non-commercial risks with regard to an investment by one of its investors in the territory of the other Contracting Party, the latter shall recognize the rights of the first Contracting Party by virtue of the principle of subrogation to the rights of the investor when payment has been made under this contract or financial guarantee by the first Contracting Party.

(2)   Where a Contracting Party has made a payment to its investor and has taken over rights and claims of the investor, that investor shall not, unless authorized to act on behalf of the Contracting Party making the payment, pursue those rights and claims against the other Contracting Party.

Article 8
Settlement of Disputes between a Contracting Party
and an investor of the other Contracting Party

(1)   With a view to an amicable solution of disputes, which arises within the terms of this Agreement, between a Contracting Party and an investor of the other Contracting Party consultations will take place between the parties concerned.

(2)   If these consultations do not result in a solution within three months from the date of request for settlement, the investor may submit the dispute either;

    (a)   to the competent tribunal of the Contracting Party in whose territory the investment was made; or

    (b)   to international arbitration of the International Centre for the Settlement of Investment Disputes (ICSID), created by the Convention for the Settlement of Disputes in respect of Investments occurring between States and Nationals of other States, signed in Washington on March 18, 1965.

(3)   Once the investor has submitted the dispute to the competent tribunal of the Contracting Party in whose territory the investment was made or to international arbitration, that election shall be final.

(4)   For the purpose of this Article, any legal person which is constituted in accordance with the legislation of one Contracting Party, and in which, before a dispute arises, the majority of shares are owned by investors of the other Contracting Party, shall be treated, in accordance with Article 25 (2) (b) of the said Washington Convention, as a legal person of the other Contracting Party.

(5)   The arbitration decisions shall be final and binding on both parties and shall be enforced in accordance with the laws of the Contracting Party in whose territory the investment was made.

(6)   Once a dispute has been submitted to the competent tribunal or international arbitration in accordance with this Article, neither Contracting Party shall pursue the dispute through diplomatic channels unless the other Contracting Party has failed to abide or comply with any judgement, award, order or other determination made by the competent international or local tribunal in question.

Article 9
Settlement of Disputes between Contracting Parties

(1)   The Contracting Parties shall endeavour to resolve any difference between them regarding the interpretation or application of the provisions of this Agreement by friendly negotiations.

(2)   If the difference cannot thus be settled within six months following the date of notification of the difference, either Contracting Party may submit it to an Ad-hoc Arbitral Tribunal in accordance with this Article.

(3)   The Arbitral Tribunal shall be formed by three members and shall be constituted as follows: within two months of the notification by a Contracting Party of its wish to settle the dispute by arbitration, each Contracting Party shall appoint one arbitrator. These two members shall then, within thirty days of the appointment of the last one, agree upon a third member who shall be a national of a third country and who shall act as the Chairman. The Contracting Parties shall appoint the Chairman within thirty days of that person's nomination.

(4)   If, within the time limits provided for in paragraph (2) and (3) of this Article the required appointment has not been made or the required approval has not been given, either Contracting Party may request the President of the International Court of Justice to make the necessary appointment. If the President of the International Court of Justice is prevented from carrying out the said function or if that person is a national of either Contracting Party, the appointment shall be made by the Vice-President, and if the latter is prevented or if that person is a national of either Contracting Party, the appointment shall be made by the most senior Judge of the Court who is not a national of either Contracting Party.

(5)   The Chairman of the Tribunal shall be a national of a third country which has diplomatic relations with both Contracting Parties.

(6)   The arbitral tribunal shall reach its decisions taking into account the provisions of this Agreement, the principles of international law on this subject and the generally recognized principles of international law. The Tribunal shall reach its decisions by a majority vote and shall determine its procedure.

(7)   Each Contracting Party shall bear the cost of the arbitrator it has appointed and of its representation in the arbitral proceedings. The cost of the Chairman and the remaining costs shall be borne in equal parts by the Contracting Parties unless agreed otherwise.

(8)   The decisions of the arbitral tribunal shall be final and binding on both Parties.

Article 10
Consultations between Contracting Parties

The Contracting Parties shall consult at the request of either of them on matters concerning the interpretation or application of this Agreement.

Article 11
Final provisions

(1)   The Contracting Parties shall notify each other when the constitutional requirements for the entry into force of this Agreement have been fulfilled. The Agreement shall enter into force thirty days after the date of the latter notification.

(2)   This Agreement shall remain in force for a period of fifteen years. Thereafter it shall remain in force indefinitely unless one of the Contracting Parties gives one year's written notice of termination through diplomatic channels.

(3)   In respect of investments made prior to the date when the notice of termination of this Agreement becomes effective, the provisions of this Agreement shall remain in force a further period of fifteen years from that date.

(4)   This Agreement shall be applicable irrespective of whether diplomatic or consular relations exist between the Contracting Parties.

Done at _____, this _____ day of _____ in duplicate in the Spanish and English languages, both texts being equally authentic.

For the Government of the Republic of Chile   For the Government of _____.

PROTOCOL

On signing the Agreement on the Reciprocal Promotion and Protection of Investments between the Government of the Republic of Chile and the Government of _____ have, in addition, agreed on the following provisions, which shall be regarded as an integral part of the said Agreement.

Ad Article 5

(1)   Transfers concerning investments made under the Chilean Program of Foreign Debt Equity Swaps are subject to special regulations.

(2)   Capital can only be tranferred one year after it has entered the territoery of the Contracting Party unless its legislation provides for a more favourable treatment.

(3)   A transfer shall be deemed to have been made without delay if carried out within such period as is normally required for the completion of transfer formalities. The said period shall start on the day on which the relevant request has been submitted in due form and may in no case exceed thirty days.

*   *   *

AGREEMENT BETWEEN

THE GOVERNMENT OF THE PEOPLE'S REPUBLIC OF CHINA

AND

THE GOVERNMENT OF _____

CONCERNING

THE ENCOURAGEMENT AND RECIPROCAL PROTECTION OF INVESTMENTS[*]

The Government of the People's Republic of China and the Government of the _____ (hereinafter referred to as the Contracting Parties),

Intending to create favorable conditions for investments by investors of one Contracting Party in the territory of the other Contracting Party;

Recognizing that the reciprocal encouragement, promotion and protection of such investments will be conducive to stimulating business initiative of the investors and will increase prosperity in both States;

Desiring to intensify the economic cooperation of both States on the basis of equality and mutual benefits;

Have agreed as follows:

Article 1

For the purpose of this Agreement,

1.   The term "investment" means every kind of asset invested by investors of one Contracting Party in accordance with the laws and regulations of the other Contracting Party in the territory of the Latter, and in particular, though not exclusively, includes:

(a)   movable, immovable property and other property rights such as mortgages and pledges;

(b)   shares, stock and any other kind of participation in companies;

(c)   claims to money or to any other performance having an economic value;

(d)   copyrights, industrial property, know-how and technological process;

(e)   concessions conferred by law, including concessions to search for or exploit natural resources.

2.   The term "investors" means:
in respect of the People's Republic of China:

(a)   natural persons who have nationality of the People's Republic of China in accordance with its laws;

---

[*]Source: Government of the People's Republic of China, Department of Treaty and Law, Ministry of Foreign Trade and Economic Cooperation [Note added by the editor].

(b)   economic entities established in accordance with the laws of the People's Republic of China and domiciled in the territory of the People's Republic of China;

in respect of the _____:

(a)

(b)

3.   The term "returns" means the amounts yielded by investments, such as profits, dividends, interests, royalties or other legitimate income.

Article 2

1.   Each Contracting Party shall encourage investors of the other Contracting Party to make investments in its territory and admit such investments in accordance with its laws and regulations.

2.   Each Contracting Party shall grant assistance in and provide facilities for obtaining visa and working permit to nationals of the other Contracting Party to or in the territory of the Former in connection with activities associated with such investments.

Article 3

1.   Investments and activities associated with investments of investors of either Contracting Party shall be accorded fair and equitable treatment and shall enjoy protection in the territory of the other Contracting Party.

2.   The treatment and protection referred to in Paragraph 1 of this Article shall not be less favorable than that accorded to investments and activities associated with such investments of investors of a third State.

3.   The treatment and protection as mentioned in Paragraphs 1 and 2 of this Article shall not include any preferential treatment accorded by the other Contracting Party to investments of investors of a third State based on customs union, free trade zone, economic union, agreement relating to avoidance of double taxation or for facilitating frontier trade.

Article 4

1.   Neither Contracting Party shall expropriate, nationalize or take similar measures (hereinafter referred to as "expropriation") against investments of investors of the other Contracting Party in its territory, unless the following conditions are met:

(a) for the public interests;

(b) under domestic legal procedure;

(c) without discrimination;

(d) against compensation.

2.   The compensation mentioned in Paragraph 1, (d) of this Article shall be equivalent to the value of the expropriated investments at the time when expropriation is proclaimed, be convertible and freely transferable. The compensation shall be paid without unreasonable delay.

Article 5

Investors of one Contracting Party who suffer losses in respect of their investments in the territory of the other Contracting Party owing to war, a state of national emergency, insurrection, riot or other similar events, shall be accorded by the latter Contracting Party, if it takes relevant measures, treatment no less favorable than that accorded to investors of a third State.

Article 6

1.   Each Contracting Party shall, subject to its laws and regulations, guarantee investors of the other Contracting Party the transfer of their investments and returns held in the territory of the one Contracting Party, including:

(a)   profits, dividends, interests and other legitimate income;

(b)   amounts from total or partial liquidation of investments;

(c)   payment made pursuant to a loan agreement in connection with investment;

(d)   royalties in Paragraph 1, (d) of Article 1;

(e)   payments of technical assistance or technical service fee, management fee;

(f)   payments in connection with projects on contract associated with investment;

(g)   earnings of nationals of the other Contracting Party who work in connection with an investment in the territory of the one Contracting Party.

2.   The transfers mentioned above shall be made at the prevailing exchange rate of the Contracting Party accepting the investment on the date of transfer.

Article 7

If a Contracting Party or its Agency makes payment to an investor under a guarantee it has granted to an investment of such investor in the territory of the other Contracting Party, such other Contracting Party shall recognize the transfer of any right or claim of such investor to the former Contracting Party or its Agency and recognize the subrogation of the former Contracting Party or its Agency to such right or claim. The subrogated right or claim shall not be greater than the original right or claim of the said investor.

Article 8

1.   Any dispute between the Contracting Parties concerning the interpretation or application of this Agreement shall, as far as possible, be settled by consultation through diplomatic channel.

2.   If a dispute cannot thus be settled within six months, it shall, upon the request of either Contracting Party, be submitted to an ad hoc arbitral tribunal.

3.   Such tribunal comprises of three arbitrators. Within two months from the date on which either Contracting Party receives the written notice requesting for arbitration from the other Contracting Party, each Contracting Party shall appoint one arbitrator. Those two arbitrators shall, within further two months, together select a third arbitrator who is a national of a third State which has diplomatic relations with both Contracting Parties. The third arbitrator shall be appointed by the two Contracting Parties as Chairman of the arbitral tribunal.

4.   If the arbitral tribunal has not been constituted within four months from the date of the receipt of the written notice for arbitration, either Contracting Party may, in the absence of any other agreement, invite the President of the International Court of Justice to appoint the arbitrator(s) who has or have not yet been appointed. If the President is a national of either Contracting Party or is otherwise prevented from discharging the said function, the next most senior member of the International Court of Justice who is not a national of either Contracting Party shall be invited to make the necessary appointment(s).

5.   The arbitral tribunal shall determine its own procedure. The tribunal shall reach its award in accordance with the provisions of this Agreement and the principles of international law recognized by both Contracting Parties.

6.   The tribunal shall reach its award by a majority of votes. Such award shall be final and binding on both Contracting Parties. The ad hoc arbitral tribunal shall, upon the request of either Contracting Party, explain the reasons of its award.

7.   Each Contracting Party shall bear the cost of its appointed arbitrator and of its representation in arbitral proceedings. The relevant costs of the Chairman and the tribunal shall be borne in equal parts by the Contracting Parties.

Article 9

1.   Any dispute between an investor of one Contracting Party and the other Contracting Party in connection with an investment in the territory of the other Contracting Party shall, as far as possible, be settled amicably through negotiations between the parties to the dispute.

2.   If the dispute cannot be settled through negotiations within six months, either party to the dispute shall be entitled to submit the dispute to the competent court of the Contracting Party accepting the investment.

3.   If a dispute involving the amount of compensation for expropriation cannot be settled within six months after resort to negotiations as specified in Paragraph 1 of this Article, it may be submitted at the request of either party to an ad hoc arbitral tribunal. The provisions of this Paragraph shall not apply if the investor concerned has resorted to the procedure specified in the Paragraph 2 of this Article.

4.   Such an arbitral tribunal shall be constituted for each individual case in the following way: each party to the dispute shall appoint an arbitrator, and these two shall select a national of a third State which has diplomatic relations with the two Contracting Parties as Chairman. The first two arbitrators shall be appointed within two months of the written notice for arbitration by either party to the dispute to the other, and the Chairman be selected within four months. If within the period specified above, the tribunal has not been constituted, either party to the dispute may invite the Secretary General of the International Centre for Settlement of Investment Disputes to make the necessary appointments.

5.   The tribunal shall determine its own procedure. However, the tribunal may, in the course of determination of procedure, take as guidance the Arbitration Rules of the International Centre for Settlement of Investment Disputes.

6.   The tribunal shall reach its decision by a majority of votes. Such decision shall be final and binding on both parties to the dispute. Both Contracting Parties shall commit themselves to the enforcement of the decision in accordance with their respective domestic law.

7.   The tribunal shall adjudicate in accordance with the law of the Contracting Party to the dispute accepting the investment including its rules on the conflict of laws, the provisions of this Agreement as well as the generally recognized principles of international law accepted by both Contracting Parties.

8.   Each party to the dispute shall bear the cost of its appointed member of the tribunal and of its representation in the proceedings. The cost of the appointed Chairman and the remaining costs shall be borne in equal parts by the parties to the dispute.

Article 10

If the treatment to be accorded by one Contracting Party in accordance with its laws and regulations to investments or activities associated with such investments of investors of the other Contracting Party is more favorable than the treatment provided for in this Agreement, the more favorable treatment shall be applicable.

Article 11

This Agreement shall apply to investments which are made prior to or after its entry into force by investors of either Contracting Party in accordance with the laws and regulations of the other Contracting Party in the territory of the Latter.

Article 12

1.   The representatives of the two Contracting Parties shall hold meetings from time to time for the purpose of:

(a) reviewing the implementation of this Agreement;

(b) exchanging legal information and investment opportunities;

(c) resolving dispute arising out of investments;

(d) forwarding proposals on promotion of investment;

(e) studying other issues in connection with investments.

2.   Where either Contracting Party requests consultation on any matters of Paragraph 1 of this Article, the other Contracting Party shall give prompt response and the consultation be held alternately in Beijing and _____.

Article 13

1.   This Agreement shall enter into force on the first day of the following month after the date on which both Contracting Parties have notified each other in writing that their respective internal legal procedures have been fulfilled, and shall remain in force for a period of five years.

2.   This Agreement shall continue in force if either Contracting Party fails to give a written notice to the other Contracting Party to terminate this Agreement one year before the expiration specified in Paragraph 1 of this Article.

3.   After the expiration of the initial five years period, either Contracting Party may at any time thereafter terminate this Agreement by giving at least one year's written notice to the other Contracting Party.

4.   With respect to investments made prior to the date of termination of this Agreement, the provisions to Article 1 to 12 shall continue to be effective for a further period of ten years from such date of termination.

In witness whereof, the duly authorized representatives of their respective Governments have signed this Agreement.

Done in duplicate at _____ on _____ , 1994 in the Chinese, _____ and English languages, all texts being equally authentic. In case of divergence of interpretation, the English text shall prevail.

For the Government of the
People's Republic of China

For the Government of _____ .

*   *   *

PROJET D'ACCORD ENTRE

LE GOUVERNEMENT DE LA REPUBLIQUE FRANCAISE

ET

LE GOUVERNEMENT _____

SUR L'ENCOURAGEMENT ET LA PROTECTION RECIPROQUES DES INVESTISSEMENTS[*]

Le Gouvernement de la République française et le Gouvernement _____, ci-après dénommés "les Parties contractantes",

Désireux de renforcer la coopération économique entre les deux Etats et de créer des conditions favorables pour les investissements français au _____ et _____ en France,

Persuadés que l'encouragement et la protection de ces investissements sont propres à stimuler les transferts de capitaux et de technologie entre les deux pays, dans l'intérêt de leur développement économique,

Sont convenus des dispositions suivantes:

Article 1

Pour l'application du présent accord:

1.   Le terme "investissement" désigne tous les avoirs, tels que les biens, droits et interêts de toutes natures et, plus particulièrement mais non exclusivement:

    a)   les biens meubles et immeubles, ainsi que tous autres droits réels tels que les hypothèques, privilèges, usufruits, cautionnements et droits analogues;

    b)   les actions, primes d'émission et autres formes de participation, même minoritaires ou indirectes, aux sociétés constituées sur le territoire de l'une des Parties contractantes;

    c)   les obligations, créances et droits à toutes prestations ayant valeur économique;

    d)   les droits de propriété intellectuelle, commerciale et industrielle tels que les droits d'auteur, les brevets d'invention, les licences, les marques déposées, les modèles et maquettes industrielles les procèdés techniques, le savoir-faire, les noms déposés et la clientèle;

    e)   les concessions accordées par la loi ou en vertu d'un contrat, notamment les concessions relatives à la prospection, la culture, l'extraction ou l'exploitation de richesses naturelles, y compris celles qui se situent dans la zone maritime des Parties contractantes.

Il est entendu que lesdits avoirs doivent être ou avoir été investis conformément à la législation de la Partie contractante sur le territoire ou dans la zone maritime de laquelle l'investissement est effectué avant ou après l'entrée en vigueur du présent accord.

Toute modification de la forme d'investissement des avoirs n'affecte pas leur qualification d'investissement, à condition que cette modification ne soit pas contraire à la législation de la Partie contractante sur le territoire ou dans la zone maritime de laquelle l'investissement est réalisé.

---

[*]Source: Government of France, Ministry of Foreign Affairs [Note added by the editor].

2. Le terme de "nationaux" désigne les personnes physiques possédant la nationalité de l'une des Parties contractantes.

3. Le terme de "sociétés" désigne toute personne morale constituée sur le territoire de l'une des Parties contractantes, conformément à la législation de celle-ci et y possédant son siège social, ou contrôlée directement ou indirectement par des nationaux de l'une des Parties contractantes, ou par des personnes morales possédant leur siège social sur le territoire de l'une des Parties contractantes et constituées conformément à la législation de celle-ci.

4. Le terme de "revenus" désigne toutes les sommes produites par un investissement, telles que bénéfices, redevances ou intérêts, durant une période donnée.

Les revenus de l'investissement et, en cas de réinvestissement, les revenus de leur réinvestissement jouissent de la même protection que l'investissement.

5. Le présent accord s'applique au territoire de chacune des Parties contractantes ainsi qu'à la zone maritime de chacune des Parties contractantes, ci-après définie comme la zone économique et le plateau continental qui s'étendent au-delà de la limite des eaux territoriales de chacune des Parties contractantes et sur lesquels elles ont, en conformité avec le Droit international, des droits souverains et une juridiction aux fins de prospection, d'exploitation et de préservation des ressources naturelles.

Article 2

Chacune des Parties contractantes admet et encourage, dans le cadre de sa législation et des dispositions du présent accord, les investissements effectués par les nationaux et sociétés de l'autre Partie sur son territoire et dans sa zone maritime.

Article 3

Chacune des Parties contractantes s'engage à assurer, sur son territoire et dans sa zone maritime, un traitement juste et équitable, conformément aux principes du Droit international, aux investissements des nationaux et sociétés de l'autre Partie et à faire en sorte que l'exercice du droit ainsi reconnu ne soit entravé ni en droit, ni en fait. En particulier, bien que non exclusivement, sont considérées comme des entraves de droit ou de fait au traitement juste et équitable, toute restriction à l'achat et au transport de matières premières et de matières auxiliaires, d'énergie et de combustibles, ainsi que de moyens de production et d'exploitation de tout genre, toute entrave à la vente et au transpot des produits à l'interieur du pays et à l'étranger, ainsi que toutes autres mesures ayant un effet analogue.

Les Parties contractentes examineront avec bienveillance, dans le cadre de leur législation interne, les demandes d'entrée et d'autorisation de séjour, de travail, et de circulation introduites par des nationaux d'une Partie contractante, au titre d'un investissement réalisé sur le territoire ou dans la zone maritime de l'autre Partie contractante.

Article 4

Chaque Partie contractante applique, sur son territoire et dans sa zone maritime, aux nationaux ou sociétés de l'autre Partie, en ce qui concerne leurs investissements et activités liées à ces investissements, un traitement non moins favorable que celui accordé à ses nationaux ou sociétés, ou le traitement accordé aux nationaux ou sociétés de la Nation la plus favorisée, si celui-ci est plus avantageux. A ce titre, les nationaux autorisés à travailler sur le territoire et dans la zone maritime de l'une des Parties contractantes doivent pouvoir bénéficier des facilités matérielles appropriées pour l'exercice de leurs activités professionnelles.

Ce traitement ne s'étend toutefois pas aux privilèges qu'une Partie contractante accorde aux nationaux ou sociétés d'un Etat tiers, en vertu de sa participation ou de son association à une zone de libre échange, une union douanière, un marché commun ou toute autre forme d'organisation économique régionale.

Les dispositions de cet Article ne s'appliquent pas aux questions fiscales.

Article 5

1. Les investissements effectués par des nationaux ou sociétés de l'une ou l'autre des Parties contractantes bénéficient, sur le territoire et dans la zone maritime de l'autre Partie contractante, d'une protection et d'une sécurité pleines et entières.

2. Les Parties contractantes ne prennent pas de mesures d'expropriation ou de nationalisation ou toutes autres mesures dont l'effet est de déposséder, directement ou indirectement, les nationaux et sociétés de l'autre Partie des investissements leur appartenant, sur leur territoire et dans leur zone maritime, si ce n'est pour cause d'utilité publique et à condition que ces mesures ne soient ni discriminatoires, ni contraires à un engagement particulier.

Toutes les mesures de dépossession qui pourraient être prises doivent donner lieu au paiement d'une indemnité prompte et adéquate dont le montant, égal à la valeur réelle des investissements concernés, doit être évalué par rapport à une situation économique normale et antérieure à toute menace de dépossession.

Cette indemnité, son montant et ses modalités de versement sont fixés au plus tard à la date de la dépossession. Cette indemnité est effectivement réalisable, versée sans retard et librement transférable. Elle produit, jusqu'à la date de versement, des intérêts calculés au taux d'intérêt de marché approprié.

3. Les nationaux ou sociétés de l'une des Parties contractantes dont les investissements auront subi des pertes dues à la guerre ou à tout autre conflit armé, révolution, état d'urgence national ou révolte survenu sur le territoire ou dans la zone maritime de l'autre Partie contractante, bénéficieront, de la part de cette dernière, d'un traitement non moins favorable que celui accordé à ses propres nationaux ou sociétés ou à ceux de la Nation la plus favorisée.

Article 6

Chaque Partie contractante, sur le territoire ou dans la zone maritime de laquelle des investissements ont été effectués par des nationaux ou sociétés de l'autre Partie contractante, accorde à ces nationaux ou sociétés le libre transfert:

a)   des intérêts, dividendes, bénéfices et autres revenus courants;

b)   des redevances découlant des droits incorporels désignés au paragraphe 1, lettres d) et e) de l'Article 1;

c)   des versements effectués pour le remboursement des emprunts régulièrement contractés;

d)   du produit de la cession ou de la liquidation totale ou partielle de l'investissement, y compris les plus-values du capital investi;

e)   des indemnités de dépossession ou de perte prévues à l'Article 5, paragraphes 2 et 3 ci-dessus.

Les nationaux de chacune des Parties contractantes qui ont été autorisés à travailler sur le territoire ou dans la zone maritime de l'autre Partie contractante, au titre d'un investissement agréé sont également autorisés à transférer dans leur pays d'origine une quotité appropriée de leur rémunération.

Les transfers visés aux paragraphes précédents sont effectués sans retard au taux de change normal officiellement applicable à la date du transfert.

Article 7

Dans la mesure où la réglementation de l'une des Parties contractantes prévoit une garantie pour les investissements effectués à l'etranger, celle-ci peut être accordée, dans le cadre d'un examen cas par cas à des investissements effectués par des nationaux ou sociétés de cette Partie sur le territoire ou dans la zone maritime de l'autre Partie.

Les investissements des nationaux et sociétés de l'une des Parties contractantes sur le territoire ou dans la zone maritime de l'autre Partie ne pourront obtenir la garantie visée à l'alinéa ci-dessus que s'ils ont, au préalable, obtenu l'agrément de cette dernière Partie.

Article 8

Tout différend relatif aux investissements entre l'une des Parties contractantes et un national ou une société de l'autre Partie contractante est réglé à l'amiable entre les deux parties concernées.

Si un tel différend n'a pas pu être réglé dans un délai de six mois à partir du moment où il à été soulevé par l'une ou l'autre des parties au différend, il est soumis à la demande de l'une ou l'autre de ces parties à l'arbitrage du Centre international pour le réglement des différends relatifs aux investissements (C.I.R.D.I.), créé par la Convention pour le réglement des différends relatifs aux investissements entre Etats et ressortissants d'autres Etats, signée à Washington le 18 mars 1965.

Article 9

Si l'une des Parties contractantes, en vertu d'une garantie donnée pour un investissement réalisé sur le territoire ou dans la zone maritime de l'autre Partie, effectue des versements à l'un de ses nationaux ou à l'une de ses sociétés, elle est, de ce fait, subrogée dans les droits et actions de ce national ou de cette société.

Lesdits versements n'affectent pas les droits du bénéficiaire de la garantie à recourir au C.I.R.D.I. ou à poursuivre les actions introduites devant lui jusqu'à l'aboutissement de la procédure.

Article 10

Les investissements ayant fait l'objet d'un engagement particulier de l'une des Parties contractantes à l'égard des nationaux et sociétés de l'autre Partie contractante sont régis, sans préjudice des dispositions du présent accord, par les termes de cet engagement dans la mesure où celui-ci comporte des dispositions plus favorables que celles qui sont prévues par le présent accord.

Article 11

1. Les différends relatifs à l'interprétation ou à l'application du présent accord doivent être réglés, si possible, par la voie diplomatique.

2. Si dans un délai de six mois à partir du moment où il a été soulevé par l'une ou l'autre des Parties contractantes, le différend n'est pas réglé, il est soumis, à la demande de l'une ou l'autre Partie contractante, à un tribunal d'arbitrage.

3. Ledit tribunal sera constitué pour chaque cas particulier de la manière suivante: chaque Partie contractante désigne un membre, et les deux membres désignent, d'un commun accord, un ressortissant

d'un Etat tiers qui est nommé Président du tribunal par les deux Parties contractantes. Tous les membres doivent être nommés dans un délai de deux mois à compter de la date à laquelle une des Parties contractantes a fait part à l'autre Partie contractante de son intention de soumettre le différend à arbitrage.

4. Si les délais fixés au paragraphe 3 ci-dessus n'ont pas été observés, l'une ou l'autre Partie contractante, en l'absence de tout autre accord, invite le Secrétaire général de l'Organisation des Nations-Unies a procéder aux désignations nécessaires. Si le Secrétaire général est ressortissant de l'une ou l'autre Partie contractante ou si, pour une autre raison, il est empêché d'exercer cette fonction, le Secrétaire général adjoint le plus ancien et ne possédant pas la nationalité de l'une des Parties contractantes procéde aux désignations nécessaires.

5. Le tribunal d'arbitrage prend ses décisions à la majorité des voix. Ces décisions sont définitives et exécutoires de plein droit pour les Parties contractantes.

Le tribunal fixe lui-même son réglement. Il interprète la sentence à la demande de l'une ou l'autre Partie contractante. A moins que le tribunal n'en dispose autrement, compte tenu de circonstances particulières, les frais de la procédure arbitrale, y compris les vacations des arbitres, sont répartis également entre les Parties Contractantes.

Article 12

Chacune des Parties notifiera à l'autre l'accomplissement des procédures internes requises pour l'entrée en vigueur du present accord, qui prendra effet un mois après le jour de la réception de la dernière notification.

L'accord est conclu pour une durée initiale de dix ans. Il restera en vigueur après ce terme, à moins que l'une des Parties ne le dénonce par la voie diplomatique avec préavis d'un an.

A l'expiration de la période de validité du présent accord, les investissements effectués pendant qu'il était en vigueur continueront de bénéficier de la protection de ses dispositions pendant une période supplémentaire de vingt ans.

Fait à _____, le _____ en deux originaux, chacun en langue française et en langue _____ les deux textes faisant également foi.

Pour le Gouvernement   Pour le Gouvernement
de la République française   _____

*   *   *

MODEL TREATY **February 1991 (2)**

TREATY BETWEEN

THE FEDERAL REPUBLIC OF GERMANY

AND

CONCERNING
THE ENCOURAGEMENT AND RECIPROCAL PROTECTION OF INVESTMENTS*

Federal Ministry of Economics
Bonn

THE FEDERAL REPUBLIC OF GERMANY

AND

desiring to intensify economic co-operation between both States,

intending to create favourable conditions for investments by nationals and companies of either State in the territory of the other State,

recognizing that the encouragement and contractual protection of such investments are apt to stimulate private business initiative and to increase the prosperity of both nations,

have agreed as follows:

Article 1

For the purpose of this Treaty

1. the term "investments" comprises every kind of asset, in particular:

   (a) movable and immovable property as well as any other rights in rem, such as mortgages, liens and pledges;

   (b) shares of companies and other kinds of interest in companies;

   (c) claims to money which has been used to create an economic value or claims to any performance having an economic value;

   (d) intellectual property rights, in particular copyrights, patents, utility-model patents, registered designs, trade-marks, trade-names, trade and business secrets, technical processes, know-how, and good will;

   (e) business concessions under public law, including concessions to search for, extract and exploit natural resources;

---

*Source: Government of Germany, Federal Ministry of Economics [Note added by the editor].

Any alteration of the form in which assets are invested shall not affect their classification as investment;

2.   the term "returns" means the amounts yielded by an investment for a definite period, such as profit, dividends, interest, royalties or fees;

3.   the term "nationals" means

    (a)   in respect of the Federal Republic of Germany:

    Germans within the meaning of the Basic Law of the Federal Republic of Germany,

    (b)   in respect of _____ :

    _____ ;

4.   the term "companies" means

    (a)   in respect of the Federal Republic of Germany:
    any juridical person as well as any commercial or other company or association with or without legal personality having its seat in the territory of the Federal Republic of Germany, irrespective of whether or not its activities are directed at profit,

    (b)   in respect of _____ :

    _____ .

Article 2

(1)   Each Contracting Party shall in its territory promote as far as possible investments by nationals or companies of the other Contracting Party and admit such investments in accordance with its legislation. It shall in any case accord such investments fair and equitable treatment.

(2)   Neither Contracting Party shall in any way impair by arbitrary or discriminatory measures the management, maintenance, use or enjoyment of investments in its territory of nationals or companies of the other Contracting Party.

Article 3

(1)   Neither Contracting Party . shall subject investments in its territory owned or controlled by nationals or companies of the other Contracting Party to treatment less favourable than it accords to investments of its own nationals or companies or to investments of nationals or companies of any third State.

(2)   Neither Contracting Party shall subject nationals or companies of the other Contracting Party, as regards their activity in connection with investments in its territory, to treatment less favourable than it accords to its own nationals or companies or to nationals or companies of any third state.

(3)   Such treatment shall not relate to privileges which either Contracting Party accords to nationals or companies of third States on account of its membership of, or association with, a customs or economic union, a common market or a free trade area.

(4)   The treatment granted under this Article shall not relate to advantages which either Contracting Party accords to nationals or companies of third States by virtue of a double taxation agreement or other agreements regarding matters of taxation.

Article 4

(1)   Investments by nationals or companies of either Contracting Party shall enjoy full protection and security in the territory of the other Contracting Party.

(2)   Investments by nationals or companies of either Contracting Party shall not be expropriated, nationalized or subjected to any other measure the effects of which would be tantamount to expropriation or nationalization in the territory of the other Contracting Party except for the public benefit and against compensation. Such compensation shall be equivalent to the value of the expropriated investment immediately before the date on which the actual or threatened expropriation, nationalization or comparable measure has become publicly known. The compensation shall be paid without delay and shall carry the usual bank interest until the time of payment; it shall be effectively realizable and freely transferable. Provision shall have been made in an appropriate manner at or prior to the time of expropriation, nationalization or comparable measure for the determination and payment of such compensation. The legality of any such expropriation, nationalization or comparable measure and the amount of compensation shall be subject to review by due process of law.

(3)   Nationals or companies of either Contracting Party whose investments suffer losses in the territory of the other Contracting Party owing to war or other armed conflict, revolution, a state of national emergency, or revolt, shall be accorded treatment no less favourable by such other Contracting Party than that which the latter Contracting Party accords to its own nationals or companies as regards restitution, indemnification, compensation or other valuable consideration. Such payments shall be freely transferable.

(4)   Nationals or companies of either Contracting Party shall enjoy most-favoured-nation treatment in the territory of the other Contracting Party in respect of the matters provided for in this Article.

Article 5

Each Contracting Party shall guarantee to nationals or companies of the other Contracting Party the free transfer of payments in connection with an investment, in particular

(a)   of the principal and additional amounts to maintain or increase the investment;

(b)   of the returns;

(c)   in repayment of loans;

(d)   of the proceeds from the liquidation or the sale of the whole or any part of the investment.

(e)   of the compensation provided for in Article 4.

Article 6

If either Contracting Party makes a payment to any of its nationals or companies under a guarantee it has assumed in respect of an investment in the territory of the other Contracting Party, the latter Contracting Party shall, without prejudice to the rights of the former Contracting Party under Article 10, recognize the assignment, whether under a law or pursuant to a legal transaction, of any right or claim of such national or company to the former Contracting Party. The latter Contracting Party shall also recognize the subrogation of the former Contracting Party to any such right or claim (assigned claims) which that Contracting Party shall be entitled to assert to the same extent as its predecessor in title. As regards the transfer of payments made by virtue of such assigned claims, Article 4 (2) and (3) as well as Article 5 shall apply mutatis mutandis.

Article 7

(1)   Transfers under Article 4 (2) or (3), under Article 5 or article 6 shall be made without delay at the applicable rate of exchange.

(2)   This rate of exchange shall correspond to the cross rate obtained from those rates which would be applied by the International Monetary Fund on the date of payment for conversions of the currencies concerned into Special Drawing Rights.

Article 8

(1)   If the legislation of either Contracting Party or obligations under international law existing at present or established hereafter between the Contracting Parties in addition to this Treaty contain a regulation, whether general or specific, entitling investments by nationals or companies of the other Contracting Party to a treatment more favourable than is provided for by this Treaty, such regulation shall to the extent that it is more favourable prevail over this Treaty.

(2)   Each contracting Party shall observe any other obligation it has assumed with regard to investments in its territory by nationals or companies of the other Contracting Party.

Article 9

This Treaty shall also apply to investments made prior to its entry into force by nationals or companies of either Contracting Party in the territory of the other Contracting Party consistent with the latter's legislation.

Article 10

(1)   Divergencies between the Contracting Parties concerning the interpretation or application of this Treaty should as far as possible be settled by the governments of the two Contracting Parties.

(2)   If a divergency cannot thus be settled, it shall upon the request of either Contracting Party be submitted to an arbitration tribunal.

(3)   Such arbitration tribunal shall be constituted ad hoc as follows: each Contracting Party shall appoint one member, and these two members shall agree upon a national of a third State as their chairman to be appointed by the governments of the two Contracting Parties. Such members shall be appointed within two months, and such chairman within three months from the date on which either Contracting Party has informed the other Contracting Party that it intends to submit the dispute to an arbitration tribunal.

(4)   If the periods specified in paragraph 3 above have not been observed, either Contracting Party may, in the absence of any other arrangement, invite the President of the International Court of Justice to make the necessary appointments. If the President is a national of either Contracting Party or if he is otherwise prevented from discharging the said function, the Vice-President should make the necessary appointments. If the Vice-President is a national of either Contracting Party or if he, too, is prevented from discharging the said function, the member of the Court next in seniority who is not a national of either Contracting Party should make the necessary appointments.

(5)   The arbitration tribunal shall reach its decisions by a majority of votes. Such decisions shall be binding. Each Contracting Party shall bear the cost of its own member and of its representatives in the arbitration proceedings; the cost of the chairman and the remaining costs shall be borne in equal parts by the Contracting Parties. The arbitration tribunal may make a different regulation concerning costs. In all other respects, the arbitration tribunal shall determine its own procedure.

(6)   If both Contracting Parties are Contracting States of the Convention of 18 March 1965 on the Settlement of Investment Disputes between States and Nationals of Other States the arbitration tribunal provided for above may in consideration of the provisions of Article 27 (1) of the said Convention not be appealed to insofar as agreement has been reached between the national or company of one Contracting Party and the other Contracting Party under Article 25 of the Convention. This shall not affect the possibility of appealing to such arbitration tribunal in the event that a decision of the Arbitration Tribunal established under the said Convention is not complied with (Article 27) or in the case of an assignment under a law or pursuant to a legal transaction as provided for in Article 6 of this Treaty.

Model I
Article 11

(1)   Divergencies concerning investments between a Contracting Party and a national or company of the other Contracting Party should as far as possible be settled amicably between the parties in dispute.

(2)   If the divergency cannot be settled within six months of the date when it has been raised by one of the parties in dispute, it shall, at the request of the national or company of the other Contracting Party, be submitted for arbitration. Unless the parties in dispute agree otherwise, the divergency shall be submitted for arbitration under the Convention of 18 March 1965 on the Settlement of Investment Disputes between States and Nationals of Other States.

(3)   The award shall be binding and shall not be subject to any appeal or remedy other than those provided for in the said Convention. The award shall be enforced in accordance with domestic law.

(4)   During arbitration proceedings or the enforcement of an award, the Contracting Party involved in the dispute shall not raise the objection that the national or company of the other Contracting Party has received compensation under an insurance contract in respect of all or part of the damage.

Model II
Article 11

(1)   Divergencies concerning investments between a Contracting Party and a national or company of the other Contracting Party shall as far as possible be settled amicably between the parties in dispute.

(2)   If the divergency cannot be settled within six months of the date when it has been raised by one of the parties in dispute, it shall, at the request of the national or company of the other Contracting Party, be submitted for arbitration. Each Contracting Party herewith declares its acceptance of such an arbitration procedure. Unless the parties in dispute have agreed otherwise, the provisions of Article 10 (3) to (5) shall be applied mutatis mutandis on condition that the appointment of the members of the arbitration tribunal in accordance with Article 10 (3) is effected by the parties in dispute and that, insofar as the periods specified in Article 10 (3) are not observed, either party in dispute may, in the absence of other arrangements, invite the President of the Court of International Arbitration of the International Chamber of Commerce in Paris to make the required appointments. The award shall be enforced in accordance with domestic law.

(3)   During arbitration proceedings or the enforcement of an award, the Contracting Party involved in the dispute shall not raise the objection that the national or company of the other Contracting Party has received compensation under an insurance contract in respect of all or part of the damage.

(4)   In the event of both Contracting Parties having become Contracting States of the Convention of 18 March 1965 on the Settlement of Investment Disputes between States and Nationals of Other States, divergencies under this Article between the parties in dispute shall be submitted for arbitration under the aforementioned Convention, unless the parties in dispute agree otherwise; each Contracting Party herewith declares its acceptance of such a procedure.

Article 12

This Treaty shall be in force irrespective of whether or not diplomatic or consular relations exist between the Contracting Parties.

Article 13

(1)   This Treaty shall be ratified; the instruments of ratification shall be exchanged as soon as possible in_____.

(2)   This Treaty shall enter into force one month after the date of exchange of the instruments of ratification. It shall remain in force for a period of ten years and shall be extended thereafter for an unlimited period unless denounced in writing by either Contracting Party twelve months before its expiration. After the expiry of the period of ten years this Treaty may be denounced at any time by either Contracting Party giving twelve months' notice.

(3)   In respect of investments made prior to the date of termination of this Treaty, the provisions of Articles 1 to 12 shall continue to be effective for a further period of twenty years from the date of termination of this Treaty.

Done at _____ on_____
in duplicate in the German and English languages, both texts being equally authentic.

For the Federal Republic of Germany   For _____.

Protocol

On signing the Treaty between the Federal Republic of Germany and _____ concerning the Encouragement and Reciprocal Protection of Investments, the undersigned plenipotentiaries have, in addition, agreed on the following provisions, which shall be regarded as an integral part of the said Treaty;

(1)   Ad Article 1

(a)   Returns from the investment and, in the event of their re-investment, the returns therefrom shall enjoy the same protection as the investment.

(b)   Without prejudice to any other method of determining nationality, in particular any person in possession of a national passport issued by the competent authorities of the Contracting Party concerned shall be deemed to be a national of that Party.

(2)   Ad Article 2

(a)   Investments made, in accordance with the legislation of either Contracting Party, within the area of application of the law of that Contracting Party by nationals or companies of the other Contracting Party shall enjoy the full protection of the Treaty.

(b)   The Treaty shall also apply to the areas of the exclusive economic zone and the continental shelf insofar as international law permits the Contracting Party concerned to exercise sovereign rights or jurisdiction in these areas.

(3)   Ad Article 3

(a)   The following shall more particularly, though not exclusively, be deemed "activity" within the meaning of Article 3 (2): the management, maintenance, use and enjoyment of an investment. The following shall, in particular, be deemed "treatment less favourable" within the meaning of Article 3: unequal treatment in the case of restrictions on the purchase of raw or auxiliary materials, of energy or fuel or of means of production or operation of any kind, unequal treatment in the case of impeding the marketing of products inside or outside the country, as well as any other measures having similar effects. Measures that have to be taken for reasons of public security and order, public health or morality shall not be deemed "treatment less favourable" within the meaning of Article 3.

(b)   The provisions of Article 3 do not oblige a Contracting Party to extend to natural persons or companies resident in the territory of the other Contracting Party tax privileges, tax exemptions and tax reductions which according to its tax laws are granted only to natural persons and companies resident in its territory.

(c)   The Contracting Parties shall within the framework of their national legislation give sympathetic consideration to applications for the entry and sojourn of persons of either Contracting Party who wish to enter the territory of the other Contracting Party in connection with an investment; the same shall apply to employed persons of either Contracting Party who in connection with an investment wish to enter the territory of the other Contracting Party and sojourn there to take up employment. Applications for work permits shall also be given sympathetic consideration.

(4)   Ad Article 4

A claim to compensation shall also exist when, as a result of State intervention in the company in which the investment is made, its economic substance is severely impaired.

(5)   Ad Article 7

A transfer shall be deemed to have been made "without delay" within the meaning of Article 7 (1) if effected within such period as is normally required for the completion of transfer formalities. The said period shall commence on the day on which the relevant request has been submitted and may on no account exceed two months.

(6)   Whenever goods or persons connected with an investment are to be transported, each Contracting Party shall neither exclude nor hinder transport enterprises of the other Contracting Party and shall issue permits as required to carry out such transport. This shall include the transport of

(a)   goods directly intended for an investment within the meaning of the Treaty or acquired in the territory of either Contracting Party or of any third State by or on behalf of an enterprise in which assets within the meaning of the Treaty are invested;

(b)   persons travelling in connection with an investment.

Done at_____on_____
in duplicate in the German and English languages, both texts being equally authentic.

For the Federal Republic of Germany   For _____.

*   *   *

AGREEMENT BETWEEN THE

PORTUGUESE REPUBLIC AND

THE REPUBLIC OF............ ON

THE MUTUAL PROMOTION AND PROTECTION OF INVESTMENTS

The Portuguese Republic and the Republic of   , hereinafter referred to as the "Contracting Parties",

Desiring to intensify the economic co-operation between the two States,

Intending to encourage and create favourable conditions for investments made by investors of one Contracting Party in the territory of the other Contracting Party on the basis of equality and mutual benefit,

Recognising that the mutual promotion and protection of investments on the basis of this Agreement will stimulate business initiative,

Have agreed as follows:

Article 1
Definitions

For the purpose of this Agreement,

(1)   The term "investments" shall mean every kind of assets invested by investors of one Contracting Party in accordance with the laws and regulations of the latter in the territory of the other Contracting Party including, in particular, though not exclusively:

   (a)   Movable and immovable property as well as any other rights in rem, such as mortgages, liens, pledges and similar rights;

   (b)   Shares, stocks, debentures, or other forms of interest in the equity of companies and/or economic interests from the respective activity;

   (c)   Claims to money or to any performance under having an economic value;

   (d)   Intellectual property rights such as copyrights, patents, utility models, industrial designs, trade marks, trade names, trade and business secretes, technical processes, know-how and good will;

   (e)   Concessions conferred by law under a contract or an administrative act of a competent state authority, including concessions for prospecting, research and exploitation of natural resources;

   (f) .   Goods that, under a leasing agreement, are placed at the disposal of a lessee in the territory of a Contracting Party in conformity with its laws and regulations.

Any alteration of the form in which assets are invested shall not affect their character as investments, provided that such a change does not contradict the laws and regulations of the relevant Contracting Party.

(2)   The term "returns" shall mean the amount yielded by investments, over a given period, in particular, though not exclusively, shall include profits, dividends, interests, royalties or other forms of income related to the investments including technical assistance fees.

In cases where the returns of investments, as defined above, are reinvested, the income resulting from the reinvestment shall also be considered as income related to the first investments.

(3)   The term "investors" means:

(a)   natural persons having the national of either Contracting Party, in accordance with its laws, and

(b)   legal persons, including corporations, commercial companies or other companies or associations, which have a main office in the territory of either Contracting Party and are incorporated or constituted in accordance with the law of that Contracting Party.

(4)   The term "territory" means the territory of either of the Contracting Parties, a defined by their respective laws, over which the Contracting Party concerned exercises, in accordance with international law, sovereignty, sovereign rights or jurisdiction.

Article 2
Promotion and Protection of Investments

(1)   Each Contracting Party shall promote and encourage, as far as possible, within its territory investments made by investors of the other Contracting Party and shall admit such investments into its territory in accordance with its laws and regulations. It shall in any case accord such investments fair and equitable treatment.

(2)   Investments made by investors of either Contracting Party shall enjoy full protection and security in the territory of the other Contracting Party.

Neither Contracting Party shall in any impair by unreasonable, arbitrary or discriminatory measures the management, maintenance, use, enjoyment or disposal of investments in its territory of investors of the other Contracting Party.

Article 3
National and Most Favoured Nation Treatment

(1)   Investments made by investors of one Contracting Party in the territory of the other Contracting Party, as also the returns therefrom, shall be accorded treatment which is fair and equitable and not less favourable that the latter Contracting Party accords to the investments and returns of investors of any third State.

(2)   Investors of one Contracting Party shall be accorded by the other Contracting Party, as regards the management, maintenance, use, enjoyment or disposal of their investments, treatment which is fair and equitable and not less favourable that the latter Contracting Party accords to its own investors or to investors of any third State.

(3)   The provisions of this Article shall not be construed so as to oblige one Contracting Party to extend to the investors of the other Contracting Party the benefit of any treatment, preference or privilege which may be extended by the former Contracting Party by virtue of:

(a)   any existing or future free trade area, customs union, common market or other similar international agreements including other forms of regional economic co-operation to which either of the Contracting Parties is or may become a Party, and

(b)   any international agreement relating wholly or mainly to taxation.

Article 4
Expropriation

(1) Investments made by investors of either Contracting Party in the territory of the other Contracting Party shall not be expropriated, nationalised or subject to any other measure with effects equivalent to expropriation or nationalisation (hereinafter referred to as expropriation) except by virtue of law for a public purpose, on a non-discriminatory basis and against prompt compensation.

(2) Such compensation shall amount to the market value of the expropriated investments immediately before the expropriation became publicly known. The compensation shall be paid without delay, shall include the usual commercial interest until the date of payment and shall have been made in an appropriate manner at or prior to the time of expropriation for the determination and payment of such compensation.

(3) The investor whose investments are expropriated, shall have the right under the law of expropriating Contracting Party the prompt review by a judicial or other competent authority of that Contracting Party of his or its case and of valuation of his or its investments in accordance with the principles set out in this Article.

Article 5
Compensation for Losses

Investors of either Contracting Party whose investments suffer losses in the territory owning to war or armed conflict, revolution, a state of national emergency or other events considered as such by international law, shall be accorded treatment no less favourable by the latter Contracting Party than the Contracting Party accords to the investments of its own investors, or of any third State, whichever is more favourable, as regards restitution, indemnification, compensation or other valuable consideration. Any payment made under this Article shall be, without delay, freely transferable in convertible currency.

Article 6
Transfers

(1) Pursuant to its own legislation, each Contracting Party shall guarantee investors of the other Contracting Party the free transfer of sums related to their investments, in particular, though not exclusively:

(a) capital and additional amounts necessary to maintain or increase the investments;
(b) the returns defined in Paragraph 2, Article 1 of this Agreement;
(c) funds in service, repayment and amortisation of loans, recognised by both Contracting Parties to be an investment;
(d) the proceeds obtained from the sale or from the total or partial liquidation of the investment;
(e) any compensation or other payment referred to in Articles 4 and 5 of this Agreement; or
(f) any preliminary payments that may be made in the name of the investor in accordance with Article 7 of this Agreement.

(2) The transfers referred to in this Article shall be made without delay at the exchange rate applicable on the date of the transfer in convertible currency.

Article 7
Subrogation

If either Contracting Party or its designated agency makes any payment to one of its investors as a result of a guarantee in respect of an investment made in the territory of the other Contracting Party, the former Contracting Party shall be subrogated to the rights and shares of this investor, and may exercise them according to the same terms and conditions as the original holder.

Article 8
Disputes between the Contracting Parties

(1)   Disputes between the Contracting Parties concerning the interpretation and application of this Agreement should, as far as possible, be settled by negotiations through diplomatic channels.

(2)   If the Contracting Parties fail to reach such settlement within six (6) months after the beginning of negotiations, the dispute shall, upon the request of either Contracting Party, be submitted to an arbitral tribunal, in accordance with the provisions of this article.

(3)   The Arbitral Tribunal shall be constituted ad hoc, as follows: Each of the Contracting Parties shall appoint one member and these two members shall propose a national of a third State as chairman to be appointed by the two Contracting Parties. The members shall be appointed within two (2) months and the chairman shall be appointed within three (3) months from the date on which either Contracting Party notifies the other that it wishes to submit the dispute to an arbitral tribunal.

(4)   If the deadlines specified in paragraph 3 of this Article are not complied with, either Contracting Party may, in the absence of any other agreement, invite the President of the International Court of Justice to make the necessary appointments. If the President is prevented from doing so, or is a national of either Contracting Party, the Vice-President shall be invited to make the necessary appointments.

(5)   If the Vice-Chairman is also a national of either Contracting Party or if he is prevented from making the appointments for any other reason, the appointments shall be made by the member of the Court who is next in seniority and who is not a national of either Contracting Party.

(6)   The chairman of the Arbitral Tribunal shall be a national of a third State with which both Contracting Parties maintain diplomatic relations.

(7)   The Arbitral Tribunal shall rule according to majority vote. The decisions of the tribunal shall be final and binding on both Contracting Parties. Each Contracting Party shall be responsible for the costs of its own member and of its representatives at the arbitral proceedings. Both Contracting Parties shall assume an equal share of the expenses incurred by the chairman, as well as any other expenses. The tribunal may make a different decision regarding costs. In all other respects, the tribunal court shall define its own rules of procedure.

Article 9
Disputes between a Contracting Party and an Investor of the other Contracting Party

(1)   Any dispute which may arise between one Contracting Party and an investor of the other Contracting Party concerning an investment of that investor in the territory of the former Contracting Party shall be settled amicably through negotiations.

(2)   If such dispute cannot be settled within a period of six (6) months from the date of request for settlement, the investor concerned may submit the dispute to:

    (a)   the competent court of the Contracting Party for decision; or

    (b)   the International Centre for the Settlement of Investments Disputes (ICSID) through conciliation or arbitration, established under the Convention on the Settlement of Investments Disputes between States and Nationals of other States, opened for signature in Washington D.C., on March 18, 1965.

(3)   Neither Contracting Party shall pursue through diplomatic channels any matter referred to arbitration until the proceedings have terminated and a Contracting Party has failed to abide by

or to comply with the award rendered by the International Centre for the Settlement of Investments Disputes.

(4)   The award shall be enforceable on the parties and shall not be subject to any appeal or remedy other than that provided for in the said Convention. The award shall be enforceable in accordance with the domestic law of the Contracting Party in whose territory the investment in question is situated.

Article 10
Application of other rules

If the provisions of law of either Contracting Party or obligations under international law existing at present or established hereafter between the Contracting Parties in addition to this Agreement contain a regulation, whether general or specific, entitling investments made by investors of the other Contracting Party to a treatment more favourable than is provided for by this Agreement, such provisions shall, to the extent that they are more favourable, prevail over this Agreement.

Article 11
Application of the Agreement

This Agreement shall apply to all investments, made by investors from one of the Contracting Parties in the territory of the other Contracting Party in accordance with the respective legal provisions, prior to as well as after its entry into force, but shall not apply to any dispute concerning investments which have arisen before its entry into force.

Article 12
Consultations

Representatives of the Contracting Parties shall, whenever necessary, hold consultations on any matter affecting the implementation of this Agreement. These consultations shall be held on the proposal of one of the Contracting Parties at a place and a time to be agreed upon through diplomatic channels.

Article 13
Entry into force and Duration

(1)   The Agreement shall enter into force thirty (30) days after the Contracting Parties notify each other in writing that their respective internal constitutional procedures have been fulfilled.

(2)   This Agreement shall remain in force for a period of ten (10) years and continue in force thereafter unless, twelve (12) months before its expiration, either Contracting Party notifies the other in writing or its intention to terminate the Agreement or any subsequent five-year period.

(3)   In respect of investment made prior to the date of termination of this Agreement the provisions of Articles 1 to 12 shall remain in force for a further period of ten (10) years from the date of termination of this Agreement.

Done in duplicate at this   day of   199 in the Portuguese, ... and English languages, all texts being equally authentic. In case of any divergence of interpretation, the English text shall prevail.

For the Portuguese Republic   For the Republic of

PROTOCOL

On the occasion of the signing of the Agreement between the Portuguese Republic and the Republic of   on the Mutual Promotion and Protection of the Investments, the undersigned duly authorised to this effect, have agreed also on the following provisions, which constitute an integral part of the said Agreement:

(1)   With reference to Article 2 of this Agreement:

> The provisions of Article 2 of this Agreement should be applicable when investors of one of the Contracting Parties are already established in the territory of the other Contracting Party an wish to extend their activities or to carry out activities in other sectors.

> Such investments shall be considered as new ones and, to that extent, shall be made in accordance with the rules on the admission of investments, according to Article 2 of this Agreement.

(2)   With reference to Article 3 of this Agreement:

> The Contracting Parties consider that provisions of Article 3 of this Agreement shall be without prejudice to the right of either Contracting Party to apply the relevant provisions of their tax law which distinguish between tax-payers who are not in the same situation with regard to their place of residence or with regard to the place where their capital is invested.

Done in duplicate in   at this   day of   199   in the Portuguese, ... and English languages, all texts being equally authentic. In case of any divergence of interpretation, the English text shall prevail.

For the Portuguese Republic   For the Republic of

AGREEMENT BETWEEN

THE SWISS CONFEDERATION

AND

_____

ON THE PROMOTION AND RECIPROCAL PROTECTION OF INVESTMENTS[*]

Preamble

The Swiss Federal Council and the Government of _____,

Desiring to intensify economic cooperation to the mutual benefit of both States,

Intending to create and maintain favourable conditions for investments by investors of oneContracting Party in the territory of the other Contracting Party,

Recognizing the need to promote and protect foreign investments with the aim to foster the economic prosperity of both States,

Have agreed as follows:

Article 1
Definitions

For the purpose of this Agreement:

(1)   The term "investor" refers with regard to either Contracting Party to

    (a)   natural persons who, according to the law of that Contracting Party, are considered to be its nationals;

    (b)   legal entities, including companies, corporations, business associations and other organisations, which are constituted or otherwise duly organised under the law of that Contracting Party and have their seat, together with real economic activities, in the territory of that same Contracting Party;

    (c)   legal entities established under the law of any country which are, directly or indirectly, controlled by nationals of that Contracting Party or by legal entities having their seat, together with real economic activities, in the territory of that Contracting Party.

(2)   The term "investments" shall include every kind of assets in particular:

    (a)   movable and immovable property as well as any other rights in rem, such as servitudes, mortgages, liens, pledges and usufructs;

    (b)   shares, parts or any other kinds of participation in companies;

    (c)   claims to money or to any performance having an economic value;

    (d)   copyrights, industrial property rights (such as patents, utility models, industrial designs or models, trade or service marks, trade names, indications of origin), know-how and goodwill;

    (e)   concessions under public law, including concessions to search for, extract or exploit natural resources as well as all other rights given by law, by contract or by decision of the authority in accordance with the law.

---

[*]Source: Government of the Swiss Confederation, Swiss Draft (1986/1995) [Note added by the editor].

(3)   The term "returns" means the amounts yielded by an investment and includes in particular, profits, interest, capital gains, dividends, royalties and fees.

(4)   The term "territory" includes the maritime areas adjacent to the coast of the State concerned, to the extent to which that State may exercise sovereign rights or jurisdiction in those areas according to international law.

Article 2
Scope of application

The present Agreement shall apply to investments in the territory of one Contracting Party made in accordance with its laws and regulations by investors of the other Contracting Party, whether prior to or after the entry into force of the Agreement.

Article 3
Promotion, admission

(1)   Each Contracting Party shall in its territory promote as far as possible investments by investors of the other Contracting Party and admit such investments in accordance with its laws and regulations.

(2)   When a Contracting Party shall have admitted an investment on its territory, it shall grant the necessary permits in connection with such an investment and with the carrying out of licensing agreements and contracts for technical, commercial or administrative assistance. Each Contracting Party shall, whenever needed, endeavour to issue the necessary authorizations concerning the activities of consultants and other qualified persons of foreign nationality.

Article 4
Protection, treatment

(1)   Investments and returns of investors of each Contracting Party shall at all times be accorded fair and equitable treatment and shall enjoy full protection and security in the territory of the other Contracting Party. Neither Contracting Party shall in any way impair by unreasonable or discriminatory measures the management, maintenance, use, enjoyment, extension, or disposal of such investments.

(2)   Each Contracting Party shall in its territory accord investments or returns of investors of the other Contracting Party treatment not less favourable than that which it accords to investments or returns of its own investors or to investments or returns of investors of any third State, whichever is more favourable to the investor concerned.

(3)   Each Contracting Party shall in its territory accord investors of the other Contracting Party, as regards the management, maintenance, use, enjoyment or disposal of their investments, treatment not less favourable than that which it accords to its own investors or investors of any third State, whichever is more favourable to the investor concerned.

(4)   If a Contracting Party accords special advantages to investors of any third State by virtue of an agreement establishing a free trade area, a customs union or a common market or by virtue of an agreement on the avoidance of double taxation, it shall not be obliged to accord such advantages to investors of the other Contracting Party.

Article 5
Free transfer

Each Contracting Party in whose territory investments have been made by investors of the other Contracting Party shall grant those investors the free transfer of the amounts relating to these investments, in particular of:

(a)   returns;
(b)   repayments of loans;
(c)   amounts assigned to cover expenses relating to the management of the investment;
(d)   royalties and other payments deriving from rights enumerated in Article 1, paragraph (2), letters (c), (d) and (e) of this Agreement;
(e)   additional contributions of capital necessary for the maintenance or development of the investment;
(f)   the proceeds of the partial or total sale or liquidation of the investment, including possible increment values.

Article 6
Dispossession, compensation

(1)   Neither of the Contracting Parties shall take, either directly or indirectly, measures of expropriation, nationalization or any other measures having the same nature or the same effect against investments of investors of the other Contracting Party, unless the measures are taken in the public interest, on a non discriminatory basis, and under due process of law, and provided that provisions be made for effective and adequate compensation. Such compensation shall amount to the market value of the investment expropriated immediately before the expropriatory action was taken or became public knowledge, whichever is earlier. The amount of compensation, interest included, shall be settled in the currency of the country of origin of the investment and paid without delay to the person entitled thereto without regard to its residence or domicile.

(2)   The investors of one Contracting Party whose investments have suffered losses due to a war or any other armed conflict, revolution, state of emergency or rebellion, which took place in the territory of the other Contracting Party shall benefit, on the part of this latter, from a treatment in accordance with Article 4 of this Agreement as regards restitution, indemnification, compensation or other settlement.

Article 7
Principle of subrogation

Where one Contracting Party has granted any financial guarantee against non-commercial risks in regard to an investment by one of its investors in the territory of the other Contracting Party, the latter shall recognize the rights of the first Contracting Party by virtue of the principle of subrogation to the rights of the investor when payment has been made under this guarantee by the first Contracting Party.

Article 8
Disputes between a Contracting Party
and an investor of the other Contracting Party

(1)   For the purpose of solving disputes with respect to investments between a Contracting Party and an investor of the other Contracting Party and without prejudice to Article 9 of this Agreement (Disputes between Contracting Parties), consultations will take place between the parties concerned.

(2)   If these consultations do not result in a solution within six months from the date of request for consultations and if the investor concerned gives a written consent, the dispute shall be submitted to the International Centre for Settlement of Investment Disputes, instituted by the Convention of Washington of March 18, 1965, for the settlement of disputes regarding investments between States and nationals of other States.

Each party may start the procedure by addressing a request to that effect to the Secretary-General of the Centre as foreseen by Article 28 and 36 of the above-mentioned Convention. Should the parties disagree on whether the conciliation or arbitration is the most appropriate procedure, the investor concerned shall have the choice. The Contracting Party which is party to the dispute can, at no time whatsoever during the settlement procedure or the execution of the sentence, allege the fact that the investor has received, by virtue of an insurance contract, a compensation covering the whole or part of the incurred damage.

(3)   A company which has been incorporated or constituted according to the laws in force on the territory of the Contracting Party and which, prior to the origin of the dispute, was under the control of nationals or companies of the other Contracting Party, is considered, in the sense of the Convention of Washington and according to its Article 25 (2) (b), as a company of the latter.

(4)   Neither Contracting Party shall pursue through diplomatic channels a dispute submitted to the Centre, unless

(a)   the Secretary-General of the Centre or a commission of conciliation or an arbitral tribunal decides that the dispute is beyond the jurisdiction of the Centre, or

(b)   the other Contracting Party does not abide by and comply with the award rendered by an arbitral tribunal.

Article 9
Disputes between Contracting Parties

(1)   Disputes between Contracting Parties regarding the interpretation or application of the provisions of this Agreement shall be settled through diplomatic channels.

(2)   If both Contracting Parties cannot reach an agreement within six months after the beginning of the dispute between themselves, the latter shall, upon request of either Contracting Party, be submitted to an arbitral tribunal of three members. Each Contracting Party shall appoint one arbitrator, and these two arbitrators shall nominate a chairman who shall be a national of a third State.

(3)   If one of the Contracting Parties has not appointed its arbitrator and has not followed the invitation of the other Contracting Party to make that appointment within two months, the arbitrator shall be appointed upon the request of that Contracting Party by the President of the International Court of Justice.

(4)   If both arbitrators cannot reach an agreement about the choice of the chairman within two months after their appointment, the latter shall be appointed upon the request of either Contracting Party by the President of the International Court of Justice.

(5)   If, in the cases specified under paragraphs (3) and (4) of this Article, the President of the International Court of Justice is prevented from carrying out the said function or if he is a national of either Contracting Party, the appointment shall be made by the Vice-President, and if the latter is prevented or if he is a national of either Contracting Party, the appointment shall be made by the most senior Judge of the Court who is not a national of either Contracting Party.

(6)   Subject to other provisions made by the Contracting Parties, the tribunal shall determine its procedure.

(7)   The decisions of the tribunal are final and binding for each Contracting Party.

Article 10
Other commitments

(1)   If provisions in the legislation of either Contracting Party or rules of international law entitle investments by investors of the other Contracting Party to treatment more favourable than is provided for by this Agreement, such provisions shall to the extent that they are more favourable prevail over this Agreement.

(2)   Each Contracting Party shall observe any obligation it has assumed with regard to investments in its territory by investors of the other Contracting Party.

Article 11
Final provisions

(1)   This Agreement shall enter into force on the day when both Governments have notified each other that they have complied with the constitutional requirements for the conclusion and entry into force of international agreements, and shall remain binding for a period of ten years. Unless written notice of termination is given six months before the expiration of this period, the Agreement shall be considered as renewed on the same terms for a period of two years, and so forth.

(2)   In case of official notice as to the termination of the present Agreement, the provisions of Articles 1 to 10 shall continue to be effective for a further period of ten years for investments made before official notice was given.

Done in duplicate, at _____, on _____, each in [French], _____ and [English], each text being equally authentic. [In case of any divergence of interpretation, the English text shall prevail.]

For the Swiss Federal Council   For the Government of _____

* * *

AGREEMENT BETWEEN THE GOVERNMENT OF THE UNITED KINGDOM OF GREAT BRITAIN AND NORTHERN IRELAND

AND

THE GOVERNMENT OF

_____

FOR THE PROMOTION AND PROTECTION OF INVESTMENTS[*]

The Government of the United Kingdom of Great Britain and Northern Ireland and the Government of _____,

Desiring to create favourable conditions for greater investment by nationals and companies of one State in the territory of the other State;

Recognising that the encouragement and reciprocal protection under international agreement of such investments will be conducive to the stimulation of individual business initiative and will increase prosperity in both States;

Have agreed as follows:

Article 1
Definitions

For the purposes of this Agreement:

(a)   "investment" means every kind of asset and in particular, though not exclusively, includes:

   (i)   movable and immovable property and any other property rights such as mortgages, liens or pledges;

   (ii)   shares in and stock and debentures of a company and any other form of participation in a company;

   (iii)   claims to money or to any performance under contract having a financial value;

   (iv)   intellectual property rights, goodwill, technical processes and know-how;

   (v)   business concessions conferred by law or under contract, including concessions to search for, cultivate, extract or exploit natural resources.

A change in the form in which assets are invested does not affect their character as investments and the term "investment" includes all investments, whether made before or after the date of entry into force of this Agreement;

---

[*]Source: Government of the United Kingdom, Department of Trade and Industry [Note added by the editor].

(b)   "returns" means the amounts yielded by an investment and in particular, though not exclusively, includes profit, interest, capital gains, dividends, royalties and fees;

(c)   "nationals" means:

   (i)   in respect of the United Kingdom: physical persons deriving their status as United Kingdom nationals from the law in force in the United Kingdom;

   (ii)   in respect of _____;

(d)   "companies" means:

   (i)   in respect of the United Kingdom: corporations, firms and associations incorporated or constituted under the law in force in any part of the United Kingdom or in any territory to which this Agreement is extended in accordance with the provisions of Article 12;

   (ii)   in respect of _____: corporations, firms and associations incorporated or constituted under the law in force in any part of _____;

(e)   "territory" means:

   (i)   in respect of the United Kingdom: Great Britain and Northern Ireland, including the territorial sea and any maritime area situated beyond the territorial sea of the United Kingdom which has been or might in the future be designated under the national law of the United Kingdom in accordance with international law as an area within which the United Kingdom may exercise rights with regard to the sea-bed and subsoil and the natural resources and any territory to which this Agreement is extended in accordance with the provisions of Article 12;

   (ii)   in respect of _____: _____.

Article 2
Promotion and Protection of Investment

(1)   Each Contracting Party shall encourage and create favourable conditions for nationals or companies of the other Contracting Party to invest capital in its territory, and, subject to its right to exercise powers conferred by its laws, shall admit such capital.

(2)   Investments of nationals or companies of each Contracting Party shall at all times be accorded fair and equitable treatment and shall enjoy full protection and security in the territory of the other Contracting Party. Neither Contracting Party shall in any way impair by unreasonable or discriminatory measures the management, maintenance, use, enjoyment or disposal of investments in its territory of nationals or companies of the other Contracting Party. Each Contracting Party shall observe any obligation it may have entered into with regard to investments of nationals or companies of the other Contracting Party.

Article 3
National Treatment and Most-favoured-nation Provisions

(1)   Neither Contracting Party shall in its territory subject investments or returns of nationals or companies of the other Contracting Party to treatment less favourable than that which it accords to

investments or returns of its own nationals or companies or to investments or returns of nationals or companies of any third State.

(2)   Neither Contracting Party shall in its territory subject nationals or companies of the other Contracting Party, as regards their management, maintenance, use, enjoyment or disposal of their investments, to treatment less favourable than that which it accords to its own nationals or companies or to nationals or companies of any third State.

(3)   For the avoidance of doubt it is confirmed that the treatment provided for in paragraphs (1) and (2) above shall apply to the provisions of Articles 1 to 11 of this Agreement.

Article 4
Compensation for Losses

(1)   Nationals or companies of one Contracting Party whose investments in the territory of the other Contracting Party suffer losses owing to war or other armed conflict, revolution, a state of national emergency, revolt, insurrection or riot in the territory of the latter Contracting Party shall be accorded by the latter Contracting Party treatment, as regards restitution, indemnification, compensation or other settlement, no less favourable than that which the latter Contracting Party accords to its own nationals or companies or to nationals or companies of any third State. Resulting payments shall be freely transferable.

(2)   Without prejudice to paragraph (1) of this Article, nationals and companies of one Contracting Party who in any of the situations referred to in that paragraph suffer losses in the territory of the other Contracting Party resulting from

(a)   requisitioning of their property by its forces or authorities, or

(b)   destruction of their property by its forces or authorities, which was not caused in combat action or was not required by the necessity of the situation,

shall be accorded restitution or adequate compensation. Resulting payments shall be freely transferable.

Article 5
Expropriation

(1)   Investments of nationals or companies of either Contracting Party shall not be nationalised, expropriated or subjected to measures having effect equivalent to nationalisation or expropriation (hereinafter referred to as "expropriation") in the territory of the other Contracting Party except for a public purpose related to the internal needs of that Party on a non-discriminatory basis and against prompt, adequate and effective compensation. Such compensation shall amount to the genuine value of the investment expropriated immediately before the expropriation or before the impending expropriation became public knowledge, whichever is the earlier, shall include interest at a normal commercial rate until the date of payment, shall be made without delay, be effectively realizable and be freely transferable. The national or company affected shall have a right, under the law of the Contracting Party making the expropriation, to prompt review, by a judicial or other independent authority of that Party, of his or its case and of the valuation of his or its investment in accordance with the principles set out in this paragraph.

(2) Where a Contracting Party expropriates the assets of a company which is incorporated or constituted under the law in force in any part of its own territory, and in which nationals or companies of the other Contracting Party own shares, it shall ensure that the provisions of paragraph (1) of this Article are applied to the extent necessary to guarantee prompt, adequate and effective compensation in respect of their investment to such nationals or companies of the other Contracting Party who are owners of those shares.

Article 6
Repatriation of Investment and Returns

Each Contracting Party shall in respect of investments guarantee to nationals or companies of the other Contracting Party the unrestricted transfer of their investments and returns. Transfers shall be effected without delay in the convertible currency in which the capital was originally invested or in any other convertible currency agreed by the investor and the Contracting Party concerned. Unless otherwise agreed by the investor transfers shall be made at the rate of exchange applicable on the date of transfer pursuant to the exchange regulations in force.

Article 7
Exceptions

The provisions of this Agreement relative to the grant of treatment not less favourable than that accorded to the nationals or companies of either Contracting Party or of any third State shall not be construed so as to oblige one Contracting Party to extend to the nationals or companies of the other the benefit of any treatment, preference or privilege resulting from

(a) any existing or future customs union or similar international agreement to which either of the Contracting Parties is or may become a party, or

(b) any international agreement or arrangement relating wholly or mainly to taxation or any domestic legislation relating wholly or mainly to taxation.

[Preferred]

Article 8
Reference to International Centre for Settlement of Investment Disputes

(1) Each Contracting Party hereby consents to submit to the International Centre for the Settlement of Investment Disputes (hereinafter referred to as "the Centre") for settlement by conciliation or arbitration under the Convention on the Settlement of Investment Disputes between States and Nationals of Other States opened for signature at Washington on 18 March 1965 any legal dispute arising between that Contracting Party and a national or company of the other Contracting Party concerning an investment of the latter in the territory of the former.

(2) A company which is incorporated or constituted under the law in force in the territory of one Contracting Party and in which before such a dispute arises the majority of shares are owned by nationals or companies of the other Contracting Party shall in accordance with Article 25(2)(b) of the Convention be treated for the purposes of the Convention as a company of the other Contracting Party.

(3) If any such dispute should arise and agreement cannot be reached within three months between the parties to this dispute through pursuit of local remedies or otherwise, then, if the national or company affected also consents in writing to submit the dispute to the Centre for settlement by conciliation or arbitration under the Convention, either party may institute proceedings by addressing a request to that effect to the Secretary-General of the Centre as provided in Articles 28 and 36 of the Convention. In the event of disagreement as to whether conciliation or arbitration is the more appropriate procedure the national or company affected shall have the right to choose. The Contracting Party which is a party to the dispute shall not raise as an objection at any stage of the proceedings or enforcement of an award the fact that the national or company which is the other party to the dispute has received in pursuance of an insurance contract an indemnity in respect of some or all of his or its losses.

(4) Neither Contracting Party shall pursue through the diplomatic channel any dispute referred to the Centre unless

(a)   the Secretary-General of the Centre, or a conciliation commission or an arbitral tribunal constituted by it, decides that the dispute is not within the jurisdiction of the Centre, or

(b)   the other Contracting Party should fail to abide by or to comply with any award rendered by an arbitral tribunal.

[Alternative]

Article 8
Settlement of Disputes between an Investor and a Host State

(1)   Disputes between a national or company of one Contracting Party and the other Contracting Party concerning an obligation of the latter under this Agreement in relation to an investment of the former which have not been amicably settled shall, after a period of three months from written notification of a claim, be submitted to international arbitration if the national or company concerned so wishes.

(2)   Where the dispute is referred to international arbitration, the national or company and the Contracting Party concerned in the dispute may agree to refer the dispute either to:

(a)   the International Centre for the Settlement of Investment Disputes (having regard to the provisions, where applicable, of the Convention on the Settlement of Investment Disputes between States and Nationals of other States, opened for signature at Washington DC on 18 March 1965 and the Additional Facility for the Administration of Conciliation, Arbitration and Fact-Finding Proceedings); or

(b)   the Court of Arbitration of the International Chamber of Commerce or;

(c)   an international arbitrator or ad hoc arbitration tribunal to be appointed by a special agreement or establishment under the Arbitration Rules of the United Nations Commission on International Trade Law.

If after a period of three months from written notification of the claim there is no agreement to one of the above alternative procedures, the dispute shall at the request in writing of the national or company concerned be submitted to arbitration under the Arbitration Rules of the United Nations Commission on International Trade Law as then in force. The parties to the dispute may agree in writing to modify these Rules.

Article 9
Disputes between the Contracting Parties

(1)   Disputes between the Contracting Parties concerning the interpretation or application of this Agreement should, if possible, be settled through the diplomatic channel.

(2)   If a dispute between the Contracting Parties cannot thus be settled, it shall upon the request of either Contracting Party be submitted to an arbitral tribunal.

(3)   Such an arbitral tribunal shall be constituted for each individual case in the following way. Within two months of the receipt of the request for arbitration, each Contracting Party shall appoint one member of the tribunal. Those two members shall then select a national of a third State who on approval by the two Contracting Parties shall be appointed Chairman of the tribunal. The Chairman shall be appointed within two months from the date of appointment of the other two members.

(4)   If within the periods specified in paragraph (3) of this Article the necessary appointments have not been made, either Contracting Party may, in the absence of any other agreement, invite the President of the International Court of Justice to make any necessary appointments. If the President is a national

of either Contracting Party or if he is otherwise prevented from discharging the said function, the Vice-President shall be invited to make the necessary appointments. If the Vice-President is a national of either Contracting Party or if he too is prevented from discharging the said function, the Member of the International Court of Justice next in seniority who is not a national of either Contracting Party shall be invited to make the necessary appointments.

(5)   The arbitral tribunal shall reach its decision by a majority of votes. Such decision shall be binding on both Contracting Parties. Each Contracting Party shall bear the cost of its own member of the tribunal and of representation in the arbitral proceedings; the cost of the Chairman and the remaining costs shall be borne in equal parts by the Contracting Parties. The tribunal may, however, in its decision direct that a higher proportion of costs shall be borne by one of the two Contracting Parties, and this award shall be binding on both Contracting Parties. The tribunal shall determine its own procedure.

Article 10
Subrogation

(1)   If one Contracting Party or its designated Agency ("the first Contracting Party") makes a payment under an indemnity given in respect of an investment in the territory of the other Contracting Party, ("the second Contracting Party"), the second Contracting Party shall recognise

(a)   the assignment to the first Contracting Party by law or by legal transaction of all the rights and claims of the party indemnified, and

(b)   that the first Contracting Party is entitled to exercise such rights and enforce such claims by virtue of subrogation, to the same extent as the party indemnified.

(2)   The first Contracting Party shall be entitled in all circumstances to

(a)   the same treatment in respect of the rights and claims acquired by it by virtue of the assignment, and

(b)   any payments received in pursuance of those rights and claims,

as the party indemnified was entitled to receive by virtue of this Agreement in respect of the investment concerned and its related returns.

(3)   Any payments received in non-convertible currency by the first Contracting Party in pursuance of the rights and claims acquired shall be freely available to the first Contracting Party for the purpose of meeting any expenditure incurred in the territory of the second Contracting Party.

Article 11
Application of other Rules

If the provisions of law of either Contracting Party or obligations under international law existing at present or established hereafter between the Contracting Parties in addition to the present Agreement contain rules, whether general or specific, entitling investments by investors of the other Contracting Party to a treatment more favourable than is provided for by the present Agreement, such rules shall to the extent that they are more favourable prevail over the present Agreement.

Article 12
Territorial Extension

At the time of [signature] [ratification] of this Agreement, or at any time thereafter, the provisions of this Agreement may be extended to such territories for whose international relations the

Government of the United Kingdom are responsible as may be agreed between the Contracting Parties in an Exchange of Notes.

Article 13
Entry into Force

[This Agreement shall enter into force on the day of signature]

or

[Each Contracting Party shall notify the other in writing of the completion of the constitutional formalities required in its territory for the entry into force of this Agreement. This Agreement shall enter into force on the date of the latter of the two notifications]

or

[This Agreement shall be ratified and shall enter into force on the exchange of Instruments of Ratification]

Article 14
Duration and Termination

This Agreement shall remain in force for a period of ten years. Thereafter it shall continue in force until the expiration of twelve months from the date on which either Contracting Party shall have given written notice of termination to the other. Provided that in respect of investments made whilst the Agreement is in force, its provisions shall continue in effect with respect to such investments for a period of twenty years after the date of termination and without prejudice to the application thereafter of the rules of general international law.

In witness whereof the undersigned, duly authorised thereto by their respective Governments, have signed this Agreement.

Done in duplicate at _____ this _____ day of _____ 19__ [in the English and _____ languages, both texts being equally authoritative].

For the Government of
the United Kingdom of
Great Britain and Northern Ireland

For the Government of
_____

* * *

April 1994

TREATY BETWEEN

THE GOVERNMENT OF THE UNITED STATES OF AMERICA

AND

THE GOVERNMENT OF_____

CONCERNING THE ENCOURAGEMENT
AND RECIPROCAL PROTECTION OF INVESTMENT[*]

The Government of the United States of America and the Government of _____ (hereinafter the "Parties");

Desiring to promote greater economic cooperation between them, with respect to investment by nationals and companies of one Party in the territory of the other Party;

Recognizing that agreement upon the treatment to be accorded such investment will stimulate the flow of private capital and the economic development of the Parties;

Agreeing that a stable framework for investment will maximize effective utilization of economic resources and improve living standards;

Recognizing that the development of economic and business ties can promote respect for internationally recognized worker rights;

Agreeing that these objectives can be achieved without relaxing health, safety and environmental measures of general application; and

Having resolved to conclude a Treaty concerning the encouragement and reciprocal protection of investment;

Have agreed as follows:

Article I

For the purposes of this Treaty,

(a)   "company" means any entity constituted or organized under applicable law, whether or not for profit, and whether privately or governmentally owned or controlled, and includes a corporation, trust, partnership, sole proprietorship, branch, joint venture, association, or other organization;

(b)   "company of a Party" means a company constituted or organized under the laws of that Party;

---

[*]Source: Government of the United States of America, Department of State [Note added by the editor].

(c)   "national" of a Party means a natural person who is a national of that Party under its applicable law;

(d)   "investment" of a national or company means every kind of investment owned or controlled directly or indirectly by that national or company, and includes investment consisting or taking the form of:

    (i)   a company;

    (ii)   shares, stock, and other forms of equity participation, and bonds, debentures, and other forms of debt interests, in a company;

    (iii)   contractual rights, such as under turnkey, construction or management contracts, production or revenue-sharing contracts, concessions, or other similar contracts;

    (iv)   tangible property, including real property; and intangible property, including rights, such as leases, mortgages, liens and pledges;

    (v)   intellectual property, including:

        copyrights and related rights,
        patents,
        rights in plant varieties,
        industrial designs,
        rights in semiconductor layout designs,
        trade secrets, including know-how and confidential business information,
        trade and service marks, and
        trade names; and

    (vi)   rights conferred pursuant to law, such as licenses and permits;

(e)   "covered investment" means an investment of a national or company of a Party in the territory of the other Party;

(f)   "state enterprise" means a company owned, or controlled through ownership interests, by a Party;

(g)   "investment authorization" means an authorization granted by the foreign investment authority of a Party to a covered investment or a national or company of the other Party;

(h)   "investment agreement" means a written agreement between the national authorities of a Party and a covered investment or a national or company of the other Party that (i) grants rights with respect to natural resources or other assets controlled by the national authorities and (ii) the investment, national or company relies upon in establishing or acquiring a covered investment.

(i)   "ICSID Convention" means the Convention on the Settlement of Investment Disputes between States and Nationals of Other States, done at Washington, March 18, 1965;

(j)   "Centre" means the International Centre for Settlement of Investment Disputes Established by the ICSID Convention; and

(k) "UNCITRAL Arbitration Rules" means the arbitration rules of the United Nations Commission on International Trade Law.

Article II

1. With respect to the establishment, acquisition, expansion, management, conduct, operation and sale or other disposition of covered investments, each Party shall accord treatment no less favorable than that it accords, in like situations, to investments in its territory of its own nationals or companies (hereinafter "national treatment") or to investments in its territory of nationals or companies of a third country (hereinafter "most favored nation treatment"), whichever is most favorable (hereinafter "national and most favored nation treatment"). Each Party shall ensure that its state enterprises, in the provision of their goods or services, accord national and most favored nation treatment to covered investments.

2. (a) A Party may adopt or maintain exceptions to the obligations of paragraph 1 in the sectors or with respect to the matters specified in the Annex to this Treaty. In adopting such an exception, a Party may not require the divestment, in whole or in part, of covered investments existing at the time the exception becomes effective.

   (b) The obligations of paragraph 1 do not apply to procedures provided in multilateral agreements concluded under the auspices of the World Intellectual Property Organization relating to the acquisition or maintenance of intellectual property rights.

3. (a) Each Party shall at all times accord to covered investments fair and equitable treatment and full protection and security, and shall in no case accord treatment less favorable than that required by international law.

   (b) Neither Party shall in any way impair by unreasonable and discriminatory measures the management, conduct, operation, and sale or other disposition of covered investments.

4. Each Party shall provide effective means of asserting claims and enforcing rights with respect to covered investments.

5. Each Party shall ensure that its laws, regulations, administrative practices and procedures of general application, and adjudicatory decisions, that pertain to or affect covered investments are promptly published or otherwise made publicly available.

Article III

1. Neither Party shall expropriate or nationalize a covered investment either directly or indirectly through measures tantamount to expropriation or nationalization ("expropriation") except for a public purpose; in a non-discriminatory manner; upon payment of prompt, adequate and effective compensation; and in accordance with due process of law and the general principles of treatment provided for in Article II(3).

2. Compensation shall be paid without delay; be equivalent to the fair market value of the expropriated investment immediately before the expropriatory action was taken ("the date of expropriation"); and be fully realizable and freely transferable. The fair market value shall not reflect any change in value occurring because the expropriatory action had become known before the date of expropriation.

3.   If the fair market value is denominated in a freely usable currency, the compensation paid shall be no less than the fair market value on the date of expropriation, plus interest at a commercially reasonable rate for that currency, accrued from the date of expropriation until the date of payment.

4.   If the fair market value is denominated in a currency that is not freely usable, the compensation paid -- converted into the currency of payment at the market rate of exchange prevailing on the date of payment -- shall be no less than:

   (a)   the fair market value on the date of expropriation, converted into a freely usable currency at the market rate of exchange prevailing on that date, plus

   (b)   interest, at a commercially reasonable rate for that freely usable currency, accrued from the date of expropriation until the date of payment.

Article IV

1.   Each Party shall accord national and most favored nation treatment to covered investments as regards any measure relating to losses that investments suffer in its territory owing to war or other armed conflict, revolution, state of national emergency, insurrection, civil disturbance, or similar events.

2.   Each Party shall accord restitution, or pay compensation in accordance with paragraphs 2 through 4 of Article III, in the event that covered investments suffer losses in its territory, owing to war or other armed conflict, revolution, state of national emergency, insurrection, civil disturbance, or similar events, that result from:

   (a)   requisitioning of all or part of such investments by the Party's forces or authorities, or

   (b)   destruction of all or part of such investments by the Party's forces or authorities that was not required by the necessity of the situation.

Article V

1.   Each Party shall permit all transfers relating to a covered investment to be made freely and without delay into and out of its territory. Such transfers include:

   (a)   contributions to capital;

   (b)   profits, dividends, capital gains, and proceeds from the sale of all or any part of the investment or from the partial or complete liquidation of the investment;

   (c)   interest, royalty payments, management fees, and technical assistance and other fees;

   (d)   payments made under a contract, including a loan agreement; and

   (e)   compensation pursuant to Articles III and IV, and payments arising out of an investment dispute.

2.   Each Party shall permit transfers to be made in a freely usable currency at the market rate of exchange prevailing on the date of transfer.

3.   Each Party shall permit returns in kind to be made as authorized or specified in an investment authorization, investment agreement, or other written agreement between the Party and a covered investment or a national or company of the other Party.

4.   Notwithstanding paragraphs 1 through 3, a Party may prevent a transfer through the equitable, non-discriminatory and good faith application of its laws relating to:

   (a)   bankruptcy, insolvency or the protection of the rights of creditors;

   (b)   issuing, trading or dealing in securities;

   (c)   criminal or penal offenses; or

   (d)   ensuring compliance with orders or judgments in adjudicatory proceedings.

Article VI

Neither Party shall mandate or enforce, as a condition for the establishment, acquisition, expansion, management, conduct or operation of a covered investment, any requirement (including any commitment or undertaking in connection with the receipt of a governmental permission or authorization):

   (a)   to achieve a particular level or percentage of local content, or to purchase, use or otherwise give a preference to products or services of domestic origin or from any domestic source;

   (b)   to limit imports by the investment of products or services in relation to a particular volume or value of production, exports or foreign exchange earnings;

   (c)   to export a particular type, level or percentage of products or services, either generally or to a specific market region;

   (d)   to limit sales by the investment of products or services in the Party's territory in relation to a particular volume or value of production, exports or foreign exchange earnings;

   (e)   to transfer technology, a production process or other proprietary knowledge to a national or company in the Party's territory, except pursuant to an order, commitment or undertaking that is enforced by a court, administrative tribunal or competition authority to remedy an alleged or adjudicated violation of competition laws; or

   (f)   to carry out a particular type, level or percentage of research and development in the Party's territory.

Such requirements do not include conditions for the receipt or continued receipt of an advantage.

Article VII

1.   (a)   Subject to its laws relating to the entry and sojourn of aliens, each Party shall permit to enter and to remain in its territory nationals of the other Party for the purpose of establishing, developing, administering or advising on the operation of an investment to which they, or a company of the other Party that employs them, have committed or are in the process of committing a substantial amount of capital or other resources.

(b)   Neither Party shall, in granting entry under paragraph l(a), require a labor certification test or other procedures of similar effect, or apply any numerical restriction.

2.   Each Party shall permit covered investments to engage top managerial personnel of their choice, regardless of nationality.

Article VIII

The Parties agree to consult promptly, on the request of either, to resolve any disputes in connection with the Treaty, or to discuss any matter relating to the interpretation or application of the Treaty or to the realization of the objectives of the Treaty.

Article IX

1.   For purposes of this Treaty, an investment dispute is a dispute between a Party and a national or company of the other Party arising out of or relating to an investment authorization, an investment agreement or an alleged breach of any right conferred, created or recognized by this Treaty with respect to a covered investment.

2.   A national or company that is a party to an investment dispute may submit the dispute for resolution under one of the following alternatives:

(a)   to the courts or administrative tribunals of the Party that is a party to the dispute; or

(b)   in accordance with any applicable, previously agreed dispute-settlement procedures; or

(c)   in accordance with the terms of paragraph 3.

3.   (a)   Provided that the national or company concerned has not submitted the dispute for resolution under paragraph 2 (a) or (b), and that three months have elapsed from the date on which the dispute arose, the national or company concerned may submit the dispute for settlement by binding arbitration:

(i)   to the Centre, if the Centre is available; or

(ii)   to the Additional Facility of the Centre, if the Centre is not available; or

(iii)   in accordance with the UNCITRAL Arbitration Rules; or

(iv)   if agreed by both parties to the dispute, to any other arbitration institution or in accordance with any other arbitration rules.

(b)   a national or company, notwithstanding that it may have submitted a dispute to binding arbitration under paragraph 3(a), may seek interim injunctive relief, not involving the payment of damages, before the judicial or administrative tribunals of the Party that is a party to the dispute, prior to the institution of the arbitral proceeding or during the proceeding, for the preservation of its rights and interests.

4.   Each Party hereby consents to the submission of any investment dispute for settlement by binding arbitration in accordance with the choice of the national or company under paragraph 3(a)(i), (ii), and (iii) or the mutual agreement of both parties to the dispute under paragraph 3(a)(iv). This

consent and the submission of the dispute by a national or company under paragraph 3(a) shall satisfy the requirement of:

(a)   Chapter II of the ICSID Convention (Jurisdiction of the Centre) and the Additional Facility Rules for written consent of the parties to the dispute; and

(b)   Article II of the United Nations Convention on the Recognition and Enforcement of Foreign Arbitral Awards, done at New York, June 10, 1958, for an "agreement in writing".

5.   Any arbitration under paragraph 3(a)(ii), (iii) or (iv) shall be held in a state that is a party to the United Nations Convention on the Recognition and Enforcement of Foreign Arbitral Awards, done at New York, June 10, 1958.

6.   Any arbitral award rendered pursuant to this Article shall be final and binding on the parties to the dispute. Each Party shall carry out without delay the provisions of any such award and provide in its territory for the enforcement of such award.

7.   In any proceeding involving an investment dispute, a Party shall not assert, as a defense, counterclaim, right of set-off or for any other reason, that indemnification or other compensation for all or part of the alleged damages has been received or will be received pursuant to an insurance or guarantee contract.

8.   For purposes of Article 25(2)(b) of the ICSID Convention and this Article, a company of a Party that, immediately before the occurrence of the event or events giving rise to an investment dispute, was a covered investment, shall be treated as a company of the other Party.

Article X

1.   Any dispute between the Parties concerning the interpretation or application of the Treaty, that is not resolved through consultations or other diplomatic channels, shall be submitted upon the request of either Party to an arbitral tribunal for binding decision in accordance with the applicable rules of international law. In the absence of an agreement by the Parties to the contrary, the UNCITRAL Arbitration Rules shall govern, except to the extent these rules are (a) modified by the Parties or (b) modified by the arbitrators unless either Party objects to the proposed modification.

2.   Within two months of receipt of a request, each Party shall appoint an arbitrator. The two arbitrators shall select a third arbitrator as chairman, who shall be a national of a third state. The UNCITRAL Arbitration Rules applicable to appointing members of three-member panels shall apply mutatis mutandis to the appointment of the arbitral panel except that the appointing authority referenced in those rules shall be the Secretary General of the Centre.

3.   Unless otherwise agreed, all submissions shall be made and all hearings shall be completed within six months of the date of selection of the third arbitrator, and the arbitral panel shall render its decisions within two months of the date of the final submissions or the date of the closing of the hearings, whichever is later.

4.   Expenses incurred by the Chairman and other arbitrators, and other costs of the proceedings, shall be paid for equally by the Parties. However, the arbitral panel may, at its discretion, direct that a higher proportion of the costs be paid by one of the Parties.

Article XI

This Treaty shall not derogate from any of the following that entitle covered investments to treatment more favorable than that accorded by this Treaty:

(a)   laws and regulations, administrative practices or procedures, or administrative or adjudicatory decisions of a Party;

(b)   international legal obligations; or

(c)   obligations assumed by a Party, including those contained in an investment authorization or an investment agreement.

Article XII

Each Party reserves the right to deny to a company of the other Party the benefits of this Treaty if nationals of a third country own or control the company and

(a)   the denying Party does not maintain normal economic relations with the third country; or

(b)   the company has no substantial business activities in the territory of the Party under whose laws it is constituted or organized.

Article XIII

1.   No provision of this Treaty shall impose obligations with respect to tax matters, except that:

(a)   Articles III, IX and X will apply with respect to expropriation; and

(b)   Article IX will apply with respect to an investment agreement or an investment authorization.

2.   A national or company, that asserts in an investment dispute that a tax matter involves an expropriation, may submit that dispute to arbitration pursuant to Article IX(3) only if:

(a)   the national or company concerned has first referred to the competent tax authorities of both Parties the issue of whether the tax matter involves an expropriation; and

(b)   the competent tax authorities have not both determined, within nine months from the time the national or company referred the issue, that the matter does not involve an expropriation.

Article XIV

1.   This Treaty shall not preclude a Party from applying measures necessary for the fulfillment of its obligations with respect to the maintenance or restoration of international peace or security, or the protection of its own essential security interests.

2.   This Treaty shall not preclude a Party from prescribing special formalities in connection with covered investments, such as a requirement that such investments be legally constituted under

the laws and regulations of that Party, or a requirement that transfers of currency or other monetary instruments be reported, provided that such formalities shall not impair the substance of any of the rights set forth in this Treaty.

Article XV

1.   (a)   The obligations of this Treaty shall apply to the political subdivisions of the Parties.

     (b)   With respect to the treatment accorded by a State, Territory or possession of the United States of America, national treatment means treatment no less favorable than the treatment accorded thereby, in like situations, to investments of nationals of the United States of America resident in, and companies legally constituted under the laws and regulations of, other States, Territories or possessions of the United States of America.

2.   A Party's obligations under this Treaty shall apply to a state enterprise in the exercise of any regulatory, administrative or other governmental authority delegated to it by that Party.

Article XVI

1.   This Treaty shall enter into force thirty days after the date of exchange of instruments of ratification. It shall remain in force for a period of ten years and shall continue in force unless terminated in accordance with paragraph 2. It shall apply to covered investments existing at the time of entry into force as well as to those established or acquired thereafter.

2.   A Party may terminate this treaty at the end of the initial ten year period or at any time thereafter by giving one year's written notice to the other Party.

3.   For ten years from the date of termination, all other Articles shall continue to apply to covered investments established or acquired prior to the date of termination, except insofar as those Articles extend to the establishment or acquisition of covered investments.

4.   The Annex [and Protocol (if any)] shall form an integral part of the Treaty.

IN WITNESS WHEREOF, the respective plenipotentiaries have signed this Treaty.

DONE in duplicate at [city] this [number] day of [month], [year], in the english and _____ languages, each text being equally authentic.

FOR THE GOVERNMENT OF THE UNITED STATES OF AMERICA:

FOR THE GOVERNMENT OF _____:

ANNEX

1. The Government of the United States of America may adopt or maintain exceptions to the obligation to accord national treatment to covered investments in the sectors or with respect to the matters specified below:

    atomic energy; customhouse brokers; licenses for broadcast, common carrier, or aeronautical radio stations; COMSAT; subsidies or grants, including government-supported loans, guarantees and insurance; state and local measures exempt from Article 1102 of the North American Free Trade Agreement pursuant to Article 1108 thereof; and landing of submarine cables.

    Most favored nation treatment shall be accorded in the sectors and matters indicated above.

2. The Government of the United States of America may adopt or maintain exceptions to the obligation to accord national and most favored nation treatment to covered investments in the sectors or with respect to the matters specified below:

    fisheries; air and maritime transport, and related activities; banking* insurance* securities* and other financial services*.

    *Note: if the Treaty Partner undertakes acceptable commitments with respect to all or certain financial services, the Government of the United States of America will consider limiting these exceptions accordingly, so that, for example, particular obligations as to treatment would apply on no less favorable terms than in the North American Free Trade Agreement.

3. The Government of _____ may adopt or maintain exceptions...

4. Notwithstanding paragraph 3, each Party agrees to accord national treatment to covered investments in the following sectors:

    leasing of minerals or pipeline rights-of-way on government lands.

*   *   *

OPIC Discussion Draft of _____ , 199__

INVESTMENT INCENTIVE AGREEMENT

BETWEEN

THE GOVERNMENT OF THE UNITED STATES OF AMERICA

AND

[NAME OF COUNTRY]*

THE GOVERNMENT OF THE UNITED STATES OF AMERICA AND THE GOVERNMENT OF [NAME OF COUNTRY];

AFFIRMING their common desire to encourage economic activities in [Name of Country] that promote the development of the economic resources and productive capacities of [Name of Country]; and

RECOGNIZINGthat this objective can be promoted through investment support provided by the Overseas Private Investment Corporation ("OPIC"), a development institution and an agency of the United States of America, in the form of investment insurance and reinsurance, debt and equity investments and investment guaranties;

HAVE AGREED as follows:

Article I

As used in this Agreement, the following terms have the meanings herein provided. The term "Investment Support" refers to any debt or equity investment, any investment guaranty and any investment insurance or reinsurance which is provided by the Issuer in connection with a project in the territory of [Name of Country]. The term "Issuer" refers to OPIC and any successor agency of the United States of America, and any agent of either. The term "Taxes" means all present and future taxes, levies, imposts, stamps, duties and charges imposed by the Government of [Name of Country] and all liabilities with respect thereto.

Article 2

(a) The Issuer shall not be subject to regulation under the laws of [Name of Country] applicable to insurance or financial organizations.

(b) All operations and activities undertaken by the Issuer in connection with any Investment Support, and all payments, whether of interest, principal, fees, dividends, premiums or the proceeds from the liquidation of assets or of any other nature, that are made, received or guaranteed by the Issuer in connection with any Investment Support shall be exempt from Taxes. The Issuer shall not be subject to any Taxes in connection with any transfer, succession or other acquisition which occurs pursuant to paragraph [c] of this Article or Article 3[a] hereof. Any project in connection with which Investment

---

*Source: The Overseas Private Investment Corporation (New York) [Note added by the editor].

Support has been provided shall be accorded tax treatment no less favourable than that accorded to projects benefiting from the investment support programs of any other national or multilateral development institution which operates in [Name of Country].

(c)   If the Issuer makes a payment of any person or entity, or exercises its rights as a creditor or subrogee, in connection with any Investment Support, the Government of [Name of Country] shall recognize the transfer to, or acquisition by, the Issuer of any cash, accounts, credits, instruments or other assets in connection with such payment or the exercise of such rights, as well as the succession of the Issuer to any right, title, claim, privilege or cause of action existing or which may arise, in connection therewith.

(d)   With respect to any interests transferred to the Issuer or any interests to which the Issuer succeeds under this Article, the Issuer shall assert no greater rights than those of the person or entity from whom such interests were received, provided that nothing in this Agreement shall limit the right of the Government of the United States of America to assert a claim under international law in its sovereign capacity, as distinct from any rights it may have as the Issuer pursuant to paragraph [c] of this Article.

Article 3

(a)   Amounts in the currency of [Name of Country], including cash, accounts, credits, instruments or otherwise, acquired by the Issuer upon making a payment, or upon the exercise of its rights as a creditor, in connection with any Investment Support provided by the Issuer for a project in [Name of Country], shall be accorded treatment in the territory of [Name of Country] no less favorable as to use and conversion than the treatment to which such funds would have been entitled in the hands of the person or entity from which the Issuer acquired such amounts.

(b)   Such currency and credits may be transferred by the Issuer to any person or entity and upon such transfer shall be freely available for use by such person or entity in the territory of [Name of Country] in accordance with its laws.

Article 4

(a)   Any dispute between the Government of the United States of America and the Government of [Name of Country] regarding the interpretation of this Agreement or which, in the opinion of either party hereto, presents a question of international law arising out of any project or activity for which Investment Support has been provided shall be resolved, insofar as possible, through negotiations between the two Governments. If, six months following a request for negotiations hereunder, the two Governments have not resolved the dispute, the dispute, including the question of whether such dispute presents a question of international law, shall be submitted, at the initiative of either Government, to an arbitral tribunal for resolution in accordance with paragraph [b] of this Article.

(b)   The arbitral tribunal referred to in paragraph [a] of this Article shall be established and shall function as follows:

> (i)   Each Government shall appoint one arbitrator. These two arbitrators shall by agreement designate a president of the tribunal who shall be a citizen of a third state and whose appointment shall be subject to acceptance by the two Governments. The arbitrators shall be appointed within three months, and the president within six months, of the date of receipt of either Government's request for arbitration. If the appointments are not made within the foregoing time limits, either Government may, in the absence of any other agreement, request the Secretary-General of the International Centre for the Settlement of Investment Disputes to make the necessary appointment or appointments. Both Governments hereby agree to accept such appointment or appointments.

(ii)   Decisions of the arbitral shall be made by majority vote and shall be based on the applicable principles and rules of international law. Its decision shall be final and binding.

(iii)   During the proceedings, each Government shall bear the expense of its arbitrator and of its representation in the proceedings before the tribunal, whereas the expenses of the president and other costs of the arbitration shall be paid in equal parts by the two Governments. In its award, the arbitral tribunal may reallocate expenses and costs between the two Governments.

(iv)   In all other matters, the arbitral tribunal shall regulate its own procedures.

Article 5

(a)   This Agreement shall enter into force on the date on which the Government of [Name of Country] notifies the Government of the United States of America that all legal requirements for entry into force of this Agreement have been fulfilled.

(b)   This Agreement shall continue in force until six months from the date of a receipt of a note by which one Government informs the other of an intent to terminate this Agreement. In such event, the provisions of this Agreement shall, with respect to Investment Support provided while this Agreement was in force, remain in force so long as such Investment Support remains outstanding, but in no case longer than twenty years after the termination of this Agreement.

IN WITNESS WHEREOF, the undersigned, duly authorized by their respective Governments, have signed this Agreement.

DONE at Washington, District of Columbia, United States of America, on the [_____] day of _____, 199___, in duplicate, in the English and _____ languages, both texts being equally authentic.

FOR THE GOVERNMENT OF   **FOR THE GOVERNMENT OF**
THE UNITED STATES OF AMERICA   **[NAME OF COUNTRY]**

_____   _____

*   *   *

Selected UNCTAD publications on
transnational corporations and foreign direct investment

A. Individual studies

World Investment Report 1998: Trends and Determinants. 465 pp. Sales No. E.98.II.D.5. $45.

World Investment Report 1998: Trends and Determinants. An Overview. 72 pp. Free-of-charge.

Handbook on Foreign Direct Investment by Small and Medium-Sized Enterprises: Lessons from Asia. 200 pp. Sales No. E.98.II.D.4. $ 48.

International Investment Towards the Year 2002. 130 pp. Sales No. GV.E.98.0.15. $29.

World Investment Report 1997: Transnational Corporations, Market Structure and Competition Policy. 420 pp. Sales No. E.96.II.D.10. $45.

International Investment: Towards the Year 2001. 81 p. Sales No. GV.E.97.0.5. $35. (Joint publication with Invest in France Mission and Arthur Andersen, in collaboration with DATAR.)

World Investment Directory. Volume VI: West Asia 1996. 192 pp. Sales No. E.97.II.A.2. $35.

World Investment Directory. Volume V: Africa 1996. 508 pp. Sales No. E.97.II.A.1. $75.

Sharing Asia's Dynamism: Asian Direct Investment in the European Union. 162 pp. Sales No. E.97.II.D.1. $26.

Transnational Corporations and World Development. 656 pp. ISBN 0-415-08560-8 (hardback), 0-415-08561-6 (paperback). £65 (hardback), £20.99 (paperback).

Companies without Borders: Transnational Corporations in the 1990s. 224 pp. ISBN 0-415-12526-X. £47.50.

The New Globalism and Developing Countries. 336 pp. ISBN 92-808-0944-X. $25.

Investing in Asia's Dynamism: European Union Direct Investment in Asia. 124 pp. ISBN 92-827-7675-1. ECU 14. (Joint publication with the European Commission.)

World Investment Report 1996: Investment, Trade and International Policy Arrangements. 332 pp. Sales No. E.96.II.A.14. $45.

World Investment Report 1996: Investment, Trade and International Policy Arrangements. An Overview. 51 pp. Free-of-charge.

International Investment Instruments: A Compendium. Sales No. E.96.IIA.12 (vols. I-III). $125.

World Investment Report 1995: Transnational Corporations and Competitiveness. 491 pp. Sales No. E.95.II.A.9. $45.

World Investment Report 1995: Transnational Corporations and Competitiveness. An Overview. 51 pp. Free-of-charge.

Small and Medium-sized Transnational Corporations: Executive Summary and Report on the Osaka Conference. 60 pp. UNCTAD/DTCI/6. Free-of-charge.

World Investment Report 1994: Transnational Corporations, Employment and the Workplace. 482 pp. Sales No. E.94.II.A.14. $45.

World Investment Report 1994: Transnational Corporations, Employment and the Workplace. An Executive Summary. 34 pp. Free-of-charge.

World Investment Directory. Volume IV: Latin America and the Caribbean. 478 pp. Sales No. E.94.II.A.10. $65.

Liberalizing International Transactions in Services: A Handbook. 182 pp. Sales No. E.94.II.A.11. $45. (Joint publication with the World Bank.)

Accounting, Valuation and Privatization. 190 pp. Sales No. E.94.II.A.3. $25.

Environmental Management in Transnational Corporations: Report on the Benchmark Corporate Environment Suvey. 278 pp. Sales No. E.94.II.A.2. $29.95.

Management Consulting: A Survey of the Industry and Its Largest Firms. 100 pp. Sales No. E.93.II.A.17. $25.

Transnational Corporations: A Selective Bibliography, 1991-1992. 736 pp. Sales No. E.93.II.A.16. $75. (English/French.)

Small and Medium-sized Transnational Corporations: Role, Impact and Policy Implications. 242 pp. Sales No. E.93.II.A.15. $35.

World Investment Report 1993: Transnational Corporations and Integrated International Production. 290 pp. Sales No. E.93.II.A.14. $45.

World Investment Report 1993: Transnational Corporations and Integrated International Production. An Executive Summary. 31 pp. ST/CTC/159. Free-of-charge.

Foreign Investment and Trade Linkages in Developing Countries. 108 pp. Sales No. E.93.II.A.12. $18.

World Investment Directory 1992. Volume III: Developed Countries. 532 pp. Sales No. E.93.II.A.9. $75.

Transnational Corporations from Developing Countries: Impact on Their Home Countries. 116 pp. Sales No. E.93.II.A.8. $15.

Debt-Equity Swaps and Development. 150 pp. Sales No. E.93.II.A.7. $35.

From the Common Market to EC 92: Regional Economic Integration in the European Community and Transnational Corporations. 134 pp. Sales No. E.93.II.A.2. $25.

World Investment Directory 1992. Volume II: Central and Eastern Europe. 432 pp. Sales No. E.93.II.A.1. $65. (Joint publication with ECE.) $65.

World Investment Report 1992: Transnational Corporations as Engines of Growth: An Executive Summary. 30 pp. Sales No. E.92.II.A.24. Free-of-charge.

World Investment Report 1992: Transnational Corporations as Engines of Growth. 356 pp. Sales No. E.92.II.A.19. $45.

World Investment Directory 1992. Volume I: Asia and the Pacific. 356 pp. Sales No. E.92.II.A.11. $65.

B. Serial publications

Current Studies, Series A

No. 30. *Incentives and Foreign Direct Investment.* 98 pp. Sales No. E.96.II.A.6. $30. (English/French.)

No. 29. *Foreign Direct Investment, Trade, Aid and Migration.* 100 pp. Sales No. E.96.II.A.8. $25.

No. 28.   *Foreign Direct Investment in Africa.* 119 pp. Sales No. E.95.II.A.6. $25

No. 27.   *The Tradability of Banking Services: Impact and Implications.* 195 pp. Sales No. E.94.II.A.12. $50.

No. 26.   *Explaining and Forecasting Regional Flows of Foreign Direct Investment.* 58 pp. Sales No. E.94.II.A.5. $25.

No. 25.   *International Tradability in Insurance Services.* 54 pp. Sales No. E.93.II.A.11. $20.

No. 24.   *Intellectual Property Rights and Foreign Direct Investment.* 108 pp. Sales No. E.93.II.A.10. $20.

No. 23.   *The Transnationalization of Service Industries: An Empirical Analysis of the Determinants of Foreign Direct Investment by Transnational Service Corporations.* 62 pp. Sales No. E.93.II.A.3. $15.

No. 22.   *Transnational Banks and the External Indebtedness of Developing Countries: Impact of Regulatory Changes.* 48 pp. Sales No. E.92.II.A.10. $12.

No. 20.   *Foreign Direct Investment, Debt and Home Country Policies.* 50 pp. Sales No. E.90.II.A.16. $12.

No. 19.   *New Issues in the Uruguay Round of Multilateral Trade Negotiations.* 52 pp. Sales No. E.90.II.A.15. $12.50.

No. 18.   *Foreign Direct Investment and Industrial Restructuring in Mexico.* 114 pp. Sales No. E.92.II.A.9. $12.

The United Nations Library on Transnational Corporations. (Published by Routledge on behalf of the United Nations.)

Set A (Boxed set of 4 volumes. ISBN 0-415-08554-3. £350):

Volume One: *The Theory of Transnational Corporations.* 464 pp.

Volume Two: *Transnational Corporations: A Historical Perspective.* 464 pp.

Volume Three: *Transnational Corporations and Economic Development.* 448 pp.

Volume Four: *Transnational Corporations and Business Strategy.* 416 pp.

Set B (Boxed set of 4 volumes. ISBN 0-415-08555-1. £350):

Volume Five: *International Financial Management.* 400 pp.

Volume Six: *Organization of Transnational Corporations.* 400 pp.

Volume Seven: *Governments and Transnational Corporations.* 352 pp.

Volume Eight: *Transnational Corporations and International Trade and Payments.* 320 pp.

Set C (Boxed set of 4 volumes. ISBN 0-415-08556-X. £350):

Volume Nine: *Transnational Corporations and Regional Economic Integration.* 331 pp.

Volume Ten: *Transnational Corporations and the Exploitation of Natural Resources.* 397 pp.

Volume Eleven: *Transnational Corporations and Industrialization*. 425 pp.

Volume Twelve: *Transnational Corporations in Services*. 437 pp.

Set D (Boxed set of 4 volumes. ISBN 0-415-08557-8. £350):

Volume Thirteen: *Cooperative Forms of Transnational Corporation Activity*. 419 pp.

Volume Fourteen: *Transnational Corporations: Transfer Pricing and Taxation*. 330 pp.

Volume Fifteen: *Transnational Corporations: Market Structure and Industrial Performance*. 383 pp.

Volume Sixteen: *Transnational Corporations and Human Resources*. 429 pp.

Set E (Boxed set of 4 volumes. ISBN 0-415-08558-6. £350):

Volume Seventeen: *Transnational Corporations and Innovatory Activities*. 447 pp.

Volume Eighteen: *Transnational Corporations and Technology Transfer to Developing Countries*. 486 pp.

Volume Nineteen: *Transnational Corporations and National Law*. 322 pp.

Volume Twenty: *Transnational Corporations: The International Legal Framework*. 545 pp.

Transnational Corporations (formerly *The CTC Reporter*)

Published three times a year. Annual subscription price: $35; individual issues $15.

Transnationals, a quarterly newsletter, is available free of charge.

United Nations publications may be obtained from bookstores and distributors throughout the world. Please consult your bookstore or write to:

United Nations Publications

Sales Section   OR   Sales Section
Room DC2-0853   United Nations Office at Geneva
United Nations Secretariat   Palais des Nations
New York, NY 10017   CH-1211 Geneva 10
USA   Switzerland

Tel: (1-212) 963-8302 or (800) 253-9646   *Tel:* (41-22) 917-1234
Fax: (1-212) 963-3489   *Fax:* (41-22) 917-0123
E-mail: publications@un.org   *E-mail:* unpubli@unog.ch

Dollar prices quoted are in United States dollars.

For further information on the work of the UNCTAD Division on Investment, Technology and Enterprise Development, please address inquiries to:

United Nations Conference on Trade and Development
Division on Investment, Technology and Enterprise Development
Palais des Nations, Room E-9123
CH-1211 Geneva 10
Switzerland

Tel.:	(41-22) 907-5707
Fax:	(41-22) 907-0194
E-mail:	karl.sauvant@unctad.org

QUESTIONNAIRE

Bilateral Investment Treaties in the mid-1990s
Sales No. E.98.II.

In order to improve the quality and relevance of the work of the UNCTAD Division on Investment, Technology and Enterprise Development, it would be useful to receive the views of readers on this and other similar publications. It would therefore be greatly appreciated if you could complete the following questionnaire and return it to:

Readership Survey
UNCTAD Division on Investment, Technology and Enterprise Development
United Nations Office in Geneva
Palais des Nations
Room E-9123
CH-1211 Geneva 10
Switzerland

1. Name and address of respondent (optional):

   _____
   _____
   _____
   _____
   _____

2. Which of the following best describes your area of work?

Government	☐	Public enterprise	☐
Private enterprise institution	☐	Academic or research	☐
International organization	☐	Media	☐
Not-for-profit organization	☐	Other (specify) _____	

3. In which country do you work? _____

4. What is your assessment of the contents of this publication?

Excellent	☐	Adequate	☐
Good	☐	Poor	☐

5. How useful is this publication to your work?

Very useful	☐	Of some use	☐	Irrelevant	☐

6. Please indicate the three things you liked best about this publication:

_____

_____

_____

_____

_____

7. Please indicate the three things you liked least about this publication:

_____

_____

_____

_____

_____

8. If you have read other publications of the UNCTAD Division on Investment, Technology and Enterprise Development, what is your overall assessment of them?

Consistently good ☐   Usually good, but with some exceptions ☐
Generally mediocre ☐   Poor   ☐

9. On the average, how useful are these publications to you in your work?

Very useful ☐   Of some use ☐   Irrelevant ☐

10. Are you a regular recipient of *Transnational Corporations* (formerly *The CTC Reporter*), the Division's tri-annual refereed journal?

Yes ☐   No ☐

If not, please check here if you would like to receive a sample copy sent to the name and address you have given above ☐